Oliver Klöckner

Buy-outs in Family Businesses

GABLER EDITION WISSENSCHAFT

Entrepreneurial and Financial Studies

Herausgegeben von
Professor Dr. Dr. Ann-Kristin Achleitner
und Professor Dr. Christoph Kaserer

Die Schriftenreihe präsentiert aktuelle Forschungsergebnisse aus dem Gebiet der Entrepreneurial und Corporate Finance. Sie greift an der Schnittstelle von Wissenschaft und Praxis innovative Fragestellungen der Unternehmensfinanzierung auf.

This series presents research results from the fields of entrepreneurial and corporate finance. Its focus lies on innovative research topics at the interface of science and practice.

Oliver Klöckner

Buy-outs in Family Businesses

Changes in Corporate Governance, Instruments of Managerial Control, and Financial Practices

With a foreword by Prof. Dr. Dr. Ann-Kristin Achleitner

GABLER EDITION WISSENSCHAFT

Bibliographic information published by the Deutsche Nationalbibliothek
The Deutsche Nationalbibliothek lists this publication in the Deutsche Nationalbibliografie; detailed bibliographic data are available in the Internet at http://dnb.d-nb.de.

Dissertation Technische Universität München, 2009

1st Edition 2009

Editorial Office: Claudia Jeske / Britta Göhrisch-Radmacher

Gabler is part of the specialist publishing group Springer Science+Business Media.
www.gabler.de

Cover design: Regine Zimmer, Dipl.-Designerin, Frankfurt/Main
Printed on acid-free paper
Printed in Germany

ISBN 978-3-8349-1627-3

Foreword

In 2005, a fierce discussion raged over the question whether private equity companies make money by firing people or whether they really create value. Dr. Oliver Klöckner and I conducted the most comprehensive study on this topic by that time. Despite data restrictions, we concluded that despite job cuts in some companies financed by private equity, the general effect on employment was positive, net of all losses. Employment growth was particularly dynamic in bought-out family businesses and exceeded growth in all other types of companies backed by private equity companies. When presenting that study to politicians, media, and fellow scholars, we were repeatedly asked for an explanation for this exceptionally strong job creation in family businesses – a question we were unfortunately not able to answer back then.

Against this background, Dr. Klöckner started his research project which resulted in this thesis. He inquired into the consequences of buy-outs in family businesses. In this thesis, he develops a comprehensive framework of analysis and bases his theoretical discussion on the comparison of the major theories for family businesses and private equity financed companies. In a detailed review of the literature, he contrasts the distinct characteristics of family businesses with the typical characteristics of bought-out companies. Based on this theoretical foundation, Dr. Klöckner conducted 32 personal interviews with managers of bought-out family businesses and investment managers backing these transactions. A thorough and diligent analysis of the results allowed him to deduct the first propositions on changes in family businesses after a buy-out. The thesis is characterized by a sound methodology, a clear and concise discussion of the theory, and a comprehensive analysis of the empirical evidence.

This thesis is the most comprehensive overview on the young, but increasingly important research field of changes after buy-outs in family businesses. I wish Dr. Klöckner's dissertation a wide and positive reception among interested scholars. I am convinced that practitioners will find the reported experiences, subtle analyses, and practical suggestions also a rewarding reading. Finally, I hope that the thesis encourages further researchers to broaden our understanding on the consequences of buy-outs as solution to succession problems in family businesses.

Munich, June 1, 2009
Prof. Dr. Dr. Ann-Kristin Achleitner

Acknowledgements

This thesis is the outcome of my work at the KfW Endowed Chair in Entrepreneurial Finance at the Technische Universität München (TUM). Although a thesis is mostly the result of many lonesome hours working on one's own, there are various crossroads, where the future scholar is thankful for help from other people – be it to decide which way to take, be it to realize that one has reached a crossroads. In the following, I will list the kind people who helped me on my academic way.

I am deeply indebted to Prof. Ann-Kristin Achleitner (TUM) for taking over the supervision of my thesis. In many discussions, she motivated me to carry on, supported me when I needed help, and inspired me to find solutions to numerous small and big problems. While carrying out the many interesting, challenging, and enriching tasks she assigned me, she granted me great liberty and showed deep trust in me. These tasks and the intriguing environment gave me many great opportunities to further develop myself. I also owe many thanks to Prof. Ralf Reichwald (TUM), the second referee of my thesis, and Prof. Gunther Friedl (TUM), the chairman of my doctoral examination committee.

I am also grateful to various scholars who helped me with their critical remarks, additional thoughts, and hints at room for improvement. Prof. Ann Huff (TUM) helped me to refine the research approach of my thesis. Prof. Sabine Klein (EBS) and Prof. Roberto Flören (Nyenrode University) provided helpful guidance in the young field of research on family businesses. Prof. Frank Wallau (Institut für Mittelstandsforschung Bonn) and Thomas Haas (University of Linz) gave me access to most recent statistics and research results. I am particularly thankful to two researchers at Nottingham University: Prof. Mike Wright invited me for a research stay in fall 2007 and gave many helpful comments on the analysis and presentation of research results. Dr. Louise Scholes acted as helpful counterpart for discussing and challenging many results of my analysis not only during our uncountable tea breaks.

This thesis also benefited from extensive support of numerous practitioners and institutions. Hans Knürr (former owner-manager of Knürr AG) and Marc Hennerkes (Buchanan Capital Group) critically reviewed the questionnaire underlying the empirical part of this thesis through the eyes of a family manager and an investment manager. I am particularly thankful to 32 anonymous interview partners who were managers of bought-out companies or investment managers who backed these buy-outs. Their time, openness, and valuable insights into the consequences of buy-outs in family businesses added the practical flesh to the theoretical bones. The two government agencies Bundesministerium für Wirtschaft und Technologie and Bayerisches Staatsministerium für Wirtschaft, Infrastruktur, Verkehr und Technologie supported the survey and, thus, helped to increase the response rate. I am also indebted to the Deutscher Akademischer Austausch Dienst and the Förderverein Kurt Fordan für herausragende Begabung for financing my research stay at Nottingham through scholarships.

I would like to express my deepest gratitude for the outstanding intellectual and emotional support in terms of academic and non-academic life to my colleagues at the KfW Endowed Chair in Entrepreneurial Finance and the affiliated Center for Entrepreneurial and Financial Studies (CEFS). In particular, I would like to thank Dr. Annabell Geidner for continuous help and motivation at the end of long office days. I am also indebted to Dr. Martin Brixner for his critical remarks and his unshakeable sense of humor and irony. For their unique team spirit, their ceaseless helpfulness, and their persistence while proof-reading, I would like to thank Markus Ampenberger, Marko Bender, Reiner Braun, Dr. Thorsten Groth, Nina Günther, Peter Heister, Bastian Hinterramskogler, Svenja Jarchow, Dr. Benjamin Moldenhauer, Dr. Kay Müller, Dr. Eva Nathusius, Monika Paul, Daniel Paulus, Stephanie Schraml, and Florian Tappeiner, as well as Jörn Block and Sebastian Stange. I also owe special thanks to my research assistants Katrin Beyer, Martin Brandstetter, and Alina Schill.

Especially in the final stage of writing-up, I was more than happy to count on the invaluable and continuous support of Sina Heller for cheering me up, putting everything into perspective, and unbiasedly reviewing the result of my research. Above all of the aforementioned, I would like to express my deepest gratitude to my beloved parents Doris and Ludwig Klöckner. This thesis is dedicated to them for endowing me with an excellent education, providing me backing when I needed it, and most notably teaching me to explore the world with my mind wide open.

Munich, June, 2009
Dr. Oliver Klöckner

Table of contents

List of Figures

List of Tables

List of Abbreviations

AC	Agency costs
AktG	"Aktiengesetz" German law on public companies
BIMBO	Buy-in management buy-out
BWA	"Betriebswirtschaftliche Auswertung" simplified overview of sales, costs and preliminary computation of earnings
CEO	Chief executive officer
CFO	Chief financial officer
CMBOR	Centre for Management Buy-out Research
EBIT	Earnings before interest and taxes
EBITDA	Earnings before interest, taxes, depreciation and amortization
EBO	Employee buy-out
EBT	Earnings before taxes
ERP	Enterprise resource planning
et seq.	and the following (page)
EVCA	European Private Equity and Venture Capital Association
FB	Family business
FM	Family manager
F-PEC (index)	Family power, experience, and culture (index)
GmbHG	"Gesetz betreffend die Gesellschaften mit beschränkter Haftung" German law on limited liability corporations
ibid.	Ibidem (at the same place)
IBO	Institutional buy-out
IfM	Institut für Mittelstandsforschung
IPO	Initial public offering
IT	Information technology
LBO	Leveraged buy-out
m	Million
M&A	Mergers & acquisitions
MBI	Management buy-in
MBO	Management buy-out
MD	Managing director
n/a	Not available

OBO	Owner buy-out
p.a.	Per annum
PEC	Private equity company
R&D	Research and development
RoI	Return on investment
UK	United Kingdom
US	Unites States (abbreviation for US American)
USA	United States of America
SFI	Substantial Family Influence
ST	Stewardship theory

List of Symbols

$MoMB_{Fam}$	Number of family members on the management board
$MoMB_{Total}$	Number of all members on the management board
$MoSB_{Fam}$	Number of family members on the supervisory board
$MoSB_{Total}$	Number of all members on the supervisory board
S_{Fam}	Stock held by the family
S_{Total}	Total stock

1 Introduction

1.1 Relevance of topic

Family businesses are a wide-spread phenomenon of significant economic importance.[1] According to the two most recent studies, between 84.0% and 95.1% of all companies in Germany are family businesses.[2] The INSTITUT FÜR MITTELSTANDS-FORSCHUNG (IfM) has estimated that there are 3.0 million family businesses in Germany (95.1% of all registered companies), employing 13.4 million individuals (57.3% of employees subject to social insurance) and contributing € 1.9 trillion (41.5%) to total sales of all German companies.[3] A comparison with other countries shows that the importance of family businesses in Germany is no exception.[4]

The integration of the family sphere and the business sphere, the emotional bond between family and business, as well as the unity of ownership and management in the hands of the family endow family businesses with distinctive characteristics: Family businesses have a reputation for efficient corporate governance[5], long-term orientation[6], trustworthiness[7], and social responsibility[8] – the list could be continued on and on. On the other side of the coin, family businesses are notorious for quarrels between family members[9], nepotism[10], closeness[11], and decisions guided by emotions,

---

1 For a definition of the term family business, see subsection 2.1.1.

2 The 84% of family businesses refers to companies with more than € 2 million (m) in sales p.a. (cf. Klein (2004), p. 42). The 95% refers to companies with at least € 17,500 in sales p.a. (cf. Kay et al. (2003), p. 49).

3 Cf. Hauser/Wolter (2007), p. 24. KLEIN has supported these figures with her estimations (accounting for the fact that these values are based on data from 1995) that family businesses employed 12.6m individuals and contributed € 1.6 trillion to total sales of all German companies (cf. Klein (2004), pp. 44 et seq.).

4 Estimations of family businesses in the USA specify their number at 10.8m, employing 77m individuals and contributing $ 5.5 trillion to the gross domestic product (cf. Astrachan/Shanker (2006), p. 62). For an overview on studies and figures relating to the significance of family businesses in different countries, see Upton/Petty (2000), p. 28; Klein (2000), p. 160.

5 Cf. Fama/Jensen (1983), p. 306.

6 Cf. Ward (1988), p. 113; Block/Thams (2008), pp. 8-14.

7 Cf. Nahapiet/Ghoshal (1998), p. 261.

8 Cf. Tagiuri/Davis (1992), pp. 46 et seq.; Donckels/Fröhlich (1991), p. 159.

9 Cf. Harvey/Evans (1994), pp. 331-334.

10 Cf. Vinton (1998), pp. 297-299.

intuition, and gut feeling[12]. All these characteristics render family businesses a fascinating and distinct phenomenon of the business world, which justifies efforts to better understand them.

Family businesses have a particular Achilles' heel: Their destiny is irreversibly tied to inter-generational succession of family members as owners, managers and in other roles in the company; otherwise, the company loses its essence of being a family business.[13] This transition is problematic as demonstrated by statistics: Only 30.0% of family businesses survive into the second generation and only 15.0% survive into the third.[14] The magnitude of this succession problem[15] is underlined by projections: FREUND expects that 17.7% of all German family businesses will need a successor within 5 years of 2004.[16]

In some family businesses no successor in the family is available, qualified or willing to take over the company.[17] Against this background, the only solution to the succession problem is liquidation or sale of the company to another company, to

---

11 Cf. Habbershon/Williams (1999), p. 2.

12 Cf. Dreux (1990), p. 228; Dyer (1989), p. 213; Schein (1983), p. 26. For a more detailed discussion of the advantages and disadvantages of family businesses compared to non-family businesses, see Bertrand/Schoar (2006), pp. 75-80; Habbershon/Williams (1999), pp. 3-5; Arregle/Durand/Very (2004), p. 36.

13 Succession in family businesses is one of the main fields of research in family businesses. In their general literature review on research in family businesses, CHRISMAN/CHUA/SHARMA found that 22% of literature in this field deals with the succession of family businesses (cf. Chrisman/Chua/Sharma (2003), p. 4). For further literature reviews, see Ip/Jacobs (2006); Le Breton-Miller/Miller/Steier (2004); Brockhaus (2004); Handler (1994).

14 Cf. Ward (1987), p. xvi; Birley/Ng/Godfrey (1999), p. 599.

15 The succession problem is defined as the problem of intergenerational continuity of family members in ownership and management.

16 Cf. Freund (2004), pp. 64 et seq. Here and in the following, statistics based on FREUND refer to family businesses with sales of at least € 50,000 (cf. Freund (2004), p. 61). This projection is supported by a survey among German family businesses that has found that 27% of family owners expect ownership succession within 5 years of 2008 (cf. PriceWaterhouseCoopers (2008a), p. 13)

The importance of succession is also reflected in research: CHRISMAN/CHUA/SHARMA found in a literature review that over 22% of scholarly publications on family businesses deal with the succession problem (cf. Chrisman/Chua/Sharma (2003), p. 4).

17 43.5% of owners of family businesses plan to hand ownership and management over to relatives (cf. Freund (2004), p. 73). However, not all these plans can be realized for diverse reasons such as surprising death of the current family manager, change in the successor's motivation, failed attempt of succession, or many more.

internal or to external managers.[18] Acquisitions of mid-sized and large family businesses by internal or external managers are mostly backed by private equity companies to secure financing – these transactions are termed buy-outs.[19]

Buy-outs are an increasingly frequent solution to the succession problem in family businesses: According to data from the CENTRE FOR MANAGEMENT BUY-OUT RESEARCH (CMBOR), the number and volume of German family businesses sold through buy-outs has more than tripled since 2000 (see Figure 1).[20] The latest estimates by FREUND predict that 35.0% of succession problems in mid-sized and large family businesses will be solved through a buy-out between 2005 and 2009.[21]

With the departure of the family and the arrival of new owners and possibly new managers, former family businesses are expected to be transformed in a multitude of ways. Will the typical characteristics of family businesses survive the buy-out? How will return expectations of private equity companies affect the companies? What are the effects of the buy-out on corporate governance? And how will post buy-out managers, either newly joining the company or being freed from restrictions imposed by the family, change their management style and restructure the company? Given the economic weight of family businesses, the urgency of the succession problem and

---

18 The IFM estimates that family businesses with a succession problem are distributed on the solutions presented above in the following way: 8.3% are liquidated, 21.1% sold to other companies, 10.2% taken over by internal managers, and 16.5% sold to external managers (cf. Freund (2004), p. 73).

19 According to statistics by the Centre for Management Buy-Out Research (CMBOR), 85.2% of buy-outs in German family businesses were backed by a private equity company over the last 10 years.

A company is considered as mid-sized or large if annual sales exceed € 5m. Despite arbitrary determination of this cutoff value, there are two arguments for stipulating the threshold at about this value: First, smaller family businesses are rather unattractive investment targets for private equity companies. The expected returns from buy-outs in smaller companies hardly suffice to cover the considerable transaction costs (due diligence, investment managers' time) and the return expectations of investors into private equity funds. Second, managers aiming at taking over smaller family businesses do not per se depend on private equity companies' financial backing, but could finance the acquisition with their private capital and bank loans.

20 The surge in buy-out activity in family businesses is not limited to Germany. On a European level, the number of buy-outs in family businesses has increased from 291 to 559 p.a. between 2000 and 2007, and deal volume has increased from € 4,155m to € 18,258m p.a. over this period (cf. Klöckner (2008), pp. 13 et seq. Europe includes Austria, Belgium, Denmark, France, Finland, Germany, Ireland, Italy, Netherlands, Norway, Portugal, Spain, Sweden, Switzerland, and UK).

21 Cf. Freund (2004), p. 73. 14% of these buy-outs will be done through internal managers and 21.0% by external managers. Figures refer to family businesses with more than € 10m in sales p.a.

some recent unlucky and widely discussed examples of buy-outs in family businesses[22], family owners, employees, journalists, politicians, researchers and the general public are increasingly interested in buy-outs in family businesses.

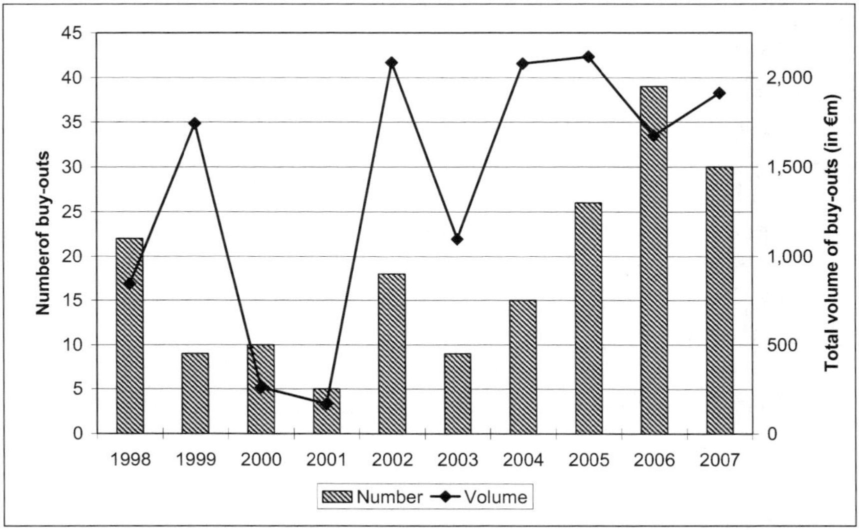

Figure 1: Development of the German market for buy-outs in family businesses

Source: Klöckner (2008), pp. 13 et seq.

Up to now, research has been unable to thoroughly answer the questions raised above. Research into buy-outs in family businesses is still nascent. Resorting to other research fields seems to be of limited help:[23] On the one hand, research into family

22 Cf. Hickey (2005), p. 31. The most prominent example is arguably Grohe AG, which was a buy-out that entailed restructuring of operations, recapitalization transferring about € 350m to the private equity company and lay-offs of 1,200 employees (cf. Kaserer et al. (2007), pp. 109-129). More recently, the buy-out of the former family business Märklin GmbH was criticized, mainly for consultants charging excessive salaries without successfully restructuring the company (cf. Iwersen (2008b); Iwersen (2008a)).

23 Cf. section 2.1.3 for a review of literature on buy-outs in family businesses. Despite the important role of buy-outs with regard to solutions to the succession problem, "there is relatively little evidence relating to this aspect of family firm succession" (Scholes et al. (2005), p. 3).

businesses is still in an early stage,[24] particularly in Germany. On the other hand, research on buy-outs has mainly focused on buy-outs of large divisions in corporations and privatizations[25] – transferability of research results seems questionable because the available results focus on larger companies and ignore the distinct character of family businesses before the buy-out.[26] However, there are considerable changes after buy-outs in family businesses: First evidence on employment growth has shown that buy-outs in family businesses outgrow buy-outs in non-family businesses by far.[27] Against this background, this thesis sets out to analyze, describe, and explain the changes after buy-outs in family businesses.

1.2 Research question

Despite the abundance of changes after buy-outs in family businesses, the following examination focuses on the most important dimensions delineated in a clear research question.

So far, research on buy-outs in general has mostly focused on two perspectives: First, the effects of buy-outs on corporate governance have been analyzed to examine whether and how buy-outs transform or improve corporate governance in bought-out companies.[28] Second, researchers have focused on the changes in financing to describe the characteristics and consequences of the typically high leverage and to find out whether changes in financial practices created value for the company.[29] Despite intense research interest in these two dimensions, they have not yet been comprehensively examined for buy-outs in family businesses with special consideration of the

24 Cf. Poutziouris/Smyrnios/Klein (2006), pp. 1 et seq.; Villalonga/Amit (2006), p. 414; Astrachan (2003), p. 567; Chrisman et al. (2008), p. 931.

25 Cf. Berg/Gottschalg (2005) for a review of the literature.

26 Cf. Malone (1989), p. 359. In 2007, the average transaction value for buy-outs in family businesses was € 32m, while average transaction value of all types of buy-outs amounted to € 120m (cf. Klöckner (2008), pp. 14 et seq.).

27 Cf. Achleitner/Klöckner (2005), p. 17. After buy-outs in family businesses, employment grew by 7.1% on average per year. This compares to the following figures of employment growth in different types of buy-outs: 3.4% in secondary buy-outs, 2.8% in going-private buy-outs, 1.6% in spin-off buy-outs, and -3.8% in turnaround buy-outs. For definitions of the different types of buy-outs, see subsection 2.1.2.

28 Cf. subsection 5.1.2.

29 Cf. subsection 7.1.2.

distinct characteristics of family businesses. Therefore, corporate governance and financing lend themselves as dimensions of analysis.

Besides these two established perspectives on buy-outs, another dimension will be added to the analysis: instruments of managerial control, which include planning, management accounting, and performance measurement.[30] This dimension seems to merit analysis for two reasons: First, instruments of managerial control are a precondition for efficient corporate governance and for the financial structures typical for buy-outs. Thus, changes in corporate governance and financial structures are likely to go hand in hand with changes in the instruments of managerial control. Second, instruments of managerial control are frequently underdeveloped in family businesses, which might suggest improvements after the buy-out.[31]

Therefore, the analysis of changes will focus on the dimensions of corporate governance, instruments of managerial control, and financing.[32] In consequence, the research question laying the foundation for further analysis is the following:

How do buy-outs in family businesses change corporate governance, instruments of managerial control, and financial practices?

1.3 Overview of research approach

As prior knowledge of the changes after buy-outs in family businesses is fairly restricted,[33] this research project is of an exploratory nature and sets out to build theory in the field delineated by the research question.

For this purpose, this thesis approaches the research question in a qualitative empirical way. An initial theoretical part provides the basic understanding by reviewing the relevant literature. Against this background, the empirical part analyzes the evidence and inductively derives propositions answering the research question (see Figure 2).

---

30 Although instruments of managerial control could be subsumed under corporate governance, they are analyzed separately as they are also highly relevant to financial practices.

31 Cf. subsection 6.1.1.

32 The order of the three dimensions is rearranged here and in the research question as the instruments of managerial control are affected by changes in corporate governance and affect changes in financial practices.

33 Cf. subsection 2.1.3.

To outline the background of this research project, the **theoretical part** builds on four streams of literature from two different levels of abstraction. On the concrete level, the literature on family businesses and buy-outs is analyzed.[34] On the abstract level, the buy-out as transition from a pre buy-out family business to a post buy-out portfolio company is theoretically approximated by the transition from a setting of stewardship theory (describing the situation in family businesses) to a setting of agency theory (describing the situation in portfolio companies).[35] On these two levels, evidence and mechanisms discussed in the literature are compiled to create a comprehensive understanding of the pre buy-out state of a family business and the post buy-out state of a portfolio company.[36] Deductively derived expectations of the changes entailed by the transition from the pre buy-out state to the post buy-out state build the theoretical background for the empirical analysis.[37]

In the **empirical part,** a qualitative research approach is chosen, which includes semi-structured interviews of managers[38] of bought-out companies and investment managers of private equity companies;[39] both interview partners have to be knowledgeable of the changes induced by the buy-out in the respective company. Interview transcripts were analyzed using qualitative content analysis according to MAYRING.[40] The resulting evidence for the pre buy-out and post buy-out states is contrasted and enriched with details of possible explanations, implementation, and

---

34 As this research project focuses on buy-outs in German family businesses, the literature reviewed consists of German literature and the broader international literature on family businesses and buy-outs, which has a particular focus on the UK and the USA (due to market maturity and multitude of publications) and German-speaking countries (for their cultural similarity with the German market) (cf. footnote 204 for the geographical delineation of this thesis and its rationale). For aspects not covered by academic literature (or where these are not the most recent publications), the theoretical approach will also include surveys and other publications by practitioners (cf. Klein/Bell (2007), p. 21).

35 For the choice and explanation of these two theories, see section 2.2.

36 This is done in the first two sections of chapters 4, 5, and 6.

37 These expectations on changes are not intended to be a pre-state of a proposition, as expected changes are too uncertain and too general to formulate propositions or hypotheses (cf. subsections 2.1.3 and 3.1.5). Expectations are merely conclusions of inductively derived changes based on the literature. These expected changes are not tested in the empirical sections of this thesis.

38 The usage of male nouns and pronouns throughout this thesis does not exclude women from the respective statements. Male forms are used for simplicity and are to be understood as gender-neutral.

39 Cf. section 3.1 for a detailed description of the empirical methodology.

40 Cf. subsection 3.1.5 for an explanation of the qualitative content analysis according to MAYRING.

other relevant comments of interviewees. To more clearly expound the changes after buy-outs in family businesses, observed changes are compared to changes in a control group. The control group consists of former family businesses that were sold to buyers that were not private equity companies.[41] Based on this empirical evidence, propositions on the changes after buy-outs in family businesses are derived inductively. Propositions focus on describing new insights and thus have to be unknown to the literature yet.

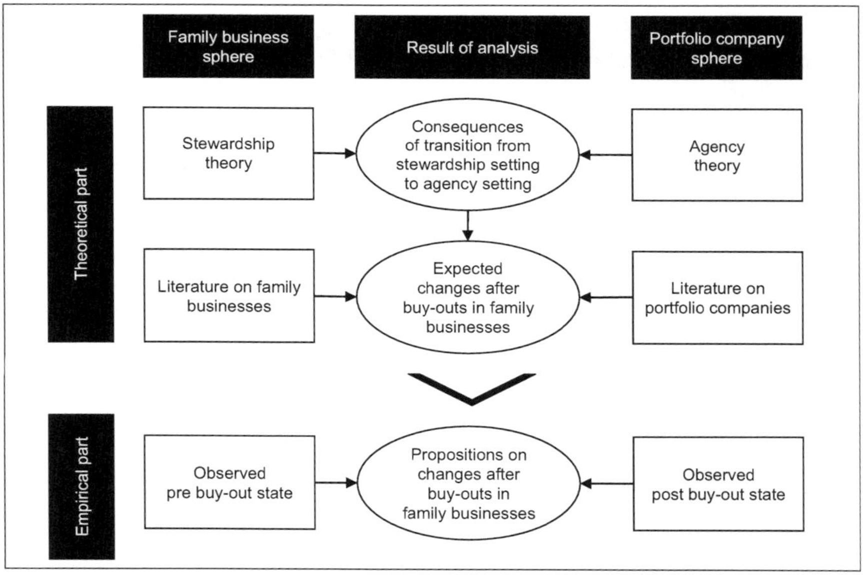

Figure 2: Elements, results and course of analysis

Source: Author's illustration

To structure the following line of argumentation, a framework of analysis is conceived based on theoretical evidence and adjusted to best fit the empirical evidence.[42] The framework is structured on two levels: The first level breaks the

[41] Holding companies or managers backed by semi-public investment companies. Cf. subsection 3.1.3 for the definition of the control group.

[42] Cf. subsection 3.1.1 for description of the framework of analysis.

research question down into its three dimensions, namely corporate governance, instruments of managerial control, and financial practices. The second level determines three to six aspects for each dimension on which the analysis focuses.

1.4 Outline of structure

After the formulation of the research question and a brief description of the research design, this section provides a general overview on the eight chapters of this thesis (see Figure 3). At the beginning of each chapter, subsection and section (where needed), the respective structure is explained in greater detail.

After the introduction in **Chapter 1**, **Chapter 2** lays the theoretical foundation for the following analysis. Section 2.1 provides basic definitions of family businesses and relevant terms relating to buy-outs. Moreover, this section comprises a review of the literature on buy-outs in family businesses and anchors this thesis in the context of other publications. Section 2.2 introduces the two theories underlying this thesis, namely agency theory and stewardship theory. In addition to a detailed explanation of each theory, the section provides background, criticism and application of the respective theory.

Chapter 3 contains the empirical foundation of this thesis. Section 3.1 explains the research approach of the empirical part of this thesis. After the research question is broken down into a framework of analysis, the research method is explained in detail. Then, the composition of the control group is presented. Next, data gathering, analysis, and presentation of results are described. The section closes with a discussion of the methodology's limitations. Section 3.2 describes the sample underlying the analysis of the empirical part.

Chapter 4 presents the background of the buy-out, which is an important prerequisite for the further analysis. Based on the literature, section 4.1 describes the two main steps preceding the buy-out: The first stage discusses the decision of family owners to sell their family business. Reasons and preparations for the sale are highlighted, and the family owners' evaluation of possible buyers is presented. The second stage examines the sale transaction. Investment criteria of private equity companies and family owners' goals in sale negotiations are analyzed. The sale process is described, including communication of and stakeholders' reactions to the buy-out. Then, the family's emotional separation and role post buy-out are discussed. Section 4.2 analyzes the buy-outs in the sample companies with regard to the aspects presented in the former section. This section does not directly relate to the research question, and it is not intended to build theory but to provide a basic understanding for the further analysis.[43] Section 4.3 summarizes.

Chapters 5, 6 and 7 constitute the main part of this thesis. The symmetrical proceedings of these chapters are reflected in their symmetrical structures. Each chapter provides findings on one dimension of the research question: Chapter 5 focuses on the changes in corporate governance after buy-outs in family businesses, Chapter 6 highlights the changes in instruments of managerial control, and Chapter 7 stresses the changes in financial practices. Sections 5.1, 6.1, and 7.1 provide a theoretical comparison of family businesses and portfolio companies with regard to the respective dimensions. Based on this comparison, sections 5.2, 6.2 and 7.2 derive expectations on changes in selected aspects of the respective dimensions according to the framework of analysis. Sections 5.3, 6.3, and 7.3 provide empirical evidence on the aspects discussed in the respective preceding sections. Presentation in these empirical sections follows the framework of presentation developed in section 3.1. Each subsection corresponds to an aspect under examination, closes with a conclusion of the key findings of the subsection and inductively derives propositions to build theory in the respective dimension of the research question. Sections 5.4, 6.4, and 7.4 summarize the respective chapters.

Chapter 8 closes this thesis. Section 8.1 summarizes the key findings and puts them into the context of overall findings. Section 8.2 carves out major implications for practitioners and researchers. Section 8.3 provides an outlook on the future of buy-outs in family businesses.

---

43 For this reason, no propositions are derived in section 4.2 and the section is termed empirical description and not empirical evidence, unlike the other sections composing the empirical part of this thesis.

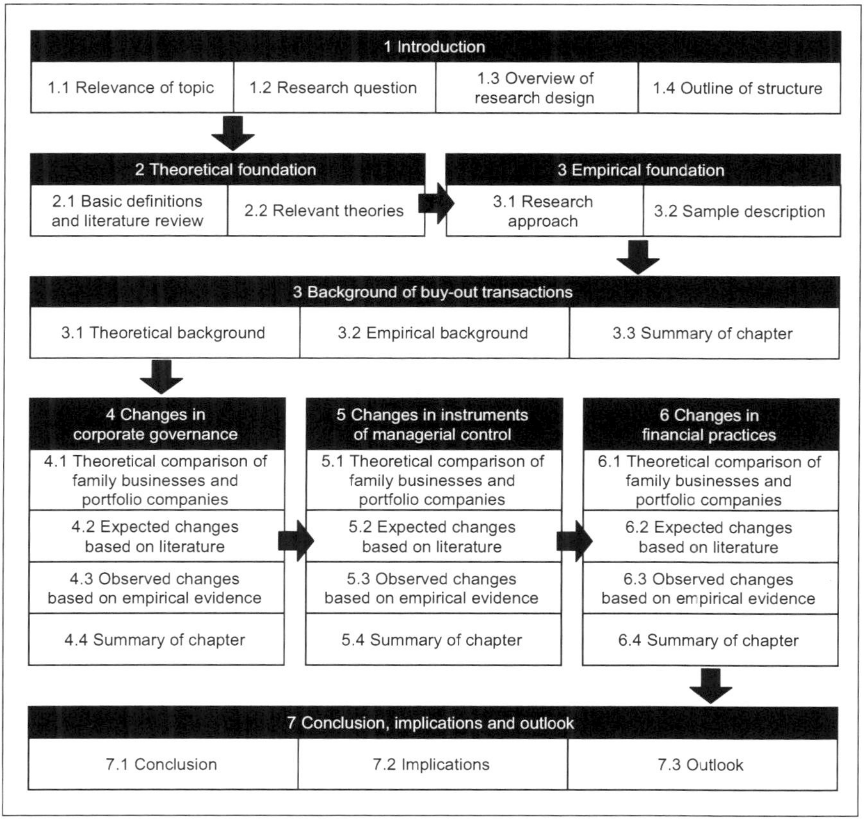

Figure 3: Structure of the thesis

Source: Author's illustration

2 Theoretical foundation

This chapter prepares the theoretical ground for this thesis. Section 2.1 defines family businesses as well as important terms relating to buy-outs and provides a review of the literature on buy-outs in family businesses. Section 2.2 introduces the two theories underlying this thesis: agency theory and stewardship theory.

2.1 Definitions and literature review

2.1.1. Family businesses

While the distinct characteristics of family businesses with regard to the research question are described in detail in the following chapters, this subsection sets out to provide an overview on definitions of family businesses and stipulates the definition underlying this thesis.[44]

A precondition for the definition of what companies qualify as family businesses is the **definition of the family**. The definition of family depends on the ethnicity of families researched, thus accounting for different delimitations of the term family.[45] As this thesis examines businesses, which belonged to central European families, FLÖREN'S definition of the term family is used: "A family is a social system consisting of individuals, related either by blood, by marriage or by legal adoption, interacting with and influencing the behavior of each other."[46] For reasons of simplicity and to focus the analysis on the changes induced by the buy-out, intra-family decision making through intra-family institutions hampered by possible

---

44 The German term "Mittelstand" refers to small and mid-sized companies, which employ less than 250 individuals and have annual sales not exceeding € 50m or a balance sheet with total assets not exceeding € 43m (cf. European Commission (2003), p. 39). Mittelstand companies are not per se equal to family businesses, as the definition of Mittelstand companies merely relates to quantitative criteria; the involvement of family members in the company, which is a constituent characteristic of family businesses, is not required. Nevertheless, as most family businesses are small or mid-sized (cf. Achleitner/Fingerle (2004), p. 9; Klein (2004), p. 42; Freund (2004), p. 64), many family businesses fulfill the criteria of Mittelstand companies.

45 Cf. McGoldrick (1992), pp. 437 et seq.; Dean (1992), p. 375; Wong/McReynolds/Wong (1992), pp. 358 et seq.

46 Flören (2002), p. 28. In the given definition, FLÖREN precises a definition by KLEIN (cf. Klein (2000), p. 158).

conflicts are not taken into account: Hence, in the following, the family is assumed to have one will and that all members pursue this will.[47]

Based on this definition of the family the task of defining a family business can be approached. However, the heterogeneous diversity of companies, which might qualify as family businesses, is reflected in a confusing variety of definitions of what is a family business. Researchers are still debating, which characteristics are essential for the definition of a family business.[48] Therefore, a brief overview on the definitional discussion is provided, before the definition underlying this thesis is stipulated.

In their review of trends in family business research, CHRISMAN/CHUA/SHARMA have subsumed **definitional attempts to the term family business** under two umbrella approaches, namely the components-of-involvement approach and the essence approach.[49]

The **components-of-involvement** approach takes the degree of family involvement as indicator whether a company is a family business or not. Family involvement

---

[47] For more details on governance, constitutions, councils, and conflict resolution in family businesses, see Koeberle-Schmid/Nützel (2005), pp. 6-77.

[48] Cf. Lansberg/Perrow/Rogolsky (1988), p. 1; Winter et al. (1998), pp. 239 et seq.; Flören (2002), p. 15; Chrisman/Chua/Sharma (2005), p. 556. This variety of definitions is seen as a result of three characteristics of research into family businesses: First, a generally accepted definition has not emerged yet, possibly because the research field is relatively young (cf. Hollander/Elman (1988), p. 145). Second, multiple reciprocal interactions between the family and the business complicate a stand-alone analysis of the family business (cf. Lansberg/Perrow/Rogolsky (1988), pp. 3 et seq.). Third, due to its multidisciplinary character, every discipline that contributes to research on family businesses focuses on different aspects of the family business and introduces a definition adequate for the analysis of the aspects examined (cf. Wortman (1994), p. 4. WORTMAN argues that there are contributions to the research on family businesses from psychology, sociology, economics, law, organization theory, organization behavior, social issues in management, policy sciences, and general systems.).

Already in the mid 1990s, when the field of research in family businesses was rather young, scholars were aware that the lack of a broadly used, consistent definition of a family business posed a problem to the research field (cf. Wortman (1994), p. 4; Winter et al. (1998), pp. 239 et seq.). Definitional cacophony hampered the development of an all-embracing research framework, sampling consistency between different studies, inadequate inferences, integration of research results, and derivation of implications for practitioners (cf. Handler (1989), pp. 259, 262; Wortman (1994), p. 3; Lansberg/Perrow/Rogolsky (1988), p. 2). The extent of definitional confusion is exemplified by WESTHEAD/COWLING/STOREY who found that the share of family businesses in their sample varied between 15% and 81% depending on the definition applied (cf. Westhead/Cowling/Storey (1997), according to Klein/Astrachan/Smyrnios (2005), p. 322).

[49] Cf. Chrisman/Chua/Sharma (2005), pp. 556 et seq.

can be exerted through family ownership, family management and the combination of both, namely ownership management (see Table 1). Despite its handy operationalization, this approach is critically based on the assumption that family involvement is sufficient to render a company a family business. This assumption reveals the lack of a theoretical underpinning, which would explain why family involvement in these components leads to company behavior that differs from non-family businesses.

The **essence approach** requires of a family business that family involvement is directed towards a behavior that entails certain distinctiveness.[50] Thus, this theory is not based on a critical assumption but is of theoretical nature. The behavior producing distinctiveness may manifest itself through familiness[51], intention of generational transfer, interdependence of the systems family and business[52], or pursuit of the objective to provide family employment. While the essence approach is theoretically convincing, practicability is restricted by the limited operationalizability of checking companies for the manifestation of behavior causing distinctiveness.[53]

Confusion over the myriad of definitions is increased by the possibility to combine several definitions through inclusion or exclusion of different definitions, thus multiplying the number of possible definitions.[54] The subsumption does not include the definitional attempt based on self-identification; despite its easy operationa-

---

50 This implies that of two companies with the same level of family involvement, one may qualify as a family business (i.e. where family involvement leads to distinct behavior) and the other one not (i.e. where family involvement does not lead to distinct behavior) (cf. Chrisman/Chua/Sharma (2005), p. 557). Distinctiveness can either be advantageous or disadvantageous for the family business.

51 Familiness is a concept developed by HABBERSHON/WILLIAMS to reflect particular resources of a given family business that distinct it from other non-family businesses. The authors define familiness as "the unique bundle of resources a particular firm has because of the systems interaction between the family, its individual members, and the business" (Habbershon/Williams (1999), p. 11).

52 Systems theory argues that interaction of the subsystems family, individual family member and family business creates individual and organizational phenomena distinguishing family businesses from non-family businesses (cf. Tagiuri/Davis (1996), pp. 201 et seq., 205 et seq.; Habbershon/Williams/MacMillan (2003), p. 453).

53 Cf. Mühlebach (2004), p. 12.

54 An inclusive combination of several definitions links these by the conjunction "or" and serves as logical statement including all objects fulfilling at least one definition. An exclusive combination of definitions is based on the conjunction "and"; the resulting logical statement only includes those objects fulfilling all definitions. See Table 1 for different combinations of definitions.

lizability, this definition lacks theoretical foundation and it is likely to lead to inconsistent results.[55]

Approach to definition	Definition category	Authors, year
Components -of- involvement	Family ownership	Mühlebach (2004) (-); Lee, S. K./Tan (2001); Littunen/Hyrsky (2000); Heck/Trent (1999) (+); Gudmundson/Hartman/Tower (1999); Smyrnios/Tanewski/Romano (1998) (+); Rue/Ibrahim (1996) (-); Flören (2002) (+); Astrachan/Kolenko (1994) (+); Lyman (1991) (-)
	Family management	Mühlebach (2004) (-); Flören (2002) (+); Heck/Trent (1999) (+); Smyrnios/Tanewski/Romano (1998) (+); Sharma/Chrisman/Chua (1997) (-); Handler (1989) (-)
	Ownership management	Donckels/Lambrecht (1999); Romano/Tanewski/Smyrnios (2001); Lansberg/Astrachan (1994); Dumas (1992) (-); Hauser/Wolter (2007)
Essence	Familiness	Habbershon/Williams/MacMillan (2003); Mühlebach (2004) (-); Westhead/Cowling (1998)
	Intention of generational transfer	Litz (1995); Shanker/Astrachan (1996); Astrachan/Kolenko (1994) (+); Handler (1989) (-); Donnelley (1964) (-)
	Interdependence of systems	Smyrnios/Tanewski/Romano (1998) (+); Sharma/Chrisman/Chua (1997) (-); Handler (1989) (-); Donnelley (1964) (-)
	Objective to employ family members	Rue/Ibrahim (1996) (-); Astrachan/Kolenko (1994) (+); Dumas (1992) (-); Lyman (1991) (-)

Table 1: Categorization of definitions in exemplary publications[56]

Source: Indicated respectively

(+) Inclusive combination of definitions (-) exclusive combination of definitions[57]

Definitions without (+) or (-) do not comprise a combination and are thus stand-alone definitions

[55] Self-identification is an approach, which defines all those companies as family businesses, which self-identify themselves as a family business (e.g. in a questionnaire or interview). Exemplary publications using this definitional approach are Gallo/Tàpies/Cappuyns (2004); Birley (2001); Johannisson/Huse (2000).

The dichotomous character of all definitions presented before, which is poorly adequate to grasp the heterogeneity of family businesses, is overcome by the latest definitional proposition, which introduced a scale of a continuous variable to measure family influence:[58] The **family-power, experience, and culture (F-PEC) index** conceived by ASTRACHAN/KLEIN/SMYRNIOS.[59] Instead of providing a precise definition of a family business, the F-PEC index is a standardized instrument to determine family influence and thus allows the comparison of research results. The F-PEC index is a scale measuring the family influence on the family business in the dimensions power, experience, and culture (see Figure 4). The power dimension measures the extent of family influence through ownership, management, and governance involvement. The experience dimension accounts for generational succession in the ownership, management, and governance, as well as the number of family members contributing to the business. The culture dimension refers to the overlap between family values and business values and the commitment of the family to the business. Being based on these three dimensions, the F-PEC index reconciles the component-of-involvement approach with the essence approach.[60] Thus, this definition is at the same time theoretically grounded and easier to operationalize than definitions based on the essence approach.

Despite the compelling character of the F-PEC index, its applicability is rather limited for two reasons, as ZELLWEGER states:[61] First, the culture dimension comprises values, which can hardly be evaluated in one time assessments, as the values measured are distorted by intertemporally variable emotions. Second, considerable data requirements to determine family influence on the three dimensions are hardly fulfillable using publicly available data, which complicates sampling significantly.[62]

---

56 For further reviews on definitions of family businesses, see Winter et al. (1998), p. 240; Chrisman/Chua/Sharma (1996), pp. 4-7; Westhead/Cowling (1998), p. 34; Flören (2002), pp. 17-22

57 For an explanation of inclusive and exclusive combinations, see footnote 54.

58 Cf. Klein/Astrachan/Smyrnios (2005), p. 323.

59 Cf. Astrachan/Klein/Smyrnios (2002), pp. 47-52.

60 Cf. Chrisman/Chua/Sharma (2005), p. 557.

61 Cf. Zellweger (2006), p. 42.

62 The exemplary questionnaire used by KLEIN/ASTRACHAN/SMYRNIOS in their validation of the F-PEC scale contains 37 items to determine the F-PEC value of a company (cf. Klein/Astrachan/Smyrnios (2005), pp. 338 et seq.).

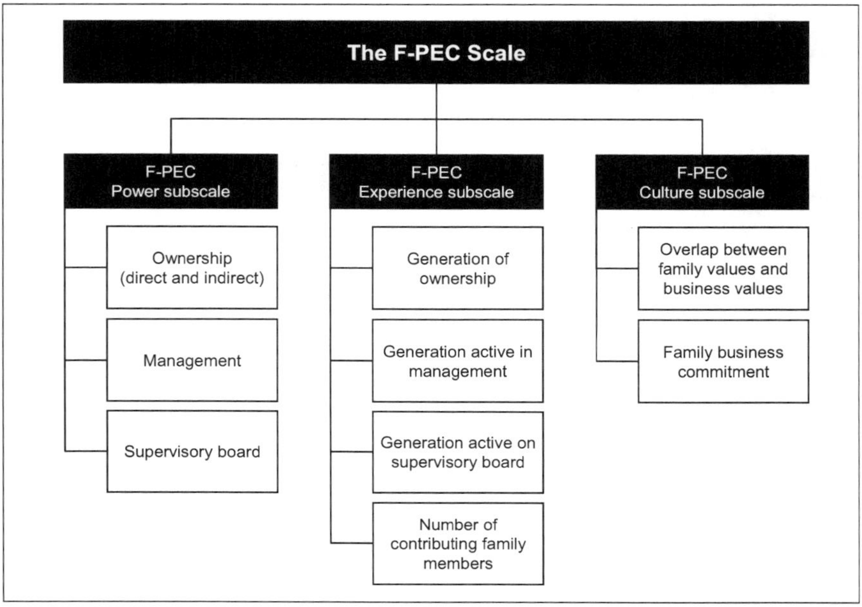

Figure 4: F-PEC scale, its dimensions, and their components

Source: Astrachan/Klein/Smyrnios (2002), p. 52

Given this problematic applicability of the whole F-PEC index, the definition underlying this thesis is based on the power dimension of the F-PEC index. This subscale was termed Substantial Family Influence (SFI) by KLEIN, in a paper preceding the definition of the F-PEC index.[63] The SFI overcomes the problematic

ZELLWEGER argues that a third constriction of the F-PEC index's applicability is the potential overlap between different dimensions that might entail potential substitutability (cf. Zellweger (2006), p. 42). However, this does not directly limit practicability of the F-PEC index. Moreover, he questions whether two companies with the same F-PEC value but different constellations, which have led to this value, can be considered the same. While this so called constriction is probably true in its essence, equal F-PEC values do not mean that companies can be considered the same and this intention was not explicitly stated by ASTRACHAN/KLEIN/SMYRNIOS (cf. Astrachan/ Klein/Smyrnios (2002)). Identical F-PEC values merely mean that family influence on the family businesses are equally strong, no matter how this influence is composed and exerted.

63 Cf. Klein (2000).

operationalizability of the whole F-PEC index, while preserving the advantages of a continuous measure of family influence and a theoretical foundation.

In this thesis, a family business is defined in line with KLEIN as "a company that is influenced by one or more families in a substantial way. [...] Influence in a substantial way is considered if the family either owns the complete stock or, if not, the lack of influence in ownership is [compensated by] influence through [the supervisory board] or influence through the management."[64]

The universe resulting from this definition is further constrained by two more characteristics: First, only those family businesses are taken into consideration with annual total sales of at least € 5 million, as smaller family businesses lack the sufficient size to be suitable for a buy-out.[65]

Second, only privately-held family businesses are taken into consideration.[66] Privately-held family businesses, which represent with about 95%[67] the lion's share of all family businesses in Germany, exhibit distinct characteristics, which stem from the owning family's particular goals and its interaction with the company – these characteristics are presented in detail later on in the thesis. In publicly-held family

---

64 Klein (2000), p. 158. This definition also embraces companies owned and managed by only one person, as these can be considered as a subset of family businesses sharing a multitude of characteristics (cf. Birley (2001), p. 75). Owner-managed companies formally qualify as family businesses according to all definitional approaches presented in this subsection. Following the components-of-involvement approach (and thus the SFI and the power subscale of the F-PEC index), unity of ownership and management in the hands of one person qualifies the company as family business. Following the line of argumentation of the essence approach (and thus of the experience and culture subscale of F-PEC index), an owner-managed company is a family business, if it shows a distinctiveness that differentiates it from non-family businesses. This distinctiveness is hardly given in case of a newly or recently founded company (which would be rather the research object of entrepreneurship). But after a certain period of time (which is still left to family researchers to define precisely), an owner-managed company will exhibit a certain culture and the owner-manager will have developed a certain experience in leading the company, so that these characteristics distinguish the company from non-family businesses.

65 This additional restriction is necessary, as buy-outs entail considerable transaction costs during the buy-out process (cf. subsection 2.1.2), which preclude profitability of buy-outs of smaller companies.

66 The distinction between privately-held and publicly-held family businesses is mostly forgone up to now, as stated by ASTRACHAN/JASKIEWICZ: "Research so far has regarded privately held businesses characterized by concentrated ownership and owner-manager duality from the same perspective as anonymously held, quoted businesses with dispersed shareholdings." (Astrachan/Jaskiewicz (2008), p. 139). See ibid. for a first discussion of the differences between both types of family businesses.

67 Cf. Klein (2004), p. 114.

businesses, the influence of minority non-family shareholders limits the effect of these peculiarities and thus limits the distinctness of family businesses from non-family businesses. In result, buy-outs in publicly-held family businesses are expected to have consequences that differ from those in privately-held family businesses. This thesis focuses on the predominating type of family businesses, namely privately-held ones.

Thus, family influence is composed of three elements: the share in total stock directly or indirectly[68] held by family members (so called family owners[69]) ($\frac{S_{Fam}}{S_{Total}}$), the share of seats on the management board held by family members (so called family managers[70]) ($\frac{MoMB_{Fam}}{MoMB_{Total}}$), and the share of seats on the supervisory board held by family members ($\frac{MoSB_{Fam}}{MoSB_{Total}}$). A company qualifies as a family business, if the following two conditions apply, where S_{Fam} refers to stock held by the family:

$$S_{Fam} > 0$$

$$SFI = \frac{S_{Fam}}{S_{Total}} + \frac{MoMB_{Fam}}{MoMB_{Total}} + \frac{MoSB_{Fam}}{MoSB_{Total}} \geq 1$$

The upper condition requires a family to own a part of the family business. The lower condition requires that the compounded share of family influence through ownership, management, and the supervisory board amounts to at least 1.[71]

The Substantial Family Influence has the advantage that it facilitates operationalization of family businesses: For sampling, data on the three elements of the definition are mostly publicly available or can be gathered without excessive effort. The resulting SFI value constitutes a continuous variable, which allows to

68 Family owners could indirectly own a company by pooling shares in an endowment, in a registered association or in another type of financial vehicle.

69 In contrast to family managers, who are family members owning and managing the family business, family owners do not manage (but merely own) the family business.

70 Cf. Chrisman et al. (2007), p. 1030; Koeberle-Schmid/Nützel (2005), p. 15. Owner-managers are also referred to by the term family managers.

71 In case no supervisory board existed, the compounded share of family influence through ownership and management was multiplied by 3/2. Supervisory boards are not mandatory for the most frequent legal incorporations of family businesses in Germany (cf. section 5.1.1).

determine family influence more precisely than a mere dichotomous variable.[72] At the same time, this definition based on the SFI is accepted among scholars.[73]

The general character of this definition permits inclusion of all the literature on family businesses for two reasons: First, the SFI embraces all definitions based on the components-of-involvement approach, as the index is based on family influence through ownership and management. Second, the substantial family influence measured by the SFI arguably entails the distinctive characteristics of family businesses demanded by the essence approach; hence, companies fulfilling the criteria of the SFI are expected to fulfill the definitional requirements of the essence approach. Therefore, the literature based on the components-of-involvement approach and the literature based on the essence approach is considered for the literature review on distinctive characteristics of family businesses.[74]

2.1.2. Private Equity, buyouts and portfolio companies

According to KASERER ET AL., **private equity** in the broader sense refers to investments into "equity or equity-like securities of private [i.e. non-publicly quoted] companies."[75] Private equity in its broader sense can be subdivided into investments in the early stage of company development (so called venture capital) and investments in the later stage of company development (see Figure 5).[76] Later stage investments,

72 Cf. Klein/Astrachan/Smyrnios (2005), p. 322.

73 Cf. Shanker/Astrachan (1996), pp. 111-114; Klein (2000), p. 158; Zellweger (2006), p. 43. The objection that the chosen definition follows the components-of-involvement approach and thus neglects the essence approach is justified. Despite criticism of the components-of-involvement approaches, family influence is a necessary precondition for the creation of the distinctness, essence approaches refer to. Although the essence approach seems attractive from a theoretical point of view, the virtually impossible applicability of these definitions (including the culture dimension of the F-PEC index), have left the SFI as the second-best solution to the definitional problem.

74 From a formal point of view, the definition used above does not embrace the approach of self-identification. However, definitional criteria provided above require a family influence of such an intensity that self-identification as family business seems to be very likely.

75 Kaserer et al. (2007), p. 14. The holding of equity in private companies refers to the situation after the acquisition. Thus, investments in public companies to take these private are also regarded as private equity investments.

76 While the first venture capital deals took place in the late 1940s, buy-outs became a phenomenon of the 1980s (cf. Gompers/Lerner (2001), p. 146; Wright/Thompson/Robbie (1992), p. 48). Both forms of private equity investments had their origin in the USA, quickly traversed the Atlantic to gain foothold in the UK, and then spread to continental Europe including Germany (cf.

which will be referred to as private equity in the narrow sense or just private equity in the following, embrace minority investments and majority investments (so called buy-outs).[77] This thesis focuses exclusively on buy-outs.[78]

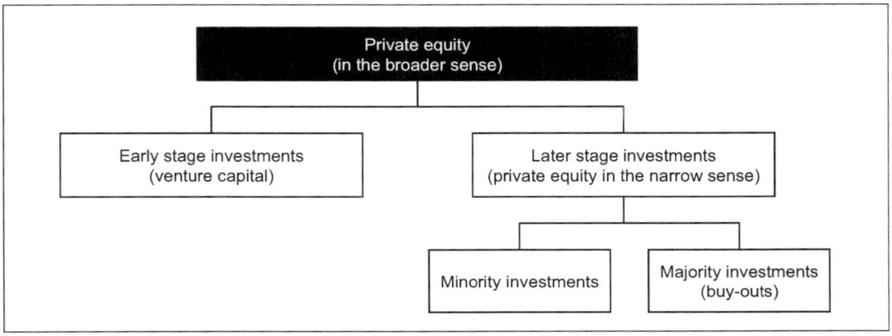

Figure 5: Definitional delineation of private equity

Source: Kaserer et al. (2007), p. 14

Private equity investments are done by **private equity companies**.[79] Private equity companies (also referred to as investors or financial investors) are financial intermediaries specialized in investing capital in a portfolio of companies (hence called **portfolio companies**) for a limited period.[80] Private equity companies aim at

Wright/Thompson/Robbie (1992), p. 48). For a history of private equity in the broader sense, see Loos (2006), pp. 10-12 and a history of private equity in the narrow sense, see Achleitner et al. (2008b), pp. 87 et seq.; Strömberg (2008), pp. 7-12.

77 Later stage investments accounted for 79.6% of all private equity (in a broader sense) investments in 2007 (cf. BVK (2008), p. 7). The term buy-out will be definied precisely later on in this subsection.

78 Cf. Achleitner/Schraml/Tappeiner (2008) for first evidence on minority investments of private equity companies in family businesses and subsection 2.1.3 for an overview on publications on minority investments.

79 Private equity companies are also referred to as buy-out specialists, LBO specialists, or private equity firms (cf. Cotter/Peck (2001), p. 103; DeAngelo/DeAngelo (1987), p. 40; Meier (2006), p. 10).

80 Cf. Meier (2006), pp. 10 et seq.; Kaserer et al. (2007), p. 16; Loos (2006), p. 12; Kitzmann (2005), p. 21. There are four different types of private equity companies (cf. Schefczyk (2000), p. 17; Meier (2006), p. 11): Independent private equity companies are not connected to their investors and gather capital from a multitude of institutional and private investors (e.g. Kohlberg, Kravis Roberts & Co. L.P.). Captive private equity companies are funded by their main shareholder (e.g.

selling their shares in portfolio companies with a capital gain at the end of the holding period, which typically lasts between three and seven years.[81] Interaction with portfolio companies is managed by senior staff of private equity companies, so called investment managers.[82] For their intermediary purpose, private equity companies typically set up closed-end funds with a lifetime of about 10 years.[83] A fund is started with the fundraising stage, in which the private equity company attracts fund investors to commit capital. In the following investment period, the private equity company draws down committed capital for investments into portfolio companies. In the succeeding holding period, portfolio companies are developed to increase company value.[84] In the final realization period, the private equity company sells the investments (also called exit); proceedings from exits are distributed to the fund investors after subtracting compensation.[85] Private equity investments bear a high risk, but compensate their fund investors through average annual net returns between 9.2% and 19.8% (internal rate of return) according to the meta study by KASERER ET AL.[86]

Barclays Private Equity GmbH). Semi-captive private equity companies raise capital from one or several shareholders and unconnected investors (e.g. EQT Partners Beteiligungberatung GmbH). Lastly, public private equity companies raise capital through the capital market (e.g. 3i).

81 Cf. Kaserer et al. (2007), p. 14.

82 Investment manager here and in the following means a representative of a private equity company, who interacts with the portfolio company on behalf of the private equity company. The term is not related to a hierarchical position of the respective investment manager within the private equity company.

83 Cf. Kitzmann (2005), p. 21; Lin/Smith (1998), p. 244. These funds are mostly organized as limited partnerships (cf. Müller (2008), pp. 16-39; Meier (2006), p. 8). By committing capital to the funds of a private equity company, fund investors delegate the labor intensive responsibilities of the investment process to the private equity company, which have comparative advantages over other investors in buy-outs due to their specialization (cf. Fenn/Liang/Prowse (2005), p. 35; Cotter/Peck (2001), p. 103).

84 See below for the discussion of value generation through buy-outs.

85 Cf. Müller (2008), pp. 19 et seq. Open-end funds (also called evergreen funds) do not have a stipulated lifetime. Thus, the previously presented stages of fund lifetime merge and take place simultaneously.

86 Cf. Kaserer et al. (2007), pp. 183-187. The high risk inherent in private equity investments is shown by the fact that standard deviation of these investments is between 17.8% and 39.0% according to this meta study. For a detailed overview of studies on returns of private equity investments, see Kaserer et al. (2007), pp. 181-188. For a literature review, see Lossen (2007), pp. 8-12.

In the investment period, private equity companies acquire other companies through **buy-outs**. In the context of this thesis, a buy-out is defined as the acquisition of a majority stake in a given company by a group of buyers including a private equity company.[87] The acquisition price of the portfolio company is typically financed through a small share of equity, which is provided primarily by the private equity company, and a significant share of debt.[88] Because of the resulting high leverage of the buy-out, these transactions are also referred to as leveraged buy-outs (LBOs).[89] Buy-outs can be categorized according to the reason for the sale and according to the buyers of the company besides the private equity company (see Figure 6).

There are six reasons for the sale of a company through a buy-out:[90] In succession buy-outs, resigning owners of family businesses sell their company.[91] In spin-off buy-outs, a corporation sells off a division or a subsidiary. In turnaround buy-outs, the portfolio company is in a distressed situation and the sale is supposed to entail a corporate restructuring. In privatization buy-outs, governments or public entities sell state-owned companies. In going-private buy-outs, public companies are bought from their shareholders and taken from the stock exchange.[92] Lastly, secondary buy-outs refer to buy-outs in former portfolio companies, which are sold by the

87 The broadness of this definition enables inclusion of the comprehensive literature on buy-outs in the USA and the UK. In general, a buy-out is the acquisition of a majority stake in a company by one or several buyers (cf. Achleitner/Fingerle (2003), p. 3; Geidner (2009), p. 7; Lütjen (1992), p. 9; Kramer (1990), p. 9). For an overview on definitions of buy-outs, see Sander (2006), pp. 9-12; Kitzmann (2005), p. 12; Webb (1985), p. 13.

SZYPERSKI/NATHUSIUS delineate buy-outs from new company foundations and acquisitions by two criteria. First, buy-outs differ from foundations of new companies by involving already existing organizations (derivative structural existence). Second, buy-outs differ from acquisitions as bought-out companies remain independent after the transaction (cf. Szyperski/Nathusius (1999), pp. 26-30).

88 For levels of leverage typical for buy-outs in family businesses, see subsection 7.1.1.

89 Cf. Kaserer et al. (2007), p. 15; Achleitner/Fingerle (2003), p. 3; Kitzmann (2005), p. 8; Webb (1985), p. 13. Particularly in studies of US authors, the term LBO is used (cf. Kitzmann (2005), p. 7). For a detailed description of the financial structure of a buy-out, see subsection 7.1.2.

90 This categorization is not mutually exclusive, as several reasons might trigger a buy-out, e.g. a buy-out in a division of a corporation, which is in a turnaround situation.

91 Reasons that lead to a succession buy-out are discussed in detail in subsection 4.2.1.1. The subsection also reveals other reasons, why a family business is sold through a buy-out.

92 For an interesting case study of a going-private buy-out, see Achleitner et al. (2008d).

formerly owning private equity company.[93] Buy-outs in family businesses are typically succession buy-outs or turnaround buy-outs.[94] These buy-outs represented 38% of all European buy-outs in 2007.[95]

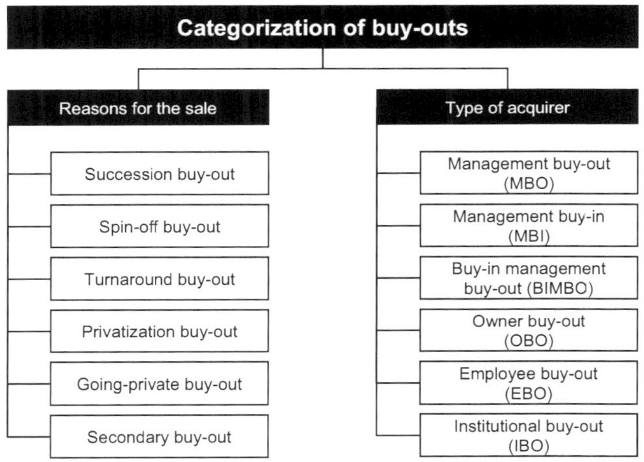

Figure 6: Categorization of buy-outs

Source: Modifiedly taken from Jakoby (2000), p. 49

Buy-outs can be also categorized according to the type of buyer besides the private equity company. In a management buy-out (MBO)[96], incumbent managers who worked with the portfolio company prior to the buy-out acquire the company with the

[93] Cf. Achleitner/Fingerle (2003), pp. 9-11; Geidner (2009), pp. 8-15; Jakoby (2000), pp. 35-48; Kitzmann (2005), pp. 15-20; Kaserer et al. (2007), p. 52; Huydts (1992), p. 21; Meier (2006), pp. 16 et seq.; Luippold (1991), pp. 18-25; Sander (2006), pp. 25 et seq. This thesis focuses on the first buy-out in a family business, as the pre buy-out state of secondary buy-outs is already biased by the changes of the first buy-out.

[94] Cf. subsection 4.1.1.1 and 4.2.1.1 for details on successions and turnaround situations in family businesses and other reasons that lead to a company sale.

[95] Cf. Klöckner (2008), p. 17. This percentage is based on the number of buy-outs; in terms of total transaction volume, buy-outs in family businesses represent 11% of all buy-outs.

[96] According to WEBB, the term "management buy-out" was coined by the British private equity company 3i about 1979 (cf. Webb (1985), p. 1).

private equity company.[97] In a management buy-in (MBI), managers who did not work with the company before the buy-out acquire the company. In case, incumbent managers as well as external managers, who did not work for the company before the buy-out, acquire a company beside the private equity company, this buy-out is referred to as buy-in management buy-out (BIMBO). In an owner buy-out (OBO)[98], the former owners of the company retain a significant stake in the company. An employee buy-out (EBO) is characterized by the fact that employees acquire a significant stake in their employing company. In an institutional buy-out (IBO), the buy-out is initiated and driven by the private equity company; incumbent and external managers are involved at a later stage of sale negotiations.[99] In practice, a clear delineation between the different buy-out types is not always possible, as there are a multitude of different mixed forms of buy-outs.[100] Throughout this thesis, the term buy-out is used as umbrella term and comprises all the definitions provided in this paragraph, if not a more precise type of buy-out is specified.

The process of a buy-out consists of four stages (see Figure 7):[101] In the first stage of target selection, private equity companies screen the market for potential companies to buy out. Investors rely on advisors, auctions and investment managers' network to source deals and critically evaluate the suitability of a company for a buy-

97 Some researches have defined a minimum threshold for the management's equity stake. If management holds at least the threshold stake, the deal is considered as an MBO; if management stake is below the threshold value, the buy-out is considered as an LBO. The threshold differs according to the author and is stipulated at 5% (cf. Kramer (1990), p. 10), 10% (cf. Jakoby (2000), p. 19), 10-20% (cf. Kohlberg Kravis Roberts (1989), p. 65), 15-25% (cf. Kropp (1992), p. 19), and even 50% (cf. Schwenkedel (1991), p. 5). This approach is not followed in this thesis, as no accepted threshold value has emerged (cf. Kitzmann (2005), p. 13).

98 This transaction is also referred to as ownership buy-out. As minority stocks of former family owners are common in buy-outs in family businesses, but these post buy-out family owners do not exert significant influence on the company after the buy-out (cf. subsection 4.2.2.5), the owner buy-out was not used to categorize post buy-out companies in the following. Cf. subsection 3.2.4 for equity stakes of family owners after the buy-out and 4.2.2.3 for the reason behind this practice.

99 Cf. Geidner (2009), pp. 15-20; Jakoby (2000), pp. 23-26; Achleitner/Fingerle (2003), pp. 8 et seq.; Kitzmann (2005), pp. 9 et seq.; Huydts (1992), p. 20 et seq.; Meier (2006), pp. 15 et seq.; Webb (1985), pp. 14-16; Sander (2006), p. 25. The institutional buy-out is also referred to as investors buy-out (cf. Huydts (1992), p. 20).

100 Cf. Achleitner/Fingerle (2003), p. 9.

101 Cf. Loos (2006), pp. 14-17; Kaserer et al. (2007), p. 14. During the investment period and the realization period, a private equity company is actively involved in several buy-outs. As these buy-outs do not take place simultaneously, the private equity company is at the same time in different stages of the buy-out process in different companies.

out.[102] In the second stage of buy-out transaction, the private equity company contacts the potential vendor, conducts a due diligence, stipulates the deal structure and negotiates and closes the sale.[103] In the third stage of post buy-out management, the private equity company supervises and supports the portfolio company. To ensure and foster development of the portfolio company in this stage, the investor influences and changes the company's corporate governance, financing, instruments of managerial control and other areas. In the last stage of exit, the private equity company sells its stake in the portfolio company and thus ends the buy-out process. The multitude of changes during the stage of post buy-out management is analyzed in this thesis according to a framework that is developed in subsection 3.1.1.

Figure 7: Stylized buy-out process of private equity companies

Source: Modifiedly taken from Achleitner/Fingerle (2003), pp. 11-13; Loos (2006), p. 16

Despite the considerable return of private equity investments in portfolio companies, there is an intense debate going on among scholars whether these returns of buy-outs are due to value capturing or value creation.[104] Proponents of the value capturing hypothesis argue that buy-outs do not create value but transfer value from other stakeholders like employees[105], vendors[106], debt providers[107], or the state[108] to the

---

[102] See subsections 4.1.2.3 and 4.2.2.3 for theoretical and empirical details on deal initiation and subsections 4.1.2.1 and 4.2.2.1 for details on investment criteria.

[103] See subsections 4.1.2.3 and 4.2.2.3 for theoretical and empirical details on deal initiation, due diligence, negotiations and closing. Apart form this stylized process, the buy-out can also be initiated by the owners of the family business or the management.

[104] Cf. Kaserer et al. (2007), pp. 94-99, 190; Berg/Gottschalg (2005), pp. 11-13. BERG/GOTTSCHALG provide the most recent literature review on value capturing and value creation in buy-outs (cf. Berg/Gottschalg (2005), pp. 31-37).

[105] Cf. Liebeskind/Wiersema/Hansen (1992), p. 82; Wright/Thompson/Robbie (1992), p. 64; Wright/ Coyne (1985), p. 130.

[106] Cf. Thompson/Wright/Robbie (1992), p. 64. The authors argue that underpricing by the vendors was more common in early buy-out years and was unlikely at the time they published their results.

private equity company and its fund investors. In contrast, proponents of the value creation hypothesis argue that buy-outs generate new value through changes in strategy and operations[109], improvements in corporate governance[110], and financial drivers[111]. While proponents of both points of view still have not settled on a compromise, this thesis might add some valuable insights into the type, degree, causes and consequences of changes induced by private equity companies in family businesses after a buy-out.

2.1.3. Review of the literature on buy-outs in family businesses

As mentioned in the introduction of this thesis, research on buy-outs has so far mainly focused on going-private buy-outs and spin-off buy-outs. The academic discussion of buy-outs followed the historical emergence of the phenomenon: Most early transactions were going-private buy-outs, until corporations embraced the instrument of spin-off buy-outs as means of corporate reorganization and divestment.[112]

Although buy-outs also have been taking place in family businesses for at least 20 years now, buy-out research has largely neglected this type of buy-outs.[113] A few researchers included family businesses in their buy-out samples[114], and even less focused on this topic. However, with the rise of research in family businesses, several

---

107 Cf. Marais/Schipper/Smith (1989), pp. 186 et seq.; Jackson-Cookland/Crowe/Pratt (1998), p. 61; Asquith/Wizman (1990), p. 212.

108 Cf. Kaplan (1989b), p. 630; Newbould/Chatfield/Anderson (1992), p. 56.

109 Cf. Heel/Kehoe (2005), pp. 24-26; Easterwood/Seth/Singer (1989), pp. 41 et seq.; Wright/Hoskisson/Busenitz (2001), pp. 121 et seq.; Phan/Hill (1995), pp. 732 et seq.; Seth/Easterwood (1993), p. 267.

110 Cf. Jensen (1986), p. 326; Easterwood/Seth/Singer (1989), pp. 35 et seq.; Cotter/Peck (2001), p. 135, 137.

111 Cf. Kaufman/Englander (1993), p. 68; DeAngelo/DeAngelo (1987), pp. 40 et seq., 43;Cotter/Peck (2001), p. 145. GEIDNER argues that in case of spin-off buy-outs, independence of the spun-off company from its former holding company also creates value. Through the buy-out, certain restrictions from the holding company are discontinued (bureaucracy, constraints in decision making, financial constraints), which strengthens the portfolio company and thus creates value (cf. Geidner (2009), pp. 132-138).

112 Cf. Geidner (2009), p. 1; Berg/Gottschalg (2005), p. 25; Kessel (1995), pp. 18-20; Hutchinson (1999), p. 354.

113 By this omission, research in buy-outs might reflect the general neglect of research in family businesses that predominated research in business administration in general.

114 Cf. Sander (2006); Achleitner/Klöckner (2005); Jakoby (2000); Gräper (1993); Luippold (1991).

scholars became interested in buy-outs in family businesses.[115] Table 2 provides an overview on the still limited number of publications on this issue.[116]

Author, year	Type of research	Description of research project	Results
Huydts (1992)	Theo-retical	Literature and interview-based description of the characteristics and success factors of buy-outs in mid-sized Swiss family businesses	• Management should be willing to take risks and must be financially motivated • Company should show scope for value creation, should be offered at a reasonable price, and must not entirely depend on the family manager • Buy-out has to be planned a considerable time in advance and needs intensive preparations
Forst (1992)	Empirical	Survey and interview-based study into the characteristics and consequences of buy-outs in German family businesses	• PECs are involved in virtually all buy-outs • Fundamental changes with regard to organization, management, and internal processes • Companies resulting from spin-off buy-outs grow faster than those from succession buy-outs
Upton/ Petty (2000)*	Empirical	Survey among PECs and family owners on financing generational transition in US family businesses	• Generational transition of family businesses mostly funded by grants of other family members, internal cash flow or bank loans • PECs look for qualified successors, companies with growth opportunities and absence of family conflicts
Howorth/ Westhead/ Wright (2004)	Empirical	Analysis of eight case studies of buy-outs in UK family businesses with regard to information asymmetries and negotiation behavior	• Information asymmetries are prevalent problem of buy-out negotiations putting the party with more information into a better bargaining position • Information asymmetries were mitigated by good relationships and trust between negotiation partners • Information asymmetries hampered knowledge transfer
Poech/ Achleitner/ Burger-Calderon (2005)	Empirical	Interview-based survey on psychological barriers hampering buy-outs in German family businesses	• Miscommunication, different social identities, prejudices, selective information processing, and cognitive dissonance hamper negotiations • Intermediaries can mitigate communication problems between both parties and address obstacles during negotiations
Silva (2006)*	Empirical	Analysis of seven case studies of PEC investments in Finish family businesses with regard to financing, corporate governance, and employment of family members	• PECs' investments facilitate access to alternative sources of capital • PECs change corporate governance by delegating members to the supervisory board • PECs' investments do not compromise employment of family members

continued on next page…

[115] An alternative explanation might be that most research issues of interest or of feasibility are answered to a sufficient degree for the other types of buy-outs.

[116] Besides scientific publications, practitioners produce a growing number of studies, e.g. Fleischhauer (2006); European Private Equity & Venture Capital Association (2005), UBS (2005), F.A.Z. Institut et al. (2004).

... continued from previous page			
Howorth/ Wright/ Westhead (2007)	Empirical	Analysis of eight case studies of buy-outs in UK family businesses with regard to professionalization and continuity of stewardship culture	• Buy-outs (and their preparations) entail significant professionalization of the former family business with regard to leadership style, internal processes and efficiency improvements • Elements of stewardship were exhibited in all surviving companies in an attachment to the company, a long-term view and prioritization of company objectives over personal ones
Scholes et al. (2007)	Empirical	Survey on information sharing and price negotiation in buy-outs in European family businesses	• Information was shared equally between negotiating parties if vendors were founders of the business or if vendors stressed market value increment • Mutually agreed sale prices were achieved if there was no family successor, if vendors stressed market value increment, or if PECs were involved in succession planning
Gossens/ Manigart/ Meuleman (2007)	Empirical	Survey on differences in efficiency and growth between succession buy-outs and spin-off buy-outs in Belgium	• Spin-off buy-outs and succession buy-outs do not differ with regard to growth • Financial backing of a PEC makes a difference: portfolio companies grow less in assets but more in employees
Scholes/ Westhead/ Burrows (2008)	Empirical	Survey on the impact of information flows and succession planning on negotiations to sell European family businesses through a buy-out	• Involvement of management in succession planning reduces information asymmetries between management and family owners and increases the likelihood of MBOs • Involvement of PECs in succession planning, reduces the likelihood of mutually agreed sale prices between family owners and management
Achleitner/ Schraml/ Tappeiner (2008)*	Empirical	Interview-based survey on the reasons for, implementation of and consequences of minority investments of PECs in German family businesses	• Family businesses mostly resorted to private equity to finance growth and ownership restructuring • Families approached PECs and based their decision on the interpersonal relationship with the PEC • PECs exert their influence through approval rights, supervisory boards and contractual stipulations • Major changes including professionalization occurred in the fields of corporate governance, instruments of managerial control and financial practices

Table 2: Overview of publications on buy-outs and private equity in family businesses

Source: Indicated respectively
PEC = private equity company
* Minority investments of private equity companies

As this review of the literature has shown, research on buy-outs in family businesses has gained momentum, especially since 2004, coming from a rather nascent state. Two streams of literature can be identified: The first stream focuses on the pre buy-out stage of buy-outs in family businesses and inquires into sale negotiations, investment criteria of the private equity company, and family owners' reasons for selling the company through a buy-out.[117] The second stream of literature covers the post buy-out stage and discusses the consequences of buy-outs with regard to efficiency and growth gains (GOSSENS/MANIGART/MEULEMANN; FORST), professionalization (HOWORTH/WESTHEAD/WRIGHT (2007)) and changes in selected areas like corporate governance and finance (FORST, SILVA, ACHLEITER/SCHRAML/TAPPEINER).

This thesis is anchored in the second stream of literature and sets out to deepen the understanding of the consequences of the buy-out on selected areas of the company (corporate governance, instruments of managerial control, and financing) and also draws on professionalization. By contributing valuable insights, the thesis attempts to enrich and incite the discussion of the consequences of buy-outs in family businesses.

2.2 Relevant theories

This section explains the two theories on which this thesis is built: agency theory in subsection 2.2.1 and stewardship theory in subsection 2.2.2. The description of each theory is structured in the following order: Background of the theory, explanation of the theory, criticism of the theory, and application of the theory.

2.2.1. Agency theory

Explanation of agency theory will start with a brief introduction to its **background**: For about three decades following World War II, mainstream economists focused on developing and expanding neoclassicism.[118] Based on the assumption that market participants have complete information, neoclassical theory praised the price mechanism of free markets as the most efficient coordination mechanism of economic transactions.[119] However, in situations of asymmetric market power, increasing returns to scale, externalities, or search and coordination problems, markets do not lead to most efficient outcomes.[120] In case of these market failures, organizational forms might be more efficient coordination mechanisms of economic transactions. In the 1970s, various economists directed their attention towards the analysis of organizations in

[117] Cf. Huydts (1992); Upton/Petty (2000); Howorth/Westhead/Wright (2004); Poech/Achleitner/Burger-Calderon (2005); Scholes et al. (2007); Scholes/Westhead/Burrows (2008).

[118] Cf. Joskow (2004), p. 1.

[119] Cf. Picot/Dietl/Franck (2005), pp. 35 et seq.; Milgrom/Roberts (1992), pp. 57-61.

[120] Cf. Milgrom/Roberts (1992), pp. 73-77.

consequence.[121] Especially in the organizational context, they relaxed the assumption concerning information to assume incomplete information of the individuals within organizations.[122] This opened a new playing field to analyze intra-organizational problems stemming from incomplete information. In particular, the role of formal legal rules and informal social norms – subsumed under the term "institutional framework" – in determining individual behavior and social interactions is examined.[123] Hence, this stream of economical thought was coined "neo-institutional economics".[124] Neo-institutional economics produced three main theories: transaction cost theory, property rights theory and agency theory.[125]

After presentation of the background of agency theory, the **theory is explained** in detail: Suboptimal behavior of one party in a cooperation was already suspected by SMITH[126] in 1776 and insinuated by BERLE/MEANS[127] in 1932. In 1976, JENSEN/MECKLING published the foundation of agency theory. In their paper, they discussed the emergence of agency problems in the cooperation between two individuals and possible solutions to these problems through contractual stipulations.[128]

---

121 Cf. Arrow (1999), p. vii; Williamson (2000), p. 595; Barney/Ouchi (1986), p. 205. There were already a few forerunners earlier, as will be pointed out later in this section. MATTHEWS notes that meanwhile "the economics of institutions has become one of the liveliest areas in our discipline [i.e. economics]" (Matthews (1986), p. 903).

122 Cf. North (1992), p. 3. Frequently, the terms "instrumental rationality" and "bounded rationality" are used instead of "complete information" and "incomplete information" to stress limited mental capacity as source of incomplete information; both words relate to the same concept.

123 Cf. North (1993), p. 6.

124 For the relation, development and differences between "neo-institutional economics" and (classical) institutional economics, see Joskow (2004), pp. 8-10.

125 Cf. Picot/Dietl/Franck (2005), p. 46. The theory of property-rights examines the distribution and transfer of rights that result from the existence or usage of commodities (cf. Picot/Dietl/Franck (2005), pp. 46 et seq.). The theory of transaction costs analyzes how different institutional arrangements affect the costs of a transaction, i.e. its efficiency (cf. Picot/Dietl/Franck (2005), pp. 56 et seq.).

126 Cf. Smith (1937), p. 700 according to Jensen/Meckling (1976), p. 305.

127 Cf. Berle/Means (1932) according to Hutchinson (1999), p. 346.

128 Cf. Eisenhardt (1989), p. 58. In 1983, JENSEN notes that two streams of literature on agency theory have emerged: Positive literature on agency theory is non-mathematical and empirically oriented, whereas normative literature on agency theory is mathematical and non-empirically oriented (cf. Jensen (1983), pp. 334 et seq.). As agency theory is used in an empirical framework in this thesis, the positive stream of literature is followed.

Agency theory examines the relationship between two parties, in which a principal, typically the owner of a company, delegates tasks to an agent, typically the manager of the company.[129] An agency conflict ensues this delegation, if two conditions are met: First, desires of the principal and the agent diverge, which results in a conflict of interests.[130] Interests may diverge as both parties behave self-servingly, which means that they attempt to maximize their personal utility regardless of effects on the utility of the other party; this is based on the assumption that every party behaves as homo oeconomicus.[131] Second, intervention of the principal to limit divergence of the agent's actions from his own goals comes at a certain cost.[132] This condition implies information asymmetries between principal and agent: The principal cannot observe effortless actions the agent takes, so that the agent could act to the principal's detriment without the latter being aware; this problem is referred to as moral hazard.[133]

---

129 Cf. Jensen/Meckling (1976), p. 308. Agency conflicts may also arise in a cooperation between two equal parties, i.e. if "there is no clear cut principal-agent relationship" (Jensen/Meckling (1976), p. 309).

This whole subsection covers the stream of literature on agency theory, which is relevant for this thesis and which is known under the term "moral hazard". The neighboring streams of literature known as "adverse selection" (which treats the misrepresentation of ability by the agent before a relationship between principal and agent is established (cf. Eisenhardt (1989), p. 61)) and "hold-up" (which deals with a principal's inability to prevent observable, adverse behavior of the agent due to dependency on the other party (cf. Picot/Dietl/Franck (2005), p. 75)), are not covered in the following as the thesis focuses on examining interactions between parties in already established and ongoing relations, which are characterized by information asymmetries. However, it should not be concealed that cases of adverse selection and hold-up are possible in buy-outs in family businesses.

130 Cf. Jensen/Meckling (1976), p. 308.

131 This behavior is also referred to as self-interested or opportunistic (cf. Milgrom/Roberts (1992), p. 601). Other explanations for the pursuit of different interests are bounded rationality of both parties or different levels of risk aversion (cf. Eisenhardt (1989), p. 58).

132 Cf. Jensen/Meckling (1976), p. 308.

133 Cf. Picot/Dietl/Franck (2005), p. 75; Jost (2001), pp. 20 et seq., 25-27, 30 et seq.; Eisenhardt (1989), p. 61. Information asymmetries can stem from two sources: First, the agent acquires information while carrying out the task; the principal is able to observe the result of the agent's behavior, but is unable to derive the information from the result (hidden information). Second, the principal cannot observe the agent's behavior and thus has no information on the agent's action (hidden action).

There are three measures to mitigate agency conflicts (see Figure 8).[134] First, the principal could set appropriate incentives for the agent to ensure that the agent acts in the principal's interest. Incentivization aligns the goals of both parties and thus mitigates conflicts of interests. Second, the principal could monitor the agents' actions to take countermeasures in case the agent does not act in the principal's interest. Monitoring mitigates information asymmetries. Third, the agent could expend resources to guarantee the principal that the agent would not take actions harming the principal or to ensure the principal compensation in case he takes such actions.[135] This measure is called bonding and prevents agency conflicts by making the agent responsible for resulting costs.

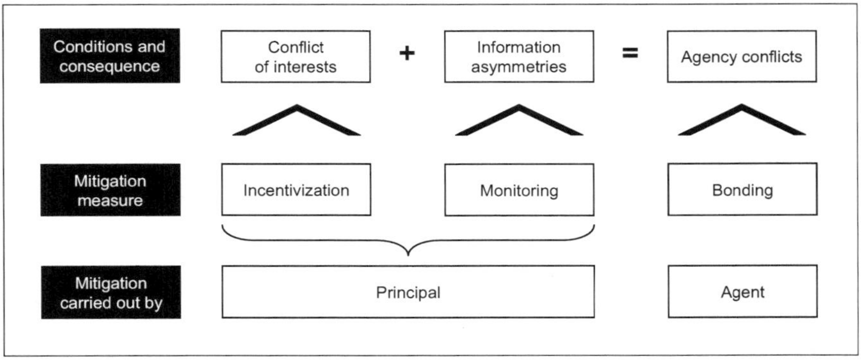

Figure 8: Stylized mitigation of agency conflicts

Source: Author's illustration

While the three measures presented above aim at mitigating agency conflicts, they come at certain costs. Regardless of the mitigating measures taken by both parties, there will still be some divergence between the agent's decisions and the decisions that would maximize the principal's utility; this reduction in the principal's

[134] This description and Figure 8 focus on the main effect of each mitigation measure. A more detailed analysis would show that each measure also affects the other conditions and consequences of agency conflicts not being the main effect.

[135] Cf. Jensen/Meckling (1976), p. 308.

utility is called the residual loss due to agency conflicts.[136] The sum of costs for monitoring, incentivization, and bonding, as well as the residual loss is called agency costs.[137]

With the rise of agency theory to its current importance in management science, the theory also raised **criticism** by some scholars. Three points of criticism will be discussed in the following. Criticism of some assumptions and methodological approach lead to stewardship theory and are discussed in subsection 2.2.2.[138]

Agency theory can be criticized for applying the thorough instruments of economics to problems already solved in the real world. The ubiquity of supervisory boards to moderate information asymmetries and the compensation standard to include variable payments to align interests signal that practitioners are aware of agency conflicts and have already taken countermeasures. In other agency-relationships, deposits and cost sharing serve as bonding instruments. As the prescriptions of agency theory are already intensively used in reality, the normative power of the theory is considerably reduced.

HIRSCH/FRIEDMAN/KOZA focus their criticism on volition. They argue that the reductionist unit of analysis, which merely focuses on the relation between an individual and another individual, neglects a number of impact factors. Career opportunities, personal values, job ladders and corporate culture further influence the behavior of managers. While recognizing the value of the clinically pure analysis of economics, the authors argue that complexity of reality calls for inclusion of the aforementioned impact factors.[139]

---

136 The principal will incur a residual loss even in case of optimal mitigation measures (cf. Jensen/Meckling (1976), p. 308). Mitigation measures merely aim at reducing the residual loss. Less efficient implementation or forgoing of mitigation measures will increase the residual loss.

137 Cf. Jensen/Meckling (1976), p. 308.

138 One point of criticism on the assumptions is not included in the discussion in subsection 2.2.2 but described in the following: LEVINTHAL criticizes that agents are typically assumed to incur disutility from effort. LEVINTHAL states that this effort aversion – though existing in reality – is overemphasized in the literature, as not lazyness is a problem principals fight against, but decisions not in the best interest of principals (cf. Levinthal (1988), pp. 181 et seq.).

139 Cf. Hirsch/Friedman/Koza (1990), pp. 90, 93 et seq.

PERROW casts severe doubts in the assumptions of agency theory. In particular, he criticizes that agents do not behave self-interestedly because this behavior is predetermined in their genomes. Instead, PERROW considers opportunistic, self-interested behavior the result of agents' bounded rationality or structural deficiencies in the organization.[140] He continues by arguing that perception of agency conflicts might follow from principals' limited ability to assess the true level of difficulty of the agents' tasks. In consequence, he discards the normative propositions of agency theory.[141]

Following explanation and criticism of agency theory, its **application** relevant for this thesis is presented. As modern organizations are characterized by the cooperation between individuals, which is typically based on the delegation of tasks, and these individuals are assumed as self-serving homini oeconomici, modern organizations serve as an almost unlimited playing field for the application of agency theory. JENSEN/MECKLING point out this general application of agency theory: Agency problems exist "in all organizations and in all cooperative efforts – at every level of management in firms [...]. The development of theories to explain the form which agency costs take [...] and how and why they are born will lead to a rich theory of organizations which is now lacking in economics and the social sciences generally."[142]

Hence, the almost universal application of agency theory is not surprising. Already in 1989, EISENHARDT[143] points out that agency theory is used in the fields of accounting[144], economics[145], finance[146], marketing[147], political science[148], organizational behavior[149], and sociology[150].

---

140 In this case, bounded rationality does not correspond to complete information but refers to rationality deficiencies stemming from cognitive incapacities (apart from this subsection, bounded rationality is defined as equal to incomplete information, see footnote 131).

141 Cf. Perrow (1986), p. 235. PERROW accepts the empirical support for agency theory – but he sees self-interested behavior not as the original source of agency conflicts. Instead, he considers self-interested behavior as an intermediary effect causing agency conflicts, while the behavior itself is caused by the problems pointed out above.

142 Jensen/Meckling (1976), p. 309.

143 Cf. Eisenhardt (1989), p. 57. A current query in the research database EBSCOhost returns more than 1,100 publications in academic journals that refer to agency theory.

144 Cf. Demski/Feltham (1978).

145 Cf. Spence/Zeckhauser (1971).

146 Cf. Fama (1980).

The application of agency theory to the relation between private equity companies and portfolio companies (respectively between investment managers and managers of the portfolio companies) is of high relevance for this thesis to examine and propose possible explanations for changes after buy-outs in family businesses. Applicability of agency theory is justified by the fact that private equity companies (the principals) delegate management of the portfolio companies to managers (the agents). In this cooperation, portfolio company's managers are likely to gain more information on the company through their involvement in daily business (hidden information) and might pursue actions without the private equity company's knowledge thereof (hidden action). These information asymmetries in combination with the conflict of interests stemming from managers' goals diverging from those of the private equity company fulfill the two conditions for the application of agency theory (moral hazard). Despite the existence of agency conflicts after buy-outs, scholars have intensively used agency theory to explain advantages of corporate governance in portfolio companies owned by private equity companies compared to corporate governance in widely held public corporations; this advantage of corporate governance after buy-outs stems from the direct relation between portfolio company and private equity company, intensity of the latter's influence given its majority stake, and the latter's experience in buy-out transactions.[151] Hence, a multitude of pieces of research into the relationship between portfolio company and private equity company employ agency theory (see Table 3).[152]

---

147 Cf. Basu et al. (1985).

148 Cf. Mitnick (1992).

149 Cf. Kosnik (1987).

150 Cf. White (1985).

151 Cf. Jensen (1986), p. 325; Sahlman (1990), pp. 516 et seq.; Berg/Gottschalg (2005), p. 10. JENSEN even argues that buy-outs are especially successful in case of formerly public corporations that exhibited significant agency costs.

152 Further publications on agency theory applied to buy-outs and portfolio companies include: Jensen (1989a); Jensen (1989b); Sahlman (1990); Simpson/Wright (1991); Wruck (1994); Denis (1994); Wright et al. (1996); Wright et al. (2001); Bruton/Keels/Scifres (2002)

Author, year	Type of research	Description of research project	Results
Jensen (1986)	Theo-retical	Theorizing about the reduction of AC in buy-outs	• Leverage, approximately equal dissemination of equity and mezzanine[153], and equity participation of managers reduce AC
Lehn/ Poulsen (1989)	Empirical	Examination of the sources of value generation in buy-outs in public corporations	• Value is generated through mitigation of AC associated with free cash flow[154] • High undistributed cash flow increases the likelihood of buy-outs
Kaplan (1989a)	Empirical	Examination of the sources of value generation in buy-outs in public corporations	• Value generation stems from reduced AC and improved managerial incentives, rejecting other possible explanations
Thompson/ Wright (1989)	Theo-retical	Formal analysis of the effect of buy-outs on agency costs	• Bonding of managers through increased leverage reduces consumption of perquisites • In contrast, injection of outside equity raises consumption of perquisites
Cotter/Peck (2001)	Empirical	Examination of the influence of private equity companies on the debt structure of portfolio companies	• Buy-outs are financed with less short term debt and have less rigid credit terms • PECs have greater representation on smaller boards compared to pre buy-out • Monitoring by PECs substitutes for tighter debt terms in monitoring and motivating managers

Table 3: Selected publications on agency theory applied to buy-outs

Source: Indicated respectively
AC = agency costs

In line with this literature, agency theory is used in the following to theoretically approach post buy-out cooperation between private equity companies and managers in portfolio companies. In this context, agency theory is contrasted to stewardship theory, which explains cooperation in pre buy-out family businesses.

The application of agency theory to family businesses is refused by FAMA/JENSEN, as the kinship bond endows family members with "advantages in monitoring and disciplining related [...] agents."[155] However, SCHULZE ET AL. extend the standard agency model with the economic building block of altruism.[156] Utility of

---

[153] For an explanation of mezzanine capital, see subsection 7.1.2.

[154] For an explanation of free cash flow, see subsection 7.1.2.

[155] Fama/Jensen (1983), p. 306. Cf. Anderson/Reeb (2003), p. 1323; Jensen/Meckling (1976), p. 330; McConaughy et al. (1998), pp. 11 et seq.; DeAngelo/DeAngelo (1985), pp. 51 et seq.

[156] Cf. Schulze et al. (2001), p. 110.

altruistic individuals is positively correlated the utility of others, i.e. the utility of one family member is linked to the utility of other family members.[157] Altruism can cause problems of self control, free riding and shirking; these problems entail agency costs through strategic inertia, misalignment of incentives, ineffective governance and other undesired adverse consequences.[158] On the other hand, reciprocal and symmetrical altruism can mitigate agency problems and endow family businesses with competitive advantages over non-family businesses in early stages of company development and in environments characterized by scarcity.[159]

Despite the merit for its early insights and its appeal, agency theory combined with altruism is still quite blurry and scientific reception questionable: The effects are ambiguous, its dissemination rather limited and research in this direction merely at its beginning. In consequence, this thesis uses the rather well established stewardship theory to explain cooperation in family businesses. This theory is presented in the following subsection.[160]

---

157 Cf. Simon (1993), pp. 158 et seq.; Becker (1981), according to Schulze et al. (2001), p. 102. SCHULZE ET AL. concede that the economic incentive of altruism may weaken over time, as personal utility and best interest of the firm and the family might blur (cf. Schulze/Lubatkin/Dino (2003a), p. 183).

158 Cf. Schulze/Lubatkin/Dino (2002), pp. 250, 253-256; Schulze/Lubatkin/Dino (2003b), pp. 477 et seq. Other consequences are difficulties to enforce contracts, generosity in terms of the consumption of perquisites and biased parental perception of child's performance (cf. Schulze et al. (2001), pp. 102 et seq., 111).

159 Cf. Schulze/Lubatkin/Dino (2002), pp. 253 et seq.; Eaton/Yuan/Wu (2002), according to Chrisman/Chua/Sharma (2005), p. 561; Carney (2005), p. 255; Schulze/Lubatkin/Dino (2003b), p. 477; Chrisman/Chua/Steier (2007), p. 5.

160 In another attempt to increase the analytical power of agency theory, another economic building block is added to the analysis, namely entrenchment. Entrenchment refers to agents' behavior detrimental to the principal and enabled by increased ownership of agents. Agents will attempt to neutralize internal control mechanism to ensure their post and their discretion (cf. Gomez-Mejia/Nuñez-Nickel/Gutierrez (2001), p. 84). However, agency theory combined with entrenchment is not further taken into account for the same reasons that apply to agency theory combined with altruism. For a review on entrenchment, see Chrisman/Chua/Sharma (2005), pp. 561 et seq.

2.2.2. Stewardship theory

Similar to the discussion of agency theory, the presentation of stewardship theory starts with the **theory's background**: While agency theory, as one of the streams of organizational economics, was applied with increasing frequency in the sphere of management research, critical voices of scholars opposing this theory became louder and louder.[161] Through an article in 1990, DONALDSON became possibly the most influential herald of critics.[162] He challenged the unadapted applicability of organizational economics and neo-institutional economics to management theory due to differences in scientific assumptions and methods.[163]

With regard to assumptions, agency theory draws upon a purely rational model of man, subsumed under the term homo oeconomicus. The homo oeconomicus pursues exclusively his self-interest and maximizes his utility thereof.[164] His quest for wealth, status, and leisure has to be confined by mechanisms to mitigate his egoistic acting and align his acting with the interest of the principal. While DONALDSON accepts existence of this model of man, he criticizes the exclusive character of this model. He argues that the range of human motives is much broader including need for achievements, responsibility, recognition, altruism, belief, respect for authority, and the intrinsic motivation of inherently satisfying tasks. In addition to that, psychologists and sociologists point to behavior that is produced through habit, emotion, unconscious

---

[161] Cf. Bettis/Donaldson (1990), p. 367; Barney (1990), p. 382; Donaldson (1990b), p. 394. The discussion between followers and critics of agency theory led to a special issue of the Academy of Management Review on "Market Discipline and the Discipline of Management" (Academy of Management Review, 1990, Vol. 15, No. 3).

[162] Cf. Donaldson (1990a).

[163] Cf. Barney (1990), p. 383. DONALDSON's criticism of the normative character of agency theory is only of minor relevance in this context and will not be dealt with in the following. Moreover, DONALDSON criticizes the evaluative language of agency theory. Linguistic nuances suggest that managers are inherently opportunistic, have a propensity to shirk, act with guile and maximize their own self-interest. DONALDSON points out that yet there is no empirical proof of these negative evaluations and casts doubt on the exclusively negative undertone of this characterization. He misses some more benign character traits like loyalty, altruism, or high ethical standards. Following the axiom underlying agency theory, all managers without any exceptions are assumed to behave in the adverse way described above (cf. Donaldson (1990a), pp. 372-374).

[164] Cf. subsection 2.2.1 and footnote 131 for details on the homo oeconomicus.

desires and further triggering factors besides rational consciousness. All these factors are ignored by the model of man behind agency theory.[165]

With regard to methods used, agency theory subscribes to the economic tradition of methodological individualism. This methodological approach analyzes systems by subdividing them into the constituent actors and analyzing each actor individually. Agency theory focuses on the relation between principal and agent, excluding all effects from outside this relation. In contrast, management theory examines organizations by treating them as systems of individuals. This systems-level analysis does not inherently assume cooperation between individual actors as problematic, as actors can (but do not always have to) jointly pursue organizational goals.[166]

Based on this criticism, **stewardship theory is explained**. DONALDSON proposes stewardship theory as countervailing view to agency theory, to overcome the aforementioned critical remarks on the latter theory. Stewardship theory was first outlined in 1991 by DONALDSON/DAVIS and formally defined by DAVIS/SCHOORMAN/DONALDSON (1997B) in 1997.[167]

Similar to agency theory, stewardship theory examines the relationship between two parties, where a principal delegates tasks to a manager, who is termed steward in this theory.[168] The essential difference between stewardship theory and agency theory is that the steward does not strive for maximizing utility through individualistic, self-serving behavior (like an agent), because he perceives greater utility from cooperative,

---

165 Cf. Donaldson (1990a), pp. 371 et seq. BARNEY replies to this criticism that bounded rational behavior of individuals is a well accepted assumption and that agency theory is well equipped to handle non-opportunistic individuals (cf. Barney (1990), pp. 384 et seq.).

166 Cf. Donaldson (1990a), p. 371. BARNEY criticizes that management theory does not always apply the holistic systems-level analysis, but partly also employs methodological individualism, which he terms reductionalism (cf. Barney (1990), p. 386).

167 Cf. Donaldson/Davis (1991); Davis/Schoorman/Donaldson (1997b). DONALDSON refers to an earlier paper from 1989, but this was only a conference presentation, which resulted in Donaldson/Davis (1991) (cf. Donaldson (1990a), p. 377). Before 1997, the theory was already applied by FOX/HAMILTON to explain company diversification (cf. Fox/Hamilton (1994)). PRESTON sees in Jones (1995) a forerunner of stewardship theory, though not naming it stewardship theory (cf. Preston (1998), p. 9).

168 Origins of the term steward are not explained in detail. However, in their earliest paper (1991), DONALDSON/DAVIS describe a manager who fits stewardship theory as "good steward of the corporate assets." (Donaldson/Davis (1991), p. 51).

collectivist behavior (see Table 4). There is a strong positive correlation between the success of the organization, the principal's satisfaction and the steward's utility thereof. Hence, the steward displays pro-organizational behavior ruling out all agency conflicts, as achievements for the company directly translate into utility gains for himself. A steward does not substitute cooperative behavior through self-serving behavior. In consequence, a steward is intrinsically motivated to act in the best interests of the principal.[169]

By this definition, stewardship theory addresses the main points of criticism of agency theory with regard to assumptions and methods, as presented before. The model of man stewardship theory is based on, assumes managers who are "motivated by a need to achieve, to gain intrinsic satisfaction through successfully performing inherently challenging work, to exercise responsibility and authority, and thereby to gain recognition from peers and bosses."[170] This model of man is an alternative to the homo oeconomicus of agency theory and originated from organizational psychology and organizational sociology.[171] Stewardship theory also breaks with the methodological individualism of agency theory. By stressing the "pro-organizational", "collective", and "cooperative" behavior of stewards, DAVIS/SCHOORMAN/DONALDSON (1997B) overcome the reductionist analysis of the isolated individual of agency theory. Stewardship theory accounts for social embeddedness of the individual steward in the organization, he works in and which is presumably owned by or under the responsibility of the principal. Thus, stewardship theory takes the perspective of a systems-level analysis.

---

169 Cf. Davis/Schoorman/Donaldson (1997b), pp. 24 et seq.; Donaldson/Davis (1991), p. 51; Corbetta/Salvato (2004b), p. 123. DAVIS/SCHOORMAN/DONALDSON emphasize that stewards are not entirely selfless, but have survival needs and strive to satisfy these. However, stewards aim at a trade-off between personal needs and organizational objectives and balance their behavior accordingly (cf. Davis/Schoorman/Donaldson (1997b), p. 25).

The assumptions of stewardship theory borrow from MCGREGOR's Theory Y of man, whereas agency theory is based on Theory X. Both theories deal with the natural attitude of man towards work (cf. McGregor (1960), pp. 33-57).

170 Donaldson/Davis (1991), p. 51. Cf. Herzberg/Mausner/Snyderman (1959) according to Donaldson/Davis (1991), p. 51.

171 Cf. Donaldson/Davis (1991), p. 51; Herzberg/Mausner/Snyderman (1959) according to Donaldson/Davis (1991), p. 51.

Aspect of differentiation	Agency theory	Stewardship theory
Percieved role of managers	Agents	Stewards
Research approach	Economic	Sociological and psychological
Assumptions of model of man	Individualist, opportunistic, self-serving	Collectivistic, pro-organizational, trustworthy
Motivation of manager	Own objectives	Organization's and principal's objectives
Relation between principal's and manager's	Diverging	Aligned
Base for relationship between principal and manager	Control	Trust
Prescribed structural setting	Monitoring and incentivization	Autonomy and empowerment

Table 4: Comparison of agency theory with stewardship theory

Source: Modifiedly taken from Vargas Sanchez (2004), p. 3

Characteristics of stewards have major implications for normative propositions on the relationship between principal and manager derived from stewardship theory. DAVIS/SCHOORMAN/DONALDSON (1997B) underline that the performance of a steward is significantly affected by his structural situation. As a steward strives for achieving organizational objectives and is inherently trustful, the authors recommend that "a steward's autonomy should be deliberately extended to maximize the benefits [i.e. utility] of a steward"[172] and thus of the organization as well as the principal. Consequently, stewardship theory suggests empowerment and autonomy of managers; these suggestions contrast those of agency theory, which promotes monitoring and incentivization of managers to overcome conflicts of interests.[173] Monitoring and incentivization are rejected by stewardship theory for two reasons: First, as interests of principal and steward do not diverge, these measures are not necessary, thus ineffective, and costs could be saved by forgoing them.[174] Second, monitoring and

172 Davis/Schoorman/Donaldson (1997b), p. 25.

173 Cf. subsection 2.2.1.

174 Cf. McClelland (1961), p. 235; Chrisman et al. (2007), p. 1032.

incentivization can even be counterproductive, as they undermine the steward's pro-organizational behavior, destroy his trust, and thus lower the steward's motivation.[175]

Given the frequent application of agency theory in management research, it is not surprising that the emergence of stewardship theory and the inherent criticism of agency theory have provoked proponents of the latter theory to **criticize stewardship theory**. Three points of criticism will be presented in the following:

First, while in particular DONALDSON criticizes the excessively gloomy, negative picture agency theory draws of managers, stewardship theory draws an excessively rosy and positive picture of managers. DAVIS/SCHOORMAN/DONALDSON (1997A) anticipate that this characterization of stewardship-minded managers might be seen as "unrealistic, naïve, and nonexistent in current business organizations"[176], but do not provide a thorough reply. Besides this immoderate praise of managers, there remain questions concerning the permanence of stewardship-minded behavior.[177] In case of impermanent behavior, a steward might turn into an agent.[178]

Second, an intensive debate is going on about the question whether stewardship theory is an independent theory or whether it can be integrated as a special case in agency theory.[179] ALBANESE/DACIN/HARRIS argue that the numerous variations of agency theory can accommodate the special case defined by stewardship theory.[180] DAVIS/SCHOORMAN/DONALDSON (1997A) retort that the difference between both theories boils down to the existence of agency conflicts:[181] As agency theory is completely built on the fundament of the existence of agency conflicts in the relation between principal and manager, a relationship free of agency conflicts is out of the

---

175 Cf. Davis/Schoorman/Donaldson (1997b), p. 25; Corbetta/Salvato (2004b), p. 360. In a laboratory experiment, TOSI ET AL. did not find support for the hypothesis described by stewardship theory that the absence of monitoring increases experimental participants' performance (cf. Tosi et al. (2003), pp. 2068-2070).

176 Davis/Schoorman/Donaldson (1997a), p. 611.

177 Cf. Albanese/Dacin/Harris (1997), p. 610; Chrisman et al. (2007), p. 1036.

178 This is of particular interest, as it might create an instable structural situation that would induce manager and principal to change to agency-minded behavior (see the third point of criticism).

179 Cf. Albanese/Dacin/Harris (1997); Davis/Schoorman/Donaldson (1997a); Preston (1998).

180 Cf. Albanese/Dacin/Harris (1997), p. 610.

181 Cf. Davis/Schoorman/Donaldson (1997a), p. 612.

scope of agency theory – instead such a relationship lends itself to stewardship theory. CAERS ET AL. depict coexistence and differentiation of both theories graphically in Figure 9.

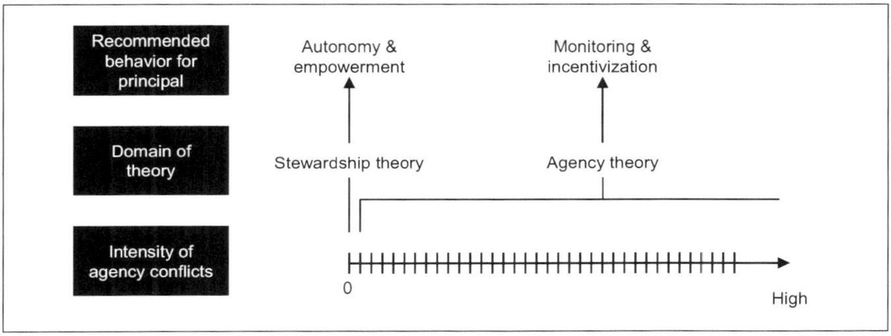

Figure 9: Differentiation between stewardship theory and agency theory

Source: Modifiedly taken from Caers et al. (2006), p. 29

Third, another point of criticism is the implication of stewardship theory recommending principals to forgo monitoring and to increase autonomy of stewards. While this stewardship-related behavior of the principal is optimal in the case of a stewardship-minded manager, the suggested structural setting would ensue an unfavorable outcome for the principal if the manager was not a steward, but an agent. In this case, the principal forgoing monitoring finds himself betrayed by an agent-minded manager maximizing the latter's self-interest (see Figure 10, quadrant 2). In response, the principal will change his mind to introduce monitoring suggested by agency theory. Similarly, a stewardship-minded manager might be frustrated by tight control installed by an agency-minded principal (quadrant 3); in consequence, the manager's frustration will turn the stewardship-minded pro-organizational behavior into agency-minded self-centered behavior. So, structural settings prescribed by stewardship-theory are only optimal if principal and manager behave stewardship-mindedly (quadrant 4), whereas structural settings prescribed by agency-theory are only optimal if principal and manager behave agency-mindedly (quadrant 1) – these two structural situations are inherently stable. In case one party behaves agency-mindedly while the other behaves stewardship-mindedly, the structural situation is instable: The stewardship-minded party will feel betrayed or frustrated and adapt behavior to follow agency theory.[182] As the principal is a priori unsure, whether the manager behaves like an agent or like a steward,[183] he rationally chooses to behave like an agent to prevent his betrayal. This severely restricts applicability of stewardship theory in practice to cases, where the principal can be a priori sure that the manager is a steward.

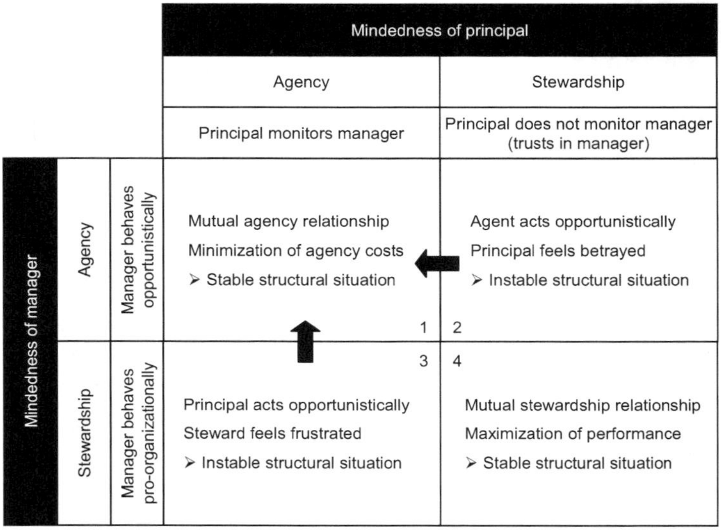

Figure 10: Cooperation between principal and manager depending on their mindedness

Source: Modifiedly taken from Davis/Schoorman/Donaldson (1997b), p. 39

182 Cf. Chrisman et al. (2007), p. 1032; Davis/Schoorman/Donaldson (1997b), p. 39. This change in the behavior of a steward who feels betrayed or frustrated is illustrated by the arrows in Figure 10. E.g. a stewardship-minded principal, who feels betrayed by an agency-minded manager, will change his behavior towards agency-mindedness, so that he moves from quadrant 2 to quadrant 1.

183 For his assessment of the manager, the principal can only resort to test the manager's trustworthiness. However, all managers will make themselves appear trustworthy. The steward is in fact trustworthy and will try to show this to the manager. The agent will pretend to be trustworthy to avoid installation of monitoring. In consequence, the principal cannot be certain, whether a manager who appears trustworthy is a steward or an agent.

After explanation and criticism of **stewardship theory**, its **application** is presented in the following: The scope of application of stewardship theory is constricted by the severe premises on which it is based: On the one hand, no agency conflicts may exist in the relation between principal and manager. On the other hand, both parties have to behave like stewards, as agency-mindedness of one party would result in the other party changing behavior towards agency-mindedness. Therefore, the scope of application of stewardship theory is constricted to few principal-manager relationships leaving the analysis of most alike relationships to agency theory.

Despite this constriction, stewardship theory has been used in such diverse fields as corporate governance in cooperative societies[184], founders' compensation and cooperation with a venture capitalist in new ventures[185], contracting of and labor relations in non-profit organizations[186], behavior of CEOs in CEO duality, at hostile takeover bids or with regard to diversification[187], effectiveness of boards of directors[188], and intercultural differences[189].

A particular application of high relevance for this thesis are family businesses. Given that ownership and control are in most family businesses in the hands of the family,[190] the kinship link will result in collective striving for objectives of the family business (pro-organizational behavior), altruism of family members and absence of agency conflicts.[191] This perfectly corresponds to a stewardship setting, which

---

[184] Cf. Vargas Sanchez (2004).

[185] Cf. Wasserman (2006); Arthurs/Busenitz (2003).

[186] Cf. van Slyke (2007); Caers et al. (2006).

[187] Cf. Donaldson/Davis (1991); Angwin/Stern/Bradley (2004); Fox/Hamilton (1994). CEO duality is a phenomenon in Anglo-Saxon corporate governance and refers to CEOs, who are at the same time chairman of the board (cf. Donaldson/Davis (1991), p. 49). According to agency theory, CEO duality undermines monitoring of the board and weakens corporate governance. In contrast, CEO duality empowers the CEO according to stewardship theory.

[188] Cf. Roberts/McNulty/Stiles (2005); Muth/Donaldson (1998).

[189] Cf. Lee/O'Neill (2003).

[190] Cf. subsection 5.1.1.

[191] Cf. Zahra (2003), p. 498; Chrisman et al. (2007), p. 1031; Greenwood (2003), p. 493; Eddleston/Kellermanns (2007), p. 548; Corbetta/Salvato (2004b), p. 123; Beehr/Drexler/Faulkner (1997), p. 309; Miller/Le Breton-Miller (2006), p. 74; Corbetta/Salvato (2004a), p. 358.

Stewardship theorists justify the absence of agency conflicts as "family managers are intrinsically inclined to pursue the interests of [family] owners; when non-financial goals are similar and important to both family business owners and family managers; and when the

DAVIS/SCHOORMAN/DONALDSON (1997B) describe as "situations in which managers are not motivated by individual goals, but rather are stewards whose motives are aligned with the objectives of their principals".[192] Due to the familiarity and intimateness of kinship links between individuals, family members as principals and managers are very likely to trust in the counterparty's stewardship-mindedness.[193] In consequence, the structural situation of both parties behaving like stewards is a priori and from then on stable.[194] Hence, it is not surprising that stewardship theory is applied increasingly over the last years by numerous scholars in family business (see Table 5).[195]

In line with this literature, stewardship theory is used in this thesis to explain pre buy-out cooperation between owners and managers in family businesses. Thus, stewardship theory is contrasted with agency theory, which theoretically explains cooperation in post buy-out portfolio companies.

relationship between family business owners and family managers is long-term and emotion laden." (Chrisman et al. (2007), p. 1032).

CHRISMAN/CHUA/SHARMA even show that stewardship theory holds, if principal and manager do not put greater value on the other party's objectives but only equal (cf. Chrisman/Chua/Sharma (2005), p. 567).

192 Davis/Schoorman/Donaldson (1997b), p. 21.

193 Cf. Corbetta/Salvato (2004a), p. 359.

194 Another argument for the applicability of stewardship theory to analyze family businesses is the systems-level approach of stewardship theory, which is particularly appropriate to inquire into non-individualistic relationships (cf. Donaldson (1990a), p. 371).

195 Further publications on stewardship theory applied to family businesses include: Klein/Bell (2007); Howorth/Wright/Westhead (2007); Schachner/Speckbacher/Wentges (2006); Blumentritt/Keyt/Astrachan (2007); Gubitta/Gianecchini (2002); Corbetta/Salvato (2004a).

However, the application of stewardship theory in research on family businesses is not unquestioned. Critics indicate that ownership and management structure might diverge from the currently predominant assumptions of one block of owners and a homogeneous group of managers with severe consequences for the applicability of stewardship theory. Moreover, critics have picked up the second point of criticism discussed above, namely the idea of integrating stewardship theory into agency theory (cf. Chrisman et al. (2007), pp. 1032, 1036; Miller/Le Breton-Miller (2006), pp. 74 et seq.; Corbetta/Salvato (2004a), pp. 360 et seq.).

Despite this criticism of the application of stewardship theory to family businesses and recent attempts to apply agency theory combined with altruism to family businesses (cf. subsection 2.2.1), it still remains a "white gap" on the map of family business scholars to empirically inquire which theoretical underpinning explains family businesses better.

Author, year	Type of research	Description of research project	Results
Corbetta/ Salvato (2004b)	Theo-retical	Conception of model to describe selection of supervisory board members based on AT, ST and resource dependence	• ST prescribes appointment of insiders or affiliated outsiders as board members to monitor management, due to greater commitment and value overlap
Chrisman/ Chua/ Sharma (2005)	Theo-retical	Overview on trends and directions in research on FBes	• ST suggested as special case of AT • Call for more research applying ST
Miller/ Le Breton-Miller (2006)	Theo-retical	Conceptualization of the consequences of different governance types on performance of FBes using AT and ST	• Large set of propositions on the relation between certain types of governance in FBes, potential agency and stewardship consequences, and impacts on company performance
Eddleston/ Kellermanns (2007)	Empirical	Survey on correlation between performance of FBes and participative strategic processes as prescribed by ST	• Higher performance of FBes applying participative strategic processes as predicted by ST
Chrisman et al. (2007)	Empirical	Survey on incentivization and monitoring in FBes to test applicability of ST and AT	• Intensive usage of incentivization and monitoring • Family owners regard family members as agents
Howorth/ Wright/ Westhead (2007)	Empirical	Analysis of eight case studies of buy-outs in FB with regard to continuity of stewardship culture (among other aspects under examination)	• Long-term view, attachement to the company, and prioritization of company objectives over personal ones exhibited stewardship-mindedness in all surviving companies
Pieper/Klein/ Jaskiewicz (2008)	Empirical	Survey on board existence and management composition in FBes based on AT and ST	• Board of directors less likely in FBes with high level of goal alignment as predicted by ST

Table 5: Selected publications on stewardship theory applied to family businesses

Source: Indicated respectively
FB = family business; ST = stewardship theory; AT = agency theory

3 Empirical foundation

This chapter prepares the ground for the empirical part of the thesis by presenting the research approach in section 3.1 and describing the sample in section 3.2.

3.1 Research approach

This section presents the research approach underlying this thesis. Subsection 3.1.1 breaks the research question down into the framework of analysis, which builds the structure of the following chapters. Section 3.1.2 explains the research method and why it was chosen. Subsection 3.1.3 defines the control group. Subsection 3.1.4 describes the process of data gathering and subsection 3.1.5 explains analysis of data and presentation of the results. Subsection 3.1.6 closes this section by discussing the limitations of this research approach.

3.1.1. Elaboration of the research question

In section 1.2, the research question guiding the following analysis was derived and formulated as: How do buy-outs in family businesses change corporate governance, instruments of managerial control, and financial practices? This research question stipulates the dimensions the following analysis will focus on: Changes in corporate governance are discussed in chapter 1, changes in instruments of managerial control in chapter 1, and changes in financing in chapter 1.

As an exhaustive discussion of all changes in these three dimensions would be lengthy and blur key findings, the analysis will focus on selected aspects only (see Figure 11).[196] These aspects were chosen based on practical relevance and theoretical interest; selected aspects reflected major changes between family businesses as a pre buy-out state and portfolio companies as post buy-out state of a given company. Further, those aspects were included in the analysis, in which observed changes were

---

[196] Similar to the limited scope of analysis with regard to the dimensions considered, there were many more aspects in each dimension that might have lent them for research. As the scope of this thesis was limited, the most promising aspects were selected and analyzed in greater detail. Thus, the scope of aspects analyzed was not intended to be exhaustively comprehensive, but rather focused and thus limited.

expected to differ from changes already known in the buy-out literature and thus enrich the discussion of buy-out consequences and value generation.[197]

In the following, the aspects analyzed are briefly introduced in the order, they will be presented in the chapters indicated. This subsection only highlights, why certain aspects merit closer examination; the relevant literature is discussed in the following chapters.[198]

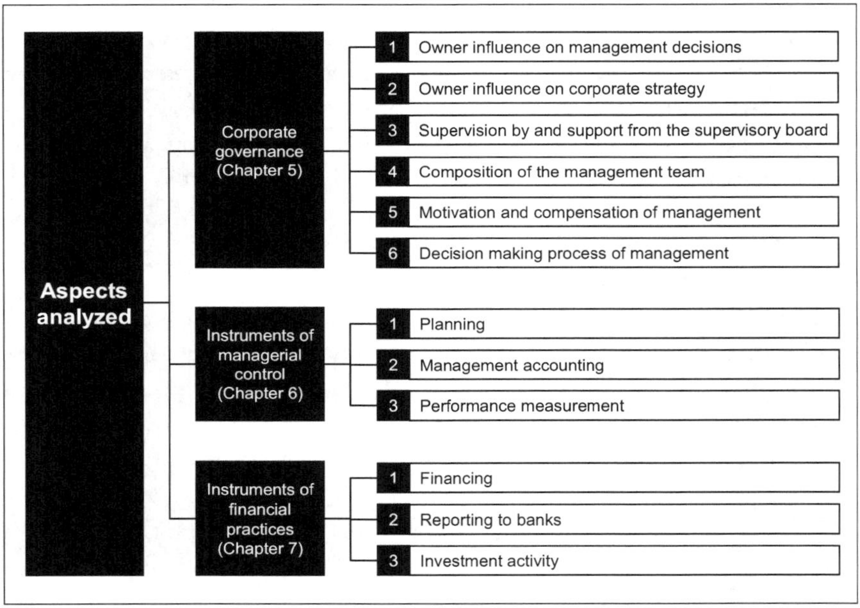

Figure 11: Framework of analysis of chapters 5 – 7

Source: Author's illustration

As explained later on in detail, **corporate governance** deals with the use of governance devices by owners to defend their interests.[199] Hence, chapter 1 focuses on

---

[197] Cf. subsection 2.1.2.

[198] Cf. the first two sections of chapters 4, 5 and 6 for literature-based comparisons between family businesses and portfolio companies with regard to the aspects covered in the respective chapter.

[199] Cf. the introduction to chapter 1 for a precise definition.

six aspects of the changes in the institutions of corporate governance, in their functions, and in their cooperation. The first two aspects examine changes in the owners' cooperation with the company and in particular with the management. The first aspect focuses on owner's influence on management decisions: Family owners exert a strong influence on management decisions, even if they are not directly involved in the company's management. Private equity companies typically exert less direct influence on management decisions, so that interesting changes may be expected. The second aspect highlights owner's influence on strategy: Pursuit of distinct, non-economic family goals[200] and inclusion of certain family interests induces family owners to influence the strategy of their family business in a certain way, while private equity companies focus on quick achievement of economic goals. After two aspects on the institution of ownership, the supervisory board is examined as third aspect. This aspect focuses on the supervisory board's supervision and support of management: In family businesses, supervisory boards are frequently not existing or not functioning adequately, while private equity companies as owners install supervisory boards and appoint valuable experts, who monitor and advise managers. After the discussion of ownership and supervisory board, focus is put on the management. The fourth aspect stresses changes in the management team: Family managers and non-family managers appointed by family owners frequently leave or are dismissed by private equity companies after the buy-out. The investor replaces the vacancies in management. The fifth aspect inquires into motivation and compensation of managers: Remaining and new post buy-out managers might show different motives for the buy-out. The sale might profoundly change managers' compensation schemes. The sixth aspect concerns decision making by managers: Family managers have a reputation for an individualistic approach to decision making, which is likely to change through the buy-out due to appointment of non-family managers, monitoring of the supervisory board, and new owners' expectations and influence.

The second dimension stressed by the research question consists of the **instruments of managerial control**. These control instruments provide information that enable management to base their decisions on and that allow owners, supervisory board members, and banks to monitor and influence company development and

[200] E.g. keeping ownership restricted to members of the family. Family owners' pursuit of non-economic goals does not imply that they do not pursue economic goals at the same time.

management behavior. The analysis focuses on three aspects of changes in the instruments of managerial control. The first aspect highlights changes in planning: Given the high leverage of buy-outs and significant return expectations of owners, financial planning is attached great importance. In family businesses, leverage and return expectations are of comparatively lower importance, as families also pursue distinct, non-economic goals. This suggests that the importance and implementation of planning might change through the buy-out. The second aspect covered is management accounting: Post buy-out non-family management as well as interaction of the different institutions of corporate governance require detailed information from management accounting, which is frequently unavailable or unneeded in family businesses. The third aspect inquires into changes in performance measurement: Due to family owners' frequent involvement in management, minor importance is attached to performance measurement in family businesses. Post buy-out, private equity companies are likely to monitor performance closely, given their considerable return expectations of portfolio companies and the expected changes in management compensation.

The third dimension of this analysis sheds light on changes in **financial practices** and focuses on the three aspects financing, reporting, and investing. The first aspect in this dimension is financing: The high leverage being a typical characteristic of buy-outs is a change to the reserved capital structure of family businesses and is likely to affect other details of companies' financing. The second aspect analyzed is reporting to banks: While family businesses are typically characterized by a very restricted reporting to banks, the high leverage typical for buy-outs forces companies to be more open towards banks. Investment activity is in the focus of analysis as third aspect: Family businesses are renowned for having a long-breath in their investments, while investing parsimoniously. Given the limited holding period of private equity companies, their return expectations and the urgent need to redeem debt after the buy-out, portfolio companies might show a rather limited and more short-term oriented investment activity.

3.1.2. Research method

This subsection describes the research method in detail. The subsection especially focuses on the reasons for choosing a particular method. Details of the implementation are discussed in the following subsections. Figure 12 provides an overview on the choices that lead to this research design.

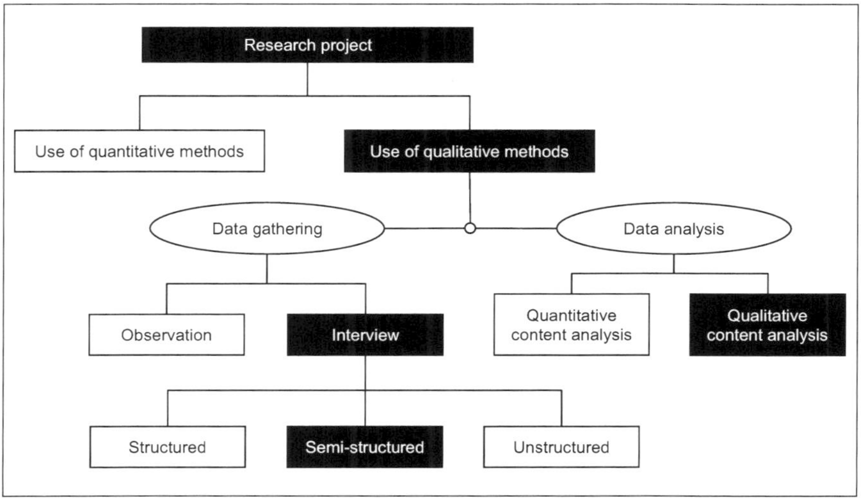

Figure 12: Selection of research methods underlying the research design

Source: Author's illustration
Black boxes represent research methods chosen

Empirical research projects employ quantitative methods, qualitative ones, or both.[201] The research question, already existing research in the field, and the nature of the research object suggest which approach might be more appropriate, though this suggestion is not compelling. In this research project, research question, already existing research and the nature of the research object all three suggested **employment of qualitative methods**. First, the research question called for examination of the comprehensive changes, their antecedents and consequences induced by a buy-out. GREEN argued that the multitude and intermingling of causal elements and effects of changes after buy-outs cannot be captured by quantitative research.[202] Second, the

201 Quantitative research methods use "statistics and replicability to validate generalization from survey samples and experiments" (Holliday (2007), p. 6). Qualitative research methods are an "array of interpretative techniques which seek to describe, decode, translate and otherwise come to terms with the meaning, not the frequency, of certain more or less naturally occurring phenomena in the social world" (van Maanen (1983), p. 9). For a comparison of both methods, see Holliday (2007), p. 6; Lamnek (2005), pp. 242-273.

202 Cf. Green (1992), p. 518; Gummesson (2006), p. 171.

review of research on buy-outs in family businesses in subsection 2.1.3 has shown that the current state of research was in general and in particular with regard to the research question very limited. Hence, there was no adequate fundament to base quantitative research on; this state called for the exploratory power of qualitative research.[203] Third, the research method should be adequate to analyze the research object. As will be shown in subsection 3.1.4, the number of identifiable buy-outs in German family businesses was rather limited to less than 100;[204] given response rates of similar research projects among portfolio companies, the sample of responding companies would not suffice minimum data requirements of quantitative methods.[205] These three reasons discourage from the use of quantitative methods and thus also from the use of a mixed methods approach.[206]

After the decision for a qualitative research approach, the methods of data gathering and data analysis had to be determined. With regard to **data gathering**, two research techniques predominate qualitative research, namely observations and interviews.[207] Interviews have two advantages of particular interest with regard to research question and research object: First, the direct interaction between researcher and interviewee allows identifying and clarifying misunderstandings that arise in the communication process. Second, this direct interaction could be used to obtain the

---

203 Cf. Lamnek (2005), pp. 90, 93.

204 Cf. subsection 3.1.4. This research project is restricted to German companies, as an international perspective might complicate the analysis of changes in corporate governance and instruments of managerial control, which are included in the research question.

205 Response rates of comparable studies are 27.5% (Geidner (2009), p. 98), 7.1% (European Private Equity & Venture Capital Association (2005), p. 29), 21.1% (Jakoby (2000), p. 111). In another study, of over 10,000 private equity companies contacted (each of it having several portfolio companies), merely 114 portfolio companies participated in a survey, despite support from the European Venture Capital & Private Equity Association (cf. Achleitner/Klöckner (2005), p. 11).

206 Besides the three arguments presented above, there was one additional advantage of qualitative methods relevant in the context of this research project. The direct interaction between researcher and people observed or interviewed for the research project ensured that data was collected from exactly the person most knowledgeable about the research object (i.e. the company and the changes induced by the buy-out); otherwise (as in case of questionnaires used in surveys), a contacted person might have delegated data provision to less knowledgeable colleagues.

207 Cf. Easterby-Smith/Thorpe/Lowe (2002), p. 85. EASTERBY-SMITH/THORPE/LOWE present diary methods (i.e. the analysis of diary of participants in a study) as third predominant qualitative method. While this method was successfully applied in social sciences, it seems inappropriate to ask participants of buy-outs for their diaries.

interviewee's trust to get access to more confidential data.[208] Besides these advantages favoring interviews, usage of the alternative technique of observations was hampered: This technique would require direct observation of the changes induced by the buy-out.[209] Direct observation was not practicable because resulting time requirements would have been excessive and because the changes within the scope of the research question might take a considerable period before becoming effective.[210] For these reasons, interviews were used to gather data.[211]

There are three **basic types of interviews** according to the rigour of structure applied. Unstructured interviews are conducted in a non-standardized, flexible way without an interview guide, in case there is not enough prior knowledge to construct a questionnaire. The opposite to unstructured interviews are structured interviews, which are highly standardized interviews exactly following a detailed, inflexible interview guide. A compromise between both types are semi-structured interviews, which allow the interviewer to diverge from a detailed interview guide to follow up new issues deepening prior understanding.[212] Despite the very early state of literature on buy-outs in family businesses, existing research results and conclusions by analogy from the literature on family businesses and buy-outs allowed derivation of expected changes.[213] While derivation of expected changes rendered unstructured interviewing futile, expected changes were too uncertain and too general to allow for structured interviewing. Given prior basic understanding and lack of detailed knowledge, semi-

---

208 Cf. Easterby-Smith/Thorpe/Lowe (2002), pp. 90-92.

209 Cf. Schnell/Hill/Esser (2005), pp. 390 et seq.

210 The time requirement could be reduced by indirect observation, i.e. comparing observations of the pre buy-out and the post buy-out state. However, pre buy-out observations necessitate identification of family businesses that would be sold in a buy-out within a certain period. This a-priori identification of relevant companies was not possible, as transactions were not disclosed before closure of the deal; moreover, before the sale was closed, it was hardly predictable whether a family business would be sold through a buy-out or not.

211 Cf. Schnell/Hill/Esser (2005), pp. 353-356, 359; Easterby-Smith/Thorpe/Lowe (2002), p. 93 for general methodological problems of interviewing.

212 Cf. Atteslander (2003), pp. 146-148; Schnell/Hill/Esser (2005), pp. 322 et seq.; Lueger (2000), p. 190.

213 Cf. subsection 1.3.

structured interviews seemed most appropriate to capture the richness and depth of the research question.[214]

Besides the method, five **details of** the implementation of **data gathering** had to be stipulated, concerning persons to interview, number of interviews, triangulation of data, pre-testing of the interview guide, and inclusion of a control group. First, interviews were to be conducted with persons who have witnessed changes after the buy-out. Thus, managers were interviewed, who had been with the company pre buy-out or who were appointed soon after the buy-out. Second, to prepare the ground for generalization of research results and to reduce biases caused by idiosyncratic effects of some buy-outs, not a few but a series of about 15 companies was aimed at to be examined.[215] Third, triangulation-within-method refers to the application of the same method of data analysis to sets of data that are different due to modifications in data gathering in order to increase reliability of data.[216] For this purpose, interviews with investment managers of the private equity companies backing the buy-out in the company examined were conducted using the same interview guide used in the interviews with the managers.[217] Fourth, to control and improve the interview guide's comprehensibility, validity and coverage of the most important changes, the interview guide was pre-tested with practitioners working in the field of buy-outs in family businesses.[218] Fifth, a control

---

214 Cf. Schnell/Hill/Esser (2005), p. 322. Two more arguments favored semi-structured interviewing for data collection: First, flexibility of the research method enabled the interview to be adjusted to peculiarities of the interviewee, the company, the buy-out, or the course of the interview. Second, the openness of the research method allowed for identifying and deducting new and potentially surprising evidence (cf. Lamnek (2005), p. 348).

215 Cf. Isenberg (1986), p. 778. The number of interviews is suggested for the chosen method of a qualitative content analysis: This number reduces the risk of missing certain aspects as it is not too small, but ensures at the same time manageability of the sample group as the number of interviews is not too large. Thus, the research design is similar to a multiple-case study approach (cf. Yin (1994), pp. 44-51).

216 Cf. Lamnek (2005), p. 278.

217 The initial design of the research project also included interviews with vendors, i.e. former family owners. Although, company managers were in most cases willing to provide contact details and a reference to approach vendors, these were hardly available for interviews. In some cases, company managers did not want former family owners to be interviewed. In consequence, the former owners of only three companies were interviewed. As most of them were not able to comment on the development of the company following the buy-out, these interviews were only of low relevance for the research question. Thus, they were not included in the following analyses and the methodology of the research project was adapted.

218 Cf. Schnell/Hill/Esser (2005), pp. 347-351.

group was established to increase distinctness of the results and differentiate between effects attributable to the sale by family owners and effects attributable to the buy-out. The control group consisted of family businesses, which were sold through transactions with buyers that were not private equity companies.[219] Managers and investment managers of some companies fulfilling the selection criteria of the control group were interviewed as well and resulting interviews were included in the analysis.

With regard to the method of **data analysis**, documents like transcripts of the interviews are typically processed by quantitative content analysis or qualitative content analysis. Quantitative content analysis deals with the "objective, systematic, and quantitative description of manifest content of communications"[220] In contrast, qualitative content analysis analyzes documents using a system of categories derived from theory and adopted to the content, the context, and the analyzer's interpretation of both.[221] As quantitative content analysis requires text documents not created for the purpose of research analysis, this method was not applicable to the interview transcripts of this research project.[222] So, interview data was analyzed using qualitative content analysis.[223] As this research project aimed at building theory, data analysis was directed to generate propositions on changes caused by buy-outs in former family businesses.[224]

While there are several approaches to qualitative content analysis, the approach of MAYRING focuses on consciously and explicitly given statements and is widely accepted; thus, this approach seems adequate to analyze the interviews.[225] As starting

---

219 Cf. Lamnek (2005), p. 727.

220 Berelson (1954), p. 488.

221 Cf. Lamnek (2005), p. 506; Bryman (2004), p. 542. For an overview on definitions, see Mayring (2003), pp. 11-13. EASTERBY-SMITH/THORPE/LOWE refer to a method very similar to qualitative content analysis as grounded analysis (cf. Easterby-Smith/Thorpe/Lowe (2002), pp. 122-127).

222 Cf. Lamnek (2005), pp. 485, 493-500. Another source suitable for quantitative content analysis might be internal documentation of the buy-out. However, this documentation would not include descriptions of the changes induced by the buy-out and was very unlikely to be accessible for research purposes given the confidential character of such transactions.

223 For criticism and disadvantages of qualitative content analysis, see Mayring (2003), pp. 109-115; Lamnek (2005), pp. 512 et seq.

224 Cf. Lamnek (2005), p. 508. Empirical evidence presented in this thesis is used to derive insights and lend them credibility, not to confirm validity of these insights.

225 Cf. Mayring (2003), pp. 56-99. For an overview on different approaches to qualitative content analysis, see Lamnek (2005), pp. 513-517, 531-542; Lueger (2000), p. 188.

point of the analysis, this approach requires the conception of a system of categories, which is deductively derived from theory and which is modified inductively throughout the analysis. Based on this system of categories, MAYRING uses three elementary techniques, to analyze given text material: First, the text material is summarized by paraphrasing content, and then selecting and consolidating important paraphrases until further reduction entails loss of essential information. This reduction facilitates understanding of the data while preserving the essential content. Second, certain passages that need clarification are explained in their respective context. Third, a structure is distilled out of the text material using pre-determined criteria based on content, typology, form, or scales – the first two criteria are used for structuring in the following. Structuring based on content assigns content elements to categories, adjusts the system of categories, defines anchor examples for each category, and delineates a certain category from others. Structuring based on typology highlights characteristics, which are extreme, of particular theoretical interest, or very frequent. The resulting system of categories comprises the distinctive characteristics of each piece of text material, can be restructured according to a particular criterion or research aspect and, thus, has prepared the ground for interpretation.[226]

3.1.3. Control group

Before data gathering, analysis and presentation of results are explained, the control group is defined as essential element underlying further steps of the research approach.

Observed changes after buy-outs in family businesses were compared to changes in family businesses, which were sold by their family owners to buyers that were not private equity companies, to differentiate between effects attributable to the sale of family owners and effects attributable to the buy-out.[227] Two relevant and comparable buyers of family businesses had been identified:[228] Financial holding

[226] Cf. Mayring (2003), pp. 53-99; Lamnek (2005), pp. 518-531; Atteslander (2003), pp. 225-229.

[227] Cf. subsection 3.1.2.

[228] Neither companies competing in the industry of the sold company nor corporations diversifying into the industry of the examined company are taken into account, as integration of an acquired family business would impede determination of post buy-out changes.

companies specialized in acquiring family businesses and private individuals, who were backed by semi public investment companies (see Table 6).[229]

Holding companies are publicly-quoted investment companies, which acquire mid-sized family businesses with foreseeable succession problems. Holding companies pursue a long-term oriented holding strategy with no pre-defined holding period (buy-and-hold strategy); this means that holding companies do not aim at selling their subsidiaries.[230] Profits of subsidiaries are reinvested into acquisitions of new companies and distributed to shareholders. Holding companies mostly cooperate with selling family owners, so that the latter remain in the management for a certain period and are followed by experienced managers appointed by the holding company, who are granted a significant equity stake. While holding companies support subsidiaries and stipulate targets for management, management acts with considerable discretion.

Possible buyers of family businesses are private individuals, who aim at becoming managers of the target company and who are backed by **semi-public investment companies**. Semi-public investment companies are subsidiaries of quasi-public saving banks or public promotional banks specialized in financing ownership successions in family businesses in order to promote economic development in certain regions.[231] Semi-public investment companies back private individuals, who want to acquire a company but cannot finance the acquisition price alone. For this purpose, they typically provide mezzanine capital or acquire minority equity stakes in the family businesses for sale. This financing behavior is the reason for two characteristics of companies backed by semi-public investment companies: First, as future management has to provide a significant share of equity capital to acquire the company, maximum size of companies to be bought is restricted by future managers' private funds.[232] Second, as semi-public investment companies typically provide capital in form of minority stakes or mezzanine contributions, their influence on sold

[229] This subsection is intended to provide details on investment behavior and purpose of different types of buyers. The differences in changes after the company sale stemming from the different types of buyers will be discussed in the course of this thesis.

[230] According to websites and investment managers of holding companies, these typically look for investments between € 10m and € 100m.

[231] Cf. Achleitner et al. (2008a), pp. 10 et seq.

[232] Semi-public investment companies rarely finance acquisitions of companies with more than € 20m in sales (cf. IMAP M&A Consultants (2008), p. 9).

family businesses is limited and managers' discretion over their company is increased. Companies acquired by managers and semi-public investment companies will be referred to as companies backed by semi-public investment companies in the following.

Companies acquired by any of these two buyers composed the control group to contrast observations in portfolio companies of private equity companies. The specific differences with regard to the aspects analyzed between both groups are discussed in the empirical sections of the thesis.

	Type of buyer organization		
Aspect considered	Private equity company	Holding company	Semi-public investment company
Type of organization	Private, closed-end investment fund[233]	Publicly-quoted, evergreen investment company	Semi-public investment company
Purpose of organization	Generate profit for fund investors through buying and selling companies	Generate profit for shareholders through buying companies and distributing profits of subsidiaries	Promote economic development through financially backing managers, who want to take over a company
Type of investment	Majority investments	Majority investments	Minority investments and mezzanine capital
Investment target (in € million in sales)	> 5	10 – 100	< 20
Holding period (in years)	3 – 7	∞	5 – 7
Interference with company	Medium	Low	Virtually none

Table 6: Comparison of different types of buyers

Source: Author's illustration; company data[234]

[233] Few private equity companies raise capital through publicly-quoted investment funds (see footnote 80).

[234] Company names are not provided to guarantee anonymity of interviewees (cf. section 3.1.5).

3.1.4. Data gathering

The process of gathering data consisted of three steps: First, relevant companies had to be identified. Second, interview partners within these companies were identified and asked for interviews. Third, the semi-structured interviews were conducted.

The **identification of family businesses** that underwent a buy-out in recent years was a challenging task, as there was no comprehensive database on these companies and vendors as well as buyers frequently did not disclose the company sale. Therefore, queries were made in several practitioners' databases, namely Zephyr, mergermarket and M&A Database.[235] Data was complemented by records from the Centre for Management Buy-Out Research (CMBOR) at Nottingham University Business School. Additional transactions were collected from various practitioners' journals and homepages of private equity companies that were known to invest in family businesses. Vendors' and buyers' reservation to disclose information on closed deals restricted the number of deals that could be identified this way; to broaden the population, all transactions after 1997 were included in this search. These sources yielded a list of 258 potentially relevant companies.

Thereafter, companies on this list were checked for their relevance with regard to the research question. To enter the sample of relevant companies, a company had to fulfill the following three criteria (see Figure 13): First, the company had to be a family business before the sale. The SFI was calculated based on data on the transaction and data from the Amadeus database. In some cases, information was not sufficient to compute the SFI so that self-identification as family business was used as an additional indicator whether a firm was a family business.[236] Second, a buy-out must have happened – though this criterion seems trivial at first sight, the quality of data in the databases used did not ensure that each transaction indicated as a buy-out was really a buy-out according to the definition in subsection 2.1.2. The hand-selected companies of the control group did not have to fulfill this criterion. Third, management had to be able to make credible statements on the state of the company

---

[235] Zephyr copyright by Bureau van Dijk Publishing; mergermarket copyright by mergerrmarket Group; M&A Database copyright Institut für Betriebswirtschaft, Universität St. Gallen.

[236] Information on the corporate website and checks through phone calls with the company were used to determine whether a company is considered a family business by self-identification.

before and after the buy-out. These statements should be based on the interviewee's direct experience and not on information from a second party, to avoid distortions. Therefore, only those companies were included in the final sample, where management worked in the company before the buy-out or entered the company directly after the buy-out.[237] 92 companies fulfilled all three criteria and thus formed the identified population of relevant companies.

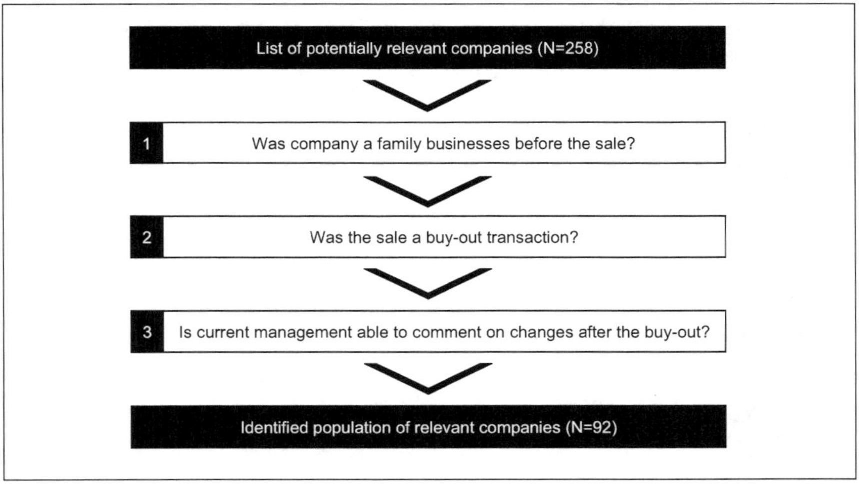

Figure 13: Checks of company for relevance

Source: Author's illustration

In the next step, **interview partners were identified** and asked for an interview. Potential interview partners with first hand experience on changes after buy-outs in family businesses were: chief executive officers (CEOs), chief financial officers (CFOs) or managing directors (MDs) of the companies, previously identified and checked for relevance. To double-check validity of answers and thus reduce inherent subjectivity of an interview-based research approach (triangulation-within-

[237] In company E, the interviewee became manager 2.5 years after the buy-out (see subsection 3.1.5 for the assignment of letters to companies). As the company was managed by the former family manager before the appointment of the new manager, many changes appeared after the change in management. Thus, the company was kept in the sample despite the late change in management.

methods), investment managers of the private equity companies backing the respective deal were interviewed using the same interview guide.[238]

Names and contact details of CEOs, CFOs or MDs (which are termed managers in the following) were available from the imprint of each company's homepage. If there were several managers, only those managers were asked for an interview that were in the company before the buy-out or entered the company directly after the buy-out.[239] In the interviews, interviewees were asked for contact details of and a reference to the investment manager of the private equity company backing the buy-out.[240]

In order to increase the likelihood that potential interview partners were willing to participate in the research project, the German Federal Ministry of Economics and Technology ("Bundesministerium für Wirtschaft und Technologie") and the Ministry of Economics, Infrastructure, Traffic, and Technology of the State of Bavaria ("Bayerisches Staatsministerium für Wirtschaft, Infrastruktur, Verkehr und Technologie") were asked for support. This support was granted, so that emblems of the two governmental institutions could be used on the cover letter (see Appendix B).

Cover letters were prepared and sent out to potential interview partners between May and July 2007. 57 companies did not respond and 9 did not want to support the research project. 4 of the remaining companies were willing to participate, but either an interview could not be arranged given interviewees' time restrictions or on closer examination, the company did not qualify as a relevant company according to the criteria discussed above.[241] In the end, interviews were conducted with managers of 17 companies, which correspond to a response rate of 18%. The companies cover a broad range of company sizes, industries, periods past between buy-out and interview, and constellations of family influence before and after the buy-out.[242]

---

[238] Cf. subsection 3.1.2. The only inconsistency between managers and investment managers was the evaluation of financial backing of the portfolio company through the private equity company, which is discussed in detail in subsection 7.3.1.

[239] Information on the tenure of managers was gathered through press clippings or phone calls to the respective company.

[240] The reference from the company's management was important as it is increasingly difficult to approach investment managers of private equity companies and convince them to be interviewed. See also footnote 205.

[241] One interviewed company did not qualify as family business pre buy-out due to an SFI index of less than 1.

[242] See section 3.2.

To compose a control group, 20 companies were contacted, which were either sold to holding companies or bought by managers, who were financially backed by semi-public investment companies. Five companies were willing to participate in the research project. This number ensured a sufficiently broad population of the control group that allowed deriving differences between sample companies and control group companies. Moreover, this number was in an appropriate proportion to the number of sample companies, which were in the research focus. In result, the total number of companies analyzed amounted to 22.

As mentioned above, interview partners were asked for contact details of their investment managers and the latter were asked for interviews. 10 investment managers were available for an interview.[243] Thus, the total number of interviews conducted and analyzed is 32.

Interviews were conducted between June and August 2007. 13 interviews were conducted by telephone, the other interview partners preferred to be interviewed in face-to-face meetings mostly in the respective company.[244]

The interviews were semi-structured based on an interview guide, shown in Appendix C.[245] This interview guide was conceived based on the literature on family businesses and portfolio companies and based on the expected changes applying the framework developed in subsection 3.1.1.[246] The interview guide consisted of 34 main questions (e.g. question 6) and 28 sub-questions, which were subordinated to the main questions (e.g. question 6.1). Primarily, main questions, which were open questions, were asked to reduce interview time; it was expected that interviewees would answer the closed sub-questions, which asked for specific details, while answering the main questions.[247] In case, an interview partner did not answer a sub-question while respon-

---

243 This number includes three investment managers responsible for companies of the control group: Two investment managers of holding companies and one investment manager of a semi-public investment company.

244 Cf. Schnell/Hill/Esser (2005), pp. 363 et seq., 368-374; Atteslander (2003), pp. 176 et seq. for description, peculiarities, advantages and disadvantages of telephone interviews.

245 Cf. subsection 3.1.2 for determination of this research method.

246 Cf. the first two sections of chapters 4, 5, 6 and 7 for literature-based comparisons between family businesses and portfolio companies with regard to the aspects covered in the respective chapter.

247 Cf. Howorth/Wright/Westhead (2007), p. 10. See Atteslander (2003), pp. 161-165 for distinction of open and closed questions and diverse sub-types of questions.

ding to a main question, the sub-question was asked individually. In some interviews, a few sub-questions were not answered because either the interview partner did not want to answer them or the interview had to be shortened for time restrictions of the interview partner. The interview guide was pre-tested with one former family manager, who sold his family business through a buy-out, and an investment manager, who has focused on buy-outs in family businesses.[248]

The interview guide was made available to the interview partners prior to the interview, so that interviewees had the opportunity to prepare and reflect their answers. Interviews lasted between 39 and 129 minutes, with an average length of 72 minutes. Interviews were recorded and transcribed. As interview partners were concerned about the confidentiality of interview content, transcriptions were sent to the interviewees for approval. Further analysis was not started before approval was received.

3.1.5. Analysis and presentation

This subsection describes data analysis, arrangement of evidence, types of empirical sections, framework of presentation and concealment of sensitive data.

As basis for the analysis, all interviews were transcribed, which yielded 513 pages of interview transcriptions. In these transcripts, motives of changes that occurred post buy-out were coded using the NVivo-software package.[249] Coding was based on the framework of analysis developed in subsection 3.1.1. This framework was amended during the coding process as new or finer patterns of changes after buy-outs in family businesses emerged from the interviews. Coding resulted in 129 categories[250] that contained in total 2,937 references[251].

The qualitative content analysis followed the approach of MAYRING presented in subsection 3.1.2: For each aspect of the framework, interview passages, which were coded as relevant, were summarized and arranged into categories exhibiting common or similar patterns of statements. These categories were structured by combining

---

248 Cf. subsection 3.1.2.

249 NVivo Version 7.0 copyright by QSR International. On the usage of computer-based qualitative content analysis, see Atteslander (2003), pp. 241-249; Easterby-Smith/Thorpe/Lowe (2002), pp. 127-129.

250 A category is a characteristic of a certain aspect.

251 A reference is a text passage in an interview that refers to a certain category.

contradicting or related passages with possible explanations for the evidence (structuring based on content). Groups relating to the same aspect were then arranged in a comprehensive and comprehensible structure for presentation. The resulting structures of evidence were the basis for the empirical sections in this thesis.

In the empirical sections, structures of **evidence are arranged** and presented on an abstract level. This abstract description is extended by worthwhile examples and verbatim quotes from the interviews to exemplify abstract evidence and to share the richness of qualitative data with the reader. However, only the most interesting examples and quotes were included to prevent redundancies and to limit total size of the thesis.[252]

Due to the character of semi-structured interviews and some interviewees' time restrictions, some aspects were not talked through in all interviews. If a company is not included in a statement, this does not mean that the opposite holds true for this company; non-inclusion in a statement merely means that the underlying evidence does not apply to that company or interviewee's opinion, but does not imply any other evidence.[253]

Some evidence might appear more than once if it is relevant for several aspects of the analysis. This evidence is discussed the first time it is mentioned or where it has the highest relevance. Other mentions are short descriptions of the evidence and refer to the detailed description.

Verbatim quotes are provided in italics and indented. Words in box brackets were not said by the interviewee but were added to facilitate understanding. Three dots in box brackets indicated that at least one word was left out. All quotes were translated from German to English with the smallest possible change in meaning to the author's best knowledge.

---

[252] In result, overviews might exhibit evidence not described in the text. This evidence does not represent inconsistencies but is not explicitly mentioned in the text to reduce redundancies.

[253] To correctly account for non-responses to certain questions, footnotes enumerating which interview partners provided a statement favoring certain evidence, are complemented by two pieces of information: First, a percentage is provided which corresponds to the share of respondents indicating this statement relative to all respondents of the specific question. Second, the total number of respondents to the specific question (accounting for non-respondents) is presented.

There are two **types of empirical sections**: The sections describing the empirical background of the buy-out in chapter 4 intend to set the ground work for the discussion of changes in succeeding chapters. Chapter 4 is not theory building and does therefore not include propositions.

The sections containing empirical findings in chapters 5, 6 and 7 directly refer to the research question and focus on different dimensions of changes in family businesses after buy-outs. They are intended to build theory in the respective aspects and therefore include propositions. Propositions focused on deriving new insights on the changes after buy-outs in family businesses. An important criterion these propositions had to fulfill was that they were unknown to the literature before this thesis. Therefore, evidence that was obvious or that was already explained by the literature is not considered for propositions.[254] In chapters 5 to 7, analysis of the changes focused on evidence in the sample companies backed by private equity companies. For greater ease of comparison, changes in companies of the control group are discussed at the end of each subsection, before propositions are derived.

A general **framework of presentation** was used in all empirical subsections of chapters 5 to 7 (see Figure 14). This framework consists of six stages, which are always presented in the same order: First, each subsection starts with a very brief overview of the subsection. Second, the pre buy-out (i.e. family business) state of the respective aspect treated in the subsection is presented.[255] Third, changes induced by the buy-out and details on the post buy-out (i.e. portfolio company) state are described and analyzed. Fourth, further details on more specific sub-aspects of the change and the post buy-out state are presented. Fifth, changes and the post-sale state[256] in companies of the control group are delineated. Sixth, a summary concludes the most important findings to derive the propositions.

---

[254] For example, the evidence that buy-outs in family businesses backed by private, closed-end private equity companies were financed using an acquisition financing structure is not surprising, but well-known in literature. Therefore, this evidence was not used to derive a proposition from.

[255] This stage of presentation is omitted in subsections 5.3.4 and 5.3.5, which focus on changes in the management team and motivation of managers for the buy-out. For the aspects examined in these subsections, there is no comparable state to describe before the buy-out.

Analysis of the pre buy-out state does not differentiate between sample companies and companies of the control group, as this thesis focuses on the differences between both groups caused by the different types of buyers and not on the differences existent before the buy-out.

[256] The post sale state for companies of the control group is the equivalent to the post buy-out state for sample companies.

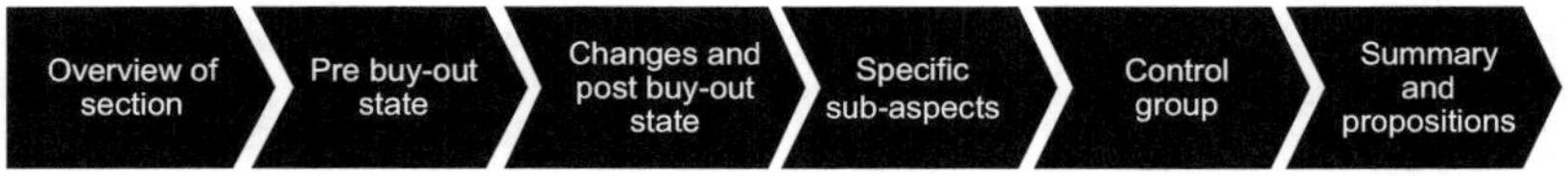

Figure 14: Framework of presentation of empirical subsections in chapters 5 – 7

Source: Author's illustration

Company names and some company characteristics have been concealed as interview partners have asked for confidentiality of their data. Therefore, all data has been made anonymous before publication, so that no inference about a specific company can be made. Thus, companies are assigned letters in alphabetic order. In the following, each company will be addressed exclusively by its respective letter. In case a group of companies is presented, companies are always enumerated in alphabetic order.

The assignment of letters to companies follows these three rules (see Figure 15): First, portfolio companies are listed in front of companies of the control group. Thus, transactions A to Q are funded by private equity companies; companies R and S are subsidiaries of holding companies; and T, U, and V are in part financed by semi-public investment companies. Second, portfolio companies that were in turnaround situations at the buy-out (company P and Q) were listed after portfolio companies that were not in turnaround situations at the buy-out (A through O). Third, companies within the group of non-turnaround companies backed by private equity companies are arranged by company size.

As another mean of concealing details on companies, no information is provided about the industry the company operates in. Data on sales, number of employees and time elapsed since the buy-out is only given in ranges. Data on sales and headcount refer to the year the buy-out took place.

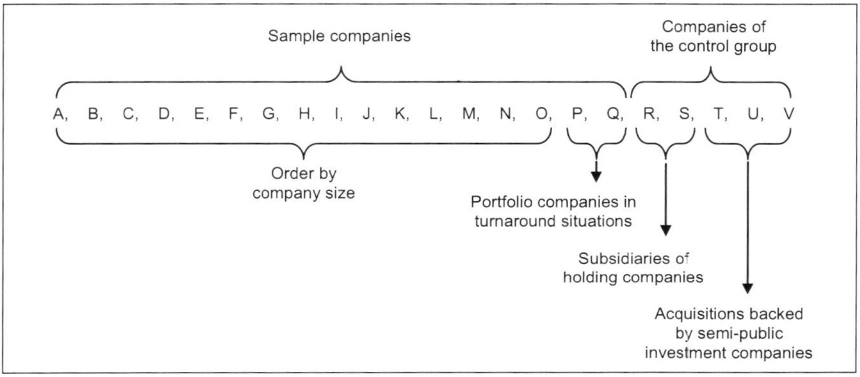

Figure 15: Assignment of letters to companies

Source: Author's illustration

3.1.6. Limitations

The nature of an exploratory, qualitative research approach and the specific design of this research project implicate limitations. These limitations can be broadly grouped by the stage of their origin, namely selection of sample companies, interviewing process and analysis of interviews.

The **selection of relevant companies** as described in subsection 3.1.3 gave rise to four limitations. First, only those companies could be identified as relevant companies, which were still in business. This bias excludes companies from the sample that went bankrupt during the holding period (survivorship bias).[257] Second, only those companies qualified for sample inclusion, where at least one manager was with the company either before the buy-out or joined the company at the buy-out. Thus, companies were excluded from the sample, where the entire management was replaced some time after the buy-out (e.g. for missing targets). Third, as only family businesses were included in the sample, availability of data to validate qualification as family business (SFI or self identification) was necessary. Some companies, which might have been relevant to the research project, were excluded for data unavailability. Fourth, possibly only those potential interview partners agreed to the interview, who

[257] Cf. Ball/Watts (1979), p. 197.

had a positive story to tell. Interview partners with negative experiences might have been unwilling to consent to be interviewed. Distorting effects of these four selection limitations are mitigated by the comprehensive empirical base of this thesis, as 32 interviews are relatively abundant for the qualitative research approach.

The process of **conducting interviews** was another source of generic limitations. A general problem of interviews on past events is hindsight bias.[258] This bias refers to a systematical distortion of past predictions and emotions due to the time past between perception of these impressions and their reporting in the interview. Another general problem of interviewing persons about their own actions and impressions is self-reporting bias.[259] This bias relates to distortions between de facto reality and reported reality, as interviewees might want to convey a picture of their actions and impressions that is better than de facto reality. Another limitation was the problem of interpersonal subjective hampering comparability. This meant that the assessment of two interview partners of exactly the same state of an object possibly diverged. Yet another problem was that some interviews left some questions open, either because of interviewees' time limitation or because of their unwillingness to answer a certain question.[260] Therefore, the number of interviewees giving a certain statement was put into relation to the total number of interview partners answering the particular question.[261] Lastly, there occurred some inconsistencies within interviews, i.e. an interviewee reported a certain fact differently at different times during the interview. This problem was accounted for by following the fact that was reported more often than the diverging fact, by logical inference or by omission. Triangulation by interviewing managers and investment managers mitigated limitations evoked in the interviews.

Finally, the **analysis of interviews** was also prone to some limitations. First, coding, summarizing, grouping of evidence and arranging evidence was done by the author alone, which exposed a significant and essential part of the analysis of evidence to the author's subjectivity and bounded rationality.[262] Second, ambiguity and

[258] Cf. Fischhoff/Bar-Hillel (1984), pp. 13-15.

[259] Cf. Ponemon/Gabhart (1990), p. 244.

[260] Cf. Schnell/Hill/Esser (2005), p. 353; Chrisman/Chua/Sharma (1996), p. 28.

[261] Cf. footnote 253.

[262] Teams of researchers analyze interviews separately and compare results to mitigate subjectivity of individual analysis (cf. Howorth/Wright/Westhead (2007), p. 11).

indistinctness in the interviews and in speech in general possibly entailed misinterpretations. Third, some issues were not exhaustively discussed, as the exploratory nature of this research approach rather aimed at providing fundamental insights and first evidence on changes through buy-outs in family businesses. Moreover, a very detailed discussion of a certain issue required the analyzed sample to be representative; although the sample did not fulfill the condition of representativity, the sample covered a broad range of diverse characteristics of portfolio companies resulting from buy-outs in family businesses and is thus appropriate for theory building to answer the research question.

To account for all these limitations as good as possible, selecting sample companies, interviewing, and analyzing were performed with especial accurateness, diligence, and prudence. Grounded in the awareness of inadequateness of these efforts to correct for the limitations, propositions in this thesis were only formulated where they were obviously not distorted by these limitations.

3.2 Sample description

This section presents the sample underlying this thesis. The section provides details on the company characteristics and the buy-out (subsection 3.2.1)[263], differentiation between sample and control group (3.2.2) as well as the degree of family involvement before (3.2.3) and after the buy-out (3.2.4). Subsection 3.2.5 contains a comprehensive sample overview showing characteristics on an individual company level (see Table 7, Table 8, Table 9, and Table 10 on pages 83 to 86).

3.2.1. Company and buy-out characteristics

Total **sales volume** of the 22 sample companies ranged from € 260m of the largest company to € 5m of the smallest company (see Figure 16), with an average sales volume of all sample companies of € 85m.[264]

With regard to the **number of employees**, the largest company counted a workforce of 1600 people, while the smallest company employed 22 (see Figure 17). Average headcount was 485 individuals.

---

[263] Reasons for the company sale will be discussed in detail in subsection 4.2.1.1.

[264] All sales figures presented in this thesis refer to the total sales volume per year. For the reason of non-inclusion of smaller companies, see subsection 2.1.1 and footnote 65.

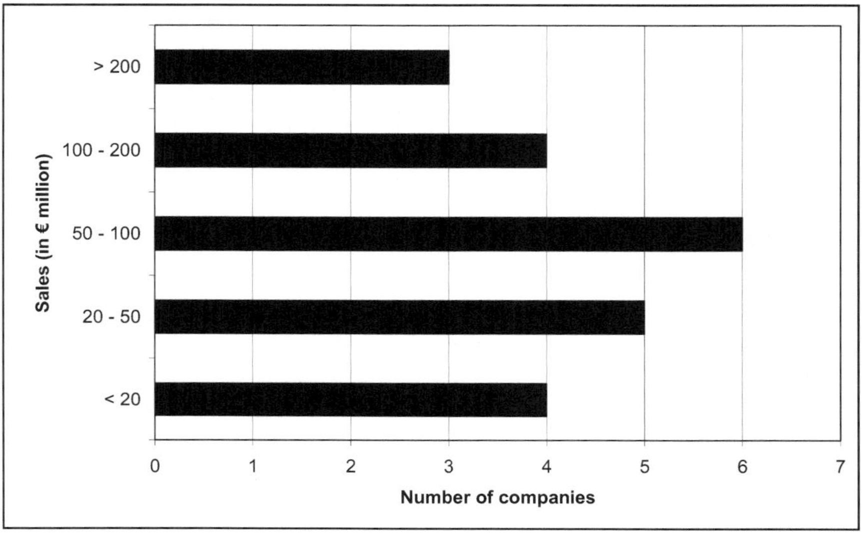

Figure 16: Company size by sales

Source: Interview data, Amadeus, CMBOR database (n=22)

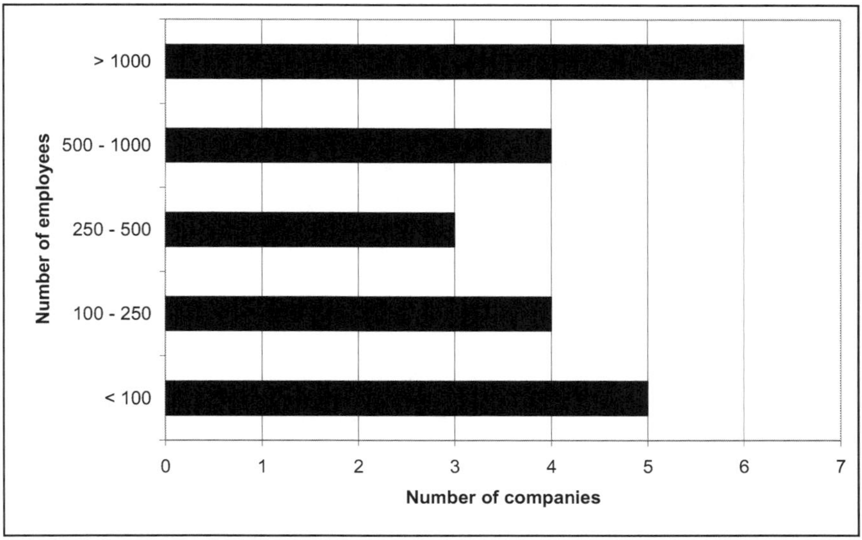

Figure 17: Company size by number of employees

Source: Interview data, Amadeus, CMBOR database (n=22)

The **time period that passed between the buy-out and the observation** of the state of the company for this research project is of great interest, as it takes some time until changes stemming from a buy-out become effective and can be evaluated. All interviews were conducted between June and August 2007. The most recent buy-out took place in December 2006, about half a year before the interview. The longest period between buy-out and interview was more than nine years in the case of a company that underwent a buy-out in 1998. The average period between buy-out and interview was 2.5 years. See Figure 18 for the distribution of sample companies by categories based on time elapsed since the buy-out.

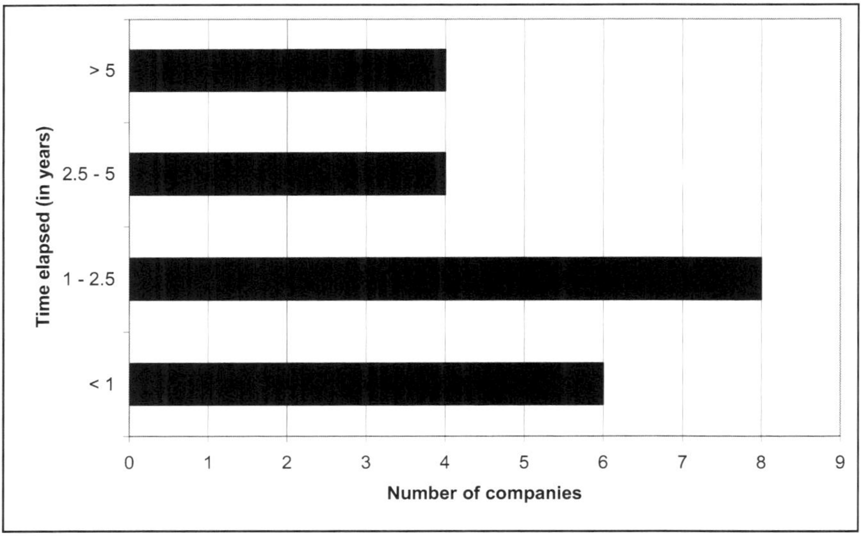

Figure 18: Time elapsed since the buy-out

Source: Interview data (n=22)

With regard to the **type of buy-out**, in seven companies a management buy-out took place.[265] In three companies, a new management bought the company, so these deals were classified as management buy-ins.[266] A buy-in management buy-out was reported in five companies.[267] In J and P, an institutional buy-out took place.[268] In company J, the manager was not involved in the buy-out transaction but was appointed later on and did not hold an equity stake. In company P, which was in a turnaround situation when the buy-out took place, an interim management was installed. The remaining companies belonged to the control group.[269]

3.2.2. Differentiation of sample and control group

Changes in portfolio companies are contrasted with changes in companies of the control group, as explained in subsection 3.1.3. The sample consisted of 17 portfolio companies[270], which were buy-outs in family businesses initiated or financed by private equity companies, and 5 companies of the control group (see Figure 19). In these companies, no buy-out took place, but they were acquired by holding companies or semi-public investment companies. Two companies of the control group were acquired by holding companies[271] and the three other companies were former family businesses sold to managers backed by semi-public investment companies[272].

265 A, D, G, H, K, M, and N; 41% of 17 respondents (portfolio companies, i.e. sample companies without the control group).

266 E, I, and L; 18% of 17 respondents.

267 B, C, F, O, and Q; 29% of 17 respondents.

268 12% of 17 respondents.

269 R, S, T, U, and V.

270 A through Q; 77% of 22 respondents.

271 R and S; 9% of 22 respondents.

272 T, U, and V; 14% of 22 respondents.

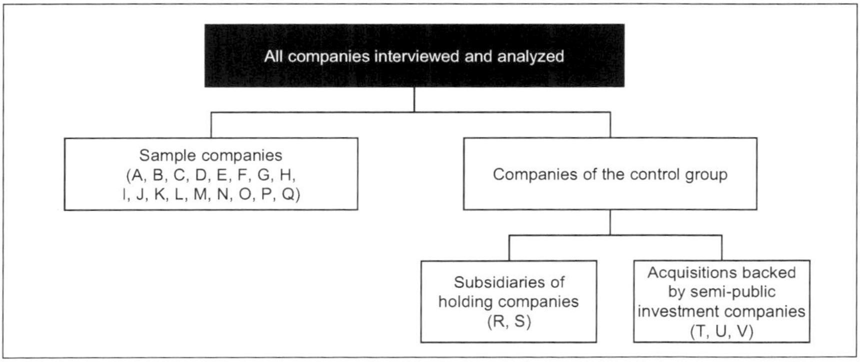

Figure 19: Differentiation between sample companies and companies of the control group

Source: Author's illustration

3.2.3. Family influence before the buy-out

Family involvement before the buy-out was exercised through three institutions of corporate governance: the equity stake owned by the family, the share of family members on the management board, and the share of family members in the supervisory board.

By definition of the SFI, families had to hold an **equity stake** in their family business.[273] 16 companies in the sample were exclusively owned by the family before the buy-out.[274] In three companies, a private equity company had already provided funds prior to the buy-out:[275] In C, the private equity company held a silent partnership in the company so that the family still possessed 100% of the control rights. In F, a private equity company held a 20% stake and in A two other private equity companies held in total 49% of equity. Besides private equity companies, wealthy individuals had invested in two companies before the buy-out:[276] In F, these private investors held

[273] Cf. subsection 2.1.1.

[274] These 16 companies are companies B, D, E, H, I, J, K, L, M, O, P, Q, R, S, U, and V; 73% of 22 respondents (all sample companies).

[275] A, C, and F; 14% of 22 respondents. All three companies were relatively large compared to the sample average in terms of sales.

[276] F and N; 9% of 22 respondents.

47% of equity along with the private equity company mentioned above. In N, private investors held 85% and thus the majority in the company.[277] In T, the family held a stake of 85% and two key employees held the remainder of equity. This ownership structure dated from the company's foundation. In G, the family held 26% of equity and 74% were held by two managers; one manager had already retired and left the company.

The distribution of the share of seats on the **management board** held by family members before the buy-out was more heterogeneous than the distribution of ownership.[278] 15 companies were (at least in part) managed by family members.[279] In seven companies, the family was not represented in the management of the company at all.[280] In eight companies, all the management power lay in the hands of the owning family.[281] In T, a non-family manager worked together with two family managers[282]: In four companies, a family manager cooperated with a non-family manager.[283] In three companies, family members formed a minority in the management.[284] As a tendency, most of the smaller companies in terms of sales were exclusively managed by family members, while in larger companies non-family managers took over some or all seats on the management board.

The last channel of family influence discussed here is the **supervisory board**. 12 companies did not have a supervisory board before the buy-out.[285] Contrary, in ten companies, supervisory boards existed.[286] In seven of these supervisory boards, the

---

277 According to the manager of N, the company needed funding for product and process innovations and the family was not able to provide this money.

278 The description in this paragraph and the details provided in Table 7, Table 8, Table 9 and Table 10 refer to the family influence in the management at the date of the buy-out. In some companies, composition of the management board had changed while the company was groomed for the sale. Subsection 4.2.1.3 contains details on these changes.

279 B, D, E, F, G, H, J, L, N, O, R, S, T, U, and V; 68% of 22 respondents.

280 A, C, I, K, M, P, and Q; 32% of 22 respondents.

281 E, J, L, N, R, S, and U; 36% of 22 respondents.

282 Family managers are managers that are members of the owning family (cf. subsection 2.1.1).

283 G, H, O, and V; 18% of 22 respondents.

284 B, D, and F; 14% of 22 respondents.

285 D, F, G, H, J, L, N, O, S, T, U, and V; 55% of 22 respondents.

286 A, B, C, E, I, K, M, P, Q, and R; 45% of 22 respondents.

family was represented.[287] In four companies, a family member was member of the supervisory board.[288] In A and B, two family representatives were among the members. In P, a supervisory board existed with at least one family member, but the interview partner could not remember the exact number of family representatives. Three companies had a supervisory board in which the family was not represented.[289]

Figure 20 shows which combinations of the different institutions of corporate governance occurred in the sample companies.[290] 13 families owned a part or the entire family business and were represented on the management board. In five companies, the family owned a stake in the family business and was represented in the supervisory board but not in the management board. Two families held stakes in their family businesses and sent representatives to the management board and the supervisory board. In two cases, family influence was restricted to the role of an owner.

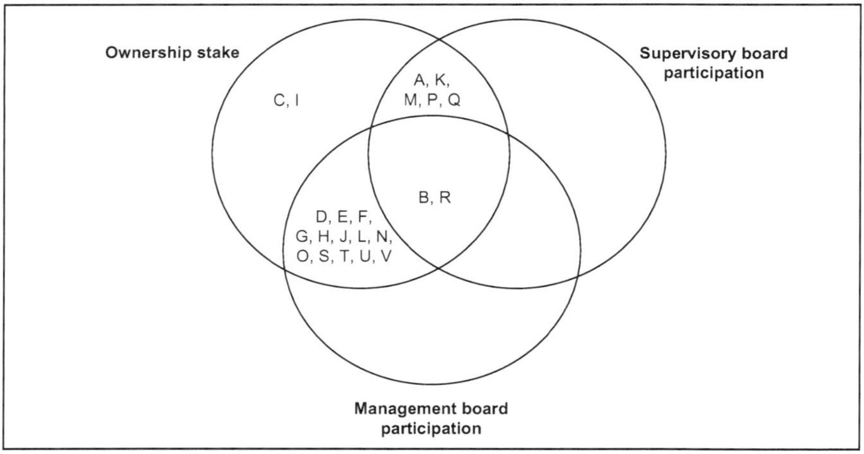

Figure 20: Family influence pre buy-out

Source: Interview data (n=22)

---

287 A, B, K, M, P, Q, and R; 70% of 10 relevant companies (sample companies with a supervisory board).

288 K, M, Q, and R; 40% of 10 relevant companies.

289 C, E, and I; 30% of 10 relevant companies.

290 As owning a certain equity stake in a company was by definition a condition to be eligible as family business, it is not astonishing that all companies are located in the circle that indicated that the family holds an equity stake in the company.

3.2.4. Family influence after the buy-out

Similar to the family influence before the buy-out, families can use the three institutions of corporate governance to have a say in shaping the company's future after the buy-out.

Former family owners held an **equity stake** in ten portfolio companies and two companies of the control group.[291] The family's stake amounted in two companies to 30% of equity (C and R)[292], in two companies to 25% (F and V)[293], in three companies to 20% (A, G, E)[294]. In three companies, families held less than 20%, i.e. 19% (H), 15% (Q) and 5% (M).[295] Interviewees in companies N and O only stated that the family held a stake in the company but did not provide more detailed data.[296] In seven sample companies and three companies of the control group, the family did not hold an equity stake in the former business after the buy-out.[297]

A family member remained on the **management board** after the buy-out in two portfolio companies and three companies of the control group.[298] In G and N, the

---

291 A, C, E, F, G, H, M, N, O, and Q; 59% of 17 respondents (of portfolio companies). The two companies of the control group are R and V.

Due to this equity participation of the former family owners, these buy-outs could be considered owner buy-outs (cf. subsection 2.1.2) besides their character of being a management buy-out or management buy-in. As the fact, whether post buy-out management came from within the company or from outside seems to have a greater effect on changes in the companies following the buy-out, the terms MBO or MBI are preferred towards the OBO.

292 6% of 17 respondents (R belongs to the control group).

293 6% of 17 respondents (V belongs to the control group).

294 18% of 17 respondents.

295 Each company represents 6% of 17 respondents.

296 12% of 17 respondents.

297 B, D, I, J, K, L, and P; 41% of 17 respondents. The three companies of the control group are S, T, and U.

298 G and N; 12% of 17 respondents. The three companies of the control group are R, V, and S. The description in this subsection and the details provided in Table 7, Table 8, Table 9, and Table 10 refer to the family influence in the management at the time of the interview. In some companies, composition of the management board had changed after the buy-out. Subsection 5.3.4 contains details on these changes.

In some cases, family members were on the management only temporary for some weeks or months until new management was found to take over as in the case of J or to facilitate transfer of responsibility to the new management as in E or U. (These temporary positions family managers held after the buy-out for up to six months are not listed in the sample description in Table 7 to Table 10 and in Figure 21). In other cases, this constellation was supposed to hold for years as in G or N.

respective family manager represented 50% of the two managers on the respective management board. In companies of the control group, the share of seats on the management board held by family members ranged from 33% in V over 50% in R to 100% in S. In F, the former family manager intended to stay but resigned after a year for having different opinions than the private equity company.[299]

A family member became member of the **supervisory board** in seven companies.[300] These companies represented half of the 14 companies, where a supervisory board existed or was installed after the buy-out.[301] In D, post buy-out management wanted the former family manager to become member of the supervisory board, though the latter did not hold a stake in the company post buy-out. In M, the former family owner and company founder left his regular position in the supervisory board after the buy-out to become honorary chairman of the supervisory board without the right to vote in decisions.

Family influence was not restricted to only one of these institutions of corporate governance but was often exerted through several institutions at a time (see Figure 21). The most frequent constellation of influence is ownership stake and participation in the supervisory board: Six portfolio companies corresponded to this pattern.[302] Family influence through a combination of ownership and management participation occurred in two portfolio companies (G, N)[303] and in two companies of the control group (R, V). In two portfolio companies, the family merely held an equity stake (H, M).[304] In D, a family member sat on the supervisory board.[305] In S of the control group, the pre buy-out family manager was manager but not owner of the company. There is no case in which the family influenced the company through all three institutions of corporate governance. Three families used exclusively one institution. Finally, in six portfolio companies and two companies of the control group, the family did not exert any influence after the buy-out.[306] Presumably, these families wanted a clear cut with their

299 Cf. subsection 4.2.2.5.

300 A, C, D, E, F, O, and Q; 41% of 17 respondents.

301 Cf. subsection 5.3.3.

302 35% of 17 respondents.

303 12% of 17 respondents.

304 12% of 17 respondents.

305 6% of 17 respondents.

306 B, I, J, K, L, P; 35% of 17 respondents.

former family business.[307] With the exception of B and P, most of these companies had sales of € 100 million or below.

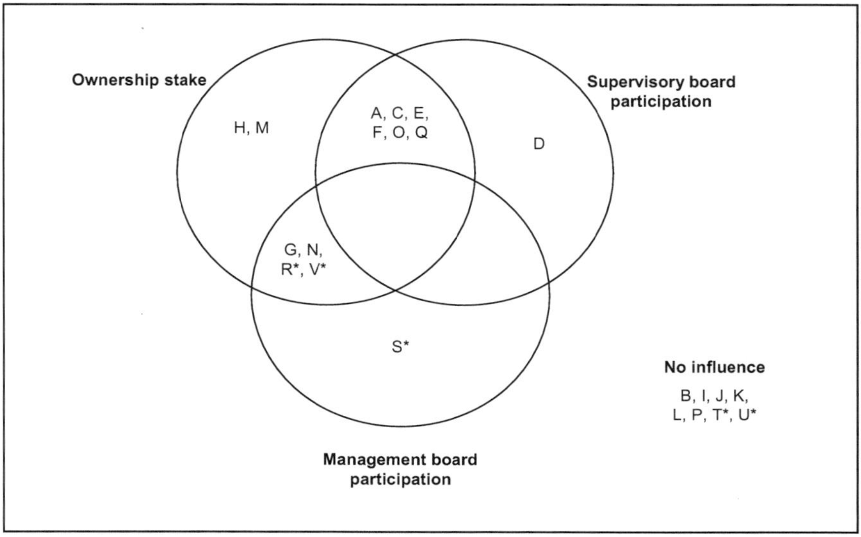

Figure 21: Family influence post buy-out

Source: Interview data (n=22)
* Company of the control group

3.2.5. Overview of interviewed companies

The tables on the following pages provide a detailed overview of company characteristics on an individual company level. Table 7, Table 8, and Table 9 describe the portfolio companies in the sample and Table 10 shows details of the companies in the control group.

[307] Cf. subsection 4.2.2.5.

		Company characteristics		Buy-out			Family involvement before buy-out			Family involvement after buy-out		
Company	Interview partner	Sales (in € million)	Number of em-ployees	Time elapsed since buy-out (in years)	Reason for sale	Type of buy-out	Owner-ship	Manage-ment	Super-visory board	Owner-ship	Manage-ment	Super-visory board
A	Manager, Investment manager	> 200	500 - 1000	1 - 2.5	Age, Opportunity to cash in	MBO	51% family; 49% 2 PEC	None	50% (2 of 4)	20%	None	33% (1 of 3)
B	Manager, Investment manager	> 200	> 1000	1 - 2.5	Age	BIMBO	100%	40% (2 of 5)	29% (2 of 7)	None	None	Board exists without family members
C	Manager	> 200	> 1000	2.5 - 5	Age, Financing problem	BIMBO	100% family; PEC held silent partnership	None	Board existed without family members	30%	None	25% (1 of 4)
D	Manager	100 - 200	500 - 1000	> 5	Age, Change in lifestyle	MBO	100%	40% (2 of 5)	No board	None	None	20% (1 of 5)
E	Manager	100 - 200	> 1000	2.5 - 5	Age, Financing problem	MBI	100%	100%	Board existed without family members	20%	None***	25% (1 of 4)
F	Manager	100 - 200	500 - 1000	2.5 - 5	Age, Financing problem	BIMBO	33% family; 47% private investors; 20% PEC	33% (1 of 3)	No board	25%	None***	33% (2 of 6)
G	Manager	50 - 100	100 - 250	< 1	Ownership restructuring ****	MBO	26% Family; 74% managers	50% (1 of 2)	No board	20%	50% (1 of 2)	No board*

Table 7: Overview of interviewed companies (1/3)

Source: Interview data

See page 85 for the reading annotations

		Company characteristics		Buy-out			Family involvement before buy-out			Family involvement after buy-out		
Company	Interview partner	Sales (in € million)	Number of em-ployees	Time elapsed since buy-out (in years)	Reason for sale	Type of buy-out	Owner-ship	Manage-ment	Super-visory board	Owner-ship	Manage-ment	Super-visory board
H	Manager	50 - 100	< 100	1 - 2.5	Change in lifestyle	MBO	100%	50% (1 of 2)	No board	19%	None	No board
I	Manager, Investment manager	50 - 100	> 1000	1 - 2.5	Insufficient management capabilities	MBI	100%	None	Board existed without family members	None	None	Board exists without family members
J	Manager, Investment manager	50 - 100	100 - 250	1 - 2.5	Age, Opportunity to cash in, Financing problem, Insufficient management capabilities	IBO	100%	100%	No board	None	None	No board
K	Manager, Investment manager	20 - 50	250 - 500	< 1	Age, Opportunity to cash in	MBO	100%	None	33% (1 of 3)	None	None	Board exists without family members
L	Manager	20 - 50	100 - 250	> 5	Age, Change in lifestyle, Opportunity to cash in	MBI	100%	100%	No board	None	None	Board exists without family members
M	Manager, Investment manager	20 - 50	250 - 500	< 1	Age	MBO	100%	None	33% (1 of 3)	5%**	None	Board exists without family members

Table 8: Overview of interviewed companies (2/3)

Source: Interview data

See page 85 for the reading annotations

Company	Interview partner	Company characteristics		Buy-out			Family involvement before buy-out			Family involvement after buy-out		
		Sales (in € million)	Number of em-ployees	Time elapsed since buy-out (in years)	Reason for sale	Type of buy-out	Owner-ship	Manage-ment	Super-visory board	Owner-ship	Manage-ment	Super-visory board
N	Manager	20 - 50	250 - 500	> 5	Opportunity to cash in, Financing problem	MBO	15% family; 85% 2 private investors	100%	No board	> 0%; details not available	50% (1 of 2)	Board exists without family members
O	Manager	20 - 50	100 - 250	> 5	Age	BIMBO	100%	50% (1 of 2)	No board	> 0%; details not available	None	> 0% (1 of n/a)
P	Manager	100 - 200	> 1000	< 1	Turnaround	IBO	100%	None	> 0% (1 of n/a)	None	None	Board exists without family members
Q	Manager, Investment manager	50 - 100	250 - 500	< 1	Turnaround	BIMBO	100%	None	33% (1 of 3)	15%	None	20% (1 of 5)

Reading annotations:

The column *Type of interview partners* contains information whether a company manager, or the manager and an investment manager has been interviewed about the respective company.

In the columns *Management* and *Supervisory board*, composition of the respective committee is indicated in brackets. The first number refers to the number of family members and the second number to the number of all members of the committee. E.g. (1 of 3) means: There is one family member in a committee, which is composed of 3 members in total. Temporary management positions held for less than six months are not taken into account.

Figures on *sales* and *number of employees* refer to the year the buy-out took place.

n/a - not available

* In company G, a board was about to be installed after the interview has taken place, according to the interviewee.

** In company M, the equity stake of 5% was promised to and planned for the former family owner, but transfer was due after the interview.

*** In companies E and F, the former family manager initially remained on the management board after the buy-out, but resigned two and a half years (E) and one year (F) after the buy-out.

**** In company G, ownership restructuring was the reason for the sale. This reason is outside the framework discussed in sections 4.1.1.1 and 4.2.1.1 (cf. footnote 403).

Table 9: Overview of interviewed companies (3/3)

Source: Interview data

Company	Interview partner	Company characteristics: Sales (in € million)	Company characteristics: Number of employees	Transaction: Time elapsed since sale (in years)	Transaction: Reason for sale	Transaction: Type of acquirer	Family involvement before the sale: Ownership	Family involvement before the sale: Management	Family involvement before the sale: Supervisory board	Family involvement after the sale: Ownership	Family involvement after the sale: Management	Family involvement after the sale: Supervisory board
R	Manager, Investment manager	50 - 100	500 - 1000	1 - 2.5	Age, Change in lifestyle, Opportunity to cash in	Holding company	100%	100%	20% (1 of 5)	30%	50% (1 of 2)	No board
S	Manager, Investment manager	< 20	< 100	2.5 - 5	Age	Holding company	100%	100%	No board	None	100%	No board
T	Manager, Investment manager	< 20	< 100	1 - 2.5	Age, Change in lifestyle, Opportunity to cash in	Semi-public investment company	85% family; 15% 2 key employees	66% (2 of 3)	No board	None	None	No board
U	Manager	< 20	< 100	1 - 2.5	Age	Semi-public investment company	100%	100%	No board	None	None	No board
V	Manager	< 20	< 100	< 1	Age, Change in lifestyle	Semi-public investment company	100%	50% (1 of 2)	No board	25%	33% (1 of 3)	No board

Table 10: Overview of interviewed companies – control group

Source: Interview data

See page 85 for the reading annotations

4 Background of buy-out transactions

This chapter examines the background of the buy-out to prepare the ground for the analysis of the changes induced by the buy-out, which will be described in the following chapters. This chapter presents the different steps of the buy-out in chronological order. The chapter analyses the decision to sell by inquiring into the reasons for selling the company, the evaluation of potential buyers and the sale preparations of the company (see Figure 22). Next, light will be shed on the sale transaction by examining private equity companies' investment criteria, family owners' goals in sale negotiations, details of the sale process, communication of and reaction to the buy-out, and family's separation from its company.

The chapter is structured as follows: At first, all aspects covered are described based on the literature in section 4.1. These explanations are complemented by empirical descriptions in section 4.2, based on evidence from the interviews. Section 4.3 summarizes the chapter.

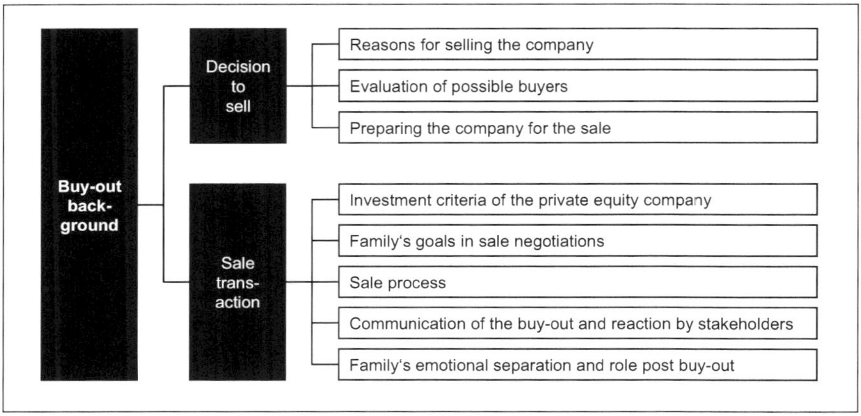

Figure 22: Structure of analysis of the buy-out background

Source: Author's illustration

4.1 Theoretical background

4.1.1. Decision to sell

4.1.1.1. Reasons for selling the company

The sale of a family business is the consequence of family managers' resigning and their inability or unwillingness to appoint an adequate family successor or non-family manager to take over company management.[308] Thus, the sale of a family business can be subsumed under a three-stage decision process of succession (see Figure 23).[309] In the first stage, the family manager contemplates to resign from the company. In the second stage, the leaving family manager scrutinizes whether a succession within the family is possible and desirable. In third step, the retiring family owner or manager, who does not hand over management to a relative, checks whether an internal or external non-family manager is available to lead the company and whether this alternative is in the owner's interest.[310]

In the following, this three-stage decision model will be discussed in detail providing a framework for the different motives and factors involved in each decision. The decision to **resign** in the first decision stage necessitates a succession in

---

308 Although this decision problem focuses on the perspective of the family manager, it also embraces the perspective of a family owner – i.e. one or several family members, who own a family business but are not actively involved in managing the company. Family owners are already in a later (the third) stage of the following decision problem, where management is delegated to non-family managers but ownership is kept in the family. The reasons for family owners to sell can be assumed to be similar to the reasons, why family managers retire from management, i.e. age, desire for a change in lifestyle, opportunity to sell, or business problems (cf. subsubsection 4.2.1.1).

309 Succession in the following refers to the handing over of management from the family manager to another person or to the transfer of ownership from a family owner to another person or party. The successor succeeds the family manager in management or the family owner in ownership and must not necessarily be a family member. A succeeding family member is termed a family successor. This usage of the term succession takes the perspective of the company that is examined – which is the research object of this thesis. This usage is in contrast to the American usage of succession, where succession is restricted to the transfer of ownership or management to family members (cf. Sharma/Chrisman/Chua (2003), p. 669).

310 According to the specific situation of the family business, family owners might find themselves at the second or third stage of the decision problem without passing through the former decision stage(s). E.g. if the only family manager of a family business died, the remaining family owners start at the second decision stage. If the family has already left management to non-family managers, family owners start at the third decision stage.

management. If management succession by family members and non-family managers is no option, a sale of the company would constitute a succession in ownership and management.

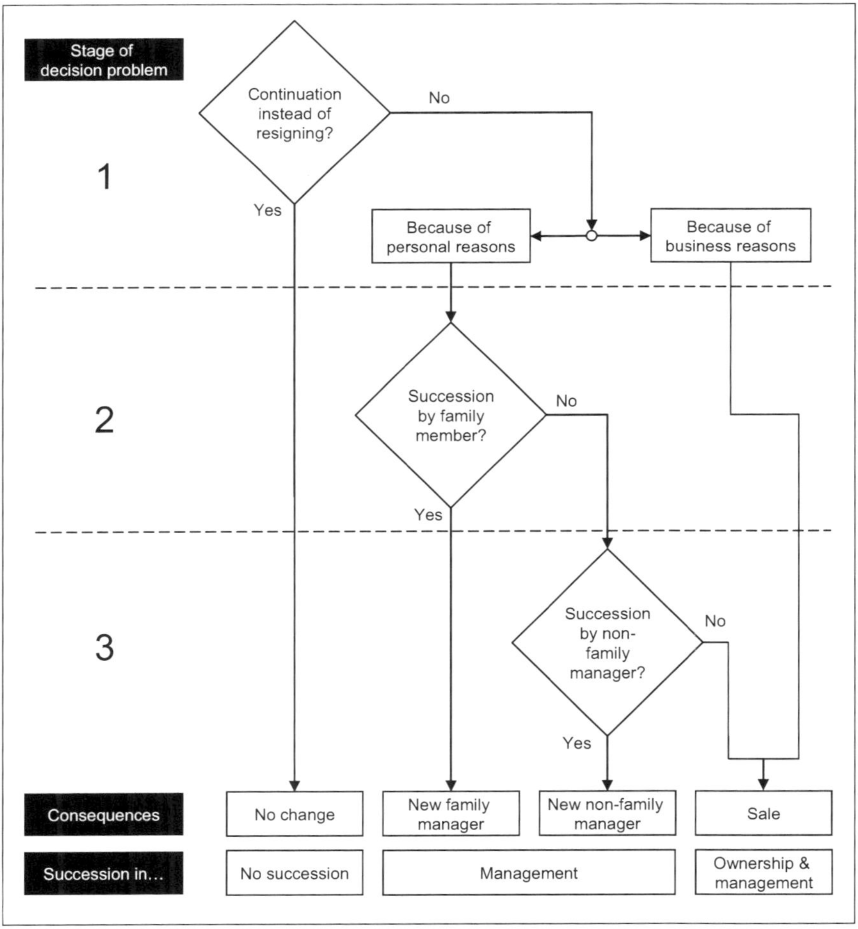

Figure 23: Decision process preceding a company sale

Source: Author's illustration
Rhombi represent decisions the family manager has to take

In the first stage of the decision process, there are numerous reasons that trigger retirement of the family manager. These reasons can be distinguished into two groups: On the one hand, reasons can be rooted in the person(s) of the family manager(s). **Personal reasons** are advanced age, desire for leisure time, health or other goals of the family manager.[311] An additional personal goal of the family manager might be to cash in his company, in case he was offered a good sale price for his company.[312] The following Table 11 summarizes some empirical studies on the family managers' reasons to retire:

Author, year	Sample composition	Reasons for resigning
Nagl (2005)	503 German family businesses	84% Age of owner 29% Desire for leisure time 18% Owner's health 13% Other reasons
PriceWaterhouseCoopers (2005)	1,342 Swiss family businesses	81.1% Age of owner 28.3% Desire for leisure time 18.5% Handover to suitable employee 17.0% Children wanted to take over 12.8% Owner's health 12.8% Possibility to sell company at a good price 4.2% Business problems 10.6% Other problems
Leyherr (2000)	122 Austrian family businesses; average value on Likert scale (1 = very important; 7 = very unimportant)	2.3 Age of owner 2.7 Other family members wanted to take over 3.2 New impulses for company 4.9 Owner was no more interested 5.0 Good opportunity at market

Table 11: Overview of surveys on family managers' reasons to resign from management

Source: Nagl (2005), p. 25; PriceWaterhouseCoopers (2005), p. 14; Leyherr (2000), p. 179

On the other hand, reasons might stem from the business itself. **Business reasons** are mostly caused by economic problems of the company or by financial shortages, which endanger company growth.[313] These business reasons are not solved through changes in the management but necessitate a sale of the company.

---

311 Especially if a retirement is not pressing, family managers tend to postpone a solution and remain in management (cf. Forst (1992), p. 78).

312 Cf. Howorth/Westhead/Wright (2004), p. 520.

313 Cf. Forst (1992), pp. 31 et seq. However, family managers might also forgo growth to retain company ownership in the hands of the family. In a survey among family businesses that received

In the second stage of the decision process, the family manager who has decided to resign might look for a suitable **successor in the family**. Passing management on to the next generation or at least other family members is an important goal for family businesses.[314] Thus, installing a child or another relative in the management seems to be the standard solution for succession in management.[315]

For handing management over to another family member, four conditions have to be met:[316] First, a relative – typically a son or a daughter – must exist and be of suitable age. Second, to replace the leaving family manager, a potential family successor must be qualified at best through studies and work experience.[317] Third, the existing and qualified family successor must be willing to take over management of the company.[318] Fourth, succession has to succeed; after transfer of management, the family successor might turn out to lack necessary skills for the position, he is supposed

financing from a private equity company, 85% of participants indicated that keeping control in the family was a very important goal. Only 45% indicated that providing capital for company growth was very important (cf. Upton/Petty (2000), p. 33).

314 Cf. Achleitner/Schraml/Klöckner (2008), p. 18; PriceWaterhouseCoopers (2005), p. 15; Tagiuri/Davis (1992), p. 48; Leyherr (2000), pp. 175-178; IMAP M&A Consultants (2008), p. 7; Mazzola/Marchisio/Astrachan (2008), p. 239. According to PRICEWATERHOUSECOOPERS, 73% of family owners desire to hand ownership and management over to an heir (cf. PriceWaterhouse-Coopers (2008a), p. 13).

315 NAGL found that in 70% of family businesses, which have made plans for succession in management, a relative of the family manager is envisaged to follow him. In 54% of cases, a son is designated, in 16% a daughter and in 3% another relative. In 14% of the family business, succession planning envisages an internal, non-family manager and in 13% an external manager to take over management (cf. Nagl (2005), p. 27).

Management succession by a family member might entail changes in the intra-family ownership structure. As family ownership is only looked at on an aggregate level in this thesis, this is not regarded as an ownership succession.

316 Another condition might be that family successors must be able to finance the succession, if the resigning owners want to be paid off (cf. PriceWaterhouseCoopers (2005), p. 21). However, as this thesis does not focus on intra-family relationships, this condition is not discussed in detail (cf. subsection 2.1.1).

317 Cf. Howorth/Westhead/Wright (2004), p. 518; Wellendorff (1999), p. 281. Family owners are advised to plan ahead for the preparation of family members that are supposed to succeed in company management (cf. PriceWaterhouseCoopers (2005), pp. 22 et seq.; UBS (2005), pp. 16-18). For an overview of desired and actual attributes of successors, see Chrisman/Chua/Sharma (1998), pp. 22-27; Leyherr (2000), pp. 184-189.

318 Cf. Howorth/Westhead/Wright (2004), p. 518; Wellendorff (1999), p. 281. HENNERKES/PLEISTER noticed that willingness of relatives to take over responsibility in the family business decreases continuously (cf. Hennerkes/Pleister (1999), p. 273).

to fill.[319] According to a survey by SCHRÖER/KAYSER among German succession advisors, management succession in the family fails in 9% of cases as children do not exist, in 33% because children are not qualified, and in 47% because children do not want to take responsibility.[320]

However, not all family owners aim at transferring the company into the next generation: Family owners in two of the eight sample companies in the study of HOWORTH/WESTHEAD/WRIGHT strived for selling the company.[321]

In the third stage of the decision process, the family manager who wants to retire and has no qualified and willing relative to take over management, might look for **non-family managers** to follow him. He might recruit these managers from within the company or outside the company. Promoting internal junior managers[322] has the advantage that family owners have better knowledge about these managers' competence and have already built trust in them.[323] Appointment of non-family managers might professionalize management, implement needed changes and provide an impetus to the company's strategy. Conservation of ownership in the hands of the family ensures a certain degree of continuity, though this degree is lower compared to succession in management by a family member. Appointment of a non-family

---

319 Cf. Howorth/Westhead/Wright (2004), p. 518. Besides incapacity of the successor, successions by family members might also fail because banks are hesitant to financially support the successor (cf. Kramer (2006), pp. 139 et seq.). A study among succession in family businesses has shown that family owners and family managers do not want to see their family business decline because of an incompetent or unskilled family successor. Therefore, 81% of family managers have the right to dismiss their successor (cf. Nagl (2005), p. 32).

The study of PRICEWATERHOUSECOOPERS has also shown that 20.3% of planned successions fail before the family successor or non-family successor takes over management. The most frequent reasons for these failures are difficulties to raise financing, diverging price expectations and different plans for the company's future (cf. PriceWaterhouseCoopers (2005), p. 22).

320 Cf. Schröer/Kayser (2006), p. 26. Figures refer to companies with more than 50 employees, as smaller companies are unlikely to be eligible for buy-outs (see subsection 2.1.1).

321 Cf. Howorth/Westhead/Wright (2004), pp. 518 et seq.

322 In corporate hierarchy, junior managers are below executive directors (referred to as managers).

323 Cf. UBS (2005), p. 36. Family owners are recommended to look for non-family managers within the company first, as forgoing of this step might frustrate incumbent junior managers and cause them to resign or not to accept the new manager.

However, junior managers of the second tier might not exist in many family businesses of the Mittelstand, as the family manager might not have developed potential internal successors adequately (cf. Zenz-Spitzweg (2001), p. 29).

manager might also serve as a temporary solution until a family member takes over management or until the family owner is emotionally ready to sell the business.[324]

A study by KAYSER/WALLAU/ADENÄUER among German family managers on management succession has found that between 2000 and 2005, 62% of former family managers were followed by family members, 14% by internal junior managers and 30% by external managers.[325] In the study by PRICEWATERHOUSECOOPERS on future management succession among German family owners, 44% of the respondents who had planned succession in management exclusively took family members into consideration, while 56% also considered non-family managers for management succession.[326]

If the decision process described above yields that the family manager wants to resign and that the options of relatives or non-family managers in the company management do not exist or are not acceptable to the family, the only solution to the family manager is to **sell the company**.[327] According to the study of PRICE-WATERHOUSECOOPERS, 70% of the respondents have planned the succession in management, but only 36% the succession in ownership. The authors interpret this difference as a sign that family owners are willing to leave management to others, but they do not want to give up ownership and thus total control of the company.[328]

---

324 Cf. Howorth/Westhead/Wright (2004), p. 511; UBS (2005), pp. 35 et seq.; KPMG (2004), p. 21.

325 Cf. Kayser/Wallau/Adenäuer (2006), pp. 52 et seq. The authors also asked respondents, who were planning management succession in the future, which solution they preferred: 48% preferred a succession by a family member, 27% by internal junior managers, 30% by external managers and 21% aimed at selling the company (cf. Kayser/Wallau/Adenäuer (2006), pp. 58 et seq.). In both statistics, respondents could give multiple answers.

In the above mentioned survey among succession advisors, respondents indicated that in non-family successions, 38% of successors came from within the company, 45% were external managers and 17% of companies were sold (cf. Schröer/Kayser (2006), p. 27).

326 Cf. PriceWaterhouseCoopers (2006), pp. 27 et seq.

327 The sale of the family business leaves the company to non-family parties and their influences and thus turns a family business into a regular company (cf. Albach/Freund (1989), p. 266). In theory, family owners could also liquidate their company to solve the succession problem. But given the emotional bond between family owner or manager and family business, this is not considered as an alternative in the following.

328 Cf. PriceWaterhouseCoopers (2006), pp. 23 et seq.

The surveys presented above show that most family managers aim at handing the company over to another family member, thus underlining validity of the presented decision process. While the depicted preference of succession is true for most family managers, some do not aim at transferring the company to the next generation.[329] In these cases, the family manager strives to sell the company, when he has taken the decision to resign from management.[330]

The following Table 12 provides an overview of surveys on reasons to sell a family business.

Author, year	Sample composition	Reasons for sale
PriceWaterhouse-Coopers (2005)	1,342 Swiss family businesses; selected reasons (multiple reasons possible)	52.2% Children not interested 18.8% No suitable employees to take over company 15.9% Children not qualified or not motivated 15.9% No children 15.9% Children too young 13.0% Employees not interested 5.8% Other reasons
European Private Equity & Venture Capital Association (2005)	117 buy-outs in European family businesses average value on Likert scale (5 = very important; 1 = very unimportant)	2.74 No suitable family successor 2.67 No family successor available 2.39 Approach by intermediary/advisor 2.37 Approach by non-family management 1.93 Need for additional capital for growth 1.56 Poor growth prospects 1.54 Death or illness of the CEO 1.46 Cash flow problems 1.34 Lack of profitability 1.23 Liquidation
Forst (1992)	24 buy-outs in German family businesses (multiple reasons possible)	79.2% No family successor 16.7% Financing problems 8.3% Insufficient profitability 4.2% Insolvency or pending insolvency 29.2% Other reasons

Table 12: Overview of surveys on reasons to sell a family business

Source: PriceWaterhouseCoopers (2005), p. 21; European Private Equity & Venture Capital Association (2005), p. 10; Forst (1992), p. 31

[329] Cf. Howorth/Westhead/Wright (2004), pp. 518 et seq.; PriceWaterhouseCoopers (2006), p. 24.

[330] Thus, the second decision stage is skipped.

4.1.1.2. Evaluation of possible buyers

Typically, there are three potential ways to sell a family business: First, the company might be sold to strategic buyer; second, the company could be sold to the general public through listing it on the stock exchange; and third, the company could be sold to a private equity company and internal or external managers through a buy-out.[331]

The sale to **a strategic buyer** is called a trade sale. Strategic buyers are other companies[332], which acquire the family business for strategic reasons. To realize economies of scale, it is not far-fetched to assume that the organization of the existing family business will be merged with the organization of the acquiring company. While this might offer several advantages to the sold company (market access, broader product range, economies of scale), this might pose a threat to the identity and brand of the company and to job prospects of employees.[333] Family owners seem especially concerned about the possibility that a competitor might take over their company – given the emotional bond between family owner and business, this could be perceived as personal defeat.[334]

Sale to **investors at the stock exchange** is also referred to as an initial public offering (IPO).[335] An IPO gives the company access to the capital market, increases reputation and attractiveness towards employees, business partners and external managers. However, requirements for a public company are high with regard to transparency, management, and expenses for investor relations. The openness towards the general public demanded from a public company by law, entails profound changes in corporate culture. Frequently, the sale to investors at the stock exchange is either unattractive or completely precluded for many family businesses for one of the

---

331 Cf. Scholes/Westhead/Burrows (2008), pp. 9 et seq.

332 Other companies can be either non-family businesses or family businesses. Family owners are frequently reluctant to sell their company to another family business; however, this issue has not been researched yet in detail.

333 Cf. Howorth/Westhead/Wright (2004), p. 511; UBS (2005), p. 36.

334 Cf. Lopes (2003), p. 62; Forst (1992), p. 80; Bousek et al. (2003), p. 5; Achleitner/Achleitner (2000), p. 132.

335 This assumes that the family business was privately held before the sale, which is true for 84% of German family businesses (cf. Klein (2004), p. 108). If the family business was public before the decision to sell, the sale to the general public would merely increase the stock floated at the stock exchange.

following reasons: First, the company does not fulfill the requirements with regard to minimum company size; second, the considerable costs of an IPO make it unattractive; third, vendors are frequently obliged to hold a significant stake in the company for a certain period post IPO.[336] Lack of feasibility or attraction of IPOs is reflected by a study among 107 German family owners, which has found that not a single family owner planned to sell his company through an IPO.[337]

As a last option, a family business can be sold to a **private equity company and internal or external managers** through a buy-out.[338] The former family owners might keep a minority stake in the company and thus keep a bond to the former family business after its sale. Given its equity participation, management is highly motivated after the deal and has access to professional know-how and support of the private equity company. A buy-out as solution to the succession problem guarantees the company's independence. In case of a management buy-out, pre buy-out managers ensure a high degree of continuity in the company. In contrast to these advantages, buy-outs put a heavy burden on the company through the high debt level and are no ultimate solution due to the limited holding period of investors.[339]

In the early 2000s, private equity companies fought against ignorance of their business model and prejudices stemming from the negative press coverage of selected transactions.[340] A more recent study by REDLEFSEN/EIBEN has shown that 85% of family owners are aware of the existence of this financing alternative, though only

---

336 Cf. Achleitner/Achleitner (2000), pp. 135-137; Howorth/Westhead/Wright (2004), p. 511; UBS (2005), pp. 37-39, 43 et seq.; Hickey (2005), p. 30; Mazzola/Marchisio (2002), pp. 139 et seq.; Dreux (1990), p. 234.

337 Cf. PriceWaterhouseCoopers (2006), pp. 23 et seq.

338 Managers could also acquire the former family business without financial backing of a private equity company. Companies T, U, and V are exemplary cases of these transactions. However, these transactions are not considered buy-outs according to the definition provided in subsection 2.1.2 and are therefore not in the focus of this thesis. Companies T, U, and V are contained in the control group to exhibit changes after these transactions.

339 Cf. Scholes/Westhead/Burrows (2008), p. 10; Howorth/Westhead/Wright (2004), p. 526; Forst (1992), p. 80; UBS (2005), pp. 39-43; Pütter (2001), pp. 3-5; Hickey (2005), p. 30; Bousek et al. (2003), p. 5; Wright/Coyne (1985), pp. 12 et seq. In case of a management buy-in, continuity in the company is lower compared to a management buy-out.

340 Cf. Burger-Calderon/Näther (2001), p. 14; Hickey (2005), p. 31. For an overview of the most notorious private equity transaction in Germany, the buy-out in the former family business Friedrich Grohe AG und Co. KG (today Grohe AG), see Frankfurter Allgemeine Zeitung (2005), p. 22 (or Madslien (2005) for an English version).

about 8% resort to it.[341] The INSTITUT FÜR MITTELSTANDSFORSCHUNG (IfM) has projected that in 2005, 21.1% of family businesses facing a succession event will be sold to another company, while 26.7% will be sold to incumbent or external managers.[342]

Besides these typical ways to sell a family business, it could be also sold to a holding company or managers backed by a semi-public investment company. Companies sold to these alternative buyers compose the control group of this thesis and are discussed in greater detail in subsection 4.2.1.2.

4.1.1.3. Preparing the company for the sale

As will be shown in the next subsections, the sale process and the investment decision by a private equity company demand certain requirements, not all family businesses fulfill before the buy-out.[343] Therefore, several measures might be taken to prepare the company for the sale process.

First, family owners are advised to sustainably **improve profitability** of the family business. Improvements in profitability might necessitate operational improvements, which family owners or family managers might oppose to, as they change the corporate structure and might entail job cuts; both consequences conflict goals family owners pursue in the sale process, as will be discussed in subsection 4.1.2.2. Nevertheless, increases in profitability are in the interest of family owners as they directly impact the sale price of the company and as they render the company more attractive to potential buyers.[344]

Second, profitability of the company is supposed to be visible to a potential buyer. Therefore, **transparency** of the company should be improved with regard to

341 Cf. Redlefsen/Eiben (2006), p. 7. This low percentage of family businesses using private equity is confirmed by a recent study of Achleitner/Schraml/Klöckner (2008), p. 28.

342 Cf. Freund (2004), pp. 86 et seq. The remaining companies will be handed over to family members (43.8%) or liquidated (8.3%). As the IfM includes all companies with sales of more than € 50.000 in its projections, the percentages provided above might overstate the number of buy-outs; a considerable share of these companies might be too small for private equity investments or might be sold to managers that are able to finance the acquisition without backing of a private equity company.

343 Cf. subsection 4.1.2.1.

344 Cf. UBS (2005), p. 14; Upton/Petty (2000), p. 36.

reporting and management accounting. Improvements in transparency are a necessary preparation for the obligatory due diligence in a sale process.[345]

Third, **composition of the management team** should be revised with an eye on manager's skills and performance. Weaknesses of the management team might entail personal changes after the sale and negatively affect the sale price or the whole investment decision of a private equity company.[346]

Fourth, before approaching private equity companies as potential buyers of the company, management should compose a **business plan** that enables a potential investor to get a comprehensive overview of business activities and the company's environment. This business plan should contain a detailed analysis of the company, its environment and a vision of the company's future development. In particular, the business plan is supposed to include forecast cash flows for several years following the buy-out and detailed discussion of the assumptions underlying the projections.[347]

Fifth, family owners and managers are advised to **disentangle their private property** from that of the company.[348]

Most of these measures are no quick wins but have a certain lead time until they unfold their full potential: Operational improvements need time to be implemented, increases in transparency might necessitate time-consuming changes in accounting or IT and new managers need time to familiarize themselves with the company.[349]

Empirical evidence on preparation of family businesses for a buy-out is scarce. The only evidence relates to changes in management pre buy-out: In the study of HOWORTH/WESTHEAD/WRIGHT, management responsibilities in a sample company were gradually handed over to a newly appointed non-family CEO, who was supposed to guarantee management continuity during transfer of ownership. In another

---

345 Cf. UBS (2005), pp. 14, 44; PriceWaterhouseCoopers (2005), pp. 18 et seq.; F.A.Z. Institut (2005), pp. 37, 48.

346 Cf. UBS (2005), p. 15; F.A.Z. Institut (2005), p. 48; KPMG (2004), p. 22.

347 Cf. Huydts (1992), p. 91; KPMG (2004), p. 22; Becker (2001), pp. 6 et seq.; Bousek et al. (2003), p. 12. For a practitioner's guide to writing a business plan, see Webb (1985), pp. 53-59; Becker (2000), pp. 106 et seq.

348 Cf. UBS (2005), p. 21.

349 Cf. F.A.Z. Institut (2005), p. 48.

company, the family owner transferred management ad hoc to a non-family senior manager, who worked in the company for a long time.[350]

4.1.2. Sale transaction

4.1.2.1. Investment criteria of the private equity company

Given the considerable risk associated with buy-outs, private equity companies have a set of criteria, companies and managers have to fulfill to be eligible for an investment of a private equity company.[351]

An investment criterion of utmost importance is the **financial strength** of the prospectively bought-out company. Given the considerable leverage typical for buy-outs, a company must show significant financial strength to ensure the company's ability to service debt after the buy-out. A strong track record proving the company's viability and profitability in the past is a good indicator that the company will show these characteristics in the future as well. Private equity companies focus especially on cash flow to assess the financial strength of a company and attempt to avoid businesses with cyclic or uncertain cash flows.[352]

The **management** is another important investment criterion for a private equity company. Management problems are one of the most frequent reasons for company failure and management is the key to implement any changes in the company. According to HUYDTS, management has to fulfill three conditions to be considered as appropriate for the buy-out by the private equity company.[353] First, managers should have industry and product know-how, profound education, excellent track record and entrepreneurial propensity. Second, managers must be able to work under the pressure of being their own boss and must be willing to bear the risk of investing their own money into the company. Third, the management team should harmonize internally

[350] Cf. Howorth/Westhead/Wright (2004), pp. 519, 522.

[351] Cf. Forst (1992), p. 90. While many investment criteria of private equity companies can be found in the literature, the following criteria are an aggregation of the most important criteria, given investment criteria are not in the main focus of the thesis. For a comprehensive framework, see Huydts (1992), pp. 61-79.

[352] Cf. Achleitner/Achleitner (2000), p. 138; Achleitner (2002), p. 740; Pütter (2001), p. 9; Arzac (2004), p. 223; Becker (2001), p. 6; Dreux (1990), pp. 232 et seq.; Bousek et al. (2003), p. 6; Forst (1992), p. 90; Huydts (1992), pp. 70 et seq.

[353] Cf. Huydts (1992), pp. 32-36.

and cover all relevant business areas. Representatives of the private equity company will hold conversations with the respective managers to get an idea of their personality and skills. Nevertheless, scrutiny of managers' quality is particularly difficult.[354]

Another criterion private equity companies assess before investing is the **product and market combination**. The family business should have products that offer a sustainable ability to create stable cash flows, at best through a competitive advantage or nonexistence of potential substitutes. With regard to the market, the family business should have a strong position in the market with growth potential.[355]

Private equity companies also like to see **potential for value creation** in the company they acquire. This might include potential for increases in sales, margins or productivity. Room for profitable investments or potential assets to sell are also seen as advantages. Investors are especially interested in opportunities for a buy-and-build strategy, which means that the base company is strengthened by acquiring competitors to grow the company and to realize synergy effects.[356]

Empirical evidence of investment criteria for buy-outs in family businesses is far from being abundant. In their study on private equity investments in US family businesses, UPTON/PETTY found that lack of the succeeding managers' qualifications was the most frequent deal killer followed by inadequate profitability or absence of growth potential.[357]

4.1.2.2. Family owners' goals in sale negotiations

For family owners, their family business is more than a mere economic vehicle: Family owners also see their company as a social entity, which people dedicate their vitality, hopes, emotions and values to.[358] The family business and the position as owner of this family business play a central role in the family manager's life.[359]

---

[354] Cf. Achleitner (2002), pp. 741 et seq.; Pütter (2001), p. 8; Dreux (1990), p. 232; Jakoby (2000), pp. 198-209.

[355] Cf. Achleitner (2002), p. 742; Dreux (1990), pp. 232 et seq.; Bousek et al. (2003), pp. 6 et seq.; Kessel (1995), p. 96.

[356] Cf. Pütter (2001), p. 9; Bousek et al. (2003), p. 6; Huydts (1992), pp. 72 et seq., 78; Kessel (1995), p. 96.

[357] Cf. Upton/Petty (2000), p. 36.

[358] Cf. Zellweger/Nason (2008), p. 212.

[359] Cf. Haubrock (2005), p. 57.

For these reasons, family owners do not exclusively focus on maximization of the transaction value when they sell their family business.[360] Instead, they also pursue other, **non-financial goals**. Continuity of the structure of the family business might be important to family owners.[361] This continuity is linked to the conservation of the company's reputation through good products or services, so that family members are able to identify themselves with the company post buy-out.[362] Conservation of employment is another goal that differentiates family owners from most other vendors.[363]

However, the **sale price** is relevant to family owners as well, since it constitutes a lion's share of their post buy-out fortune.[364] Intertwined with the goal of achieving a high sale price, some family owners might pursue the objective of a fast closing of the deal in negotiations, e.g. if the family manager has fallen seriously ill or if he has died.[365] Pursuit of one or several of the non-financial goals described above might lower the financial outcome of the sale. So, family owners have to consider carefully which objectives to emphasize.

The following Table 13 provides an overview of surveys on objectives the family pursued at the sale of the company. While earlier studies show that family owners attached high importance to financial goals in negotiations, more recent surveys suggest that non-financial goals are more important than financial goals.

[360] Cf. Forst (1992), p. 80; Hickey (2005), p. 30.

[361] Cf. Howorth/Westhead/Wright (2004), p. 526; Forst (1992), p. 79; Huydts (1992), p. 28.

[362] Cf. Kayser/Wallau/Adenäuer (2006), p. 57.

[363] Cf. Hickey (2005), p. 30.

[364] Cf. Forst (1992), p. 79; Huydts (1992), p. 28; Achleitner/Achleitner (2000), p. 132.

[365] Cf. Forst (1992), pp. 78 et seq., 81.

Author, year	Sample composition	Objectives
Kayser/Wallau/ Adenäuer (2006)	1,102 German family businesses; average value on Likert scale (5 = very important; 1 = very unimportant); Selected objectives	4.63 Continuity of the company 4.29 Conservation of reputation 4.22 Conservation of independence 4.20 Conservation of corporate culture 4.13 Conservation of jobs 2.98 Minimization of tax payments 2.92 Creation of new jobs 2.54 Maximization of sale price
PriceWaterhouse-Coopers (2005)	1,342 Swiss family businesses; average value on Likert scale (5 = very important; 1 = very unimportant); Selected objectives	4.28 Continuity of company 4.25 Independence of company 4.02 Building a financial reserve for family 3.84 Conservation of jobs 3.19 Continuity of company name
Forst (1992)	24 Buy-outs in German family businesses; rates of approval to reasons for selling through a buy-out	62.5% Continuity of the company 41.7% Quick sale decision 33.3% Not selling to competitor 29.2% Highest sale price
Gräper (1993)	36 Buy-outs in German family (23) and non-family (13) businesses; average value on Likert scale assigned to reasons for selling through a buy-out (1 = very important; 5 = very unimportant)	2.6 Speed of offer 2.9 Highest sale price 3.2 Less guarantees 3.3 Reputation of buyer 3.3 Conservation of jobs 3.4 Limited public attention 3.5 Conservation of reputation

Table 13: Overview of surveys on objectives at the sale

Source: Kayser/Wallau/Adenäuer (2006), p. 57; PriceWaterhouseCoopers (2005), p. 15; Forst (1992), p. 80; Gräper (1993), p. 104

4.1.2.3. Sale process

Following the decision to sell the family business through a buy-out, the sale process starts. Figure 24 shows the different stages of the sale process.

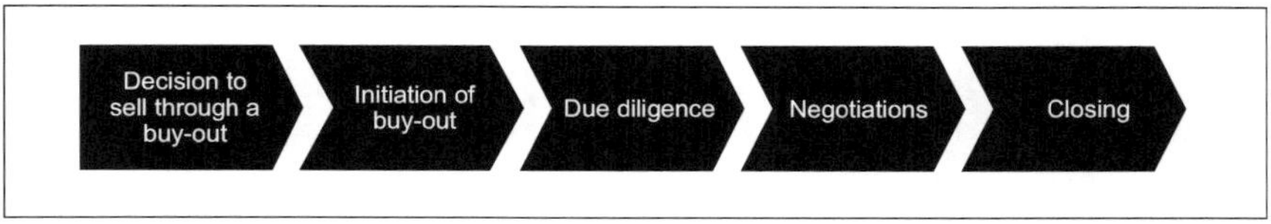

Figure 24: Stylized sale process of family owners

Source: Modifiedly taken from Hill (2003), p. 143

There are three different parties to **initiate the buy-out**: The selling family owners, private equity companies and management. According to a study of the

EUROPEAN PRIVATE EQUITY AND VENTURE CAPITAL ASSOCIATION (EVCA) among buy-outs in former family businesses, only 26% of the buy-outs in the sample were initiated by non-family management through approaching the former family owners. In contrast, 64% of buy-outs were initiated by the former family owners; to sell their company, family owners contacted independent advisors (28%), private equity companies (17%) or non-family managers (17%).[366]

Deal initiation through managers seems to be hampered by three possible reasons: First, the typical authoritative leading style of family managers might not leave enough space for internal managers to develop the proactive, creative behavior that characterizes an entrepreneur, who would be willing to take the risk of doing a buy-out.[367] Second, management might be reluctant to initiate a buy-out given the low likelihood of success, as family owners in general aim at handing the company over to the next generation.[368] Third, managers might not want to put their senior management position at risk by proposing family owners to sell the company and being uncertain about their reaction.[369]

If family owners have contacted a private equity company exclusively through a direct contact, the latter will perform a due diligence and negotiations will start afterwards.[370] If there is no direct contact to an investor, the sale process starts with the identification of potential buyers. This identification is mostly done by financial intermediaries who have a market overview on potentially interested candidates and might have contacts to these parties. In sales of family businesses, auctions seem to be the predominant process.[371]

---

366 Cf. European Private Equity & Venture Capital Association (2005), p. 13. The article leaves unanswered how buy-outs in the remaining 10% of cases were initiated.

367 Cf. Huydts (1992), pp. 40-43.

368 Compare to the discussion of objectives family owners pursue in sale negotiations in the subsection 4.1.2.2.

369 Cf. Pütter (2001), p. 14; Bousek et al. (2003), p. 12.

370 Cf. Arnet/Hartmann (2004), p. 838. Reasons for exclusive sale talks can be that the vendor strives for the greatest degree of confidentiality possible or that only one potential buyer is interested in the company (ibid.).

371 Cf. Pütter (2001), p. 6. However, not all sale processes of family businesses are organized as auctions.

In an **auction**, the company to be sold prepares an information memorandum, which is sent to potential buyers. These return an unbinding bid for the company in case of interest. Low bids are excluded from the auction process and the remaining potential buyers get access to further data on the family business for analysis in greater detail; possibly, the potential buyer might have to accept a confidentiality agreement before the vendor grants access to sensitive information. Ultimately, the vendor assures exclusivity to the potential buyer with the most favorite offer; exclusivity means that this potential buyer is the only one to have access to relevant data and to enter sale negotiations with family owners.[372]

To reduce the high level of uncertainty inherent in the acquisition of a complex entity like a company, the private equity company will commission different service providers (auditors, lawyers, etc.) to carry out a **due diligence** before the deal is closed. The due diligence is a process that aims at systematically collecting, verifying and analyzing data of the company to be acquired, especially to reveal potential risks of the transaction and thus reduce later conflicts between vendor and buyer. The due diligence covers legal, financial and taxation aspects and includes analyses of the company's environment, market, and strategy. Service providers carrying out these tasks are investment banks, strategy consultancies, law firms, auditing firms, and others.[373] In an earlier study among managers of bought-out companies, participants complained about the considerable time consumed by the work of lawyers and advisors. Further, the transaction could have been speeded up by a better relation between management and family owners.[374]

Due to a subjective point of view, the family owners' idea of a fair company value frequently exceeds the result of objective calculations of the company value.[375]

[372] Cf. Achleitner (2002), pp. 205-210; footnote 460. Besides the presented auction process, the family business might also be sold in a parallel or exclusive sale process. In the first process, family owners are in talks with exclusively one potential buyer and in the second, with only a small number of potential buyers. An auction process has the advantage of ensuring family owners the highest likelihood of completion of the transaction and the highest sale price.

[373] Cf. Achleitner/Achleitner (2000), pp. 138 et seq.; Achleitner (2002), pp. 177-183; Zenz-Spitzweg (2001), pp. 2-14; Becker (2001), pp. 11 et seq.

[374] Cf. European Private Equity & Venture Capital Association (2005), p. 16.

[375] Cf. Huydts (1992), pp. 44 et seq.; Hickey (2005), p. 31; Lopes (2003), pp. 59 et seq. Different authors recommend family owners considering a sale of their company to obtain an objective valuation of the company through an expert (cf. F.A.Z. Institut (2005), p. 49; UBS (2005), pp. 22

Vendor loans or earn-out agreements are possible solutions to overcome significant differences in price expectations.[376]

Sale negotiations end with the acquisition agreement and deal closing, which refers to conferring the company on the buyer. Throughout this entire process, private equity companies have to pay particular attention to respecting the family owner's feelings about the business – disrespect might end negotiations despite a financially, very attractive offer.[377]

ACHLEITNER/POECH have identified four reasons for **family owners' prejudices** towards private equity that complicate negotiations: First, opinions between both parties diverge with regard to time horizon of ownership, goals and leadership style. Second, family owners might interpret the sale to a private equity company as a personal failure. Third, revelation of weaknesses of the company by a potential buyer can be understood as critique of the family manager's past actions. Fourth, conflicts might be anticipated about future control rights and information rights of the private equity company.[378] SANDER has found that private equity companies attempt to mitigate the negative attitude among family owners by building sympathy and trust, appreciating the family owners' work of a lifetime, and underlining social responsibility and long-term interest in the company.[379] Studies on information sharing between selling family owners and buyers through a buy-out have shown that family owners exhibited patriarchal features and unwillingness to share information in

et seq.). MERTENS presents a model-based analysis of the process that leads to an agreement on the sale price (cf. Mertens (2004), pp. 95-128).

376 A vendor loan is a loan the vendor contributes to the financing of the transaction. The loan is frequently endowed with the right to participate in future profits of the sold company. A vendor loan is to be paid back within one to three years. An earn-out agreement grants the vendor the right to participate in the bought-out company's profits, in case these exceed a pre-defined threshold value (cf. Bousek et al. (2003), p. 9; Beitmann (2003), pp. 102-105; Mertens (2004), p. 130).

377 Cf. Hickey (2005), pp. 30 et seq. For an interesting example, how disregard of family concerns can impact negotiations and results, see Steen/Welch (2006). For further details on the acquisition agreement, see Becker (2001), pp. 12 et seq.

378 Cf. Achleitner/Poech (2004), pp. 4-7. These findings contradict earlier research by HUYDTS, who concluded that negotiations and closing of a buy-out in family businesses are very similar to a normal acquisition without the involvement of a private equity company (cf. Huydts (1992), p. 173). Although ACHLEITNER/POECH have examined transactions in which the private equity companies held minority stakes, these findings are relevant for the buy-outs in the sample companies, as the families remain involved in their former family businesses in the majority of sample companies (cf. subsections 3.2.4 and 4.2.2.5).

379 Cf. Sander (2006), p. 135.

negotiations; however, if these owners were founders of the company or if they aimed at maximizing the sale price, information was shared equally.[380]

4.1.2.4. Communication of the buy-out and reaction from stakeholders

After the buy-out, the academic and practitioners' literature recommend a clear communication strategy to avoid rumors that might irritate business partners and employees. Therefore, employees should be informed in detail and in person through a staff meeting or any other mean of internal communication. Business partners should be noticed of the buy-out by a personal letter of the retiring family owner or family manager. In this letter, the former owner might explain his reasons for selling the party and express confidence in the company's future. This letter is important to ensure that business contacts devolve to post buy-out managers. The general public is informed best through a press release to local and national media.[381]

The buy-out might also be expected to have an impact on the bought-out company's **relations to customers and suppliers**. In family businesses, these business relations are characterized by a high level of flexibility and personal interaction of family managers with business partners.[382] Family owners assign great importance to customers' satisfaction with their products.[383] Continuity in family ownership and management enable creation of trust and strong relations with business partners.[384] After the buy-out, family influence can be expected to decrease or even vanish. This development might negatively affect the above mentioned strengths of family businesses' relations to business partners.[385]

---

[380] Cf. Howorth/Westhead/Wright (2004), pp. 515 et seq., 526-528; Scholes et al. (2007), p. 342.

[381] Cf. Huydts (1992), pp. 174 et seq.; Haubrock (2005), p. 79; UBS (2005), pp. 12 et seq.; Webb (1985), pp. 101 et seq.

[382] Cf. Lyman (1991), pp. 321 et seq. These characteristics contrast the formalized and more impersonal relations towards business partners in non-family business. Contrary to these findings that emphasize strength of relations between family businesses and customers, WESTHEAD has found no differences between family and non-family businesses with regard to product range, development and warranties (cf. Westhead (1997), p. 147).

[383] Cf. Tagiuri/Davis (1992), p. 46.

[384] Cf. Family Business Center/Ernst & Young (2005), p. 13; Mühlebach (2004), pp. 93 et seq.

[385] According to a survey among buy-out managers in the UK, satisfaction of 60% of customers and 38% of customers increased. However, this study focused on divestments of corporations, so that results do not seem to be transferable to buy-outs in family businesses (cf. Wright/Thompson/Robbie (1992), pp. 62 et seq.).

The buy-out might also mark a change for **employees**. Family owners and managers are not only concerned about their own personal wellbeing, but also about that of the family business as a whole and their employees.[386] Private equity companies focus more on value creation and their return. This change in goals might entail measures to improve operational performance, which might result in layoffs. Anecdotal evidence has shown that employees might react shocked to the buy-out with anxiety about the company's future.[387]

4.1.2.5. Family owners' emotional separation and role post buy-out

As described in subsections 2.1.1 and 4.1.2.2, the relation between families and especially family managers and their family businesses is very special. Given the intensive involvement of business issues and personal issues of family members, the divorce of the family from its business is not an easy operation.[388] However, this separation is a critical step in the emancipation of the business from its family. This step is especially important to private equity companies, as the family owners' willingness to let go is a critical factor that determines whether a buy-out is funded or not.[389] Separation can be facilitated if family influence on the business is already reduced prior to the sale, for example by replacing family members on the management board or supervisory board with non-family members.

At the buy-out, there are two strategies for the separation of the family from their former family business. Either family owners make a clear cut and put a sudden end to all influence on the company; or family owners prefer a smooth transition through a fading, minor influence after the buy-out as discussed in subsection 3.2.4.

---

[386] Cf. Mühlebach (2004), pp. 93 et seq.; Günther/Gonschorek (2006), p. 7; Tagiuri/Davis (1992), pp. 46 et seq.; Donckels/Fröhlich (1991), p. 159. See also the family owners' objectives in sale negotiations described in subsection 4.1.2.2.

[387] Cf. F.A.Z. Institut (2005), p. 33.

[388] For a discussion of the tensions within a parting family manager, cf. Sonnenfeld/Spence (1989), pp. 355-357, 370 et seq.; Klughardt (1994), pp. 112 et seq. SONNENFELD/SPENCE point out that retirement is extremely difficult for family managers who founded the business, as "their identities have become intertwined with those of their firms." (Sonnenfeld/Spence (1989), p. 371).

[389] Cf. Upton/Petty (2000), pp. 36 et seq.

The strategy of a **clear cut** has the advantage that there is no ambiguity for business partners and employees, whether the former family manager or a new manager is in charge of the company at any time during the buy-out process.[390] Further, this sudden change might prevent family members from suffering to see changes in their former family business happen, which they might possibly oppose to but do not have the power to stop these changes.

The alternative strategy of a **fading, minor family influence** could facilitate the transfer of social capital[391] from former family managers to the post buy-out managers.[392] Post buy-out managers appreciate access to the experience and know-how of former family managers.[393] Through this strategy, family owners could remain in contact with their company and would not need to cut the emotional bond to their former company.[394] A disadvantage of the strategy of fading, minor influence is that the family's ongoing influence might lead to conflicts between former family owners or managers and post buy-out management.[395] Moreover, the ongoing presence of the former family manager or family owner might limit the authority of new post buy-out managers.[396]

Empirical results on family influence after the buy-out suggest that the strategy of fading influence is preferred by family owners. According to NAGL, only 21% of family owners pursue the strategy of a clear cut. The remaining 79% of family owners interfere with the company post buy-out through ownership (21%), management

---

390 Cf. Haubrock (2005), pp. 78-81.

391 The concept of social capital refers to "the actual and potential resources individuals obtain from knowing others, being part of a social network with them, or merely from being known to them and having a good reputation." (Baron/Markman (2000), p. 107).

392 Cf. Haubrock (2005), pp. 78-81; Hickey (2005), p. 31.

393 Cf. F.A.Z. Institut (2005), p. 49; UBS (2005), p. 19.

394 Cf. Achleitner et al. (2008c), p. 95; PriceWaterhouseCoopers (2005), p. 23. FORST interprets the fact, that 21% of former family managers became consultants to the new management after the buy-out, as indicator for the ongoing interest of the family members in the company (cf. Forst (1992), p. 85).

395 Conflicts might arise from differences between the former family owners' vague expectations, how succeeding managers should act, and actions of the post buy-out managers (cf. Haubrock (2005), p. 65).

396 Even if the former family owner or manager is not involved in the company's management post buy-out, employees might ask him for his opinion or decisions. Employees might refer to the answers they receive, given their loyalty and orientation towards the former family owner or manager. Thus, the position of new management might be undermined (cf. UBS (2005), p. 19).

(45%), or supervisory board (6%).[397] LEYHERR has shown in his survey that only 12.2% of family owners planned a clear cut with the company, while 58.3% wanted to keep some influence as advisors to the company and 29.5% aimed at continuing their work in the company.[398] SONNENFELD/SPENCE found that 52% of family managers held a formal position and 72% remained on the supervisory board after the sale.[399] Despite these results suggesting active involvement, FORST found that 89.2% of former owners do not hold an equity stake in the company after the buy-out.[400] HOWORTH/WESTHEAD/WRIGHT might propose an explanation under which circumstances family owners preferred a clear cut over fading, minor influence. They have shown that family involvement after a management buy-out seems to be linked to mutual satisfaction with the buy-out: Fading, minor influence post buy-out occurred if both management and former family owners had a good relationship whereas a clear cut was reported in the cases of poor relationship between both parties after the sale.[401]

---

397 Cf. Nagl (2005), p.33. The remaining 7% of family owners indicated interference through another way (e.g. advisor to the management). Respondents could indicate multiple answers.

398 Cf. Leyherr (2000), pp. 187 et seq. LEYHERR does not specify in which position family owners wanted to advise the company.

399 Cf. Sonnenfeld/Spence (1989), p. 362.

400 Cf. Forst (1992), pp. 30, 86. This percentage has to be interpreted with caution, as the results are rather old and the author does not clearly distinguish between buy-outs in family businesses and non-family businesses.

401 Cf. Howorth/Westhead/Wright (2004), p. 529. Other factors increasing the likelihood of family involvement after the buy-out are high levels of mutual trust, fair information sharing, and cooperative behavior in negotiations.

However, in case a non-family management performs a management buy-out, the relationship between managers and family owners might be stressed through management's behavior in negotiations. In this situation, the management has a conflict of interests with regard to the sale price of the company: On the one hand, managers represent the company and grant access to information underlying valuation of the company. This way, they act in the interest of family owners, who aim at a high sale price. On the other hand, managers cooperate with the private equity company to acquire the company. Thus, they are interested in a lower sale price (cf. Bousek et al. (2003), p. 12; European Private Equity & Venture Capital Association (2005), p. 16; Howorth/Westhead/Wright (2004), p. 532).

4.2 Empirical background

4.2.1. Decision to sell

4.2.1.1. Reasons for selling the company

As all sample companies were sold in a buy-out, interview partners were able to provide insights into the reasons that led family managers to sell their family businesses. The three-stage decision process of succession, which was presented above, is used as a framework for discussing the reasons behind this decision.

In the first stage of the decision process, family managers contemplated **retirement**.[402] Reasons to retire could be either related to the person or to the business. In the interviews, three different **personal reasons** were mentioned:[403] First, the most frequent reason was the age of the family manager that was named by 15 companies as a trigger for the sale.[404] Most of these family managers were in their sixties or late fifties, as they had postponed their resigning despite approaching or passing retirement age. Perpetuity of the family business was a goal many former family managers seemingly subscribed to, but succession in management by the next generation seemed hampered for several reasons that will be discussed later. As succession seemed obstructed, family members continued their work in the hope that a potential family successor would develop a motivation or would prove his qualification to take over the company. In the buy-outs of the sample companies, this hope was not fulfilled.

Second, some interview partners brought up that the sale was a decision to change the vendor's lifestyle. This reason was mentioned in total six times and it was the exclusive reason for the sale in two cases (H, V).[405] The manager of H characterized the founder and former family manager:

---

[402] Some former family owners had already left management before the buy-out, but kept ownership of their companies. These cases will be discussed in the third stage of the decision problem.

[403] Interview partners could indicate multiple reasons for the sale. A reason for the sale outside these three main reasons was reported by the pre and post buy-out manager of company G: While a former non-family manager still held a significant stake in the company and the other active non-family manager was also approaching retirement, they came up with the idea of selling the company.

[404] The 15 companies are A, B, C, D, E, F, J, K, L, M, O, R, S, T, and U. These 15 companies correspond to 68% of the 22 respondents to this question.

[405] D, H, L, R, T, and V; 27% of 22 respondents.

He has built the company over the last twenty-five years and if you knew him, you would know that he is always into starting something new, something different. He is bored by some routines, even if the company is doing quiet fine.

Third, a concrete opportunity to cash in the value of the company triggered the sale in seven companies.[406] The opportunity was either a concrete offer of a private equity company, or a successful year yielding good results and thus promising a high valuation in case of a sale. A concrete offer led to the sale of J by its family owner, after he was disappointed by two family successions that failed. The family owner of T, who had been ill for some years before the sale, sold with an exceptionally good order backlog. In five of the seven cases, the succession problem was already visible at the horizon with the family manager aging and no qualified and motivated family successor available. In contrast to these sales triggered by family owners, the sale in company N was driven by two individuals who held a stake in the company and wanted to sell.

Besides the personal reasons, buy-outs could be also triggered by **reasons stemming from the business**.[407] Interviewees reported three different kinds of business reasons: First, the obviously most important business reason why a family sold its company was that the company got into a crisis and the family was unable to rescue the company. In such a turnaround situation, a private equity company could acquire the company and restructure it. In P, adverse market developments and fierce competition caused the crisis. In Q, mismanagement and too many acquisitions gave rise to the crisis. In both cases, the banks put the owning families under pressure to sell a significant stake to an investor.

Second, financing problems called for the sale in five companies. These can be broadly separated into financing problems that stemmed from renewing loans[408] and obtaining funding for growth[409]. Both problems occurred in the interaction with the companies' banks. When companies applied for revolving loans, banks did not only

[406] A, J, K, L, N, R, and T; 32% of 22 respondents.

[407] Interview partners could indicate multiple reasons for the sale.

[408] C and J experienced the problem of renewing loans.

[409] E, F, and N experienced the problem of not receiving funding for growth.

check the business situation but also the management to determine the credit worthiness of the respective family business. While the family manager of J was applying for a new credit, the bank asked him to solve the foreseeable succession problem in the company. In rapidly growing companies, banks became cautious to provide debt, as high growth might increase the risk of credit default. An example for this financing problem is E, whose manager reported:

> *Back then, the company grew at 15-20% p.a. organically and through acquisitions. Then, the banks became more cautious and didn't want to finance this development any more. So, the idea was born to look for a new investor.*

Third, insufficient management capabilities to develop the company were a last business reason for selling the company in two companies.[410] While the first two business reasons could only be mitigated by selling the company, this third could also be solved by hiring managers with the needed capabilities; however, this was not done in the following cases: Managers might lack the skills necessary for the company's further development. Market pressure forced company J to internationalize, but neither the family manager nor any other manager in the company had the needed language skills or experience in international negotiations. In I, two junior managers were appointed to the management board after the family managers death. Both had never executed this responsibility under the family manager and lacked the capabilities required by their position. These managers were described as unable to initiate the steps needed by the post buy-out manager of I.

Comparing the importance of personal reasons and business reasons to resign shows that resigning was mostly triggered by personal reasons (see Figure 25). In 13 companies, personal reasons alone led to the buy-out. A combination of personal and business reason appeared in five cases. Only in three cases, business reasons drove the sale.[411]

---

[410] I and J; 9% of 22 respondents.

[411] When interpreting this result, it should be noted that only those companies qualified for entering the sample, which were targets of a buy-out. This means that possibly far more companies were sold for business reasons; but as these transactions did not materialize as buy-outs, they were not eligible for the sample underlying this thesis.

In the second stage of the decision process of succession, family managers attempted to **find a successor** in management **within the family**. Interview partners in 11 companies commented on the diverse problems that precluded management succession by a family member.[412] As explained in the theoretical foundation to this subsection, four conditions had to be fulfilled so that management could be handed over to a family member.

The first condition is that a family member had to exist and be of suitable age. In four companies, no potential family successor was born.[413] In three companies, potential family successors existed but were too young.[414] The family manager of S said:

> *I was 55 [at the decision to sell the company] and when I considered the age of my children, the education they were to receive, and the experience they were to gather, then I would be 75 and manage the company as an old fool.*

The second condition relates to qualification and skills of potential family successors. Two interview partners reported of potential family successors, who were either not qualified as managers or not considered to be qualified for this position.[415] In the family owning D, there was no son but a daughter – however, she was not taken into consideration to succeed as family manager. The son of family owner R was a skilled engineer, but his father recognized that he lacked the necessary skills of a manager. These two examples suggest that family members' decisions whether a potential family successor was sufficiently qualified did not only depend on the latter's objective qualification and skills, but also on the perception of these qualities.[416]

Condition three is the potential family successor's motivation to succeed in management. In three companies, potential family successors of suitable age existed but were not willing to take over the company.[417] In L, two sons had already worked in

---

412 A, B, C, D, K, M, L, O, R, S, and U; 50% of 22 respondents.

413 A, B, M, and O; 36% of 11 respondents.

414 C, K, and S; 27% of 11 respondents.

415 D and R; 18% of 11 respondents.

416 Infrequent statements concerning the lack of family successors' qualification might be explainable by the fact that succession problems were well foreseeable and thus preparation of potential successors could be initiated at time.

417 L, R, and U; 27% of 11 respondents.

the company before a potential succession was discussed, but neither one wanted to manage the company. The daughter of the family owning R worked in a different industry and said that she did not want to do the father's job to herself.

The fourth condition is that the succession from senior family managers to the juniors had to succeed. In two cases, potential family successors were available of suitable age, needed motivation and required qualification and experience, but failed to take over the company in practice.[418] The family manager of J gave some responsibility to his son and his daughter, but both did not manage to win the confidence of customers and the acceptance of employees. In T, which was a company jointly held by the family and two key employees, the son and the key employees wanted to acquire the company but failed to convince banks and potential investors to fund the deal and did not want to bear the risk all alone.

The third and last stage of the decision process of succession was that the family checked whether **leaving management to non-family managers** while retaining ownership was a solution that was possible and acceptable to the family.

In five companies, family managers were not active in the management at the time of the buy-out, but had installed non-family managers some years before the buy-out.[419] In four of these companies, the former family manager had retired and opted for this solution to the succession problem. In I, the founder and family manager surprisingly died of stroke on a business trip abroad. Neither his wife nor his daughters were qualified to take over management and left it to the two junior non-family managers.

Although, non-family management successfully steered the company (with the exception of I), these families decided to eventually sell the company. This sale some years after retirement of the family manager could be seen as a "delayed sale". The delay might be explainable by the fact that the former family manager did not want to sell his company due to an emotional bond between the family and its business.[420] Over the course of years, the emotional bond might have loosened opening up the way for a sale: In A, the family owner got the opportunity to cash in; in I, family owners

418 J and T; 18% of 11 respondents.

419 A, C, I, K, and M; 23% of 22 respondents.

420 Cf. subsection 4.2.2.5.

wanted to sell the company, as they could not develop the company to its full potential; and in M, the non-family manager, who had a long relationship with the family owner, approached retirement age.

The other family managers still actively working in company management before the buy-out decided against the appointment of non-family management for two reasons: On the one hand, some owning families did not want to hold a stake in a company that was completely managed by non-family managers, as this might put the family estate at risk. The argument was brought up in interviews with four companies, which were 100% family owned and where the majority of management lied in the hands of family managers before the buy-out.[421]

On the other hand, family owners did not find suitable managers to lead the family business on their behalf.[422] While families knew potential candidates among junior managers[423] in the company and these persons had established a good relationship to the family over past years, the question remained whether these candidates had the profile and skills to manage the company successfully. In V, the family manager had tried out to delegate responsibility to his deputy but this attempt failed. Besides the necessary qualification, a potential candidate should have been young enough so that the candidate did not need to be replaced after a short period. Companies I and M reported that there were qualified and experienced non-family managers but they were about the same age as the family manager and about to retire soon. If no candidate for a non-family manager was available within the company, this candidate could join the company from outside.

To many family owners, the alternative to remain owner of the company but delegate the management to non-family managers seemed to be acceptable as an interim solution at best. The family manager and later manager of S seriously considered installing a non-family manager but discarded this idea. He regarded this constellation merely as an interim solution, which he found not satisfactory given that none of his children might follow in his footsteps and the company would need to be sold eventually.

---

421 B, J, O, and S; 18% of 22 respondents.

422 I, M, and V; 14% of 22 respondents.

423 Junior managers are second-tier managers (cf. footnote 322).

This analysis of the interviewees' statements concerning reasons for the sale has proven the applicability of the three-stage decision process derived beforehand. Arguments of interview partners provided the rationale, why former family owners of the sample companies decided to sell. Figure 25 summarizes the arguments.

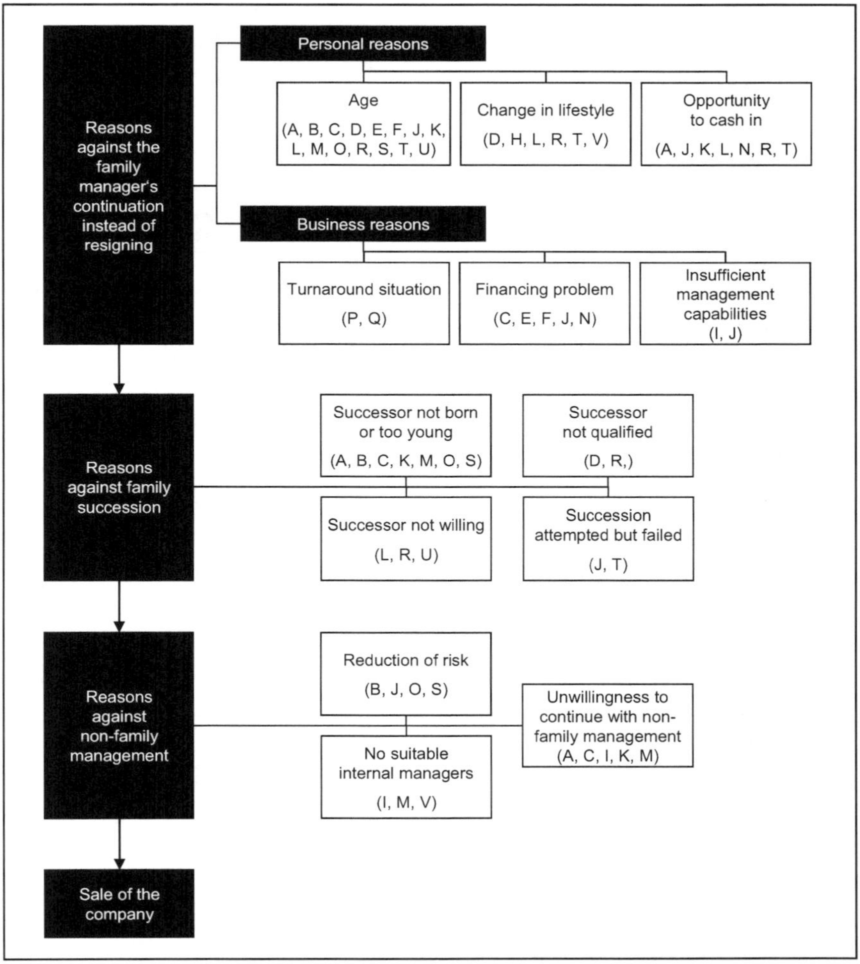

Figure 25: Overview of reasons for selling a family business

Source: Author's illustration

Multiple indications were possible

4.2.1.2. Evaluation of possible buyers

As discussed in subsection 4.1.1.2, there are several buyers family owners could sell their company to. This subsection discusses why former family businesses were sold to private equity companies and not to another potential buyer. The subsection also explains why companies of the control group were sold to holding companies or managers backed by semi-public investment companies.[424]

Interview partners mentioned two main arguments in favor of **selling the family business to a private equity company**: First, the company would continue to exist as an independent company. This argument was mentioned by five interview partners.[425] As the manager of M quoted the former family owner:

> *He wanted to keep the company in the market and wanted to see it prosper. This was his baby and that was the reason to look for a partner.*

Family owners and managers regarded the company as the result of their lifetime's work; therefore, the company's name should continue to exist beyond the sale. Private equity companies respected these concerns by leaving the company on a stand-alone basis during the holding period.[426] However, independence was not guaranteed infinitely, as the holding period of a private equity company was limited and after this period, the company would be sold – potentially to a strategic buyer.[427]

---

424 No information can be provided on the reasons and opinions of the families that have chosen another solution to the succession problem, as the sale to a private equity company was a criterion a company had to meet in order to be eligible for the sample. For sample criteria, see subsection 3.1.3.

425 D, H, I, K, and M; 23% of 22 respondents.

426 This argument would not hold in case of an add-on acquisition that complements a company undergoing a buy-and-build strategy (buy-and-build strategies aim at developing a portfolio company by merging it with other companies in related business fields to grow the company size (cf. Loos (2006), p. 15)). However, no transaction of a sample company was an add-on acquisition to complement another portfolio company.

427 According to manager M, this argument did not weaken the attraction of private equity, as the postponed decision to sell the company to a strategic buyer would not be taken by the former family owner.

Second, a more trivial argument for selling to a private equity company was that the investor bid a higher price for the company than competing potential buyers.[428] For family owners, a higher sale price reflected appreciation of the time and effort the family invested into the family business. Thus, a high sale price mitigated the emotional pain of losing the family business. However, only two interview partners stated the highest bid as argument for the sale to a private equity company.[429]

An argument not mentioned by interview partners was familiarity with private equity if a private equity company had held a minority stake before the buy-out. Theoretically, family owners of companies with participation of a private equity company might have been familiar with the business model of private equity and might be more likely to sell their company to an investor. Although three family owners, who had cooperated with private equity companies pre buy-out (A, C and F), sold their company through a buy-out, interviewees' statements did not allow to derive, whether pre buy-out cooperation affected the likelihood of the buy-out.[430]

Two arguments from the literature were not mentioned by interview partners: Neither post buy-out professionalization and accelerated development nor the high burden of debt were mentioned as advantage or disadvantage of the sale to a private equity company. This might indicate a lack of understanding of how private equity works at the time, negotiations were conducted.[431]

---

428 However, this might be a sample bias, as only those companies entered the sample, which were sold to private equity companies. If other buyers made a higher bid and the family business was not sold to a private equity company, the transaction would not qualify for the sample.

429 A, and M; 9% of 22 respondents. Possibly, the sale price might have been an important reason for more family owners, but they did not want to comment on this and thus answers were biased (cf. subsection 3.1.6).

430 The interview partner in F did not comment on the relation between private equity company and management and its impact on the sale decision. In the other two companies, cooperation led to very different results: In company C, the private equity company held a silent partnership before the buy-out. Cooperation was described as good and trust developed between both parties, which facilitated the sale. In A, where two private equity companies held a stake of 49% in the company, cooperation was described as difficult because opinions diverged on company development and the way how to deal with entrepreneurial opportunities. The manager of A indicated that stress in this relationship led to the sale of the company. While company C was sold to the private equity company that provided the silent partnership before the buy-out, company A was sold to another private equity company.

431 However, the absence of references to these two arguments may not be overinterpreted, as the former family owners or managers who sold the company were not directly interviewed.

A potential **sale to a strategic buyer** was the most frequently mentioned alternative to the sale to a private equity company. However, this option did not materialize as there was no potential buyer, the family manager objected, or negotiations failed.

Some companies did not have the option of selling to a strategic buyer, as they were operating in industries where there was no potential buyer. Company O was already the largest company in its industry, so that competitors would hardly have been able to submit a competitive offer. S was active in a niche market with a very small number of competitors worldwide. Neither company was an attractive target for corporations looking to diversify.

For most companies, a potential strategic buyer existed, but the family decided not to sell to it for one or several of the following three reasons: First, the family owners feared that the company would be integrated into the buyer's organization and thus vanish from the market, as mentioned above. Especially mergers of corporate functions to gain synergies, appointments of new managers from the parent company, and potential close-downs of the whole company after exploiting their technology were seen as critical. Second, for many family owners, a sale to a direct competitor seemed to be out of question. This might be seen as sign of personal pride of the family: The company should eventually not be sold to a competitor the company fought with fiercely for a long time. Moreover, the due diligence process would require the family business to open its strictly confidential books to their competitor. Third, stakeholders might prevent a sale to a strategic buyer. In L, which was an exclusive trading partner for a large corporation, the main supplier had a veto right to a company sale, which could reduce the number of potential buyers, while the corporation itself was not interested in buying L.

In two cases, there was a potential strategic buyer and the family was willing to sell to this potential buyer. Negotiations had started but eventually failed. In the case of company F, vendor and buyer could not agree on the terms of sale. Company K had already been sold by a verbal agreement between the family owner and the CFO of an acquiring group. Surprisingly, the CFO was dismissed and his successor cancelled the deal. Both vendors turned to a private equity company thereafter.

Although interviewees provided various arguments against selling to a strategic buyer, six family owners pursued a dual track strategy and negotiated at the same time with strategic investors and financial investors, i.e. private equity companies.[432] All companies that pursued a dual track approach eventually sold to the private equity company as it made a higher bid.[433]

The owning family might have also sold the company to the capital market through an **IPO**. Only the manager of D indicated that this option was taken into consideration. But even D, which was a rather large and promising company in the sample with sales between € 100 and 200 million and fast growth, was not considered as acceptable for a going-public.

A comparison of the arguments, which favor a sale to a private equity company and which were mentioned by interview partners, with the arguments in the literature yields that continuity and independence of the company can be confirmed to be major reasons for a sale to a private equity company. The possibility to retain a minority influence on the family business after the sale did not seem to be very important, as this argument was never mentioned. This is surprising, given that 14 family owners were still involved in the business after the buy-out, what would be highly unlikely if they sold to a strategic buyer.[434] In general, the decision to sell to a private equity company seemed to be a decision against strategic buyers, given the numerous objections of family owners against these buyers. Figure 26 provides an overview of the reasons for the sale to a private equity company.

---

432 A, B, D, H, M, and Q; 27% of 22 respondents.

433 This association cannot be generalized, as it is distorted by the sample selection bias (cf. subsections 3.1.4 and 3.1.6).

434 Cf. subsection 3.2.4.

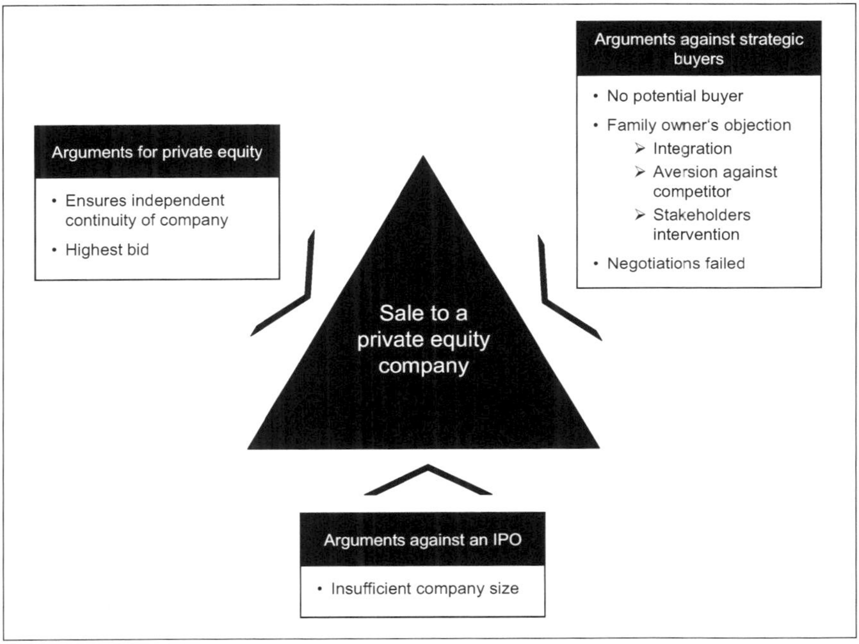

Figure 26: Reasons for the sale to a private equity company

Source: Author's illustration

Besides the sample companies sold to private equity companies, five companies of the control group, which were not sold to private equity companies, were analyzed: R and S were sold to holding companies and buy-outs of managers in T, U, and V were backed by semi-public investment companies.[435]

The family owners of R and S were both looking for buyers that would hold the company for a rather long period. Before approaching **holding companies**, both family managers negotiated with private equity companies, but were displeased by the lack of respect and trust negotiation partners showed them.[436] The family manager of R had the impression that negotiation partners rather thought about a potential exit

[435] Cf. subsection 3.1.3.

[436] Cf. subsection 4.2.2.2.

than about developing the company. Thus, both family owners eventually decided to sell their companies to holding companies.

As described in subsection 3.1.3, these holding companies pursued a buy-and-hold strategy, were not exit-oriented and funded new acquisitions from profits of their portfolio companies. Both family managers liked this long-term holding strategy, the managerial discretion and trust they were granted and especially the possibility to remain in the company's management until retirement.[437] The manager of S summarized:

> *If you are merely interested in sale price maximization, you can sell to anyone. If you want to remain in the company and want to keep on living close to the headquarters, you are very interested that the company will prosper. And then, the selection of a partner is crucial.*

The decision that the buy-outs in T, U, and V were financed by **semi-public investment companies** was made by the respective acquiring managers. These deals were not initiated by a private equity company but by the managers who wanted to buy a company and were looking for funding. The managers wanted to maximize their equity stake and the semi-public investment companies agreed to provide financing mainly through silent partnerships. The semi-public investment companies backing the buy-outs in T and V did not hold any shares in these companies. Other arguments in favor of this type of private equity company were the low degree or absence of involvement of the private equity company, the fixed interest rate on the mezzanine capital provided, and support like consulting services. The three companies backed by semi-public investment companies were the smallest companies in the sample and the only companies management held majority stakes in.[438]

---

[437] The family manager of R was to retire two years after the buy-out and was followed by a close relative.

[438] If management wants to hold the majority of shares in a company, managers' personal funds restrict the maximum company size, these managers can afford. The size of sample companies sold to managers backed by semi-public investment companies suggests that a company size of less than € 20m in sales might be the maximum company size acquirable.

4.2.1.3. Preparing the company for the sale

In 11 sample companies measures of preparation were taken to enable or facilitate the sale process. Analog to the measures derived from the literature, these can be differentiated into measures aimed at improving operational performance, revising the business plan, increasing transparency, and changes in the management.

Operational changes to increase profitability were mentioned by only two interview partners. One of the first tasks of a newly appointed non-family manager of C was to minimize all risks as far as possible, so that they were manageable for the buyer. The non-family manager of V achieved better conditions in contract renegotiations with suppliers and started an initiative to improve the outdated IT infrastructure.

As discussed above, the **business plan** is the key document to arouse interest among potential buyers. Three interview partners confirmed changes to the business plan as a preparation of the sale: The business plan was extrapolated for a longer period into the future (B), planning was done in greater detail (G), and in the turnaround buy-out Q, a new business plan was written.[439]

Improvements in transparency were reported by three managers. The need for improvement even existed in A, though two private equity companies were among the shareholders before the buy-out. V said that without the improvements in management accounting, management would not have been successful with the buy-out. The manager of U explained the rationale behind these activities, namely that the company had to become transparent, so that a buyer could assure himself that the product portfolio was sustainable and that corporate finance and management accounting were in order.

The most frequent measures of preparation were **changes in the management**. In eight companies, family influence on the management board was reduced.[440] This

---

439 Given the importance of the business plan for the sale process, it might be expected that every business plan was revised before the buy-out in case of a management buy-out, although this revision was not always mentioned.

440 B, C, D, G, K, M, O, and Q; 36% of 22 respondents. As a result of the changes on the management board, family influence through the management was in these companies significantly lower than in other sample companies. The family was not represented in the management of four companies and held a minority of management positions in four companies following these changes.

was in the interest of the private equity company, as the investment manager backing company K explained:

> *We find it difficult to invest if the family manager who is very active and solely responsible for the business leaves the company upon sale. We like to see that the vendor considers his succession at the age of fifty or fifty-five and that he has gathered a team over the past five years, which handles the day-to-day business.*

Family influence was reduced by replacing family managers with non-family managers or appointing additional non-family managers to the management board. In C, the family manager and two other non-family managers were replaced with a non-family CEO. In D, three managers were added to the management board, while two family managers remained on the board until the buy-out.

New managers could be attracted to the management board by promoting internal or hiring external managers. Only in two companies, new managers came from within the company. In B, two non-family managers were promoted to senior managers one year before the buy-out. The family manager of G joined the company about seven years before the buy-out and was appointed to the management board five years later.[441]

In seven companies, managers were hired from outside the company. Five managers were hired for the purpose of leading the company after the buy-out.[442] These five managers were employed about six to twelve months before the buy-out. The managers of F and V were hired as deputy or non-family successor for the family manager three (F) and four (V) years before the company sale; however, a buy-out was not explicitly planned, when these managers were appointed.

An **analysis of the managers that prepared the company** for the sale yields a very interesting result: With the exception of the family manager of G, all preparations not relating to changes in the management (operational improvements, rewriting the

[441] In G, the leaving manager retired and wanted to sell his stake. The newly appointed family manager took over his position and initiated the owner buy-out to pay out the retiring manager.

[442] C, K, M, O, and Q; 23% of 22 respondents. In M, another non-family manager was on the management board besides the newly hired manager. The former manager was about to retire within the next years following the transaction, so that the new manager was hired as his successor.

business plan, improving transparency) were initiated and carried out by non-family managers. Family managers and family owners focused on appointing new managers and reducing family influence on the management board. This forgoing of preparations by family managers and owners might be either explainable by the fact that they did not want the respective changes, or that they did not have the know-how to improve the company.[443] Forgoing preparations in general was somewhat surprising, as this was a chance to increase the sale price.

To **conclude**, this subsection has shown that most measures, which were derived from the literature to prepare the company for the sale, were reported in the sample companies. Only the measure of disentanglement of the company's and the family's property was not reported by interview partners before the buy-out. The measures of preparation were a possibility for family owners to advance a part of the value creation of a buy-out before the company sale and thus increased the company value. Although the changes described were first steps that seemed sufficient for the company sale, all private equity companies went beyond this state after the buy-out as will be shown in the following chapters. All 11 companies, in which interview partners indicated that sale preparations took place before the buy-out, were management buy-outs.[444]

4.2.2. Sale transaction

4.2.2.1. Investment criteria of the private equity company and buyers of the control group

Interviewed investment managers were asked about the investment criteria, which companies were expected to fulfill to be eligible for an acquisition. Answers by the ten

---

443 An extreme example of family owners forgoing operational improvements is company U: Before the buy-out, the former family manager of U learned about potential for efficiency gains from the consultant, who later on acquired the company as post buy-out manager. However, the family manager did not want to realize these efficiency gains despite the foreseeable sale.

444 The fact that no changes prior to the buy-out were reported in companies that underwent a management buy-in, could be explained by the fact that in a management buy-in, the managers did not work for the company before the buy-out by definition; thus, they might possibly not have known about changes that happened before the sale of the family business.

investment managers interviewed allowed comparing investment criteria in the literature with those applied to buy-outs in family businesses.

The **combination of** the **product** the acquired company offered **and** the **market** this company operated in was of highest importance – six investment managers indicated that this criterion was crucial for their investment decision.[445] Presumably, this criterion seemed so important, as it served as a potential indicator for future company development. When assessing the product portfolio of the company, investment managers looked for the products offered by the company and the strengths and weaknesses of these products. High brand recognition, widespread reputation for quality or technology and a low substitutability made a product especially valuable and attractive for a private equity company. While all these aspects concerned a theoretical potential of a product, the current market position was also important – especially market leadership at best in several geographical regions or segments.

Besides the product portfolio and market position, general market trends were also in the focus of interest of private equity investors. Investment managers considered future market trends and development of demand for the company's products. Bargaining power of customers and suppliers as well as the level of competition were also analyzed. Finally, two investment managers backing companies A and M indicated that the potential for market consolidation increased the attraction of the deal significantly. This could be explained by the fact, that private equity companies often motivated their portfolio companies to grow through acquisitions after the buy-out.[446]

Aspects of the **management team** were mentioned by four investment managers as decisive investment criteria.[447] Investment managers expected managers of portfolio companies to have proven their qualification for the position: Managers should have profound understanding of the relevant or a similar market, and show a track record of past successes, at best with expertise in the areas the company had to improve after the buy-out. Management and potential buyer should agree on the future

---

445 A, B, I, J, K, and M; 86% of 7 respondents.

446 Cf. subsection 5.3.2.

447 A, I, J, and K; 57% of 7 respondents.

strategy of the company. Further, management's ability to implement the changes envisaged was of utter importance as the investment manager backing A said:

> *There is no point in appointing a management that conceives amazing plans and strategies but fails to deliver on them. Sometimes, the third best strategy that is in fact implemented is the better and more effective solution.*

Besides these requirements of qualification, investment managers were also looking for soft factors, like the managers' personalities or their motivation to do the buy-out. The investment manager backing company T underlined the importance of personality especially in the case of management buy-ins, as new managers had to have the wits to win employees' confidence and sympathy. If a private equity company wanted to bring in a new manager and the candidate was initially not enthusiastic about this opportunity, this lack of motivation was not an obstacle as long as motivation could be aroused. An example for this was the later manager of J, who did not want to participate in the buy-out initially. As the manager fitted perfectly to the company, the investment manager worked hard to persuade him and finally succeeded.

It is interesting that Huydts' criterion of harmony in the management team was not mentioned by a single investment manager. Although qualification and personality of the management in place seemed to be important factors in assessing a deal, private equity companies did not refrain from replacing managers, as will be discussed in subsection 5.3.4.

Less frequently named investment criteria were financial strength and potential for value generation. **Financial performance** of a company was reported by three private equity companies to be checked before investing.[448] Investment managers examined the past track record of the potential portfolio company and looked for companies that grew steadily and profitably and that generated stable cash flows without high volatility in parallel. The fact that this criterion was only mentioned by three investment managers surprises, given it is an essential prerequisite for applicability of the typical buy-out financing structure.[449]

---

[448] I, K, and M; 43% of 7 respondents.

[449] Cf. subsection 7.1.2.

Three investment managers mentioned foreseeable levers of **value generation** as reason to invest.[450] The investment manager backing B stated that the company had an immense potential for value generation by increasing commercialization of its products and by adjusting investments, as he considered the company as overinvested. The investment manager backing J saw potential in the company's international strategy and management.[451]

The investment decision in the turnaround company Q was exclusively determined by the scope for operational improvements according to the investment manager backing the company. Thus, investment decisions in this turnaround company differed significantly from those in other companies. Neither quality of the management, which was completely replaced, nor financial strength, which was weak due to the turnaround situation, deterred the private equity company from its investment.

Holding companies and semi-public investment companies seemed to have additional investment criteria. Holding companies looked for three particular criteria: First, pre buy-out family managers had to be willing to continue managing the company after the sale. This arrangement enabled the holding company to become familiar with the market and business partners; the arrangement required that the family manager must accept changes in the company and support them. Second, investment managers looked for the state of professionalism in a potential subsidiary. As holding companies aimed at cooperating with pre buy-out managers, a significant move towards professionalization would be unlikely, if the company was managed unprofessionally pre buy-out.[452] Third, family managers should appreciate the business model of the holding companies, so that they were willing to accept the lower sale price these investors offered.

Semi-public investment companies had two particular investment criteria. First, the acquiring manager should not pay too much but an adequate price for the company that was in line with current market valuations. Second, the acquiring manager should be motivated by making money and not by fulfilling his dream of an own company.

---

[450] B, J, Q; 43% of 7 respondents.

[451] Cf. subsection 5.3.2.

[452] To determine the state of professionalism in the portfolio companies, investment managers checked the quality of junior managers, the company's organization (investment manager backing R), and the management information system (investment manager backing R).

This check for goal alignment between investor and manager could presumably be necessary as semi-public investment companies typically invested through silent partnerships and thus only had limited control over the manager.

To **conclude**, this subsection has shown that private equity companies mainly looked at the product-market combination, the management quality and – to a lower degree – at the financial strength and the potential for value generation, when they decided about an investment decision (see Figure 27 for an overview). While these three criteria are in line with theory, the literature does not reflect investment criteria relating to turnaround companies or investments of holding companies or semi-public investment companies.

Investors' interest in the financial strength and the potential for value generation is based in the high leverage and investors' aim to create value after the buy-out. But why did private equity companies have high requirements with regard to the product-market combination and the management? At first sight, these aspects could be changed the same way, all the other changes are initiated. There might be two reasons for the particular interest in these two criteria: First, market was an externally given parameter which the private equity company could hardly influence. Second, private equity companies acted under severe time pressure, as profit was measured relative to the investment period. Thus, it was difficult for a private equity company to change products or management. Product development and market launch would have taken a considerable time. It would have also taken new managers a considerable time to become familiar with the company and run it efficiently.

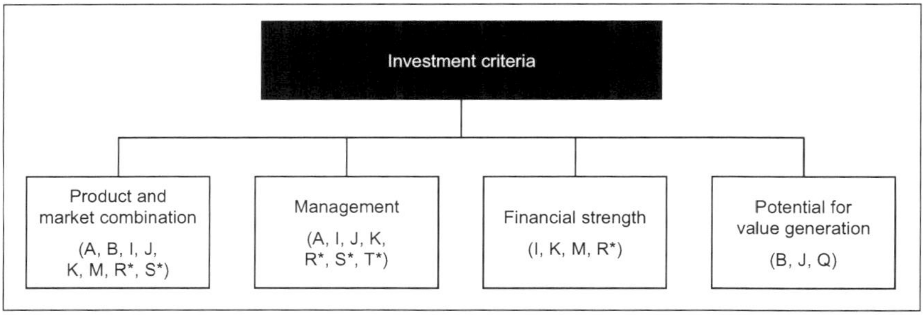

Figure 27: Major investment criteria reported by investment managers

Source: Author's illustration

* Investment managers of buyers different from private equity companies

4.2.2.2. Family owners' goals in sale negotiations

The review of the literature has shown that family owners' goals can be split into two groups: financial and non-financial goals. With regard to **financial goals**, families were interested in a high valuation of the company, as confirmed by five interviewees.[453] Financial interest was further underlined by the fact, that six family owners offered their companies to strategic buyers beside the private equity company, but sold to the latter as the investors offered a higher price.[454] However, only three interview partners directly mentioned valuation or payment modalities[455] as a crucial objective in sale negotiations.[456]

Non-financial goals were pursued by 14 family owners in sale negotiations. These goals mostly related to the company's future development and the wellbeing of employees.[457] Achievement of these goals mostly entailed restrictions on internal measures private equity companies might pursue in the company after the buy-out.[458] A first potential restriction could be to rule out lay-offs post buy-out. Second, cost cutting programs could be excluded to protect long lasting business relationships, e.g. with suppliers in the case of G. Third, adherence to an existing investment plan or continuity of company expansion could be another objective in negotiations. Interviewees also reported a non-financial goal, which cannot be subsumed under the umbrella of social responsibility: Avoidance of guarantees which are linked to indemnification through the former family owners.

While most non-financial goals might seem rather altruistic at first sight, they might also be a mean to conserve the family owners' reputation post buy-out and

---

[453] F, J, M, P, and Q; 36% of 14 respondents. This surprisingly low number could be biased (cf. subsection 3.1.6)

[454] Cf. 4.2.1.2.

[455] The private equity company could demand that the family held a stake in the company after the buy-out, provided a vendor-loan or agreed to an earn-out rule. Cf. subsection 4.2.2.3.

[456] With reference to company valuation, the former owner and manager of S said that it made a big difference which party suggested the deal in negotiations with strategic buyers. If a potential strategic buyer approached the owning family, the sale price was very likely to be higher compared to a case in which the owning family offered its company for sale to a strategic buyer.

[457] A, F, G, H, M, P, Q, R, S, and V; 71% of 14 respondents.

[458] These objectives were likely to conflict with objectives of the private equity company and were therefore a matter of sale negotiations. Cf. subsection 4.2.2.3.

prevent public reproaches why he sold the company. As the investment manager backing company A explained:

> *The family owner lives in the town, where the company is located. Therefore, it was very important for the selling family manager that he would be able to walk through the streets and look his neighbors in the eyes after the buy-out.*

The importance family owners assign to non-financial versus financial goals varied significantly. For some family owners, social responsibility did not seem to be more than a lip service. The investment manager backing company S stated that family representatives frequently pretended that the company's continuity was of high importance to them. But when they were told that any restriction might lower the sale price, some negotiations were stopped. Other family owners, for instance the two that sold to holding companies, were willing to pay the price for the non-financial goals and accepted a lower sales price. The investment managers backing companies R and S argued that family owners who emphasized their social responsibility were mainly located in rural areas and not in metropolitan areas, where anonymity might dilute social responsibility.

The goals family owners of the sample companies pursued in sale negotiations correspond to the goals derived from the literature. Interestingly, non-financial goals do not only seem to be driven by social responsibility of the family owner, but seem to be also a preparation for a peaceful evening of life.

4.2.2.3. Sale process

After presenting the goals family owners pursued in negotiations, this subsection discusses the different ways of deal initiation, interviewees' opinions on and experience with the due diligence, potential obstacles in sale negotiations and the importance of trust and respect in the sale process.

Four **different ways a buy-out was initiated** emerged from the interviews. Seven former family owners sold their family business in an auction process.[459] After the decision was taken to sell the company, they hired an M&A advisor to arrange the auction process. The auction process fairly corresponded to the description in the

[459] A, B, G, H, K, Q, and S; 32% of 22 respondents.

respective theoretical subsection.[460] An auction process offers family owners two advantages, namely maximization of the sale price and opportunity to become familiarized with the private equity company before negotiations start.

The buy-out in three companies was initiated by direct contact between the family owners and private equity companies.[461] The family manager of L approached an investment manager whom he knew from a hobby both shared. The family manager of R was told about the possibility to sell to a holding company by another entrepreneur and started negotiations, after several negotiations with private equity companies had failed. The manager of F mentioned that the family owners wanted to save the considerable fees for advisors by exclusively negotiating with an investment manager whom one family owner knew. No other potential buyers were contacted in the first two cases, which presumably led to a lower sale price eventually. The high degree of credibility and trustworthiness inherent in personal contacts could be a possible explanation for the exclusivity of negotiations.

Some buy-outs were not initiated by the family owners but by the private equity company or an advisor. Although this way of deal initiation was not mentioned in the empirical study by the EVCA[462], this route was chosen by four companies.[463] The family manager of J received a request to sell his company from an M&A advisor, who passed the company on to the private equity company that eventually bought J. The private equity company backing M initially screened the industry while attempting to acquire a direct competitor; when these negotiations ended unsuccessfully, the investor approached M through the company's bank. In C, a private equity company had held a silent partnership for seven years and offered to take over the entire

---

460 Cf. subsection 4.1.2.3. Interview partners unanimously described the auction process the following way: After the vendor due diligence, an information memorandum was compiled that was sent out to about 10 to 30 potentially interested buyers (private equity companies and strategic investors) who had guaranteed confidentiality. If the potential buyer was interested, he made a non-binding offer. Based on these non-binding offers, about five to ten potential buyers were selected for the short-list. Pre buy-out management of the company gave management presentations to the short-listed potential buyers, which had to make a new bid, in case they were interested. Based on these bids, the vendor selected the potential buyer with the best offer, who started the due diligence afterwards.

461 F, L, and R; 14% of 22 respondents.

462 Cf. European Private Equity & Venture Capital Association (2005), p. 13; subsection 4.1.2.3.

463 C, J, M, and V; 18% of 22 respondents.

company.[464] According to interview partners, no other potential buyer was contacted in these cases, though this way of deal initiation could lead to lower sale prices compared to an auction process.

Two transactions were initiated by the acquiring management.[465] The manager of T was looking for an opportunity to acquire a company in a buy-out and learned about the company from business contacts. The acquiring managers of U worked as consultants on preparing the company for sale; when they had analyzed the company, they intimated to the family owner that they wanted to acquire the company. Both cases were management buy-ins in rather smaller companies and were financially supported by semi-public investment companies. The fact that only two transactions were initiated by management underlines the reasons hampering this initiation in family businesses as discussed above.[466]

Although family businesses were very restrictive with regard to disclosing data on their company, the willingness to grant private equity companies access to sensitive information was a precondition for the **due diligence**. If a family owner was not willing to cooperate, this would entail failure of the sale negotiations.[467]

In line with the literature, family owners and sometimes also new managers complained about the due diligence. Time consumption and fees for service providers were seen very critical. This might be in part explainable by the family businesses' unfamiliarity with a due diligence process. Another explanation might be that private equity companies were particularly thorough in the due diligence process; this was suggested by the manager of K, who indicated that the due diligence by the last potential strategic buyer only took about half the time.[468] Length and intensity of the

---

464 This case does not imply that all private equity companies holding minority stakes or silent partnerships, take over the company they backed before the buy-out. E.g. company A was sold to a different private equity company than the investor that backed the company pre buy-out. Cf. footnote 430.

465 T and U; 9% of 22 respondents.

466 Cf. subsection 4.1.2.3.

467 An exceptional counterexample was company J: The former family owner gave the private equity company access to all information, but did not allow the investor to talk to any employee prior to the sale; the investor agreed despite considerable uncertainty about the deal.

468 Holding companies can be even faster, which was exemplified by the due diligence of R, which took six hours. A possible explanation for this short due diligence might be that in case of company R, the family manager of this company remained in his position as manager after the

due diligence might be explained by the prudence of private equity companies about reliability of financial figures and the transparency in family businesses especially with regard to reporting and management accounting, which had not fulfilled the buyers' expectations in some cases.[469]

The managers of the two management buy-ins in companies L and U worked for the respective company as consultants before they became managers. In this role, they got access to company data and all areas of the company. The new manager of L used this opportunity to conduct a management due diligence, a market study and a study on customer satisfaction.

As described in the theory subsection, **negotiations** for buy-outs in family businesses had to take the family owner's feelings for his business into account. If investment managers failed to show adequate respect, this might jeopardize the whole deal. The investment manager backing A said:

> *We had to convince the former family owner, that we had the right ideas for this company and wanted to develop it accordingly. And we also had to show him that we accept his ideas and jointly aim at framing the company's future in a new way.*

As the family owners have worked in their companies for so many years, they were very demanding negotiation partners. Thus, it sometimes seemed uncertain, whether family owners would sell their business at all. Empathy and wit could have a very strong impact, which was exemplified by sale negotiations of company E: The family owner initially wanted to sell a minority stake to the private equity company. Given the foreseeable succession problem, the company's financing problem and presumably a smart negotiation strategy by the private equity company, the family owner eventually gave away a majority stake.

The sale price was one of the main reasons why negotiations broke up. An earn-out agreement or a vendor loan were possible solutions to different ideas about a fair company value.[470] While both solutions allowed family owners to participate in the

buy-out. Post buy-out cooperation might have mitigated potential information asymmetries and might have built trust in negotiations.

[469] K, N, and O; 14% of 22 respondents.

[470] Cf. footnote 376.

future development of the company, they also served as risk limitation for the private equity company if the company's performance was below the vendor's projections. Another possibility for the family owner to participate in the future company development was an equity stake in the portfolio company, which 12 companies reported.[471] However, family owners might object the typical inclusion of earn-out agreements, vendor loans or equity stakes in negotiations:[472] The former family manager of U did not want any participation in the company after the sale. The family manager of S would have liked to keep an equity stake, but refrained from it for tax reasons.

Although family owners were very interested in guarantees concerning indemnification, interviewed investment managers indicated that they would not grant any guarantees, e.g. guarantees not to dismiss employees or not to relocate the headquarters. Investment managers argued that guarantees would constrict the private equity company's freedom to develop the company and that former family owners would receive too much money for having the right to demand guarantees.

A potential obstacle in deals was fragmented ownership. Different opinions of the multitude of owners of company P hampered the deal, as family members had different perceptions about the state of the company and about a fair valuation. In companies B and R, the different family clans were represented by a single family member who acted as lead negotiator (in both cases the former family manager) facilitating the sale process.

Although management did not hold an equity stake before the buy-out, managers also had a minor influence on the decision to sell the company. Managers were mainly interested in the conditions of their future involvement, their equity stake, and how the private equity company approached them.[473]

The whole sale process took between 8 (R) to 24 (K) months and typically about 11 months, depending on the state of the management information system, sale

---

471 A, C, E, F, G, H, M, N, O, Q, R, and V; 55% of 22 respondents (2 of the 12 companies belong to the control group). In case, the potential buyer was not a private equity company but one or several managers, a post buy-out equity participation of the selling family owner might have rendered the deal feasible in the light of potentially limited financial resources of the managers.

472 Cf. subsection 4.2.2.2.

473 Non-family managers could influence sale negotiations, because company value would be severely affected if management threatened to resign (cf. Forst (1992), pp. 83 et seq).

preparations and whether the company was sold to the first negotiation partner or not. All family owners besides those of F and J engaged advisors – mostly M&A advisors and lawyers – whose advices and experience were highly appreciated in the process.

Managers as well as investment managers stressed the outstanding **importance of soft factors** as trust and respect **in negotiations**. These factors seemed to be frequently neglected, which might have led to failure of negotiations. The family manager of R said:

> *I was asked to give all kind of guarantees, e.g. that I never went bankrupt. I said: But I am no rogue. The lawyer explained that we had to keep this rogue paragraph. So, I got up and said: I wanted trust and not this!*

Particularly the two family managers of R and S complained about the lack of respect of private equity companies in negotiations: Investment managers made disrespectful comments on their family businesses or merely focused on the exit without understanding the company. The problem that family owners and investment managers lacked a common business language was discussed in subsection 4.1.2.3 and also mentioned by interview partners: Representatives of private equity companies aroused antipathy by employing anglicisms and financial terms, or would not lead negotiations in German.

Most of the investment managers interviewed were aware of this problem and developed certain strategies to build trust. First, the personal contact and understanding of the family owner's situation were emphasized. The investment manager backing J explained:

> *While the [sale] process has become somewhat more professional in recent years, the issues of mutual trust and personal interaction are very important.*

Second, the private equity company could present its track record to underline that it had gathered experience in this market. Third, industry or operational experience or cooperation with an expert in relevant fields could lend credibility to the potential buyer. Fourth, a negotiation style, that started slowly and focused on company history and business model, expressed greater respect for the company than negotiations that quickly approached valuation issues. Fifth, the possibility to retain a minority stake in the company after the buy-out mitigated the emotional ache of family owners to let their family business go.[474] Last, the private equity company could allow the family owner and management to talk to other portfolio companies in the absence of a representative of the private equity company to learn about what these managers think about the potential buyer.

In consequence of these strategies, the level of trust could change quickly. The investment manager backing B reported that at first, his private equity company had difficulties to get access to financial data of the company. Later on, there was such a confidence that the family owners wanted to make sure that the private equity company knew about everything in the company. The investment manager presumed that this change was triggered by the family's intention to ensure the company's future.

Holding companies had fewer difficulties to convince family owners of their trustworthiness given their particular business model, their track record, their quick and unbureaucratic due diligence, and their willingness to make concessions addressing the personal needs of the family owner.

This subsection has shown that initiation of buy-outs was mostly in line with the literature. One aspect not discussed in the literature is that buy-outs can be triggered by private equity companies or M&A advisors, if they proposed an acceptable offer to family owners who were rather aged or who looked for changing their lifestyle. Figure 28 shows the different impact factors that influence sale negotiations. All of these factors were already discussed in the theoretical subsection.[475] Investment managers as well as family managers underlined the particular importance of soft factors like trust and respect in negotiations. While investment managers had developed strategies to build trust and respect, family managers still complained about adverse or disrespectful behavior of private equity companies.

---

[474] Cf. subsection 4.2.2.5.

[475] Guarantees aimed at stipulating non-financial goals of the family owners (cf. subsection 4.1.2.2).

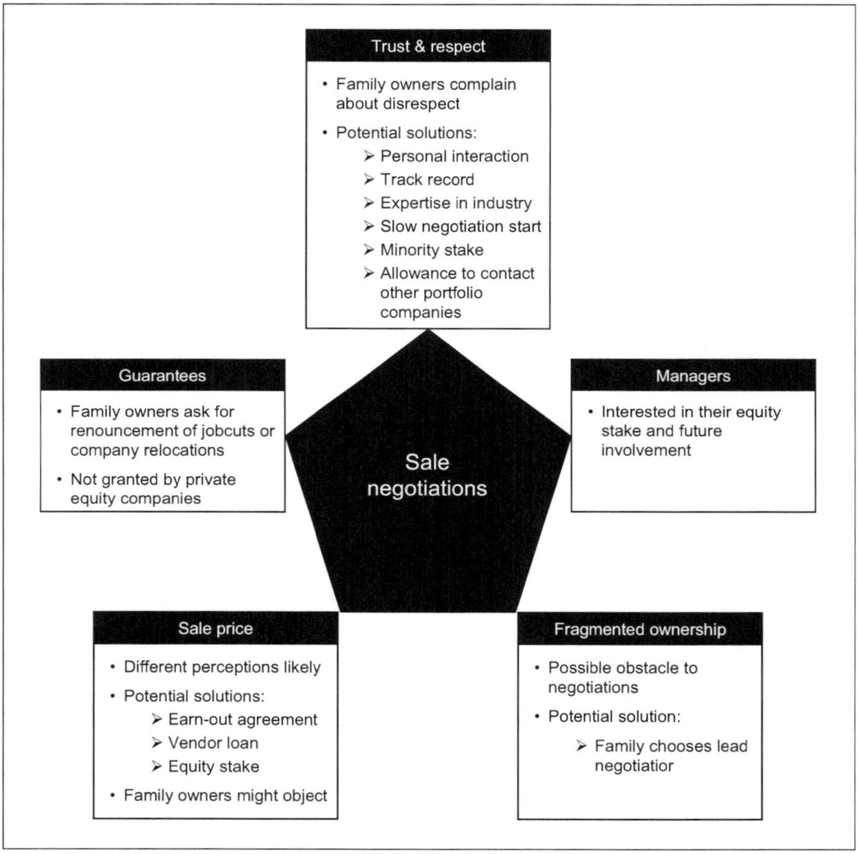

Figure 28: Factors influencing sale negotiations

Source: Author's illustration

4.2.2.4. Communication of the buy-out and reaction from stakeholders

The following procedure emerged as the typical **communication strategy** of buy-outs from the interviews (see Figure 29). After the management team and the private equity company agreed to do the transaction, stakeholders of the company were informed about the buy-out in the following order: Junior management, employees, customers and suppliers, and finally general public. Communication of junior management and general public are not treated in the literature according to the literature review in subsection 4.1.2.4. Junior management was informed on the day of the buy-out or one day in advance. Senior management informed junior managers in detail, as this was typically a small circle.

Figure 29: Stylized strategy to communicate the buy-out

Source: Author's illustration

Employees learned about the buy-out mostly the day the sale became effective. Communication took place through a staff meeting, in which post buy-out management informed about the transaction and about future plans. In three of these meetings, the new management was accompanied by the former family owner, who explained the reasons for the sale.[476] In another company, an investment manager attended the meeting (I).[477] In the staff meetings, two managers invited employees to call at their office and ask further questions concerning the buy-out and the company's future (H, K).[478] In companies L and M, which were spread over several locations, managers announced the sale in person in all branches. As an exception from announcing the buy-out in a staff meeting, employees in A were informed by letter.

In the next step, customers and suppliers were informed. Information policy towards these stakeholders varied: Company A did not inform its customers or suppliers about the buy-out, and B only informed the business partners on request and through the press. Other companies sent emails or letters to regular business partners and management informed important business partners through phone calls or personal

---

[476] K, M, and J; 18% of 17 respondents.

[477] The private equity company sent a representative to the staff meeting to support management, possibly because the former family manager could not attend this meeting as he had passed away years before.

[478] While in H not a single employee used this opportunity and asked the manager questions, in K, several employees used the manager's offer and informed themselves about the buy-out.

meetings.[479] Communication of the buy-out to customers and suppliers could be simultaneous with the general public.[480]

In a last step, the media was informed through press releases, which were distributed by the private equity company and the portfolio company. Content of the press releases varied. In the case of M, financial backing to support further growth was stressed instead of the succession problem, as the sale of the company was seen as personal decision of the family owner. In contrast, the succession problem was clearly addressed in C and O. Press releases were sent to national as well as regional newspapers, as the latter were of special importance to some family owners. Only the manager of company H did not want to inform the public about the buy-out, as he did not expect a positive effect as reaction; however, he gave an interview and released a press statement as a journalist found out about the buy-out.

In two cases, the communication strategy did not succeed as planned. In an interview with a local newspaper, the former manager of A talked ambiguously about the possibility of a company relocation, which was misinterpreted by a journalist. The management had to correct the statement to appease the general public. In company P, several members of the fragmented family ownership gave non-coordinated interviews, which aroused a chaotic impression of the buy-out.

Reactions of customers and suppliers to the buy-out varied widely, as interview partners reported positive as well as negative reactions. Six interviewees indicated that business partners reacted positively to the buy-out.[481] Customers and suppliers were especially positive, if the buy-out solved a succession problem or a financing problem in the bought-out company. Some business partners that were also family managers of other family businesses well understood the personal decision of family owners to sell the company and retire, or enjoy their evening of life. Some business partners were pleased to learn that the family sold the company as relations between these business partners and the respective family manager were described as difficult. Customers and suppliers were pleased about the changes in the company

[479] I, K, and L; 18% of 17 respondents.

[480] A pattern that appears from the interviews is that the closer relationship and interaction between company and business partner were, the more intensive was the buy-out communicated towards the respective business partner.

[481] F, G, I, K, L, and Q; 46% of 13 respondents.

after the buy-out: In L, management took more intensive care of customers; in K business partners appreciated the increased entrepreneurial spirit; and in I, customers were happy about improved reliability and quality.[482]

Contrary to these positive reactions, two interviewees also reported initially negative reactions, particularly by managers of other family businesses.[483] But negative reactions were only of temporary nature and later on, business partners were neutral, as the manager of C said:

> *In the beginning, the change in ownership caused irritations among our costumers, who are mainly owner-managed companies; especially, if you are sold from a private owner to a financial investor. [...] The problem is an emotional problem. But as we are [...] a good supplier and a good customer the problem is controllable.*

While reasons for this irritation mostly remained unclear, one reason seemed to be that business partners were insecure about the company's future and whether the company would pay its liabilities. In J suppliers' confidence was restored quickly when the private equity company provided enough money and a credit line to assure payment of liabilities. Nevertheless, some of J's business partners defected to a competitor, as post buy-out management abolished special discounts, which the family manager offered to loyal long-term business partners. J was also the only case, where competitors unsuccessfully attempted to convince customers to defect with the argument that the competitor was still a family business. Irritations in general seemed to increase with spatial proximity: Business partners geographically closer to the bought-out company were more likely to show a negative reaction; possibly because relations between the former family manager and business partners in the neighborhood were among the closest.

Interview partners of five companies stated that there was a neutral reaction from business partners.[484] In company A, the manager attributed this reaction to the atomistic customer structure with customers not caring about company ownership. In some companies, the owner had already left company management or did not have

---

[482] Cf. subsection 5.3.6 for a discussion of the evaluation of business relations after the buy-out.

[483] C and J; 15% of 17 respondents.

[484] A, B, D, M, and O; 38% of 17 respondents.

customer contact for years before the buy-out, so that customers were already used to not talking to the family owner or family manager (A, M).

Interview partners also mentioned some ways to mitigate potential irritations of business partners following the buy-out. Post buy-out managers of two companies had a good reputation in the industry due to their previous activity and this reputation was honored by customers and suppliers (J, L). Three managers stressed that business partners did not react as products remained unchanged and customers' demands were satisfied (K, M, O). Another way to mitigate potential irritations was to retain a reduced family influence post buy-out through ownership, participation on the supervisory board or management board.[485] Presumably, the effect of this mitigation was correlated to visibility of family influence to business partners.

Family businesses sold to holding companies reported positive reactions of suppliers and customers. Business contacts appreciated the solution of the foreseeable succession problem and the financial backing of the private equity company.[486] Interview partners in companies funded by semi-public investment companies reported a positive reaction from business partners, as new managers acted more entrepreneurially, were already known in the industry and had the advantage of being younger, which facilitated talks and negotiations.[487]

In contrast to the reaction of business partners, **employees'** negative **reactions** were rather homogeneous. All 13 interview partners answering this question reported that employees were shocked by the sale of the company.[488] Employees were

485 Cf. subsection 3.2.4.

486 The manager of R explained that a corporation R supplied was concerned whether the company was financially able to build a new plant in the USA to supply the corporation there. After the new owners took over, these concerns vanished.

487 The manager of V elaborated on this point by saying that customers frequently had doubts to enter a long-term contract with a small company owned by a family manager in his sixties. As these long-term contracts involved technical dependency of the business partner, the latter one was concerned about sustainability of company management and the whole company due to its limited size. The buy-out brought in two younger managers, therefore solved this problem and thus, enabled considerable growth.

488 A, C, D, F, G, I, J, K, L, M, O, P, and Q; 100% of 13 respondents.

particularly afraid of private equity companies as new owners in consequence of the negative media coverage in Germany after summer 2005.[489] The manager of I said:

> *What was the employees' reaction to the buy-out? At first, insecurity. "Oh my god, we are taken over by a private equity company. They are going to cut jobs."*

The shock was the more intensive, the worse employees were prepared for the buy-out, as the manager of J reported, in whose company not even senior managers were informed about the sale process in advance. On announcement of the buy-out, some employees started to weep, work atmosphere deteriorated, and productivity decreased significantly. Interview partners attributed strong emotional reactions to the long tradition and thus security assigned to family businesses, to the long period some employees worked in the company, and to the close relations between employees and family owners or managers.

However, this shock reaction was in all cases only of temporary nature, as employees' confidence in the company was restored when they saw, that jobs were not cut and that the private equity company did not interfere directly with the business. In two companies, employees even welcomed the buy-out after some time, as it solved the succession problem and increased the company's independence of the former family manager and brought new impetus into the company.[490] The shock reaction seemed also the smaller, the lower the degree of the family manager's or owner's involvement in the company was before the buy-out.

Interview partners stated that there were four factors mitigating employees' reactions: First, continuity of management was a very positive sign for employees. Trust in long-serving managers translated into confidence about the company's future. This effect was stronger, if managers held a significant stake in the company.

---

489 In summer 2005 started the so called locust debate ("Heuschrecken Debatte") – a rather biased and negative public debate on private equity, raised by the politician Franz Müntefering's critique on the private equity investment Grohe AG (see footnote 340 on page 96) (cf. Achleitner (2005), pp. 327-329). The effect of this discussion can be seen by employees' reaction in O, where the buy-out took place well before the locust debate. The manager indicated that employees were uncertain about the company sale but not particularly terrified by being bought by a private equity company.

490 G and M.

Second, continuity of family influence eased emotional reactions. The former family owner or manager was an important person of identification for employees. The manager of C explained:

> *If a former family member is still holding a stake – even if this stake is quite small –, there is a certain potential for identification and we play this vis-à-vis the employees.*

Third, presence of the private equity company restored employees' confidence. Private equity companies talked on the staff meeting when the buy-out was announced, sat in on meetings of junior managers, talked to the mayor, or spent time in the company in another way. At these occasions, representatives of the private equity company explained the rationale for the buy-out and outlined the company's future strategy. Fourth, cooperation with the works council was another way to mitigate employee's reactions. In I, the formerly restricted information flow to works council was improved and in B, the investment manager backing this company continued the formerly family managers' close contact with representatives of the council.

Calming employees was especially challenging in management buy-ins (or institutional buy-outs), where new managers were appointed from outside the company. Continuity of family influence and presence of the private equity company were also used in these cases to mitigate the transition. The manager of L talked to many junior managers about the company's growth strategy and that jobs were not in danger. Junior managers in turn were expected to pass the key message on to employees.

In the two companies, which were in a turnaround situation, employees' reaction was different from the pattern of negative reactions described above. In P, the works council organized a demonstration to demand that the family sold the company. However, this positive atmosphere favoring a private equity company as owner exacerbated when jobs were cut due to the corporate crisis post buy-out. In Q, the situation was rather similar with employees reacting positive to the sale by the family but fearing next steps of the new owner. In both cases, hard measures were taken given the turnaround situation of the company: In P, about one third of employees were dismissed, and in Q, labor time was increased without increases in salary.

In family businesses sold to holding companies, employees' reactions were similar to reactions following sales to private equity companies. Employees were shocked at first about the sale, but when they noticed that the management remained in the company and changes in their daily work were insignificant, they calmed down. The long-term orientation of investors and the close monitoring and frequent presence of investment managers in the companies also eased the shock. In the companies backed by semi-public investment companies, reactions varied. In V, the pre buy-out family manager participated in the buy-out and employees reacted positively, as they had expected this succession and were pleased not to be sold to a competitor. Employees showed a negative reaction to the management buy-ins in T and U because of the fact of being sold. But also in these cases, employees calmed down after some time.

This subsection has shown that the typical communication strategy reported by interview partners was an extended version of the strategy recommended in the literature. The recommended strategy was extended by including junior management and the general public in the dissemination of the buy-out. However, according to the literature stakeholders' reactions were expected in a different way. The presented literature underlined the advantages which family businesses had in their relation to business partners and employees. This positive impact on relations would imply that stakeholders reacted negatively if families sold the company. Evidence from interviews contradicted this presumption. Reactions by business partners were mixed: The majority of interview partners reported positive or neutral reactions and only a few interviewees indicated the expected negative reactions. Employees showed homogeneously a shock at first, but calmed down after some time. These limited occurrences of negative reactions could be possibly seen as result of a successful communication strategy or as an indication that the advantages of family businesses with regards to their relations to stakeholders might be overemphasized. The occurences of these shock reactions after sales to private equity companies and holding companies suggests that employees' shock was not due to the type of buyer but rather evoked by the fact that the family business was sold at all.

4.2.2.5. Family owners' emotional separation and role post buy-out

After the sale of the company, the formerly owning family and the company developed into different directions. There were several reasons for the family owner, why this **separation** was **emotionally** very difficult.[491] The main reason was that the family business was considered the result of hard work of one or several family members, potentially even of various generations. As the investment manager backing company M said:

> *[The company] is the life's work of the [vendor]. He worked there for 20, 30 or even 40 years.*

This combination of reminiscence of time and energy invested into the company and of pride in the result created an intensive emotional bond between the family owners and their company.[492]

Another reason complicating emotional separation was that the family manager did not want to retire though he knew that the sale of the company was a necessary step. As the family manager of S explained:

> *I didn't want to quit. I didn't want to stop working there. I didn't want to do nothing – I wanted to continue. [...] This letting go is a very emotional thing.*

The process of separation from the company was especially hard, if the company was shortly before an important step in its development or if several projects launched by the former family manager were near completion.

However, there were also other factors that mitigated the emotional ache of separation. First, the sale released a lion's share of the family fortune bound in the family business before. The released capital was no more at risk and independent of the company's further development. Second, the family owners were assured that they did not follow the example of other family businesses, which were led by an overaged

---

491 An anecdote of the manager of S showed how difficult the emotional separation was for some family owners or family managers: The manager was talking to one of his customers, who was a 74 years old family manager and kept on working in his company every day. When the customer learned that the family manager of S had sold his company, the customer patted the manager of S on the back and said: "Well done!" The manager of S interpreted into this, that the old customer was unhappy that he had not been able to sell his company.

492 Cf. subsection 4.2.1.1.

family manager into decline. Third, the sale could be a release from potential business problems depressing family owners.[493]

Against this background, family owners had the choice between two strategies how to separate from their company as described in the theoretical subsection (see Figure 30).[494] The first option was a "**clear cut**" of all links to the company. As described in subsection 3.2.4, eight families had taken this option.[495] In the long run, this option prevented any conflicts between the family as minority owner and the private equity company as majority owner. However, in the short run, it was a hard cut for family owners. The manager of E explained:

> *It must have been very hard for the family manager to answer on the phone: "Listen, please. We have worked together for 20 years, but I'm not your contact person any more – would you mind to call [the new manager]." [...] That wasn't easy for him.*

The alternative strategy was a **minor influence fading over time**. This strategy was chosen by the remaining 14 families.[496] This involvement as junior partner compared to the private equity company as senior partner seemed to be frequently driven by concerns about the company's future. The family's involvement and interest decreased when family owners were convinced that their former family business prospered under the influence of the private equity company. While the latter option mitigated the emotional stress for the family from losing its influence, cooperation might entail future conflicts between family and private equity company.

---

493 Cf. subsection 4.2.1.1.

494 Although choice between the two strategies presented was theoretically at hand of the family owners, the private equity company might have demanded the family to keep a stake in the company after the buy-out or that the family manager remained on or joined the management board or the supervisory board, to facilitate the transition or reduce the risk of the buy-out.

495 B, I, J, K, L, P, T, and U; 36% of 22 respondents.

496 A, C, D, E, F, G, H, M, N, O, Q, R, S, and V; 64% of 22 respondents (cf. subsection 3.2.4).

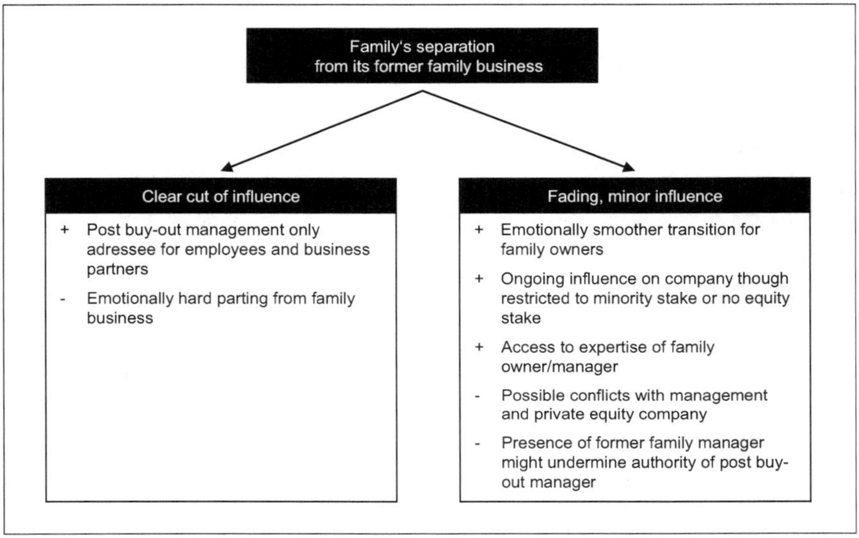

Figure 30: Family owners' strategies of separation from the former business

Source: Author's illustration
+ advantages - disadvantages

In case the family had chosen the strategy of fading, minor influence after the buy-out, **conflicts between family members and the private equity company** seemed especially likely if a family member remained on the management board.[497] In F, the former family manager remained on the management board, but noticed that he did not agree with the private equity company about how to take decisions and how to lead the company; as this dissent was a constant source of conflict between both parties, the former family manager resigned one year after the buy-out. The manager of F commented:

[497] However, there were also positive comments on former family members still being related with the company after the sale. The manager of H appreciated that the former family manager still remained a close relationship with him beyond the shareholders' meeting and thus served as a sparring partner.

Family managers, who are materially absolutely independent and who are used to manage their companies their way for more than 20 years, are unable to deal with the significant interference of the private equity company.

Interview partners formulated three solutions that led to a good cooperation between a family manager and the private equity company: First, the private equity company did hardly or never interfere with the company; this was only acceptable to a private equity company if company development was in line with the business plan. Second, the family manager had to accept and comply with the monitoring requirements and management principles of the private equity company. Third, the family manager's employment could be limited, as in case of company V.

Conflicts might also arise between family managers and non-family managers. A potential conflict was that family members might be reluctant to accept changes, as they might regard changes as criticism of their past decisions like in O and T.[498] Family managers might not accept new arrangements but stick to the traditional way. Conflicts could also arise from different opinions on strategic decisions stemming from different time horizons considered. In company V, the management wanted to enter a new market segment, which would take years to pay off; the post buy-out family manager objected this step, as the investment was unlikely to become profitable during the remaining time he wanted to hold his stake. Some problems can be mitigated by explaining changes to family managers and thus increasing their acceptance. Another way of mitigation was assigning responsibility for a more technical department to a family manager, as most conflicts arised from commercial issues.

To **conclude**, this subsection has provided empirical evidence on the emotional hardship family owners and managers felt when separating from their company and what factors might have mitigated this emotional stress. The subsection has also proven applicability of the two strategies of separation of family owners or managers from their company: While 8 companies had chosen a clear cut with their former family business, 14 had chosen to let their influence fade slowly. Although the second strategy of fading, minor influence seemed emotionally less demanding, this strategy

[498] In T, one family manager remained in the company though not as member of the management board.

was prone to conflicts between family members and the private equity company or post buy-out managers, if family members remained on the management board post buy-out.

4.3 Summary of chapter

This chapter aimed at examining the background of the buy-out and thus laying the foundation for the analysis of changes in subsequent chapters.

The first part of the chapter focused on the decision to sell, which was the result of a three-stage decision process. In the first stage of the decision process, the family manager faced the decision to continue in his position or to retire. Retirement could be driven either by personal reasons, which included age, desire for a change in lifestyle, and opportunity to cash in, or by business reasons, which included corporate crises, financing problems or insufficient management capabilities. Personal reasons seemed to be the main triggers for the sale. In the second stage of the decision process, the retiring family manager checked whether a family member could succeed in management. To succeed, a candidate from within the family had to be of suitable age, qualified as well as motivated. Moreover, the succession had to work. In the third stage, the parting family manager checked whether appointment of a non-family manager was possible and acceptable for the family. If the family manager wanted or needed to retire, and neither the appointment of family members nor non-family managers to succeed in management was possible or acceptable, sale of the family business was the logical consequence.

In theory, the family business could be sold to a strategic buyer, to the general public or to the management backed by a private equity company. There were several arguments in support of a sale to a private equity company: This option ensured continuity and independence of the company after the sale. Private equity companies might have made the highest bid. Moreover, this option seemed obvious to family owners who cooperated with private equity companies as minority owners. Given sampling criteria, interviewed companies were not sold to strategic buyers, either because no potential buyer existed or because the family objected to selling to a strategic buyer, as the company would be dissolved or sold to a competitor the family manager had fought with for a long time. IPOs were in general not a feasible alternative given sample companies were too small.

Two thirds of family owners and managers prepared the company for the sale to facilitate the sale process and possibly increase the sale price. Four ways of preparations were identified: First, operational changes were initiated to increase profitability of the company. Second, the business plan was revised to elaborate the company's potential. Third, transparency of the company was increased. Fourth, changes in management took place to reduce family influence and facilitate transition in management following the buy-out.

The second part of this chapter deals with the sale transaction. At first, the criteria for an investment decision of private equity companies are discussed. Investors wanted to see in future portfolio companies a strong market position with products that had a high brand recognition and reputation. Investors also looked for managers with strong personalities and the qualification to carry through with the buy-out. Moreover, portfolio companies were expected to show financial strength and potential for value generation. Especially the first two characteristics might have been decisive for an investment decision, as changes in products or management would take too long given the limited holding period of investors.

A pivotal factor in negotiations were goals the vendor pursued with the sale. Family owners did not exclusively aim at financial goals. Only a few interviewees mentioned this goal, though the lion's share of family fortune was bound in the family business. Besides, family owners pursued non-financial goals which related to prevention of lay-offs, restriction of cost cutting, continuation of company expansion, and avoidance of guarantees. The first three goals could be subsumed under the umbrella of social responsibility and could be explained by stewardship theory. However, interviewees also reported that some family owners only intimated these goals at the beginning of sale negotiations, but preferred a higher sale price instead of insisting on them.

After presenting the investment criteria of private equity companies and the goals of family owners, the sale process was analyzed. Former family owners decided to sell the company in an auction process or approached exclusively one private equity company, with the latter approach suggesting non-professional selling behavior. Few sales were initiated by the private equity company, an advisor or later post buy-out management. In sale negotiations, private equity companies had to pay special attention to their behavior towards family owners. While interviewed investment managers presented several strategies to facilitate negotiation, family managers and post buy-out managers frequently complained about a lack of trust and respect in sale talks. Negotiation partners' perceptions on company value might diverge. Given the sale price was a critical element of sale talks, several solutions to overcome diverging valuations were at hand for negotiation partners, like earn-out agreements, vendor loans and post buy-out equity stakes. Fragmented ownership of the family might have hampered sale negotiations and were overcome by family owners settling on a lead negotiator. Guarantees mostly relating to the non-financial goals discussed before were generally refused by private equity companies.

Interview partners mostly agreed on a uniform communication strategy for the buy-out. The buy-out was at first communicated within the company, starting with junior management and followed by employees. Then, external stakeholders were informed including customers and suppliers as well as the general public through the media. Reaction from business partners was mostly positive or neutral, as it frequently meant a solution to the succession problem. Only a few interview partners initially showed negative reactions that disappeared shortly afterwards. Employees in virtually all companies were initially shocked when they learned about the sale but calmed down, when no lay-offs took place. Employees' shock was triggered by the fact of being sold not by the fact of being sold to a private equity company. The fact that business partners and employees were rather neutral about the sale after some time shows that loss of status as a family business had no significant effect for stakeholders.

With the buy-out, the family had to separate from the company. This process was especially hard given the intensive intermingling of family and family business before the buy-out. Two strategies are presented for this separation: A clear cut put a sudden end to any family influence on the company. The strategy of "fading, minor influence" allowed the family to retain some influence after the sale. While the second strategy limited the emotional ache for the family to let go, it sometimes gave rise to conflicts over decision making and necessary changes, especially if a family member remained on the management board.

These summarized findings lend themselves to draw some conclusions: This chapter has presented several peculiarities of buy-outs in family businesses stemming from the interaction with the families. The sale of a family business is a second-best solution for family owners if management succession by family members or non-family managers is not possible or wanted. If the family business needs to be sold, family owners' striving for continued independence and development of the family business suggest private equity companies are preferred buyers. Although family owners and managers could facilitate the sale and increase the sale price through preparing the company, they frequently forgo these measures – possibly because families want to ignore the forthcoming sale. Family owners pursue non-financial goals in sale negotiations, which are mostly driven by social responsibility and caring for the company. In negotiations, private equity companies have to pay special attention to the feelings of family members; otherwise, negotiations might fail. Families frequently wish to stay involved in their family business, to monitor company development after the sale.

All these peculiarities in the transaction suggest that buy-outs in family businesses are different from other types of buy-outs. The particular behavior of family owners as vendors differs from that of regular vendors like corporations in case of spin-off buy-outs or anonymous shareholders in case of going private buy-outs. While family behavior might seem unprofessional at times, this behavior is driven by the multitude of in part non-economic goals families pursue through their business. Negotiation partners might have difficulties to understand the importance of these non-economic to families and might therefore perceive negotiation behavior of family owners irrational or incomprehensible; however, given the influence of non-economic goals on the utility function of family owners, their behavior is rational and maximizing their utility.

5 Changes in corporate governance

This chapter sheds light on changes in selected aspects of corporate governance after buy-outs in family businesses.[499] After a theoretical comparison of corporate governance in family businesses and portfolio companies in section 5.1, expected changes in the selected aspects are derived from the literature in section 5.2. Section 5.3 contains the empirical part of this chapter: Changes in the above mentioned aspects, which were observed in sample companies, are analyzed and discussed, so that propositions on major changes are eventually derived. Section 5.4 closes the chapter with a summary.

Figure 31 presents the six aspects analyzed in this chapter and integrates them into a framework of corporate governance. The selected aspects are: Owner influence on management decisions; owner influence on corporate strategy; supervision by and support from the supervisory board; composition of the management team; motivation and compensation of management; and the decision making process of management.

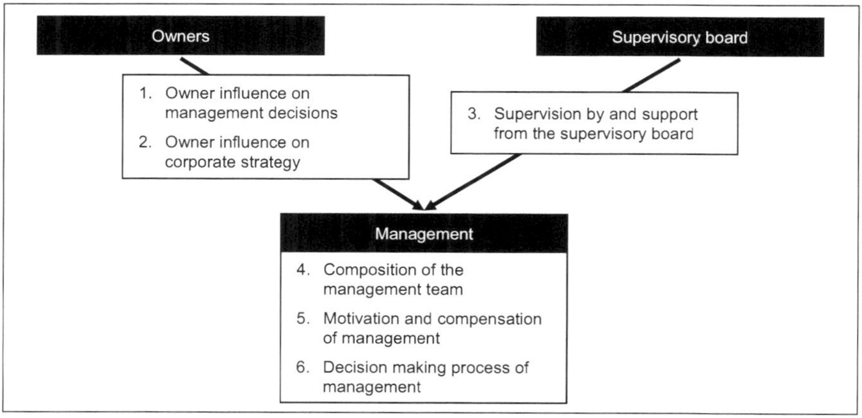

Figure 31: Analyzed aspects of corporate governance

Source: Author's illustration

---

[499] Corporate governance is defined as the defense of owners' "interests by the use of governance devices" (Brunninge/Nordqvist/Wiklund (2007), p. 295) and thus deals with holding management accountable for their doings and enabling management to exercise enterprising spirit (cf. Uhlaner/Wright/Huse (2007), pp. 226 et seq., 239). For further definitions on corporate governance, see Shleifer/Vishny (1997), p. 737; Filatotchev/Wright (2005), pp. 1-5; Moldenhauer (2007), pp. 11-14.

5.1 Theoretical comparison of family businesses and portfolio companies

5.1.1. Corporate governance in family businesses

This subsection discusses the corporate governance in family businesses with regard to its institutions, their cooperation and related theories.

The first institution under examination is **ownership**. "Ownership in German family businesses is very closely held."[500] This statement by KLEIN is underlined by results of the two surveys presented in Table 14. More than 80% of German family businesses are exclusively held by family members and family owners hold a majority in almost all remaining companies. Family owners hold a minority stake in only one out of fifty family businesses.[501]

		Percentage of family businesses, in which the family holds the indicated equity share (in %)				
Author, year	Sample composition	1 – 25%	26 – 50%	51 – 75%	76-99%	100%
Achleitner/ Schraml/ Klöckner (2008)	237 German family businesses	0.8	2.6	5.1	6.4	85.1
Klein (2004)	669 German family businesses (data from 1995)	1.9		9.7	8.3	80.1

Table 14: Share of equity held by family owners

Source: Achleitner/Schraml/Klöckner (2008), p. 15; Klein (2004), p. 109[502]

[500] Klein (2000), p. 164.

[501] This result might be partly due to the definition of a family business employed in this thesis, namely that a company's SFI must be at least 1 to qualify as a family business. (cf. subsection 2.1.1). The lower the total equity stake held by the family, the greater family involvement in the management or supervisory board must be to result in an SFI of greater or equal 1. In contrast, if the family only holds a minority stake and non-family members hold the majority, the latter might be more likely to appoint non-family members to the management and supervisory board, as his decisions are not affected by any kinship links. Appointment of non-family members to the management and supervisory board would further decrease the SFI, so that the company might not qualify as a family business any more.

As this thesis only considers family ownership as if it was held by a single individual, distribution of the equity stake among family members is not taken into account. For details on this see Klein (2000), pp. 164-167. For literature on ownership dispersion in family business, see Schulze/Lubatkin/Dino (2003a).

[502] Size categories in Klein (2004) do not perfectly match those of Achleitner/Schraml/Klöckner (2008). The category borders of the more recent study were taken.

In general, owners of family businesses[503] attempt to prevent any influence of non-family parties and thus object spreading equity stakes outside the family.[504] However, financial needs of the family or the family business might necessitate selling a stake to non-family members.[505] Another possible reason for selling a stake to non-family members is that the family needs additional capital to pay-out a family owner who wants to sell his stake.[506] Family businesses with non-family owners are arguably in the transition process to non-family business, as the trend of declining ownership in family's hands is rarely inverted.[507]

The second institution of corporate governance discussed in the following is the **management board** ("Geschäftsführung"). Following the definition of a family business underlying this thesis, it is not obligatory for a family business to be managed by family members. Although almost every second family business is managed exclusively by family managers (i.e. managers who are at the same time family members), non-family managers are not a rare phenomenon in family businesses:[508] Table 15 shows that about two-fifth of family businesses are managed jointly by family and non-family managers. However, the whole management board is left to non-family managers only in every tenth company.[509] Non-family managers are

---

503 For clarification of the focus of analysis (changes in family businesses after buy-outs), the family is assumed to have one will and that all members pursue this will before and after the buy-out. Hence, intra-family dynamics are excluded from further analysis (cf. subsection 2.1.1).

504 Cf. Achleitner/Schraml/Klöckner (2008), p. 19; subsection 7.1.1; Tagiuri/Davis (1992), p. 16; Westhead/Cowling (1996), p. 19. KLEIN has shown that the greater the number of family members family ownership is distributed to, the lower is the total stake of the whole family (cf. Klein (2004), p. 191). As ownership dispersion might indicate alienation of family members to their company, the before mentioned correlation could be explained by the fact that family members more distant to the family business might have sold their stake.

505 Cf. subsection 4.2.1.1 for financing problems in the sample companies.

506 Cf. Achleitner/Schraml/Tappeiner (2008), p. 19; Klein (2004), p. 191.

507 Cf. Klein (2004), p. 194. Although minority shareholders in family businesses are expected to demand consideration in corporate governance, the resulting changes on corporate governance are not discussed in detail in the following, as minority stakes seem a rather infrequent phenomenon. For further information on minority shareholders impact on corporate governance, see Achleitner/Schraml/Tappeiner (2008), pp. 41-68.

508 Non-family managers are also referred to as professional managers in the literature (cf. Chittoor/Das (2007), pp. 67, 69; Songini (2006), p. 270).

509 HENNERKES argues that non-family management might be advisable for even a greater number of family businesses. If evaluated objectively, family members would not always be the first choice

recruited almost equally from within and outside the family business.[510] As discussed in subsection 4.1.1.1, appointment of non-family managers might be a consequence of the retirement of a family manager combined with the absence of a qualified and motivated family successor within the family. KLEIN has found a significant negative correlation between involvement of family members in the management and company size.[511]

<table>
<tr><th></th><th></th><th colspan="6">Share of positions on the management board held by family members</th></tr>
<tr><th>Author, year</th><th>Sample composition</th><th>0%</th><th>1 – 25%</th><th>26 – 50%</th><th>51 – 75%</th><th>76-99%</th><th>100%</th></tr>
<tr><td>Achleiner/ Schraml/ Klöckner (2008)</td><td>237 German family businesses</td><td>6.1%</td><td>6.6%</td><td>28.8%</td><td>9.6%</td><td>2.2%</td><td>46.7%</td></tr>
<tr><td>Schachner/ Speckbacher/ Wentges (2006)</td><td>132 Austrian and German family businesses</td><td>14.4%</td><td colspan="4">19.7%</td><td>65.9%</td></tr>
<tr><td>May/Redlefsen/ Knappe (2005)</td><td>361 German family businesses</td><td>10.2%</td><td colspan="4">30.7%</td><td>59.1%</td></tr>
<tr><td>Klein (2004)</td><td>669 German family businesses (data from 1995)</td><td>14%</td><td>7%</td><td>27%</td><td colspan="2">8%</td><td>44%</td></tr>
</table>

Table 15: Share of family members on the management board

Source: Achleitner/Schraml/Klöckner (2008), p. 15; Schachner/Speckbacher/Wentges (2006), p. 597; May/Redlefsen/Knappe (2005), p. 101; Klein (2004), p. 131

There are several reasons why non-family managers are appointed to the board: Owning families might not have enough adequately qualified members to fill all seats on the management board.[512] Company growth might necessitate professional

to succeed a resigning family manager. However, he concedes, resigning family managers are likely to be biased in the assessment of their sons or daughters (cf. Hennerkes (1998), p. 182).

510 Cf. May/Redlefsen/Knappe (2005), p. 105.

511 Cf. Klein (2000), p. 171. This correlation is not supported by May/Redlefsen/Knappe (2005), p. 101. Besides other possible explanations, KLEIN argues that family involvement might entail lower company growth due to lack of professionalism or higher risk aversion. However, an empirical study has shown that there is no difference in performance of high growth companies led by family or non-family managers; family managers are assumed to adapt to the changes in the company and its environment (cf. Willard/Krueger/Feeser (1992), p. 190).

512 Cf. Chrisman/Chua/Sharma (1996), p. 19; Dyer (1989), p. 222; May/Redlefsen/Knappe (2005), pp. 102 et seq.

management expertise from outside the company.[513] Non-family managers may bring about a desired change in attitudes from family values to business values like profitability and efficiency.[514] Installation of non-family management could be a measure to prepare the company for management succession or sale.[515] Non-family managers can play an important role in reconciling and coordinating antipathetic family managers.[516] Finally, non-family managers can easily be replaced if their performance is not satisfactory; replacement of family managers might be rather difficult.[517]

But there are also arguments against non-family managers: Family managers might display higher motivation due to their identification with and attachment to the company, which might be irrelevant for non-family managers.[518] External non-family managers are less likely than family members to adhere to values or strategic visions of the family.[519] Following agency theory, non-family managers might also pursue goals diverging from those of family owners.[520] Lastly, family owners might be afraid to lose control of the company.[521]

Hiring talented non-family managers might be a challenge for family businesses. Potential non-family managers might consider family businesses as less attractive, because selection, compensation and disciplining of management frequently differ between family and non-family members.[522] Family businesses are also less

---

513 Cf. Hennerkes (1998), p. 181; Sharma/Chrisman/Chua (1997), p. 16; Ward (1988), p. 115.

514 Cf. Dyer (1989), p. 223.

515 Cf. subsection 4.2.1.1; Hennerkes (1998), p. 181; Dyer (1989), p. 223.

516 Cf. Hennerkes (1998), p. 181; Klein (2004), p. 254.

517 Cf. Klein (2004), p. 254; Ensley/Pearson (2005), p. 279.

518 Cf. Menendez-Requejo (2006), p. 577; Davis/Schoorman/Donaldson (1997b), pp. 24 et seq.; Ram/Holliday (1993), p. 635.

519 Cf. Dyer (1989), pp. 223 et seq.; Poza/Alfred/Maheshwari (1997), p. 148. Non-family managers from within the company are more likely to perpetuate family values (cf. Dyer (1989), p. 229).

520 Cf. Dunemann/Barrett (2004), p. 12.

521 Cf. Perrigo (1975) according to Chrisman/Chua/Sharma (1996), p.19. This fear of losing control might induce family managers to forgo growth in order to conserve family control over the company, as a larger company might outgrow the family's managerial capacities (cf. Allen/Panian (1982), p. 546).

522 Cf. Menendez-Requejo (2006), p. 577; Carney (2005), p. 256; Carney/Gedajlovic (2002), p. 126; Mühlebach (2004), p. 99; Schulze et al. (2001), p. 111; Poza/Alfred/Maheshwari (1997), pp. 141, 150 et seq.

likely to grant equity stakes to non-family managers due to the fear of losing control.[523]

The third institution of corporate governance is the **supervisory board**, whose members oversee and advice management.[524] German companies are governed by a two-tier board system; while the management board is responsible for managing the company, the supervisory board ("Beirat")[525] promotes the interests of owners and supervises managers.[526] Supervisory boards are not mandatory for limited liability corporations ("GmbHs") and limited partnerships with a limited liability corporation as general partner ("GmbH & Co. KG"), which are the two dominant legal incorporations of German family businesses.[527] Only about one third of German family businesses have a supervisory board.[528] If a supervisory board exists, there are mostly family and non-family members on it.[529] KLEIN has found that the presence of family members on the management board is negatively correlated with the existence of a supervisory board.[530]

There is a multitude of reasons, why the installation of a supervisory board is advisable, even if it is not required by law: Depending on the composition of the

523 Cf. subsection 5.2.5; Carney (2005), p. 256; May/Redlefsen/Knappe (2005), p. 107.

524 Cf. Johnson/Daily/Ellstrand (1996), p. 411; Shleifer/Vishny (1997), pp. 750 et seq.

525 The term "Aufsichtsrat" refers to a mandatory supervisory board in public corporations, whereas the term "Beirat" is employed for voluntary supervisory boards of companies organized as a different legal form. As most family businesses are not public companies, only the German translation "Beirat" is provided. See also footnote 527.

526 Cf. Witt (2003), p. 79.

527 In Germany, 52 % of family businesses are organized as limited liability corporation and 30 % as limited partnerships with a limited liability corporation as general partner. Only in exceptional cases, these two types of legal corporation are obliged to appoint a supervisory board (§52 GmbHG; cf. Achleitner/Schraml/Tappeiner (2008), p. 49). A supervisory board is mandatory for public corporations, though this legal form is rare among German family businesses (4%) (cf. Klein (2004), pp. 113 et seq.; §111 I AktG).

528 Cf. Achleitner/Schraml/Klöckner (2008), p. 15; Klein (2000), p. 167. The share of family businesses with a supervisory board is relatively low compared to the fact that two-thirds of non-family businesses have a supervisory board (cf. Klein (2000), p. 167).

529 Cf. Redlefsen (2004), p. 155. In REDLEFSEN's survey of 55 German family businesses, 6% of supervisory boards exclusively comprised family members, 16% exclusively comprised non-family members, and 78% were mixed boards with family and non-family members.

530 Cf. Klein (2000), p. 167. Further, KLEIN has shown that the larger a company is in terms of sales or the lower total equity held by the family, the more likely is the company to have a supervisory board (cf. Klein (2004), p. 137; Klein (2000), p. 167).

supervisory board, this institution might gather greater expertise to supervise and support the company than a committee of family owners.[531] A supervisory board can serve as sparring partner for managers and thus increase quality of management decisions.[532] In case some family members have fallen out with others or cannot settle on a decision, a supervisory board can restore actionability of the family business.[533] Lastly, the supervisory board assures control of managers' performance by stipulating and monitoring targets.[534]

Despite these reasons favoring a supervisory board, there are other reasons against it: Particularly family managers do not like to be supervised, regardless whether supervision is delegated to non-family or family members.[535] Family managers and owners might be discouraged by the increase in complexity and costs the installation of a supervisory board means for the company.[536]

Analysis of the **cooperation between the institutions of corporate governance** in family businesses is complicated by the heterogeneity of family influence on the institutions and by the fact that family members take positions in all three institutions.[537] Both characteristics blur relationships between the institutions of corporate governance.

To simplify the discussion of pre buy-out corporate governance, some types of family businesses will be outlined. The statistics provided above have shown that German family businesses are typically exclusively owned by the family and rarely

531 Cf. Corbetta/Salvato (2004b), p. 218; Hennerkes (1998), p. 165.

532 Cf. Lehmann-Tolkmitt (2008), p. 353; May (2001), pp. 361 et seq.

533 Cf. Hennerkes (1998), pp. 165 et seq.; Redlefsen (2004), p. 69; Lehmann-Tolkmitt (2008), p. 353.

534 Cf. Hennerkes (1998), p. 166; Hinterhuber/Minrath (1994), p. 77.

535 Cf. Johannisson/Huse (2000), p. 361; Klein (2000), p. 167.

536 Cf. Lehmann-Tolkmitt (2008), p. 353; Schwartz/Barnes (1991), p. 276.

537 Cf. Mustakallio/Autio/Zahra (2002), p. 205. Family businesses are also heterogeneous with regard to family characteristics like degree of family dispersion, ownership dispersion, simultaneous presence of several generations, or other family-related variables (cf. Uhlaner/Wright/Huse (2007), p. 231). However, these variables are not taken into consideration here, as they are not the focus of this thesis.

have a supervisory board.[538] With regard to management three different types of family businesses can be distinguished:[539]

In the first type of family businesses, management lies exclusively in the hands of the family. This is the typical constellation in companies led by an owner-manager; these companies can be regarded as newly founded family businesses.[540] The unity of ownership and control in the hands of the family prevents any actions undesired by the family; however, if a supervisory board is not installed in this constellation, decisions by the family – possibly merely by the single owner-manager – will not be checked by another institution of corporate governance.

The second type of family businesses is characterized by a mixed management board comprising family and non-family members. Mixed management boards are likely to be either dominated by family managers or based on equality of family and non-family managers.[541] While a mixed management board combines the experience of non-family managers from other companies with the influence of the family, cooperation between non-family and family managers might not be easy: Internal non-family managers, who have been working in the family businesses for several years and were promoted to managers, are frequently regarded as subordinated to family members.[542] External non-family managers, who joined the family business from a large corporation, might be frustrated by their limited discretion and non-acceptance of their propositions by family managers or owners.[543] Further, family managers might be reluctant to share information with non-family managers to preserve privacy of information or their power.[544] A strong supervisory board could mitigate conflicts or disequilibria between family and non-family managers.

---

538 Exclusive ownership by the family applies to about 80% of family businesses. In further 18%, the family holds a majority. KLEIN has discussed several stipulations to limit control rights of non-family owners in these companies, so that influence of the owning family is affected to a minor degree by the minority owners (cf. Klein (2004), pp. 191 et seq.).

539 Cf. Klein/Bell (2007), p. 20.

540 Cf. Klein (2004), pp. 160 et seq.

541 Cf. Becker (2007), pp. 213 et seq.; Goffee/Scase (1985), p. 88; Redlefsen (2004), pp. 66 et seq., 153. A mixed management board dominated by non-family managers is unlikely to occur in family businesses, given the family typically holds the majority stake in the company (as discussed earlier in this subsection) and might be represented on the supervisory board.

542 Cf. Klein (2004), p. 250.

543 Cf. Klein (2004), pp. 247 et seq.

544 Cf. Upton/Teal/Felan (2001), p. 61.

In the third type of family businesses, only non-family members are in the management. As in the second type, non-family managers can be recruited from within or outside of the family business. Through this separation of ownership and control, a family business approximates a public company with the family as majority block-holder.[545] As discussed above, this governance constellation is more likely to occur in large family businesses than in small companies. Further, absence of family representation on the management board makes the installation of a supervisory board more likely to control management.[546] Despite the formal separation of ownership and control, family owners – especially those that are retired family managers – can be assumed to interfere with management decisions, as is discussed in subsections 5.2.1 and 5.3.1.

These three types of family businesses can be **related to the theories underlying this thesis**: stewardship and agency theory (see Figure 32). Stewardship theory is frequently applied to family businesses, in which ownership and control are united in the hands of the family.[547] In these constellations, stewardship theory is used to explain corporate governance and behavior of the different institutions of corporate governance. Unity of ownership and control in the hands of the family eliminates agency conflicts, which limits applicability of agency theory.[548] If ownership and management are assigned to several members of the family, the family's shared vision and joint goals reduce conflicts of interests between the different family members.[549] A mixed management dominated by family managers is likely to behave alike, as agency conflicts resulting from cooperation with non-family managers are minimized by

545 Cf. Moldenhauer (2007), pp. 79-81.

546 Cf. Klein (2000), p. 167.

547 Cf. subsection 2.2.2. If ownership and management are concentrated in the hands of one person, behavior of this owner-manager is neither captured by stewardship nor agency theory. Both theories are applied to predict behavior of several individuals if ownership and control are split between them. In case of an owner-manager, behavior of one individual does not need to be coordinated and therefore does not lend itself to neither one of these theories.

548 Cf. Jensen/Meckling (1976), pp. 317 et seq., 327 et seq., 350; Fama/Jensen (1983), pp. 306 et seq.; Kellersmann/Winkeljohann (2007), p. 407; Wagner (2008), p. 187. Several empirical studies have supported this argument: Chrisman/Chua/Litz (2004), p. 349; Anderson/Reeb (2003), p. 1323; Ang/Cole/Lin (2000), p. 106.

549 Cf. Uhlaner/Flören/Geerlings (2007), p. 286; Stewart (2003), pp. 389 et seq.; Mustakallio/Autio/Zahra (2002), p. 218; Habbershon/Astrachan (1997), p. 47.

dominating family managers. Control through a supervisory board contradicts individual altruism predicted by stewardship theory; thus, supervisory boards contribute less, the smaller dispersion of family ownership and management is.[550]

Agency theory explains the coordination of owners and managers if ownership and control are separated.[551] The theory is appropriate to explain the behavior of parties involved in case the family business is exclusively managed by external non-family members or an equally mixed management board with external non-family managers. These constellations give rise to two problematic situations: First, non-family managers might pursue their own interests, which might diverge from those of the family. Second, non-family managers might not exert full effort in managing the company. Both situations constitute cases of moral hazard.[552] The lower family influence on the company is, the more likely moral hazard occurs.[553] Installation of a supervisory board or grant of an equity stake to non-family managers can reduce resulting agency costs.[554]

In two constellations, it is a priori unclear which theory to apply. The two constellations are mixed management with internal non-family managers that is not dominated by family managers, and exclusive non-family management with internal managers (hatched areas in Figure 32). In these constellations, applicability of stewardship or agency theory depends on the respective internal non-family managers: Given imprinting by the family culture during his tenure with the company, an internal non-family manager might behave according to stewardship theory.[555] However, adherence to agency theory might also be thinkable. Which theory describes the internal

---

[550] Cf. Fiegener (2005), p. 645.

[551] Cf. subsection 2.2.1.

[552] Cf. Klein/Bell (2007), p. 24; Bhattacharya/Ravikumar (2004), pp. 29, 36; Chua/Chrisman/Sharma (2003), pp. 96-101; Hennerkes (1998), p. 191. CHUA/CHRISMAN/SHARMA assume that agency conflicts and agency costs increase, the more power is delegated to non-family managers (cf. Chua/Chrisman/Sharma (2003), p. 98).

[553] Cf. Corbetta/Salvato (2004b), pp. 128 et seq.

[554] Cf. Corbetta/Salvato (2004b), p. 127; Hennerkes (1998), p. 192. The grant of an equity stake to non-family managers turns these persons into minority stakeholders. However, families are unlikely to grant a significant stake to non-family managers, as this might limit family influence on the company. Thus, grant of equity stakes to non-family managers does neither contradict the above statistics on ownership stake held by the family nor does it turn the company into a non-family business.

[555] Cf. Klein/Bell (2007), p. 28; subsection 5.3.5.

non-family manager better depends on personal characteristics, tenure in the family business, and intensity of family culture. If internal and external non-family managers are on the management board in both constellations, presumably agency theory might be more applicable.

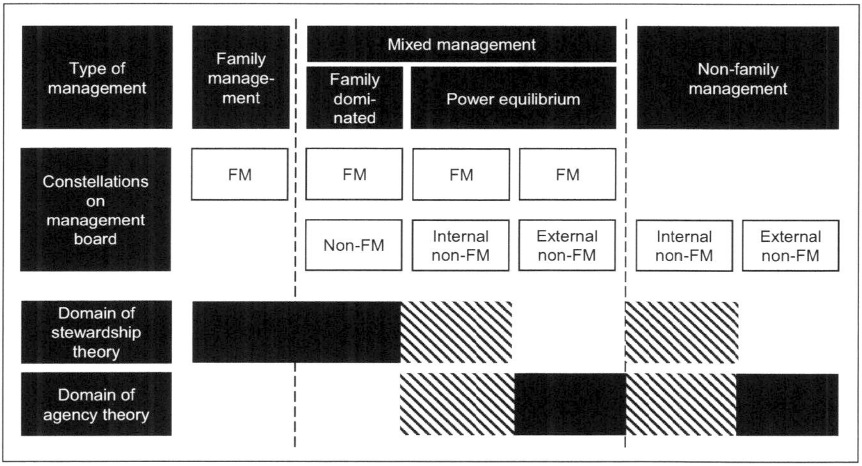

Figure 32: Management constellations and related theories

Source: Author's illustration
Hatched areas can be related to both theories; FM = family manager

Although management constellations which suggest applicability of agency theory are possible, they are not very likely to occur for two reasons: On the one hand, statistics on family involvement in management in Table 15 have shown that family members manage the family business either exclusively or jointly with non-family managers. On the other hand, through their role as owners of the company, family members can be expected to influence management, given the close relationship between owners and managers in private companies and the fact that family owners either hold all or a majority share of family business' equity; the influence of family members on management can be assumed to entail management behavior according to stewardship theory.

5.1.2. Corporate governance in portfolio companies

Analysis of the corporate governance in portfolio companies will also start with the institutions of corporate governance. The first institution under scrutiny is **ownership structure**. Portfolio companies are owned by at least two parties: one or a small group of private equity companies and the management team.[556] Investors typically hold majority stakes to control portfolio companies.[557]

Equity participation of management is expected and promoted by the private equity company, to ensure motivation of the management.[558] Management's equity stake puts a part of the managers' personal wealth at risk and renders a positive company development more profitable for managers.[559] However, some managers are reported not to favor equity participation, given it puts a considerable share of their tangible fortune at risk of the buy-out in addition to their personal human capital.[560]

While these two types of owners occur in the ownership structure of all types of buy-outs, a third type of owner is particular to buy-outs in family businesses: the former family owner. Empirical evidence on equity participation of the former family owners post buy-out is rather scarce: While many earlier studies neglected this type of owner, 8 (13%) former family owners held a stake post buy-out in the survey of JAKOBY and 12 (55%) companies of the sample underlying this thesis.[561] As discussed

556 Cf. Jensen (1989b), p. 65.

557 Cf. Shleifer/Vishny (1997), p. 766. For first research on minority stakes of private equity companies in family businesses, see Achleitner/Schraml/Tappeiner (2008). Private equity companies might syndicate their investments with other private equity companies to increase quality of their deal flow, to improve funding capacity vis-à-vis the portfolio company, and to reduce risk (cf. Hug/Ernst (2003), pp. 445 et seq.; Lerner (1994), pp. 17 et seq.; Nathusius (2005), pp. 79-103). However, WRIGHT/LOCKETT found that syndication in mature buy-out companies is less frequent than in more risky, early stage investments (cf. Wright/Lockett (2003), p. 2076).

558 Cf. Jensen (1986), p. 326. Private equity companies promote the acquisition of equity stakes by management through granting sweet equity (i.e. management invests predominantly into nominal capital and not into capital reserves) and exempting management from providing shareholders' loans (cf. Kitzmann (2005), p. 30; Bächle/Hager (1999), pp. 83 et seq.).

559 Cf. Cotter/Peck (2001), p. 102; Tobler (1998), p. 46.

560 Cf. Forst (1992), p. 107; Howorth/Westhead/Wright (2004), p. 526.

561 Cf. Jakoby (2000), p. 281; subsection 3.2.4. JAKOBY indicates that equity stakes held by former family owners varied between 5% and 60%. In this study, equity stakes varied between 5% and 30% (a majority stake held by former family owners is excluded by definition, cf. subsection 2.1.2).

in subsection 4.2.2.5, equity stakes for former family owners serve to reduce the risk for private equity companies and let the family participate in the post buy-out development of the company.

Table 16 provides empirical data on average equity stakes of private equity companies and management after the buy-out. As the studies until 2000 do not reflect current market trends, the results of GEIDNER are the most recent and thus appear to be the best indicator of the distribution of ownership between private equity company and management.[562] According to GEIDNER, management holds on average a significant minority stake. Presumably, the remainder or a large fraction is held by the private equity company. Although GEIDNER looks at larger spin-off buy-outs and argues that management stake is negatively correlated with company size, companies underlying this sample underline the validity of her results by the fact that management held between 0% and 40% (although sample companies were smaller than in GEIDNER'S sample).[563]

---

[562] A trend over the last years is the increased activity of more private equity companies in the market for succession in German family businesses (between 2000 and 2007, the number of buy-outs in family businesses has tripled from 10 to 30 and total deal volume has increased by seven times from € 258m to € 1914m (cf. Klöckner (2008), pp. 13 et seq.)). Increased activity of private equity companies might favor more frequent participation and higher equity stakes of investors in buy-outs in family businesses.

[563] Cf. Geidner (2009), p. 145. GEIDNER'S findings are further backed by the survey of FORST, who found that private equity companies held the majority stake in 52.5% of buy-outs in family businesses compared to managers holding majority stakes in 43.5% (cf. Forst (1992), p. 72).

		Average equity stakes (in %) held by	
Author, year	Sample composition	Private equity company	Management
Geidner (2009)	24 Buy-outs in German non-family businesses	n/a	17.0
Jakoby (2000)	62 Buy-outs in German family and non-family businesses	n/a	74.4
Vest (1995)	29 Buy-outs in German non-family businesses	47.9 (13)	51.7 (16)
Luippold (1991)	19 Buy-outs in German family and non-family businesses	50.5 (14)	39.3 (18)

Table 16: Survey results on equity distribution between management and private equity companies after the buy-out

Source: Geidner (2009), p. 228; Jakoby (2000), p. 276; Vest (1995), p. 248; Luippold (1991), p. 342
Numbers in brackets indicate the number of respondents/cases underlying the particular question; Missing equity stakes to 100% are held by other owners[564]

The second institution of corporate governance is **management**. Investment managers of private equity companies are not directly involved in the management of portfolio companies. On the one hand, staff of private equity companies is so limited in numbers that investors cannot afford to delegate investment managers for a longer period to the company. On the other hand, private equity companies are not allowed to directly interfere with portfolio companies, if they do not want to lose a tax privilege according to German law.[565]

Therefore, private equity companies rely on managers, who have been with the portfolio company already before the buy-out (so called management buy-outs) or who joined the company after the buy-out (management buy-ins).[566] In case of management buy-outs, managers are familiar with the company and its environment; thus, they have an advantage over the management team of a management buy-in, as the latter are

564 JAKOBY did not provide an average percentage for the equity stake held by private equity companies.

565 Cf. Bundesministerium der Finanzen (2003), p. 5.

566 Cf. Wright et al. (1993), p. 93.

ignorant of much company-specific knowledge that will be lost through the replacement of pre buy-out management.[567] Yet, pre buy-out management might not be willing to run the risk of a buy-out, which might leave a management buy-in as last option.[568] Managers in a management buy-in are more opportunistic, more proactive and willing to take a greater risk.[569] However, private equity companies have difficulties to assess the quality of these managers, given they have no opportunity to observe them in the potential post buy-out position.[570]

Figure 33 shows the relation of management buy-ins to all buy-outs in terms of numbers. The figure shows that over the last years, management buy-ins have become more frequent for all buy-outs and buy-outs in family businesses. Until 2005, management buy-ins used to be more frequent among buy-outs in family businesses than among the other types of buy-outs. Since 2005, every second buy-out in family businesses is a management buy-in. Possibly, private equity companies were not convinced by pre buy-out managers, so that they chose to install new managers increasingly frequent.[571]

---

567 Cf. Robbie/Wright (1995), p. 532.

568 Cf. Robbie/Wright (1996), p. 20

569 Cf. Robbie/Wright (1995), pp. 532 et seq. These characteristics might be reflected in the fact that operational changes in portfolio companies seem greater after management buy-ins compared to management buy-outs (cf. Robbie/Wright/Thompson (1992), pp. 450 et seq., 454 et seq.).

570 Cf. Robbie/Wright/Thompson (1992), p. 455; Robbie/Wright (1995), p. 533. This might be a possible explanation, why performance of management buy-ins frequently falls short of expectations and is below performance of management buy-outs (cf. Robbie/Wright/Thompson (1992), pp. 453, 455).

571 Private equity companies are free to choose between continuing with pre buy-out management and replacing it with new management, as sale negotiations take place between family owners and the private equity company and managers are typically only marginally involved in the sale process (cf. subsection 4.2.2.3).

Figure 33: Number of management buy-ins relative to buy-outs

Source: Klöckner (2008), p. 21 (n=12,600 (all buy-outs); n=3,900 (buy-outs in family businesses))[572]

Another peculiarity of buy-outs in family businesses is continued family involvement in company management after the buy-out. A survey of the EVCA has shown that family involvement does not discontinue at the buy-out, but rather fades out over time.[573] The only anecdotal evidence on this issue provided HOWORTH/WESTHEAD/WRIGHT, who have shown that family members remained on the management board in four of their eight sample companies. In two of these four sample companies, private equity companies replaced family managers within two years after the buy-out for their poor management skills.[574]

---

[572] In the CMBOR database, the group of management buy-ins also comprises buy-ins management buy-outs (BIMBOs) and institutional buy-ins (cf. subsection 2.1.2).

[573] Cf. European Private Equity & Venture Capital Association (2005), p. 19.

[574] Cf. Howorth/Wright/Westhead (2007), pp. 14, 30. In the third sample company, the family manager left management eight years after the buy-out, and in the fourth sample company, family members bought the company back and took over the entire management board.

The third institution of corporate governance analyzed is the **supervisory board**. Private equity companies frequently delegate representatives to supervisory boards of portfolio companies.[575] Board representation is needed to monitor management, as private equity companies are not allowed to interfere with management directly but are heavily invested in portfolio companies.[576] Besides this monitoring task, supervisory board also gives advice to management and thus plays the role of a sparring partner.[577] Although empirical evidence on the frequency of supervisory boards in German portfolio companies does not exist[578], ACHLEITNER/SCHRAML/TAPPEINER found that installation of a supervisory board is a requirement private equity companies demand before buying a minority stake in German family businesses.[579] Members of the supervisory board are frequently representatives of the private equity company, but also independent businessmen, who contribute expertise in certain fields relevant for the company and who represent the private equity company.[580]

Similar to their involvement in ownership and management board, former family owners can join or remain on the supervisory board after the buy-out. Only SANDER provides empirical evidence for this possibility and reports of a bought-out company, whose former family owner sat on the supervisory board post buy-out.[581]

Analysis of **cooperation between the institutions of corporate governance** in portfolio companies is more straightforward than in family businesses, due to the considerable degree of homogeneity between portfolio companies. By the definition of a buy-out underlying this thesis,[582] private equity companies hold majority stakes in

575 Cf. Sander (2006), p. 171; Singh (1990), pp. 117, 126; Cornelli/Karakas (2008), pp. 70, 74.

576 Cf. Cotter/Peck (2001), pp. 135, 137; Wright et al. (1996), pp. 361 et seq.; Kessel (1995), p. 143; Denis (1994), p. 204; Smith (1990), p. 144; Baker/Wruck (1989), pp. 181, 189; DeAngelo/DeAngelo (1987), p. 43. Representation on the supervisory board does not endanger the tax exemption of private equity companies but is explicitly admitted (cf. Bundesministerium der Finanzen (2003), p. 5).

577 Cf. Achleitner/Schraml/Tappeiner (2008), pp. 52 et seq.; Baker/Wruck (1989), p. 189.

578 This statement reflects the author's best knowledge.

579 Cf. Achleitner/Schraml/Tappeiner (2008), p. 50.

580 Cf. Sharp (2003), p. 100; Achleitner/Schraml/Tappeiner (2008), p. 51; Cornelli/Karakas (2008), p. 66.

581 Cf. Sander (2006), p. 171.

582 Cf. subsection 2.1.2.

portfolio companies and delegate representatives to the supervisory board. Management holds a minority stake and leads the portfolio companies. This separation of ownership and control and the absence of a kindredship link between both parties calls for the **application of agency theory** in portfolio companies.[583]

A large stream of literature has discussed how buy-outs in public companies reduce agency conflicts that existed in these companies before the buy-out. BERG/GOTTSCHALG have subsumed measures to reduce agency costs into three groups of measures:[584] First, the equity stake of management aligns interests of owners and managers.[585] Second, intensive and skilled monitoring of private equity companies mitigates information asymmetries between owners and managers.[586] Third, the increased level of debt typical in buy-out transactions limits managerial discretion.[587]

Given the scarcity of research on buy-outs in family businesses, it is not surprising that agency theory has yet not been applied to portfolio companies, which were former family businesses. With the change of the starting point from a widely held public corporation with an atomistic shareholder structure to a privately held family business controlled by a close circle of kindred family owners, effects of two of the three measures to reduce agency costs are inverted. While management holds an

583 HOWORTH/WESTHEAD/WRIGHT have found that stewardship characteristics could be found in former family businesses which were sold without the involvement of private equity companies. In contrast, managers of portfolio companies backed by private equity companies showed traits that are better explained by agency theory (cf. Howorth/Wright/Westhead (2007), pp. 16-18, 30).

Despite the separation of ownership and control, private equity companies and managers of portfolio companies retain a working relationship incomparably closer compared to a relationship in public corporations (cf. Sharp (2003), p. 96). This closeness is due to the close cooperation between both parties and the ownership concentration in the hands of the private equity company.

584 Cf. Berg/Gottschalg (2005), pp. 20-23. This subsumption follows Wright et al. (1996), pp. 60-62.

585 Cf. Cotter/Peck (2001), p. 166; Lichtenberg/Siegel (1990), p. 102; Hite/Vetsuypens (1989), p. 955; Bull (1989), p. 264; DeAngelo/DeAngelo (1987), p. 41; Jensen (1986), p. 326.

586 Cf. sources in footnote 576. For this involvement and intensive monitoring, private equity companies are also regarded as active investors (cf. Jensen (1989a), p. 36; Wright et al. (1996), pp. 61 et seq.).

587 Cf. subsection 7.1.2; Fox/Marcus (1992), pp. 67 et seq.; Stulz (1990), p. 23; Smith (1990), p. 163; Baker/Wruck (1989), p. 189; Jensen (1986), pp. 323 et seq.;

equity stake post buy-out, this stake is presumably lower than it was before the buy-out, if the family business was led by family managers.[588] In consequence, interests of owners and managers in the portfolio company are aligned to a lower degree compared to the pre buy-out state.[589] The argument for monitoring follows a similar line: Despite intensive monitoring of management by private equity companies, this monitoring is unlikely to attain the same intensity and profoundness of monitoring by family owners, given family owners' frequent involvement in the company pre buy-out.[590] Only debt as measure to reduce agency costs can be assumed to positively affect managerial behavior after buy-outs in family businesses. Thus, two of the three levers of value creation in buy-outs explained by agency theory hardly reduce agency costs of buy-outs, when contrasting buy-outs in family businesses with those in public companies (see Figure 34).

The conclusion of this discussion of agency theory is the following: While buy-outs in public companies reduce agency conflicts, buy-outs in family businesses potentially create new agency conflicts. Thus, agency theory lends itself to analyze post buy-out characteristics of portfolio companies. A synthesis of the theories best describing the situation of a bought-out family business pre buy-out and post buy-out suggests that buy-outs in family businesses correspond to a transition of the companies from a stewardship-minded setting to an agency-minded setting. This transition serves as background of argumentation throughout the following chapters of the thesis.

---

[588] Only about 10% of family businesses are exclusively managed by non-family managers (cf. subsection 5.1.1).

[589] Minority stakes of management do not completely eliminate agency conflicts (Cf. Jensen/Meckling (1976), p. 317).

[590] Involvement can take place either directly through family owners being members of the management board or indirectly through influencing management decisions as will be discussed in subsection 5.2.1.

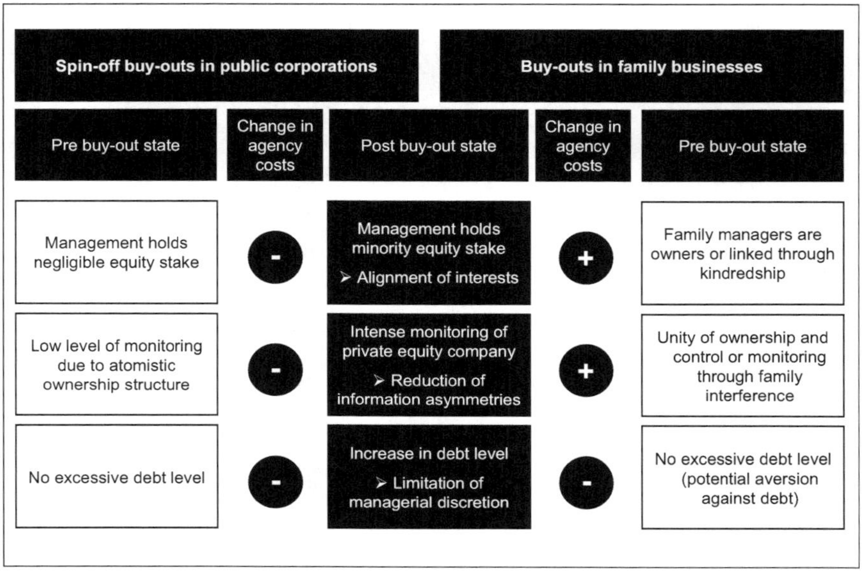

Figure 34: Comparison of changes in agency costs after buy-outs in public corporations and family businesses

Source: Author's illustration

5.2 Expected changes based on the literature

5.2.1. Owner influence on management decisions

Although the separation of ownership and control results in two autonomous institutions of corporate governance, namely ownership and management, this separation does not imply that no interaction between both parties takes place. In fact, interaction is necessary for owners to ensure that managers know what goals they are expected to pursue. However, the degree of this interaction may be expected to differ between family businesses and portfolio companies.

In family businesses, owner influence differs according to the constellation of management board composition: In case management lies exclusively in the hands of the family, unity of ownership and management provides owners with the maximal influence on management decisions. But also in case of mixed or exclusive non-family management, family owners or fellow family managers are frequently tempted to intervene in management decisions.[591] Family members might intervene to prevent decisions detrimental to family wealth, to enforce pursuit of particular family goals or to support non-family managers.[592] Especially former family managers who retired might interfere with management decisions because they are used to do so.[593] After the buy-out, private equity companies do not directly interfere with the management.[594] Investment managers give managers high discretionary room over operational decisions, as long as the performance targets are achieved.[595] As explained above, investment managers do not interfere with operative management decisions because they are deterred by law and because they lack thorough understanding of the company and its environment.[596] However, investment managers provide advice to the management on critical or far-reaching decisions through the supervisory board or through approval rights reserved for private equity companies.[597] So, owner influence on management decisions seems to decrease significantly through the buy-out.[598]

5.2.2. Owner influence on corporate strategy

Strategy can be seen as an important link between owners' goals for the company's future and management's decisions in day to day operations.[599] While family owners aim at making profits and several other, equally important goals like achieving

---

591 Cf. Hennerkes (1998), pp. 192 et seq.; Mertens (2004), pp. 28 et seq. The first author recommends stipulation of rights and obligations of non-family management and family members to prevent this undermining of the power of non-family managers.

592 Cf. subsection 5.1.1; Hall/Nordqvist (2008), pp. 61 et seq.; Klein/Bell (2007), pp. 28 et seq.; Harvey/Evans (1994), p. 341.

593 Cf. Sonnenfeld/Spence (1989), pp. 368 et seq.; Holland/Boulton (1984), pp. 20 et seq.

594 Cf. Achleitner/Achleitner (2000), p. 140; Sander (2006), p. 174.

595 Cf. Singh (1990), p. 126.

596 Cf. subsection 5.1.2; Sharp (2003), p. 97.

597 Cf. Sharp (2003), p. 87; Webb (1985), p. 101.

598 This formulation of an expected change is not intended to be a pre-state of a proposition. This (and alike) statements are merely a conclusion of the changes that might be expected from literature. This (and alike) sentences are not tested in the empirical section(s). See section 1.4 and footnote 37.

599 Due to the multitude of possible strategies a company can pursue, this subsection only considers those strategies, which were pursued by sample companies either before or after the buy-out (cf. subsection 5.3.2).

excellence, handing the company over to the next generation, or conserving employment, private equity companies merely aim at maximizing company value.[600] In consequence, changes in the strategy can be expected after the buy-out.

The most generic strategy is organic growth.[601] DAILY/DOLLINGER have found two contradictory characteristics influencing this strategy in family businesses. On the one hand, family managers foster innovations within the company as a base for further growth.[602] On the other hand, family businesses tend to pursue a rather conservative strategy not explicitly aiming at growth, thus forgoing the strength from innovations.[603] This reservation towards growth might be explainable by the fact that family managers are unwilling to let the company outgrow their own capabilities, what would necessitate installation of non-family managers.[604] Post buy-out, private equity companies pressure portfolio companies towards growth in order to increase the latter's value.[605] A study on business strategy by the EVCA has shown that growth related objectives became more important after the buy-out.[606] So, former family businesses are expected to pursue a strategy of more aggressive growth post buy-out.

Given portfolio companies' strong market positions, which were expected as investment criterion by private equity companies, internationalization might be more

---

600 On the goals of family businesses, see Achleitner/Schraml/Klöckner (2008), p. 18; Tagiuri/Davis (1992), p. 46. On the goals of private equity companies, see Becker (2000), p. 30; Sharp (2003), p. 45; Kessel (1995), pp. 129 et seq.

Besides these differences in goals, there are also differences in terms of pressure to reach these goals. Family managers are accountable to family owners; both are linked through kindredship, so that family owners might be expected to be more forgiving in case targets are missed. In contrast, private equity companies are accountable to their investors and pass this pressure on to managers.

601 In this context, organic growth means growth in the domestic market by expanding company activities excluding growth through acquisitions. In contrast, internationalization means growth in foreign markets by expanding company activities.

602 Cf. Daily/Dollinger (1992), pp. 123, 133; Donckels/Fröhlich (1991), p. 156; PriceWaterhouseCoopers (2008a), p. 20. This is in line with family businesses' goal to strive for excellent products (cf. Tagiuri/Davis (1992), p. 46).

603 Cf. LeCornu et al. (1996), p. 11; Dreux (1990), p. 228; Daily/Dollinger (1992), pp. 123, 133; Donckels/Fröhlich (1991), p. 159.

604 Cf. Whisler (1988), pp. 311, 313; Daily/Dollinger (1992), p. 133; Dreux (1990), p. 228.

605 Cf. Sharp (2003), p. 17; Wright/Hoskisson/Busenitz (2001), p. 118. Post buy-out, non-family managers have a self-interest to pursue ambitious growth targets, as this reflects their own power, increases their compensation and creates new positions for managers within the organization (cf. Daily/Dollinger (1992), pp. 122 et seq.).

606 Cf. European Private Equity & Venture Capital Association (2005), p. 20.

promising than further growth in markets, where the company is already active.[607] Family businesses internationalize with caution and mostly concentrate on a small number of foreign markets.[608] Possible reasons for this might be that family businesses try to avoid excessive risk or that they lack know-how and financial resources to internationalize.[609] In their striving for growth, private equity companies might push managers to expand into new markets after the buy-out.[610] But internationalization brings about several pitfalls, which make it less attractive to investors, like a high degree of uncertainty, considerable front-up costs and a potentially long lead time until it pays off.[611] Thus, it is unclear whether buy-outs foster or inhibit internationalization of a portfolio company.

Besides organic growth, companies can grow through acquisitions. Family businesses seem to be hesitant towards acquisitions: In a recent survey, only every fifth family business considered acquiring another company.[612] Possibly, family businesses refrain from acquisitions as they consider buying other companies not their core competence and might have no experience in post-merger integration. After the buy-out, private equity companies motivate portfolio companies to grow through acquisitions.[613] Investors can actively support acquisitions through their experience in this field and their financial backing.[614] The fact that private equity companies look for potential portfolio companies in consolidating industries as discussed in subsection 4.2.2.1 underlines this argument. In a survey, KITCHING found that 30% of UK portfolio companies made acquisitions in the aftermath of the buy-out.[615] So, portfolio companies are expected to pursue acquisitions post buy-out.

---

607 Cf. subsection 4.2.2.1.

608 Cf. Zahra (2003), p. 507; Fernández/Nieto (2005), p. 86; Harris/Martinez/Ward (1994), pp. 166 et seq.

609 Cf. Donckels/Fröhlich (1991), p. 159; Cappuyns (2006), pp. 445, 456 et seq.; Gallo/Sveen (1991), pp. 185 et seq.

610 Cf. Pütter (2001), pp. 9 et seq.; F.A.Z. Institut (2005), pp. 34 et seq.

611 Cf. Sharp (2003), p. 18.

612 Cf. PriceWaterhouseCoopers (2006), p. 16.

613 Cf. Sharp (2003), p. 17; Liebeskind/Wiersema/Hansen (1992), pp. 82 et seq.

614 Cf. Achleitner/Schraml/Tappeiner (2008), p. 70; Pütter (2001), p. 10.

615 Cf. Kitching (1989), p. 79. The percentage given compares to about 10% of US portfolio companies doing acquisitions post buy-out. The author does not provide possible explanations for this difference.

Another strategy ensuing the buy-out might be reorganization to increase organizational efficiency and profitability. As described above, family businesses pursue a multitude of goals and are thus less focused on maximizing profits than non-family businesses.[616] This might lead to family owners' and managers' focusing rather on sales and production than on organizational efficiency and profits.[617] After the buy-out, managers are expected to increase organizational efficiency and, thus, improve profitability and cash flows.[618] To achieve this goal, typical measures include lying off employees, reducing wages, decreasing marketing and sales costs, and reducing inventory.[619] Typically, buy-outs also entail selling of unused assets and divisions; given the moderate company size of typical family businesses sold through buy-outs, scope for these sales seems rather limited among sample companies.[620] In consequence, the buy-out is expected to intensify efforts to increase profitability in portfolio companies.

5.2.3. Supervision by and support from the supervisory board

In family businesses, supervisory boards are rather the exception than a widespread institution, as explained in subsection 5.1.1. Only about one third of family businesses have a supervisory board, possibly due to the frequent unity of ownership and management in the hands of the family and the stewardship relation between family owners and non-family managers.[621] As explained in subsection 5.1.2, portfolio companies typically have a supervisory board for two reasons: First, board members support managers by contributing their expertise. Second, board members mitigate

---

616 Cf. Donckels/Fröhlich (1991), p. 159. In contrast, DREUX does not support this argument but argues that profitability of family businesses exceeds that of non-family businesses, without supporting it with evidence (cf. Dreux (1990), p. 228). However, this objection does not affect the further line of argumentation, as portfolio companies differ significantly from typical non-family businesses.

617 Cf. Dreux (1990), p. 228.

618 Cf. Fox/Marcus (1992), p. 75; European Private Equity & Venture Capital Association (2005), p. 20. For the rationale to improve cash flows, see subsection 7.1.2.

619 Cf. Vest (1995), pp. 159-168; F.A.Z. Institut (2005), p. 34; Sharp (2003), pp. 17 et seq.

620 Cf. Liebeskind/Wiersema/Hansen (1992), p. 75 et seq., 82 et seq.; Berg/Gottschalg (2005), pp. 19 et seq.; Sharma/Manikutty (2005), p. 305.

621 The stewardship relation means that the manager does not give in to its self-interest but pursues the goals of the family owners. A monitoring supervisory board would constitute an agency relation-oriented control of the manager, and induce the latter to diverge from the behavior predicted by the stewardship relation (cf. Davis/Schoorman/Donaldson (1997b), p. 39).

agency conflicts by monitoring managers and thus ensuring that managers do not act to the detriment of the private equity company. Thus, after the buy-out, supervisory boards are expected to be installed in portfolio companies.

Board composition is a major determinant of the contribution, a supervisory board can make to the company. Independent board members with experience in areas relevant to the company would be desirable.[622] Table 17 shows that many seats on supervisory boards of German family businesses are assigned to confidants of the family: Family members, bankers, auditors, and lawyers.[623] Their contribution to the board is doubtful, given they might lack the above described independence and expertise.[624] In contrast, private equity companies typically send investment managers, industry experts, experienced entrepreneurs or other individuals with relevant expertise to the supervisory board.[625] Differences in the strategy of appointment suggest that the composition of supervisory boards is expected to change from confidants of the family to individuals supporting the company.

Type of member of the supervisory board	Frequency
Family member	65%
Active manager	38%
Lawyer	32%
Banker	30%
Entrepreneur	30%
Auditor	26%
Retired manager	19%

Table 17: Classification of members in supervisory boards of family businesses

Source: Klein (2004), p. 145 (n=200 companies)

[622] Cf. Ward/Handy (1988), p. 304.

[623] This data is supported by the survey of SCHWARTZ/BARNES, who found that 69.1% of supervisory boards of US family businesses do not comprise non-family members besides bankers, lawyers and auditors (cf. Schwartz/Barnes (1991), p. 275).

KLEIN provides two reasons for representation of these professions: First, they are confidants of family managers or owners. Second, appointment of external experts (like external managers or entrepreneurs) could be understood as revelation that the expertise expected from a supervisory board might not be available in the owning family (cf. Klein (2000), p. 169).

[624] Cf. Schwartz/Barnes (1991), p. 283; Hennerkes (1998), p. 166.

[625] Cf. Achleitner/Schraml/Tappeiner (2008), pp. 50 et seq.; Sharp (2003), pp. 99 et seq.

Fulfillment of the supervisory board's functions, supervising and supporting management, depends on the composition of the supervisory board. Composition of the board in family businesses presented above make execution of these functions less likely: While family members might not support the board with genuinely diverse resources and insights, bankers, auditors, and lawyers might be guided by their own interest instead of that of the company.[626] Further, bankers, lawyers, auditors, and friends are prone to be mere followers of the family manager or owner and might not question decisions.[627] Independence and thus supervision of the remaining board members may be doubted as well.[628] Post buy-out changes in board composition also influence the board's ability to exert supervision and provide support. The absence of a relationship based on business relations or kinship grants members of the supervisory board the independence they need to effectively supervise management.[629] Selection of board members according to qualification instead of familiarity endows the board with the resources needed to support management.[630] In a survey, managers appreciated the installation of a sound board as most important non-financial contribution of the private equity company.[631] In consequence, supervisory boards monitor more tightly and support management better after the buy-out than before.

5.2.4. Composition of the management team

As buy-outs significantly transform former family businesses, they might be expected to have an impact on the composition of the management team for two reasons: On the one hand, pre buy-out management might not want to continue leading the company given family managers are no longer majority owners of the company and pre buy-out

[626] Cf. Corbetta/Salvato (2004b), p. 129; Klein (2000), p. 169; Schwartz/Barnes (1991), p. 283; Hennerkes (1998), p. 166. In contrast, another empirical study has shown that performance of family businesses with non-family members on the supervisory board was lower than companies without non-family members on the board (cf. Schulze et al. (2001), p. 111).

[627] Cf. Brunninge/Nordqvist/Wiklund (2007), p. 304; Hennerkes (1998), p. 166.

[628] Non-family members on the supervisory board of family businesses can only make their full contribution if their interference is honestly desired by family managers (cf. Schwartz/Barnes (1991), p. 283).

[629] Cf. Achleitner/Schraml/Tappeiner (2008), pp. 53, 68; Sharp (2003), pp. 100 et seq.

[630] Cf. Baker/Wruck (1989), pp. 181 et seq.; Sharp (2003), pp. 101 et seq.; Webb (1985), p. 101.

[631] Cf. European Private Equity & Venture Capital Association (2005), p. 26.

non-family managers might not want to run the risk of a buy-out.[632] On the other hand, private equity companies look for managers with profiles and qualifications, who seem more adequate to make the buy-out work.[633] Thus, numerous changes in the composition of the management team may be expected; some of these changes already occurred before the buy-out as reported in subsection 4.2.1.3.[634] HOWORTH/WESTHEAD/WRIGHT found changes in the management team in seven of the eight sample companies examined after the buy-out.[635] A survey among buy-outs in German family businesses found that in 55% of portfolio companies, composition of the management team was changed after the buy-out.[636]

Family managers following the strategy of a clear cut with the family business might want to resign from management at the buy-out. In case they follow the strategy of a fading, minor influence, pre buy-out family managers might wish to remain on the management board. However, private equity companies might object due to doubts whether the respective manager is the right person to lead the company through the buy-out. Another reason for objection might be the fear of conflicts between family managers and private equity companies or non-family managers; these conflicts might also convince family managers to leave the company after the buy-out.[637] In consequence, family managers are expected to leave the management board at or some time after the buy-out.

Despite the advantage pre buy-out non-family managers have with regard to their intimate knowledge of the company and its environment, they are frequently replaced. These managers might not fulfill investors' expectations of buy-out

---

632 Cf. subsection 5.1.2 for reasons why managers might not want to participate in the buy-out and subsection 4.2.2.5 for family owners' and managers' separation from the company.

633 Cf. subsection 4.2.2.1; Huydts (1992), pp. 32 et seq.; Sharp (2003), pp. 19-21.

634 The fact that most buy-outs in the sample companies are management buy-outs does not indicate that there were no changes in the management team induced by the buy-out; management buy-out in this context merely means that at least one team member has not been replaced directly after the buy-out.

635 Cf. Howorth/Wright/Westhead (2007), p. 30. ROBBIE/WRIGHT support this high figure of management turnover by finding that management changes occurred in 74% of UK management buy-ins examined (cf. Robbie/Wright (1996), p. 87).

636 Cf. F.A.Z. Institut (2002), p. 18. A study by the EVCA has shown that on average, one of four managers leaves the company and two others join management after the buy-out (cf. European Private Equity & Venture Capital Association (2005), p. 18).

637 Cf. subsection 4.1.2.5 for family's strategies on separation from the family business and subsection 4.2.2.5 on conflicts between private equity companies and family managers.

managers, as family owners or fellow family managers might have based their recruiting decision on different criteria. Family owners or managers might look for non-family managers who subordinate their opinion to those of family members, who are entrepreneurial but leave final decisions to family members, or who are very experienced in their function or industry but might lack experience in leadership.[638] Non-family managers might not be used to shoulder responsibility, as some family managers refrain from delegating it.[639] In contrast, private equity companies typically look for managers, who are risk takers, have proven their leadership skills and have gathered industry and functional experience.[640] Pre buy-out managers fulfilling these criteria can be expected to remain on the management board. The network and personal experience of investment managers further facilitate changes on the management board and represent an advantage family owners lack.[641] All these factors can be expected to explain changes in the management team after the buy-out.

While all the reasons explaining changes in the management team stated above hold in general for most non-family managers, they might be particularly true for Chief Financial Officers (CFOs).[642] In many family businesses, the responsible person for financing is a family manager who resigns after the buy-out and who, thus, has to be replaced.[643] If financing is the responsibility of a non-family manager or a non-resigning family manager, doubts might be cast whether this person fulfils the requirements a buy-out entails.[644] Given the importance and specialty of the financial structure of buy-outs, a CFO is supposed to be able to improve financial practices in the company, internally supervise the financial soundness of the company, and

---

638 Cf. Klein/Bell (2007), p. 30; Hennerkes (1998), p. 185; Westhead (1997), pp. 129 et seq.

639 Cf. Hickey (2005), p. 31; Huydts (1992), pp. 41-43; Schachner/Speckbacher/Wentges (2006), pp. 603 et seq. The last authors add that likelihood and intensity of delegation increase with company size.

640 Cf. subsection 4.2.2.1; Huydts (1992), pp. 32 et seq.; Sharp (2003), pp. 19-21.

641 Cf. Achleitner/Schraml/Tappeiner (2008), p. 69.

642 For simplicity, the term CFO embraces in the following also the head of accounting, management accounting and financing, if this person is no senior manager and thus not member of the management board.

643 Cf. Achleitner/Schraml/Klöckner (2008), pp. 22 et seq. In contrast, a survey among Spanish family businesses showed that 81% of CFOs in family businesses are non-family managers (cf. Gallo/Tàpies/Cappuyns (2004), p. 313); however, this survey focuses on large family businesses.

644 Cf. Filbeck/Lee (2000), pp. 212 et seq.

communicate with financial partners - in particular banks and private equity companies.[645] So, especially the CFO is expected to be replaced in the buy-out.

5.2.5. Motivation and compensation of management

Buy-outs put severe pressure on managers and imply high risk. Nevertheless, a multitude of motivations makes managers endeavor to do a buy-out. Table 18 provides an overview of surveys on the different motivations:[646] First, managers might be fascinated by the opportunity to develop the company they want to buy out.[647] Second, managers might want to become entrepreneurs to take their decisions independently.[648] Third, managers might be intrigued by the financial rewards buy-outs promise.[649] Fourth, managers might feel personally committed to the company and its employees; especially long-serving, internal managers, who acted as stewards and forwent self-interest for the sake of family owners and the company, might feel personally committed to keep the company going, when family owners have to retire.[650] Fifth, managers might long for self-fulfillment in doing a buy-out and leading their own company.[651] Sixth, management buy-outs can prevent other companies from taking over the respective company and thus help incumbent managers to remain in their position.[652] So, there are several motivations that are expected to induce managers to perform a buy-out.

---

645 Cf. Webb (1985), p. 47.

646 Cf. European Private Equity & Venture Capital Association (2005), p. 14. For further surveys, see Forst (1992), p. 87; Luippold (1991), p. 340.

647 Cf. Kitching (1989), p. 75.

648 Cf. Becker (2000), p. 22; Forst (1992), p. 87. Being an entrepreneur also brings about a certain status and prestige, managers might like (cf. Huydts (1992), p. 37; Luippold (1991), p. 42). Entrepreneur in this context does not refer to an owner-manager of a newly or recently founded company (cf. subsection 2.1.1). The entrepreneur is a person who accepts risk to exploit an opportunity without regard to the resources to do so (cf. Dees (2001), pp. 2,5; Achleitner/Heister/Stahl (2007), p. 6).

649 Cf. Luippold (1991), pp. 42 et seq.; von Boxberg (1991), p. 204 et seq. In a survey, KITCHING found that making a fortune is the most important goal for buy-out managers in the USA, whereas it ranked third among buy-out managers in the UK (Kitching (1989), p. 75).

650 Cf. European Private Equity & Venture Capital Association (2005), p. 14; Howorth/Westhead/ Wright (2004), p. 526.

651 Cf. Huydts (1992), p. 37; Luippold (1991), p. 25.

652 Cf. Luippold (1991), p. 42.

Author, year	Sample composition	Motivation for the buy-out
European Private Equity & Venture Capital Association (2005)	117 European family businesses; average value on Likert scale (5 = very important; 1 = very unimportant)	4.3 Opportunity of company 3.8 Being entrepreneur 3.6 Financial rewards 2.9 Commitment to company/employees 2.8 Self-fulfillment 1.8 Fear of new owner
Jakoby (2000)	62 Buy-outs in German family and non-family businesses; selected average values on Likert scale (5 = very important; 1 = very unimportant;)	4.2 Being entrepreneur 3.3 Commitment to company/employees 3.0 Fear of new owner 2.7 Financial rewards
Vest (1995)	16 Buy-outs in German non-family businesses; percentage of respondents confirming a motivation (multiple answers possible)	37.9% Opportunity of company 75.9% Being entrepreneur 31.0% Financial rewards 34.5% Commitment to company/employees 20.7% Fear of new owner
Gräper (1993)	36 Buy-outs in German family (64%) and non-family (36%) businesses; selected average values on Likert scale (1 = very important; 5 = very unimportant);	3.6 Self-fullfilment 2.8 Fear of new owner 2.3 Financial rewards 2.0 Being entrepreneur 1.3 Opportunity of company

Table 18: Surveys on motivation of managers for the buy-out

Source: European Private Equity & Venture Capital Association (2005), p. 14; Jakoby (2000), p. 182; Vest (1995), p. 190; Gräper (1993), p. 100

The financial rewards of the buy-out for managers depend on their compensation scheme. In family businesses, compensation of non-family managers is rather moderate compared to non-family businesses.[653] Compensation of non-family managers seems to be influenced by compensation levels of family managers.[654] The latter accept lower pecuniary compensation, as they benefit from capital gains and dividends and draw additional utility from achievement of non-financial goals and wellbeing of the company.[655] Family businesses seem reluctant to grant equity stakes to non-family managers.[656] Although family businesses intensively use the instrument of variable

[653] Cf. Carrasco-Hernandez/Sánchez-Marín (2007), p. 224; Anderson/Reeb (2003), p. 1318; Werner/Tosi (1995), pp. 1685 et seq.

[654] Cf. Gomez-Mejia/Larraza-Kintana/Makri (2003), p. 234.

[655] Cf. Uhlaner/Wright/Huse (2007), p. 235; McConaughy (2000), pp. 124, 130. As family managers are typically also owners of the family business, they might be rather indifferent between financial compensation through a fixed salary and bonus payments, or capital gains of their share in the family business.

[656] Cf. PriceWaterhouseCoopers (2006), p. 36; Gubitta/Gianecchini (2002), p. 293. A reason for this might be that family owners emphasize the goal of not giving equity out of the hands of the family (cf. subsection 7.1.1).

shares of compensation, these shares amount to about 30% of total salary and are lower than in non-family businesses.[657] Private equity companies can be expected to increase compensation significantly. Following agency theory, they tie compensation strongly to achievements of certain goals to align managers' interests with their own.[658] Private equity companies also demand and support managers to acquire equity in the portfolio company, so that managers have an additional incentive to prevent buy-out failure and participate in the exit price.[659] So, compensation in portfolio companies is expected to include participation in equity and to increase significantly in terms of total compensation and variable payments.

5.2.6. Decision making process of management

In line with the separation of ownership and control and the changes in the management team, changes in the decision making process of the management can be expected. Before the buy-out, family managers as well as mixed, family dominated management teams are often said to base their decisions on gut feeling, intuition and emotions.[660] Possible explanations for this decision making are that this approach might be driven by personal, estate or tax considerations of the family manager; that the family as a subsystem of the family business acts non-rational; or that this approach might be the unchanged continuation of decision making of the company's early days though meanwhile being inadequate.[661] Although this style of decision making leads to fast results, it might be hard to comprehend for others and might thus

[657] Cf. Günther/Gonschorek (2006), pp. 14 et seq.; Gubitta/Gianecchini (2002), p. 293; PriceWaterhouseCoopers (2008b), p. 11; Schulze/Lubatkin/Dino (2003b), p. 487.

[658] Cf. Becker (2000), p. 90; Wright/Thompson/Robbie (1992), p. 61. Although 85% of family businesses use variable compensation elements for incentivization, the ratio of variable to fixed compensation is expected to increase through the buy-out (cf. PriceWaterhouseCoopers (2006), p. 36; Denis (1994), p. 204).

[659] Cf. Cotter/Peck (2001), p. 102; Bächle/Hager (1999), pp. 381-384; Lee et al. (1992), p. 59. Typical equity investments of buy-out managers correspond to one or two annual net salaries; this might illustrate the consequences of a failed buy-out for managers (cf. Oberpracht/Engelstädter (2006), p. 71).

[660] Cf. Schachner/Speckbacher/Wentges (2006), p. 606; Zenz-Spitzweg (2001), p. 26; Forst (1992), pp. 32 et seq.; European Private Equity & Venture Capital Association (2005), p. 21; Dreux (1990), p. 228; Dyer (1989), p. 213; Schein (1983), p. 26.

[661] Cf. Dreux (1990), p. 228; Forst (1992), p. 33; Hollander/Elman (1988), p. 147; Welsch (1993), p. 45; Ward (1997), p. 324.

seem arbitrary.[662] After the buy-out, managers are expected to base their decisions on data and decision making tools, so that decisions are comprehensible for others.[663] This can be seen as consequence of the agency relationship between management on the one side and private equity companies as well as members of the supervisory boards on the other side. Management is accountable to the latter two groups, which monitor managers' actions closely. FORST reports that post buy-out managers reported more non-emotional, rational decisions based on figures after the buy-out.[664] So, the decision making process post buy-out can be expected to be rather non-emotional and based on verifiable data.

5.3 Observed changes based on empirical evidence

5.3.1. Owner influence on management decisions

In this subsection, the influence of family owners on management decisions pre buy-out is compared to the influence of private equity companies post buy-out. To enable a more detailed analysis of the changes, strategic management decisions pursuing long-term objectives are differentiated from operational decisions taken in the day-to-day business.[665]

A strong influence on strategic decisions was exerted by family owners in six companies **before the buy-out** (see Table 19).[666] While family owners frequently stipulated a concrete strategy, management was not included in the decision making but was merely supposed to implement. No or a weak influence of family owners was

---

662 Cf. Mühlebach (2004), pp. 25 et seq., 109; Klein (2000), p. 161.

663 Cf. Wright et al. (2000), p. 592; Baker/Wruck (1989), p. 182. Taking rational, comprehensible decisions can be seen as the effect of installing non-family managers in the portfolio company. The discussion of decision making in the general buy-out literature focuses on liberating decision making in the company examined from its former holding company and is thus hardly transferable to buy-outs in family businesses (cf. Malone (1989), p. 357).

664 Cf. Forst (1992), pp. 39 et seq.

665 In the following, a management decision with a time horizon of less than a year until execution is defined as operational decision; a decision with a longer time horizon is defined as strategic decision (cf. Weber/Schäffer (2006), pp. 263, 301 et seq.). Family businesses exclusively managed by family managers are not included in this analysis, as owner influence in these cases is obvious.

666 B, D, F, H, K, and M; 55% of 11 respondents.

reported in two companies. In I, the family manager died and heirs did not entirely take over responsibility, and in Q, the family had discredited itself by mismanagement in the past.

Influence of the family on operational decisions was reported to be strong in seven companies (see Table 20).[667] The former family manager of M, who had left the management board for the supervisory board, still commented certain activities in the company; these comments were taken as orders by most employees. In K, the former family owner visited the company once a week after he resigned from the management board and presented certain ideas that had to be implemented. In three companies, the family's influence on operational decisions was described as low. These were companies I and Q, which already indicated a low strategic influence by the family, and A, whose former family manager had left the company seven years before the buy-out and had meanwhile given up all influence on operations.

After the buy-out, influence of the private equity company on strategic management decisions was reported as strong by eight companies.[668] Thus, intensity of owner influence on strategic decisions remained unchanged through the buy-out. A possible explanation for this unchanged owner influence might be that managers of mid-sized companies simply lacked strategic experience; this lack could be compensated by experienced investment managers or members of the supervisory board. This was underlined by some managers that appreciated the strategic support and advice, like the manager of I, who stated:

> *Sometimes, I am grateful for having a partner on the other side to discuss profoundly some strategic projects.*

However, owner influence was more based on interaction: The private equity company wanted management to prepare decisions. Based on these drafts, investment managers led intensive discussions with managers or provided suggestions how to adapt decisions. Thus, the process of conceiving a strategy became an interactive process between two almost equal partners. Only three companies indicated that strategic influence of the private equity company was low: The pre and post buy-out family

---

[667] B, C, D, F, H, K, and M; 54% of 13 respondents.

[668] B, H, I, K, M, O, P, and Q; 73% of 11 respondents.

manager of G reported no significant influence of the new owners. This absence of influence was not surprising given that the family owner particularly looked for a private equity company promising low or no influence. In D and F, managers noted that private equity companies agreed to the initial business plan and did not take any further influence on corporate strategy.

Operational influence of new owners was described as non-existent by all 13 managers.[669] Private equity companies never intervened in decisions related to the day-to-day business of the company; this behavior marked a sharp difference to the owners' influence before the buy-out. Interview partners explained this absence of operational influence with prohibition of investors' influence by law[670], investment managers' lack of know-how on operations, company and market, and the demotivating effect of investors' influence on managers.[671] This decrease in owner influence on operational decisions increased managers' freedom, as the manager of B noted:

> *In many areas, we have a higher degree of freedom, which we didn't have in the past, and from our ongoing talks with the former family owners [...] we know, that we wouldn't have this freedom today.*

This was also in the interest of the private equity company, as the investment manager backing B explained:

> *Incumbent management approached us after the two family managers had left and we understood from their questions that the former family owners had taken operational decisions we never wanted to take. So, we explained [to the incumbent management] that they had to take these decisions on their own.*

With regard to the **control group**, owner influence in the family businesses sold to holding companies was completely in line with the findings presented above. Holding companies took influence on strategic management decisions through discussions and suggestions but left all operational decisions to management.

Interview partners in the three companies financed by semi-public investment companies, reported neither strategic nor operational influence. On the one hand, this

---

669 A, B, C, D, F, G, H, I, K, M, O, P, and Q; 100% of 13 respondents.

670 Cf. section 5.1.2.

671 Cf. subsection.5.3.5.

might be explainable by the fact that semi-public investment companies held either no or a minority stake in former family businesses, so that their influence was limited anyway. On the other hand, investment managers in semi-public investment companies were responsible for a greater number of portfolio companies, what restricted their involvement.[672]

		Post buy-out influence of private equity company	
		Influence	No influence
Pre buy-out influence of family owners	Influence	B*, H*, K, M	D*, F*
	No influence	I, Q	
	No comment provided	O*, P	G*

Table 19: Change in strategic influence

Source: Interview data (n=11)
* Mixed management pre buy-out

		Post buy-out influence of private equity company	
		Influence	No influence
Pre buy-out influence of family owners	Influence		B*, C, D*, F*, H*, K, M
	No influence		A, I, Q
	No comment provided		G*, O*, P

Table 20: Change in operational influence

Source: Interview data (n=13)
* Mixed management pre buy-out

The comparison of influence on management decisions by family owners with the influence by private equity companies can be **summed up** by the following: While investors exerted an equally high influence on strategic decisions in portfolio companies, private equity companies ceased the considerable influence on operational decisions of former family owners. However, also influence on strategic decisions changed as investors exerted their influence through discussions and suggestions. This approach was different from the family owners' direct stipulation of strategic

672 While in German private equity companies, 8.9 investment managers are responsible for 20.6 portfolio companies on average, in semi-public investment companies, 8.6 investment managers are responsible for 220.3 portfolio companies on average (cf. Achleitner/Ehrhart/Zimmermann (2006), pp. 15, 18).

measures. Possibly, influence of family owners on strategic and operational decisions before the buy-out could be seen as expression of family members' emotional attachment to the company. These considerations lead to the following propositions:

Proposition 1A:	*Private equity companies' influence on strategic decisions is as intensive as the influence of former family owners.*
Proposition 1B:	*Private equity companies influence strategic decisions through an interaction-oriented approach, whereas family owners stipulate a concrete strategy.*
Proposition 1C:	*Private equity companies do not exert influence on operational decisions.*

5.3.2. Owner influence on corporate strategy

As subsection 5.3.1 has shown, private equity companies influenced the strategy of their portfolio companies. Internationalization, acquisitions, and increases in profitability emerged as major post buy-out strategies. Before these strategies of portfolio companies are discussed, light is shed on the attitude of family businesses towards these strategies pre buy-out.

Before the buy-out, the family businesses in the sample mainly pursued a strategy of organic growth.[673] Especially manufacturing companies relied on the quality and innovativeness of their products to achieve considerable growth.

With regard to internationalization, six family businesses already operated abroad before the buy-out.[674] Company B was already present on all continents, but sales and profit contribution of non-European subsidiaries was very low compared to European activities. While some companies followed a clear strategy to grow abroad (V), others followed customers into foreign countries as suppliers (V). In contrast to these internationalizers, three companies did not internationalize at all.[675] The investment manager backing company K explained that some family owners did not see the necessity to go abroad:

---

[673] For the differentiation between internationalization and organic growth, see footnote 601.

[674] B, D, H, K, I, and V; 35% of 17 respondents.

[675] A, J, and K; 18% of 17 respondents.

There are many family owners of mid-sized companies that are happy with their market position, especially if they are market leader in Germany or in German-speaking Europe. Most of them lack the experience to expand into Europe or globally. Moreover, there is frequently a certain fear to do it.

Other family managers did not internationalize to forgo the strain and stress linked to traveling, as the investment manager of S stated:

A family manager at the age of 65 frequently doesn't want to travel any more. And he doesn't feel like acquiring customers. [...] He might also have a language problem because his English isn't that good.

Acquisitions were a mean only three companies resorted to before the buy-out.[676] In M, this strategy significantly contributed to company growth. For other companies, acquisitions were the beginning of financial difficulties. Company E acquired excessively, until the financial situation became problematic given some acquired activities were less successful. A similar development combined with mismanagement led Q into a crisis and made it a turnaround case. The investment manager backing company M explained that the lack of experience and tight financial resources made acquisitions a risky endeavor potentially endangering the family owner's work of a lifetime.

Interview partners did not comment on family owners' attitude towards profitability before the buy-out. However, from the fact that many interview partners considered the post buy-out focus on increases in profitability a new strategy, it can be inferred that maximizing profitability was not in the focus of all family owners before the buy-out.

After this discussion of the family's influence on corporate strategy, the influence of the private equity company on strategy **after the buy-out** is presented in the following. The first main strategy, private equity companies wanted their portfolio companies to pursue, was **growth through acquisitions**. In ten companies, this strategy was newly launched or intensified.[677] An example of this strategy was company B, which was in negotiations to close its third acquisition within 13 months

---

[676] E, M, and Q; 18% of 17 respondents.

[677] A, B, C, F, H, I, J, K, L, and M; 59% of 17 respondents.

after the buy-out.[678] Acquisitions resulted in significant company growth: In B, sales doubled within 13 months and in C, sales tripled within four years. Acquisitions were needed to fulfill the ambitious plans for portfolio companies according to the investment manager of M:

You can only achieve growth of 20% or 30% through acquisitions; otherwise that's normally impossible. You can't get 20% out of a well-run company all of a sudden.

In companies, where acquisitions were made before the buy-out, intensity and speed of this strategy increased, the manager of H explained:

We have done [acquisitions] already before [the buy-out] and had bought two companies in three years. This was part of our strategy. But [the private equity company] is more on the lookout for it because they have the know-how in this area: How to find targets? Where to find them? How to talk to them? How to succeed?

Private equity companies supported growth through acquisitions in three ways. First, they had expertise in acquisitions as the quote above underlines. Second, investors used their network to have a good market overview of companies that were for sale. Thus, they could identify possible target companies and report these to their portfolio companies. Third, private equity companies could provide financial backing for acquisitions, so that portfolio companies could target larger companies to take over.[679]

Investors supported growth through acquisitions as this strategy was a major lever of value generation and an advantage for portfolio companies stemming from their new owners, as the investment manager of I said:

The family owner would have never bought a company. Meanwhile, we are in talks to acquire the third company – this way, we play more keys on the piano.

---

[678] The manager of B gave three reasons for this aggressive growth strategy: First, the company wanted to move closer to the market by acquiring distributors. Second, B entered markets for similar products that were not targeted before the buy-out. Third, acquisitions of foreign companies fostered internationalization.

[679] Nevertheless, private equity companies ensured that portfolio companies grew healthily: E, which had financial difficulties after a long series of acquisitions, focused on consolidating the business after the buy-out.

The second main strategy private equity companies demanded from their portfolio companies was **internationalization**. Despite fostering organic growth in the markets the portfolio companies already served before the buy-out, private equity companies also demanded entering new markets. Launch or intensification of this strategy was reported in eight companies.[680] Internationalization was achieved by rolling out existing products to new foreign markets; setting up production facilities abroad; or acquiring foreign companies.[681] The change in mindset that went along with this strategy was summarized by the manager of B:

Now, we are a global company with headquarters in Germany. Beforehand, we were a German company with some subsidiaries abroad.

Interview partners that strived for internationalization before the buy-out, reported an increased verve and pressure by the private equity company to work towards this goal. Company B closed down its slowly-developing joint-venture with a local partner in China and opened a wholly-owned foreign enterprise to boost growth. The former family owner of K insisted on in-house production and sale representatives abroad; after the buy-out, in-house production was reduced, products were sourced from global suppliers, and cooperation with local trading partners in other countries were set up, thus creating significant savings. The manager of K explained:

From a strategic point of view, we have a much better position than we had [before the buy-out]. It is not, that we didn't have these thoughts and ideas, but we were simply unable to implement them under the former owner.

Interview partners stated two reasons for internationalization: On the one hand, going abroad enabled a company to expand its market leadership in new geographic areas and open up further growth potential.[682] On the other hand, the company became more independent of the home market.[683]

---

680 A, B, C, D, E, H, J, and K; 47% of 17 respondents.

681 An example for the first approach was company A, which offered its services in Germany pre buy-out and entered three more markets after the buy-out. The second approach was exemplified by company C which established a new plant in Eastern Europe.

682 Company E, which was described as very "Germany-focused" before the buy-out, could not have sustained growth without internationalization. After entrance into several markets, 90% of its growth came from abroad.

683 This was particularly important for company J, which saw it confronted with a forthcoming change in regulation that would adversely affect demand for its products in its domestic market.

Private equity companies supported internationalization in three ways: First, through acquiring companies abroad and thus employing investors' expertise in the field of acquisitions; second, through appointing specialists with international experience to the management board or supervisory board and employing consultants[684]; and third, through providing direct support to the company.[685]

The third strategy private equity companies demanded was **improving profitability** in terms of EBITDA to increase exit valuation, as reported by six interviewees including in particular the portfolio companies in turnaround situations.[686] The focus on performance improvement was new to many companies.[687] The investment manager backing company B explained:

> *This company didn't work with performance indicators. They didn't focus on margin, but on sales – they were totally sales-focused. And they have primarily bought sales-volume. We don't renew some contracts in the US, which are simply unprofitable. In these cases we say: If you don't raise the price by 30%, we don't need to do business with you.*

Interview partners did not report support from private equity companies to achieve this strategy, possibly because support necessitated operational involvement by investors, which they were unwilling and prohibited to provide.[688]

Despite striving for increasing profitability, only three companies indicated operational improvements like selling of unused assets or divisions.[689] In P, two plants

---

[684] Cf. subsection 5.3.3.

[685] In B, the investment manager directly intervened in the dissolution of an unsuccessful joint-venture in China (as stated above). He negotiated with the joint-venture partner with support from the local branch of his private equity company.

[686] A, B, C, M, P, and Q; 35% of 17 respondents.

[687] Cf. subsection 6.3.3. Either companies focused on different performance indicators or they put less emphasis on them.

[688] Cf. subsection 5.1.1.

[689] L, P, and Q; 18% of 17 respondents. Companies P and Q were in turnaround situations when being sold. In these companies, growth through acquisition and internationalization had to be postponed until weaknesses in the operational performance were overcome.

were closed and in L, two unprofitable business divisions were sold.[690] This low number of companies selling unused assets might be explainable by lean operations in the family businesses pre buy-out, or by the limited size of family businesses before the buy-out. Rareness of these measures was interesting as it differed from buy-outs in large corporations.[691]

With regard to the **control group**, subsidiaries of holding companies and bought-out companies backed by semi-public investment companies did not report pressure towards growth through acquisitions or internationalization. The former did not change their strategy after the sale and continued to pursue profitable, organic growth. Their holding companies demanded information on corporate strategy but did no interfere.[692] The semi-public investment companies did neither interfere with strategic decisions of the management, as described in subsection 5.3.1.

To sum up, this subsection has shown that private equity companies pressured their portfolio companies to launch or intensify growth through acquisitions and internationalization and to increase profitability (see Figure 35). Investors provided their companies more valuable support for the two former strategies than former family owners. All strategies aimed at increasing company value with regard to the foreseeable exit. Operational improvements were reported only by very few companies, possibly because operations were efficient before the buy-out.

---

690 In L, the two divisions had been unprofitable for long. The former family owner was aware of the problems in these divisions but lacked pressure to become active and capital needed to solve these problems.

691 Cf. subsection 5.2.2.

692 Although no direct influence on corporate strategy was reported, the manager of R appreciated the financial support that facilitated the company's steps towards internationalization.

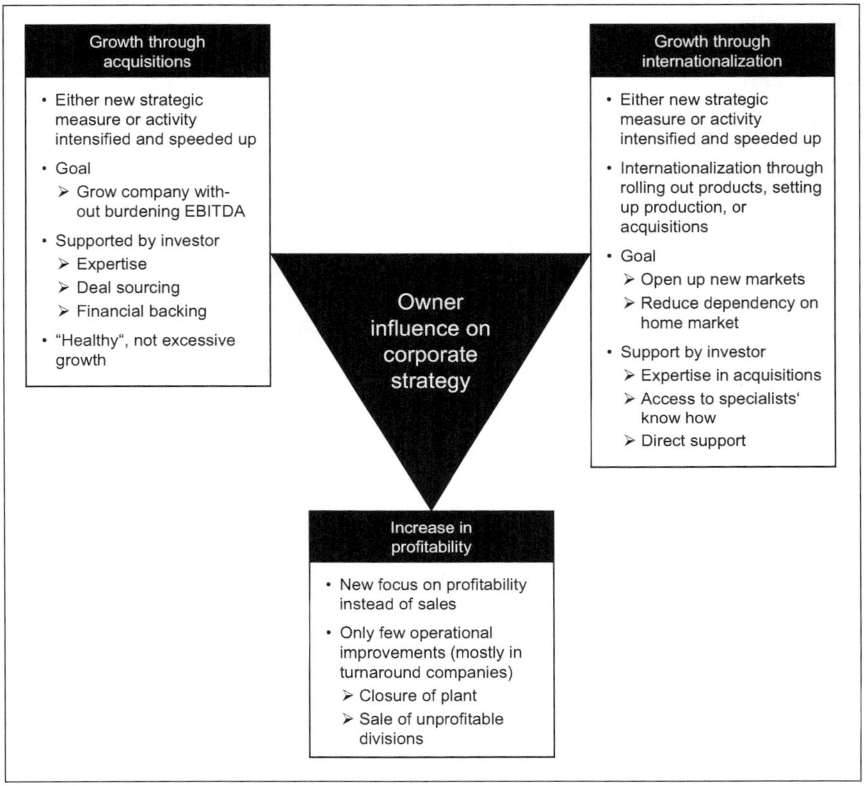

Figure 35: Corporate strategies induced by private equity companies

Source: Author's illustration

Predominance of the strategies of internationalization and acquisitions can be seen as logical consequence of the investment criteria of private equity companies.[693] Portfolio companies were supposed to have a good financial track record and a strong market position, thus limiting potential for operational improvements and organic

693 Cf. subsection 4.2.2.1.

growth.[694] Acquisitions and internationalization served as means to grow into new market segments, enter foreign markets, and strengthen the position in markets the company was already present. Acquisitions were a favorable strategy as they burdened cash and financing, but not EBITDA, which company valuation at exit was based on. In contrast, internationalization was somewhat less favorable due to its high costs and long lead time until profitability. However, these disadvantages might have been overcompensated by increased attraction to potential buyers due to a broader position and future returns expected from international activities. These considerations lead to the following proposition:

Proposition 2A: *Private equity companies urge their portfolio companies to grow through acquisitions and/or internationalization and/or increase profitability.*

Proposition 2B: *Apart from portfolio companies in turnaround situations, private equity companies hardly demand operational improvements following buy-outs.*

5.3.3. Supervision by and support from the supervisory board

This subsection analyzes the board structure pre buy-out, changes in the board, types of new board members and functions of the supervisory board post buy-out.

As described in subsection 3.2.3, ten family businesses already had a supervisory board **before the buy-out**.[695] In seven of these, the family was represented by one or two members; the majority of members of the supervisory board were non-family members.[696] In the remaining three companies, there were no family members on the supervisory board.[697] The other seats on the supervisory boards were held by auditors, lawyers, bankers, friends or acquaintances of the family. In some cases the latter had relevant industry or technical experience, in other cases they were appointed

[694] This statement does not apply to portfolio companies in turnaround situations. Excellence in operational efficiency was not expected as investment criterion from these companies (cf. subsection 4.2.2.1), so that improvements in operational efficiency might have been expected and were observed as described before.

[695] 45% of 22 respondents.

[696] A, B, K, M, P, Q, and R; 70% of 10 respondents.

[697] C, E, and I; 30% of 10 respondents.

to the board for having long relationships to the family or being prominent persons in the company's home region.

Interviewed non-family managers were mostly skeptical about the supervisory boards' contribution to company success before the buy-out. Supervisory boards often lacked entrepreneurial thinking or experience in the areas, in which management would have needed support. Members of the supervisory board did not challenge management's decisions or opinions, as the manager of company C explained. The manager of B stated:

> *The old supervisory board hardly had a supportive function. They met twice a year and were quite satisfied with the results, so that they didn't see the necessity to further develop the company. They were pleased with the positive development and let the management act with great discretion. This was quite comprehensible, given that [family managers] owned 66.6% of the company.*

The weak role some supervisory boards played might be explainable by their problematic task to control family managers, who appointed board members in their function as owners.[698] The supervisory board was further weakened by members that were not independent of family owners (i.e. auditors, friends, potentially even bankers) or by a family member being chairman of the board. In two companies, former family managers who joined the board after resigning used their position to take influence on operational decisions in the company.[699] Weak supervisory boards might be explainable by family owners not wanting to be supervised by a strong board or difficulties of family businesses with attracting strong, independent board members.[700]

The buy-out severely **changed** the existence and composition of the supervisory board in every single company. In five companies a supervisory board was

---

698 Boards that controlled family managers existed in companies B, E, and R.

699 K and M (cf. subsection 3.2.4).

700 In some cases, the supervisory board was strengthened before the buy-out. In company E, banks pressured the family manager to replace friends of the family and local dignitaries with independent, external board members. In Q, a restructuring expert was on the supervisory board given the critical situation the company was in. In A, the private equity companies that held minority stakes sent one representative each to the supervisory board, though they were described as very passive. All these changes were initiated by non-family parties or company crises.

newly installed.[701] Out of the ten pre buy-out supervisory boards, one board was dissolved[702] and in the remaining nine boards, fundamental personal changes took place.[703] The magnitude of change can be seen in the fact that only one of all members of these supervisory boards was not replaced after the buy-out.

Three companies did not have a supervisory board when interviews were conducted, because the investor was looking for members to appoint to the new board (G), considered the company too small for a board (H), or had a very good relationship with and trust in the manager (J).[704] Managers of H and J did not miss support of a supervisory board as they could purchase specific advice from consultants when needed.

After the buy-out, **supervisory boards were composed** of mainly three types of members: investment managers, experienced managers and former family owners (see Table 21). Investment managers were on ten supervisory boards, independent experts on twelve and members of the formerly owning family on seven.

Company	Investment managers	Experienced managers	Former family owners	Others
A	2		1	
B	2	2		1
C		1	1	2
D		2	1	2
E	2	1	1	
F	4		2	
I	1	1		1
K		3		1
L	1	1		
M	2	3		1
N		3		
O	≥ 1	1	1	
P	1	1		
Q	2	2	1	

Table 21: Composition of supervisory boards post buy-out

Source: Interview data (n=14)
Others include former owners of acquired companies, lawyers, and former non-family mangers

701 D, F, L, N, and O; 29% of 17 respondents.

702 The supervisory board was dissolved in company R, which was acquired by a holding company. The case is discussed in detail later on in this subsection.

703 A, B, C, E, I, K, M, P, and Q; 53% of 17 respondents.

704 18% of 17 respondents.

Investment managers served as contact persons for the management to the private equity company and sat on ten supervisory boards.[705] Private equity companies seemed to have different policies with regard to the number of investment managers they sent to the supervisory board: On the one hand, the investor backing M had the restriction that less than half of the board seats were allowed to be held by investment managers. On the other hand, four of the six supervisory board members in F were investment managers delegated by the two private equity companies that bought the company. In large sample companies, private equity companies were represented by two investment managers on the supervisory board.[706] If new managers were appointed to the management board after the buy-out, representation of the private equity company on the supervisory board seemed more likely.[707] Given the additional risk of these transactions, investors possibly preferred tighter control.[708]

Experienced managers sat on 12 supervisory boards.[709] Interview partners highly appreciated experienced managers as members of the supervisory board. Most of them were industry experts, functional experts or former entrepreneurs. Private equity companies assessed portfolio companies and managers' competencies to identify areas where support was needed. Based on this analysis, investors appointed board members with the specific expertise needed.[710] The investment manager backing K explained:

> *The supervisory board supports the management board in key areas, e.g. sourcing from Asia, internationalization, operations and other issues. [...] We look for areas, where the company needs support: Operations, sales, human*

---

705 A, B, E, F, I, L, M, O, P, and Q; 71% of 14 respondents. The manager of L complained that representatives of the private equity company were replaced very often, which presumably hindered him to establish a good and stable relationship. These frequent changes can be expected to have complicated monitoring for the private equity company.

706 A, B, E, and F.

707 Investment managers were on the board of 100% of MBIs (E, I, and L), 75% of BIMBOs (F, O, and Q), 50% of IBOs (P), and 40% of MBOs (A and M).

708 Managers of management buy-ins do not know the company, products and industry to an extent, managers of management buy-outs know their company. Further, they might struggle to be accepted by employees (cf. Robbie/Wright (1995), p. 544).

709 B, C, D, E, I, K, L, M, N, O, P, and Q; 86% of 14 respondents.

710 If some managers were replaced and the search for new managers needed more time, an experienced manager who was member of the supervisory board might take over operational responsibility in the interim, as in the case of B.

resources? In our circle of experienced managers, we have specialists with diverse backgrounds and we consider for each transaction, what does the company need and who can support it best.

The appointment of experienced managers depended on two conditions: First, whether the company needed support which the private equity company was unable to provide. Second, whether the private equity company had an experienced manager with the needed skills at hand. Thus, private equity companies compensated their own lack of industry or company know-how by appointing specialists in these areas.

Not every former top manager was adequate for a position on the supervisory board as the candidate had to internalize the objectives of the private equity company and should not have an inclination towards showmanship. Thus, the search process for adequate board members became a complex challenge in small industries with only a few available experienced managers, as the manager of F told:

You don't want to have suppliers or customers [on the supervisory board]. You don't want a competitor. This makes it very hard to find good people who have the experience and are willing to contribute in such a small industry we operate in. Now, we are thinking towards [a similar industry], which might fit to our industry...

Therefore, private equity companies often cooperated with the same experienced managers or resorted to professional members of supervisory boards. To make the position more attractive, board members had the chance to invest in the respective portfolio company.

Members of the formerly owning family sat on seven supervisory boards.[711] Post buy-out management had an ambivalent attitude towards this presence of family members on the board: While a few managers were happy about family members' involvement (A) or even requested it (D), others objected representation of the family on the board post buy-out (G, Q). Objecting managers argued that family members would not contribute as much as investment managers or experienced managers, and that family members were likely to live in the past and would not contribute to solving current problems.

[711] A, C, D, E, F, O, and Q; 50% of 14 respondents.

Representation of former family members on the supervisory board was highly correlated with holding an equity stake in the company (see Table 22). Only in company D, family members that were not holding a stake were on the supervisory board. There are two explanations for this observation: On the one hand, family members were mostly sitting on the board to represent their equity share and not to contribute their experience. If their expertise was indispensable, family members would sit on more boards. On the other hand, families adhered to the two strategies of separation from the company presented in subsection 4.2.2.5: Either they participated neither in equity nor in the supervisory board (strategy of clear cut), or they participated in both equity and supervisory board (strategy of fading, minor influence). Both explanations were backed by the two major groups of companies in Table 22: In six companies the family held a stake in the company and was represented on the supervisory board. In five companies, family members were neither among the owners nor among the board members.

		Family on the supervisory board		
		Yes	No	No board
Family among owners	Yes	A, C, E, F, O, Q	M, N	G, H
	No	D	B, I, K, L, P	J

Table 22: Family ownership and supervisory board representation post buy-out
Source: Interview data (n=17)

In line with the new composition of the supervisory board, the **functions of the supervisory board** and the process of board meetings changed. After the buy-out, the supervisory board was installed or improved to supervise and support management. Private equity companies delegated supervision to the board and stipulated a list of management decisions, which had to be approved by the board. Post buy-out supervisory boards carried out this duty with a greater degree of professionalism than pre buy-out boards as the manager of C stated:

The level of control exerted is much more intensive compared to before [the buy-out]. Requirements for financial and strategic documentation as well as intensity of discussions have increased considerably.

This increase in the effectivity of monitoring by the supervisory board is due to two changes: On the one hand, the frequent pre buy-out unity of ownership and control in the hands of family managers, which limits power of supervisory boards and thus hinders effective monitoring, was broken up.[712] On the other hand, power of the supervisory board was further increased by the presence of investment managers on the board, who unified ownership and supervision in one person (see Figure 36).

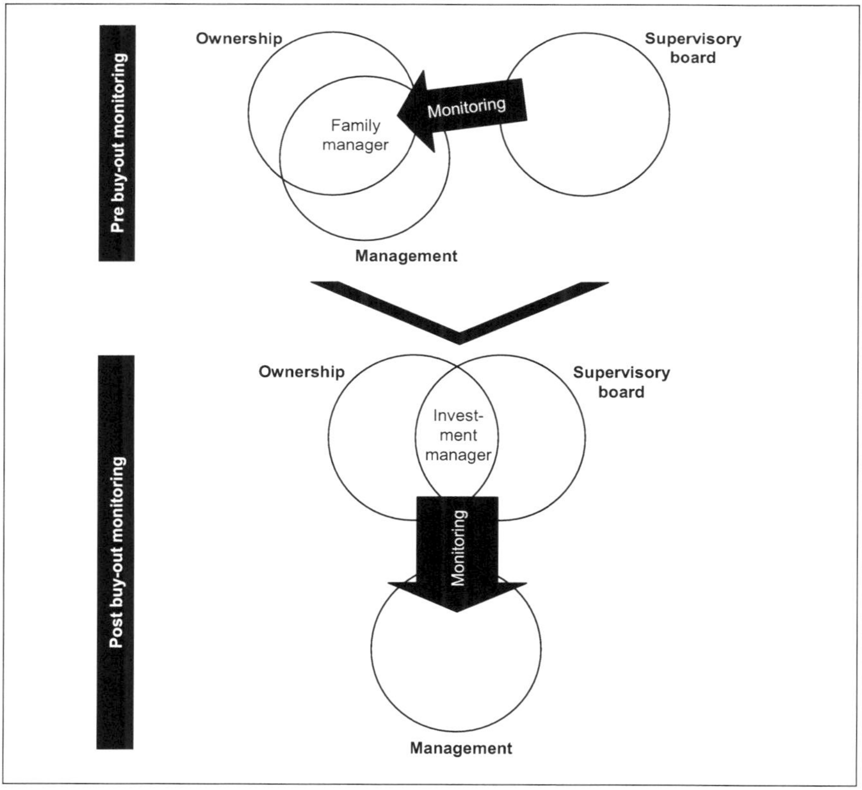

Figure 36: Changes in supervisory board composition and impact on monitoring

Source: Author's illustration

[712] Cf. subsection 5.1.1.

Four managers appreciated monitoring by the supervisory board as it motivated them to be more disciplined and structured.[713] Moreover, interviewees stressed that the intensive monitoring by board members increased the transparency for investors, which they assumed as a critical prerequisite for their increased managerial discretion after the buy-out.[714]

Based on the new composition of supervisory boards, members supported managers by providing advice and acting as sparring partners in the fields of general management, corporate functions or industry trends.[715] Board members rarely made propositions but focused on reviewing prospective decisions management was about to take. In these discussions, members of the supervisory board contributed their own experiences from similar cases, a fresh look from an outsider, and benchmark know-how. The permanent and intensive challenging of decisions made supervisory board meetings for the management very demanding and stressful, yet very valuable, as the manager of O said:

> *Typically, the supervisory board is a committee of experts, which makes interaction very challenging and tough, but characterized by expertise. You might not have this in family businesses, as their committee isn't only marked by expertise.*

Board members also supported management by providing business contacts. In M, experienced managers on the board helped management to get into contact with potential customers, which they could not have contacted without this help.[716]

---

[713] B, I, L, and N; 29% of 14 companies (with a supervisory board).

[714] These statements by interviewees could also allow an inference about supervisory boards pre buy-out: Pre buy-out boards, which were also composed of family members, exerted operational influence that was discontinued after the buy-out (cf. subsection 5.3.1). The discontinuation of the owners' operational influence implied greater discretion for managers post buy-out.

[715] The manager of company F noted that the contribution of the supervisory board depended very much on the private equity company: While he was not satisfied with the support by the investors, which bought the company from the family, the owners after the secondary buy-out provided valuable support.

[716] Contrary to this, the manager of A did not recognize this support of business contacts by saying that he already knew all relevant persons in his industry and would be very surprised to learn about a new contact he did not know. This might be possibly explainable by the facts that company A was the largest sample company and the manager held his position for a long time.

Meeting frequency of the supervisory board was kept constant at mostly three or four times a year. Shortly after the buy-out or at important turning points, meetings were held more often, in some cases on a monthly basis. Especially after the buy-out, duration of meetings increased as the new members of the supervisory board had to familiarize them with the respective business model. The atmosphere of meetings was described as more open and informal, and at the same time more professional and more structured than before the buy-out.

Supervisory boards seemed of lower importance in the companies of the **control group**. None of the two holding companies employed a supervisory board in a subsidiary. Holding companies exerted control and support through a very close and direct relationship to portfolio companies.[717] Investment managers stated that this direct contact would be more adequate for the mostly smaller subsidiaries and fitted better the thinking of family businesses. However, both portfolio companies were not completely satisfied with this support: The manager of R missed the support and decision challenging, he was used to from the supervisory board before the sale, and the manager of S disapproved the holding company's lack of industry knowledge.[718]

Similar to the subsidiaries of holding companies, companies backed by semi-public investment companies neither had supervisory boards. Even if a board had existed, the investment company would not have insisted on being represented according to the investment manager backing T. Support and monitoring seemed to vary: While no support or monitoring was reported by companies T and U, the management of V had monthly meetings and a consulting contract with the investment company.

In conclusion, this discussion has shown that buy-outs in family businesses had a severe impact on the supervisory board. Before the buy-out, supervisory boards infrequently existed. If a family business had a board, it was less professional in its composition of members and, thus, its work. These boards were composed of people mostly depending on the family, who lacked the background to support management efficiently. Presumably, the weakness of supervisory boards before the buy-out was

[717] In S, a junior investment manager visited the headquarters on a monthly basis to discuss financial statements and a senior investment manager once or twice a quarter to discuss strategy and other important issues.

[718] It should be noted that company S operated in a highly specialized niche market.

explainable by family managers' dislike to be supervised by board members. After the buy-out, private equity companies newly installed a supervisory board or replaced virtually all members. Post buy-out boards comprised investment managers, experienced managers and sometimes former family owners. The board was professionalized through appointment of new board members, who contributed their experience and intervened to monitor and support management. A high correlation between family ownership post buy-out and family representation on the supervisory board suggests that family members were on the board to represent their equity stake instead of supervising and supporting management. These arguments lead to the following propositions:

Proposition 3A:	*Private equity companies professionalize the supervisory board by appointing experienced and intervening members to the board.*
Proposition 3B:	*Post buy-out supervisory boards tighten supervision and stronger support management compared to pre buy-out supervisory boards.*
Proposition 3C:	*Family members remain on supervisory boards post buy-out to represent their equity stake and keep in touch with the company rather than to contribute their experience.*

5.3.4. Composition of the management team

In this subsection changes in the management composition and reasons for these changes will be discussed with a special look at the position of the CFO. The analysis continues with the assessment of pre buy-out management and the attraction of new managers.[719]

Buy-outs changed the composition of the management team in all 17 companies. In nine companies (53%), the entire management team was replaced and in eight companies (47%), a part of the management team was replaced.[720] Changes took

[719] This subsection only takes those changes in management into consideration that had taken place at the earliest 24 months before the buy-out and all changes after the buy-out. Changes in the management more than two years before the buy-out are considered as no preparation for the buy-out.

[720] The large share of companies, in which the whole pre buy-out management was replaced, contradicted the opinion of some interviewed managers about pre buy-out managers' importance

place either before the buy-out to prepare the company for the sale, after the buy-out, if private equity companies or new managers triggered changes, or before and after the buy-out.[721] Table 23 shows an overview of the degree of and timing of changes.

		Time of changes		
		Before the buy-out	Before and after the buy-out	After the buy-out
Degree of changes	Replacement of all managers		B, C, D, O, Q	E, I, J, P
	Replacement, dismissal, or appointment of a part of the management team	A, G, M	F, K	H, L, N

Table 23: Degree and time of changes in management of portfolio companies

Source: Interview data (n=17)

In the following, some examples of changes in the management are provided. In three companies, some managers were replaced before the buy-out. These measures were initiated by family owners to facilitate the sale process.[722] In M, a second non-family manager was hired before the buy-out as the incumbent non-family manager approached retirement age.

In seven companies, changes in the management took place before and after the buy-out. In five companies, the entire management was changed: In D, the two family

for the company. The manager of F argued that private equity companies would be well advised not to replace managers. He said that the management of a Mittelstand company was the "personification of the company", which employees depended on. Obviously, the private equity companies that replaced pre buy-out managers had a different point of view.

721 Changes in the composition of the management team that took place after the buy-out could occur either directly (i.e. they were triggered by the transaction and had an immediate effect) or they could occur some time after the buy-out. Distinction between both alternatives was not applied to data presented in this subsection, as some changes took effect with a delay that made it impossible to determine whether a given change was a direct consequence of the transaction or triggered later on. In other cases, changes in the management that were triggered directly by the buy-out were postponed to ensure a good transition in management.

722 Cf. subsection 4.2.1.3.

managers appointed three non-family junior managers[723] to the management board to enable a buy-out; the family managers retired after they sold the company. In two companies, not all managers were replaced: In K, the family owner hired an additional non-family manager as CEO to prepare the buy-out.[724] While this new manager remained after the buy-out, the family manager retired, two non-family managers were dismissed due to their lack of qualification and a third non-family manager left the board and became junior manager.

Changes in the management team occurred exclusively after the buy-out in seven companies. In four companies all managers were replaced. In I, both non-family managers were close to retirement age and replaced.[725] In three companies, a part of the management team was replaced: In H, the family manager, who was CEO of his company, left the company at the day of the buy-out. The other non-family manager remained on the management board and became CEO of the company.

In total, 29 managers retired or were dismissed from the management board.[726] This means that three of four managers are replaced after a buy-out. The high proportion of managers who are replaced through the buy-out is in line with a peculiarity of buy-outs in family businesses discussed in chapter 4: Other types of buy-outs are frequently driven by pre buy-out managers, who only strive for a buy-out if they expect to remain on the management after the transaction. Buy-outs in family businesses are initiated by selling family owners or by private equity companies and not by pre buy-out managers.[727] This reservation of pre buy-out managers might be explainable by managers' doubts whether they fulfill expectations of post buy-out owners or whether they want to run the risk of a buy-out – obviously, these concerns are justified.

---

723 In corporate hierarchy, junior managers are below executive directors (referred to as managers) (cf. footnote 322).

724 At that time, there were already three non-family managers in the management.

725 At the buy-out, the commercial manager was replaced with an external manager and one year later, the technical manager was replaced. In four companies, only some managers were changed.

726 At the time interviews were conducted, company P was managed by an interim management team and new permanent managers were not yet appointed. Therefore, this company did not count to the appointments but only to dismissals. Further, this company was not included in the figures on changes in the size of the management team or family influence.

727 Cf. subsections 4.1.2.3 and 4.2.2.3.

11 of the dismissed managers were family managers that left deliberately, 2 family managers were dismissed or asked to retire by the private equity company, though they were initially supposed to remain on the management.[728]

29 managers were appointed to the management board. 1 of these newly appointed managers was a family manager and 8 worked in the company before their appointment. 9 managers were on the management board before and after the buy-out. The number of managers on the management board increased in 6 companies, decreased in 3 companies and remained unchanged in 7 companies.

Family influence in the management board increased in 2 cases, decreased in 10 cases and remained unchanged in 4 cases. Through these changes, families ceased to be on the management board of 12 companies. Table 24 provides details on the changes in each company.

Company	Dismissals, retirements	Appointments	Pre and post buy-out position on the management board
A	Non-family CEO (-4)	Non-family manager (-4)	Non-family manager
B	2 family managers (0; 0), non-family CFO (0)	Non-family CEO (5), non-family CFO (8), 4 non-family managers (-12*; - 12*; 8; n/a)	
C	Family CEO, 2 non-family managers	Non-family CEO (-12), non-family CFO (0), 2 non-family managers*	
D	2 family managers (0; 0)	3 non-family managers* (-24; -24; -24)	
E	Family CEO** (30), non-family CFO (48)	Non-family CEO (30), non-family CFO (48)	
F	Family CEO** (12), family manager (0)	Non-family CEO (12), non-family manager (0)	2 non family managers
G	Non-family manager (-24)	Family manager* (-24)	Non-family manager
H	Family CEO (0)		Non-family manager
I	2 non-family managers (0; 12)	2 non-family managers (3; 12)	
J	Family manager	Non-family manager	
K	Family manager (0), 3 non-family managers (0; 0; 0)	Non-family CEO (-9)	Non-family manager
L	Family CEO (0)	Non-family CEO (0)	Non-family manager
			continued on next page...

[728] E and F.

... continued from previous page			
M		Non-family manager (-3)	Non-family CEO
N	Non-family manager (24)		Family manager
O	Family manager	2 non-family managers	
P	3 non-family managers (0; 0; 0)	Interim management	
Q	Non-family CEO (3)	2 non-family managers (-6; 3)	

Table 24: Changes in the composition of management in portfolio companies

Source: Interview data (n=17)
Numbers in brackets indicate the number of months after the buy-out, when managers were dismissed or appointed (if information was reported; negative numbers indicate months before the buy-out)
* Promotion of an internal manager
** In E and F, former family managers initially remained in the management post buy-out, but resigned one year (F) and two and a half years (E) after the buy-out

A position of special importance for the private equity company was the **CFO** or head of accounting, managem ent accounting or financing; this manager was responsible for ensuring transparency and providing information on the company to the investor, supervisory board members and banks.[729] Given this important role, high expectations and requirements were linked to the position of a CFO – however, these expectations were frequently not met by pre buy-out CFOs, as the investment manager backing K said:

> *CFOs in family businesses are frequently the 60 years olds, who started their first job in the family business. Actually, they rather had the family owner's confidence instead of professional competence.*

In nine companies, the CFO was replaced by the private equity company after the buy-out.[730] Pre buy-out CFOs in these companies were either family members,

[729] As an exception from footnote 642 (the term CFO embraces in the following also the head of accounting, management accounting and financing, if this person is no senior manager), in Table 24, the term CFO indicates that this person was also member of the management board.

[730] B, C, E, F, I, J, N, O, and P; 53% of 17 respondents. In E, replacement of the CFO was triggered by the CEO, while the private equity company did not complain about the CFO.

Profiles of the newly appointed CFOs could be seen as the optimal qualification private equity companies expect: New CFOs had learned their tasks in corporations and had at best already cooperated with a private equity company. They had considerable experience in accounting and management accounting at best gathered in the relevant industries.

who left the company at the buy-out and had to be replaced; or pre buy-out CFOs had to be replaced for their insufficient qualification with regard to knowledge in the fields of reporting, management controlling or capital markets. In eight companies, the CFO was not replaced.[731] In these companies, the CFO had the qualifications needed.[732]

The increased importance of the CFO for external stakeholders was reflected by an appreciation of the position within the organization. While pre buy-out CFOs were frequently excluded from important meetings and major decisions, post buy-out CFOs participated in both. In company B, the CFO became the second most important senior manager after the CEO. In some companies, this appreciation took place after some time: In C, the CFO position was upgraded to member of the management board to attract better candidates – initially the CFO was envisaged to be a junior manager.

There are **reasons for and against changes** in the management (see Figure 37). Major reasons for replacing managers included family managers' resigning, insufficient qualification, poor cooperation with family managers, and non-family managers' age. At the buy-out, most family managers resigned voluntarily because they approached retirement age or wanted to change their lifestyle.[733] Though not mentioned explicitly, another reason for retirement was possibly that after the sale, former family managers were no longer owners of the company and thus possibly neither had the motivation nor the obligation to manage it.

Poor cooperation with family managers that remained in the company after the buy-out entailed their dismissal. Private equity companies had a hard time to assess family managers' willingness and ability to adopt their management style and carry out the new owners' strategy. In F, the family manager did not adopt his management principles and decision making, what led to his resigning a year after the buy-out.[734] In E, the family manager lacked the skills to internationalize the company as envisaged

[731] A, D, G, H, K, L, M, and Q; 47% of 17 respondents. The CFOs in companies D and Q joined these companies 24 and 6 months before the buy-out respectively.

[732] In H, the CEO wanted to keep the incumbent CFO and the investor did not object.

[733] Cf. subsection 4.2.1.1.

[734] Cf. subsection 4.2.2.5.

by the investor; in consequence, the family manager was replaced with a non-family manager experienced in doing business abroad.[735]

Insufficient management skills were frequently named as causes for replacement of managers. In turnaround companies P and Q, insufficient skills could have been derived from past management performance demonstrated for instance by poor productivity indicators. But even if managers showed good performance pre buy-out, investment managers possibly assessed managers' qualification inadequate for upcoming challenges of the company, e.g. internationalization. This indicated that family owners and managers based their recruiting decisions on different criteria. As family owners and managers often took decisions in the areas assigned to non-family managers, the former possibly accepted managers with some weaknesses or who merely carried out their decisions.[736] The investment manager backing J provided support for this argument:

> *The former family owner told them what to do and that's it. Management was not involved in decisions. We [the investment managers] were really surprised by the low level of their contribution.*

Age was also a reason why non-family managers were replaced in three companies.[737] Despite the theoretical possibility to participate in the buy-out, these non-family managers had to be replaced because they approached retirement age. A last reason already described in subsection 4.2.1.3 was that family owners replaced managers to prepare their companies for sale.[738]

Besides these reasons favoring changes in the management, interviewees also brought up reasons for keeping pre buy-out management. First, pre buy-out managers had valuable knowledge of the company, the market and competitors. The investment manager backing B explained:

---

[735] However, cooperation with family managers could also work out. Cooperation was successful in G, where the family owner paid special attention to determine whether his strategy and management style were in line with the private equity company when choosing an investor.

[736] Indications for this assessment were found in companies B, C, and J. For characteristics private equity companies expected from post buy-out managers, see subsection 4.2.2.1.

[737] A, I, and M.

[738] D, K, and O.

We don't want to run the business without the two incumbent managers, who have been in this business that long. [One incumbent manager] is a top sales manager who knows the customers' needs inside-out.

Second, replacing single managers could possibly damage the whole management team, as newly appointed managers might not get along with remaining managers. Third, new managers might not feel committed to former managers' plans, which would thus become obsolete. However, thorough changes in the business plan might endanger the post buy-out financial structure of portfolio companies, as banks tie debt provision to managers' plans.[739] Fourth, managers were a strong link to employees and, thus, an important backbone of the organization.[740]

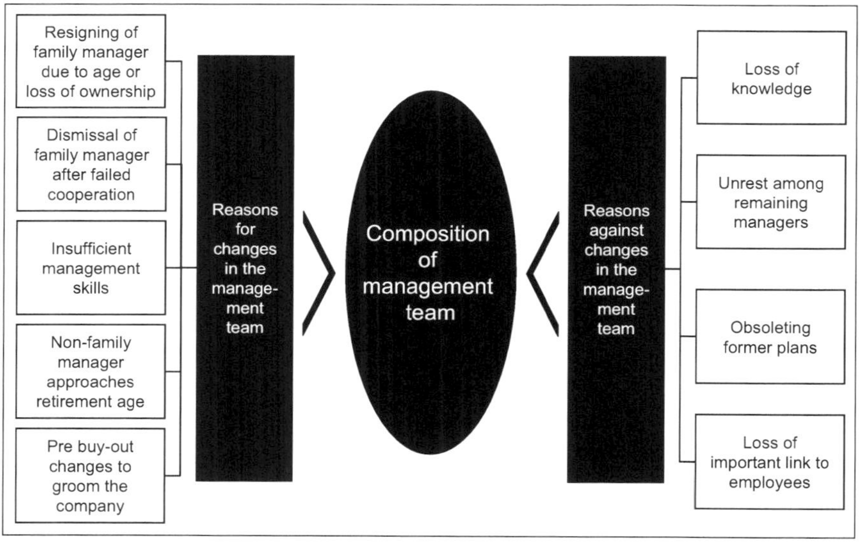

Figure 37: Reasons for and against changes in the management team

Source: Author's illustration

[739] Cf. subsection 7.1.2.

[740] Cf. subsection 4.2.2.4. These four reasons might possibly explain why private equity companies rarely changed the entire management right after the buy-out (this happened only in I, J, and P). Instead, many investigated each manager's skills and decided after a certain period whether the respective manager was to be replaced or not. However, if there was no doubt about insufficient qualification of a manager, this person might be fired right away after the buy-out.

Evaluation of pre buy-out managers is crucial for the private equity company to identify weaknesses in the management team and initiate a search for adequate candidates to overcome these weaknesses. Investment managers based their assessment on the due diligence process and their own and colleagues' personal impressions. In case of doubts about a manager's capacity, private equity companies also resorted to management audits by external parties. Nevertheless, in some cases the assessment was not right and a replacement seemed unavoidable: In Q, the pre buy-out CEO was fired three months after the buy-out. The investment manager backing this company explained:

> *We simply haven't known the management team enough. In a due diligence, you have about four meetings with the management – who arrogates [to know] how good a manager is? [...] All these due diligences and management audits are only theoretical. You get to know managers best when you cooperate with them.*

If managers did not qualify but wanted or expected to participate in the management team post buy-out, investors were advised to remove these managers from the company as they might have caused severe unrest within the company otherwise. In J, a junior manager, who was not appointed CEO despite aspirations for this position, tried to convince fellow junior managers to defect with him to a competitor.

To overcome weaknesses in the management team, private equity companies strived to **attract new managers**. Although candidates from within the company and outside the company were eligible to join the management board, in the sample companies only 8 internal managers were promoted compared to 21 appointments of external managers. The investment manager backing S commented on this preference for external managers:

> *A frequent problem is that there is no junior management with the skills needed. Or there are junior managers that have the right skills but lack entrepreneurial thinking. Moreover, there is a problem if the candidate is asked to buy shares in the company [...] and he has to bear risk. Many refrain from this opportunity in consequence.*

External candidates for the management were identified through headhunters, private equity companies' networks of interested managers[741], former colleagues of post buy-out managers, or could be recruited from acquired companies. Despite highly attractive compensation schemes, candidates might refrain from becoming managers in portfolio companies due to uncertainty about the long term perspective and the next career steps.[742] In case a preferred candidate declined to participate in the buy-out, investors could approach managers in competing large corporations or look for managers in related industries. This search process was not always successful, as the example of F shows: After a family manager resigned, an external manager was appointed CEO, who was described as completely unqualified due to his lack of industry know-how and experience in Mittelstand companies. This CEO was dismissed in the secondary buy-out of the company.[743]

With regard to the **control group**, in the family businesses sold to holding companies, changes in the management team varied (see Table 25). S was the only

[741] Three managers that did a management buy-in actively looked for an opportunity to do a buy-out (one of them with backing of a semi-public investment company): The later manager of I was an experienced manager in restructuring. He had been in contact with the private equity company for fifteen years and had already been in talks about buy-outs in companies he had been with before. Eventually, the private equity company asked him to join the management of company I.

The later manager of L worked as a consultant before the management buy-in. Over the years, he set up a network of about fifty private equity companies and M&A advisors. Before the buy-out in L, he had a closer look at three companies to take them over. The family owner of the first company was unwilling to open the books for due diligence. The second company did not seem to be a promising opportunity. In the third company, a private investor was faster to acquire the company.

Similarly, the later manager of T had examined about one hundred companies as potential buy-out targets. He decided to buy a company with his own equity and financial backing by a semi-public investment company. Thus, he avoided the influence of a private equity company as majority owner, though this independence meant that he could only become manager of a smaller company. He learned about the opportunity of a buy-out in company T through a local savings bank and the industry association the company was member of.

[742] The manager of E argued that a candidate with comparable job offers from a well-established corporation and a Mittelstand company backed by a private equity company would probably join the corporation. The manager of J supported this point of view: When he had learned that the company was owned by a private equity company, he contemplated once more about becoming manager or forgoing the offer.

[743] The manager of F assumed that a personal obligation of an investment manager brought this CEO into his position. This personal obligation prevented the CEO's dismissal before the secondary buy-out, as the interviewed manager and his fellow senior manager demanded the private equity company to withdraw the CEO, after they had realized the CEO's weaknesses.

sample company without a change in management. In R, the holding company appointed an external non-family manager to the management board to reduce dependency on the family manager. Later on, the second cousin of the family manager joined management in anticipation of the latter's retirement.[744]

In contrast, management changed significantly in the buy-outs backed by semi-public investment companies (see Table 25). In T and U, buy-out managers replaced the parting family managers. Management transition was ensured by regular meetings with former family managers (T) or by a consulting contract with former family owners (U). In V, the two internal buy-out managers joined the family manager on the management board.[745]

Company	Dismissals, retirements	Appointments	Pre and post buy-out position on the management board
R		Non-family manager (10), Family manager	Family CEO
S			Family manager
T	2 family managers (0; 0), non-family manager (0)	Non-family manager (0)	
U	2 family managers (0; 0)	2 non-family managers (0; 0)	
V		Non-family manager* (0)	Family manager, non-family manager

Table 25: Changes in the composition of management in companies of control group

Source: Interview data (n=5)
Numbers in brackets indicate the number of months after the sale, when managers were dismissed or appointed (if information was reported; negative numbers indicate months before the sale)
* Promotion of an internal manager

744 Both family owners achieved the goal they pursued with the buy-out: The family manager of R ensured a smooth transition to his relative and the manager of S could remain on the management board after the sale. In the subsidiaries of holding companies, no replacement of a CFO was reported. In S, the family manager acted as CFO and in R, the investor was satisfied with the pre buy-out CFO.

745 At the buy-out, non-family managers asked another internal non-family manager to join the management board. He rejected this offer for lacking financial means needed and avoiding personal risk.

In the companies backed by semi-public investment companies, replacements of the CFO occurred but were linked to the complete replacement of management in the management buy-ins (U, T). In V, the CFO was not changed.

To sum up, this subsection has shown that changes in the management team after the buy-out were immense. Changes in the management were reported in all portfolio companies. And these changes were very profound, as only 9 (24%) of initially 38 managers remained on the management board. The intensity of changes was surprising, given that quality of management was a major investment criterion for private equity companies, as discussed in subsection 4.2.2.1.

These changes could be explained by considerable differences between the requirements for managers in family businesses and portfolio companies. Private equity companies required managers that were able to carry out the strategy conceived with the investor. Managers were supposed to have a professional, accountable and transparent management style. These criteria were not fulfilled by all pre buy-out managers. Therefore, three of four pre buy-out managers were replaced at the buy-out, though investment managers recognized advantages of keeping pre buy-out managers. Especially CFOs were replaced (53% in the sample) and their positions upgraded, to reflect the increased importance of financing and strengthen the interface to investors and banks.

Proposition 4A: *Private equity companies have requirements for managers of portfolio companies that differ from requirements demanded by family owners.*

Proposition 4B: *Pre buy-out managers seldom fulfill the requirements expected by private equity companies and are therefore replaced.*

Proposition 4C: *In particular, CFOs are replaced by more competent managers and their position is upgraded.*

Most family managers left deliberately as they approached retirement age or wanted to change their lifestyle. If family managers decided to remain in the management, cooperation failed in two of three cases.

Proposition 4D: *Most family managers leave deliberately due to incapacity to carry out the strategy agreed on, or after a conflict with the private equity company about different management styles.*

Private equity companies employed their experience, and resorted to external specialists and their broad networks to shape the management team according to their requirements and the companies' needs. Despite some managers' reservation towards private equity, investors had arguably an advantage in recruiting over family businesses because of their skills and resources to assess pre buy-out managers and because of their ability to attract new managers. Family businesses might have appeared less attractive to potential managers due to lower salaries and subjectivity in the decisions who is promoted. Moreover, family managers might have preferred hiring weak managers, who did not challenge them.

Proposition 4E: *Private equity companies have an advantage over family businesses in composing a management team suitable for implementing needed changes.*

Three of four newly appointed managers came from outside the company. Internal junior managers either did not have the management skills needed or were unwilling to take the risk. External managers – especially from corporations – were used to work more transparently and could be chosen based on the skills needed in the respective company.

Proposition 4F: *Private equity companies prefer appointing external managers over promoting internal junior managers to the management.*

Some changes in management teams were initiated by the family before the buy-out in order to increase the salability of the company. However, in six of the nine companies, in which changes in the management occurred pre buy-out, management had to undergo further dismissals and appointments after the buy-out. But no manager appointed to the management board before the buy-out, was dismissed thereafter.

Proposition 4G: *Family owners appoint non-family managers before the sale to ensure continuity and thus increase salability of the company.*

Proposition 4H: *Private equity companies continue to change the management in most companies in which management was already changed before the buy-out.*

5.3.5. Motivation and compensation of management

This subsection presents the main drivers of motivation why managers participate in buy-outs and their compensation thereafter.[746]

Interviewed managers indicated the following **motivations** for the buy-out: become an entrepreneur, commitment to the company, make money, follow the owner's decision, and discontent with former job (see Table 26).[747]

	Managers' tenure in the company...		
Motivation for buy-out	...at least one year before buy-out	...less than a year before buy-out	...since buy-out
Become an entrepreneur	A, B, F, H	C, K, O	I, J, L
Commitment to company	B, D, F, G, H, M		
Make money	H	K	E, I
Follow owner's decision	A, B	Q	
Discontent with former job		O	E

Table 26: Managers' motivation for the buy-out

Source: Interview data (n=15; multiple motivations possible)
The managers of N and P were not asked for their motivation

Ten managers stated the aim to become an entrepreneur as motivation to do the buy-out.[748] They seized the opportunity to take over responsibility in an established company, which they could direct independently after the buy-out. Managers were especially intrigued by the discretion they had after the buy-out, as the manager of I explained:

---

[746] Most of these managers participated in the buy-out, but did not trigger the buy-out (cf. subsection 4.2.2.2).

[747] Motivation of the managers that were not interviewed could not be inferred. Therefore only the motivation of interviewed managers is discussed in this subsection.

[748] 67% of 15 respondents. Three of the managers mentioning this motivation were entrepreneurs some time before the buy-out and longed for becoming entrepreneurs again (H, J, and L).

> *This [company] was a very attractive opportunity, where I had the possibility to shape the company from the beginning on and where I had immense freedom in this reorganization. I've almost unlimited freedom here. [...] In a broader sense, I've to coordinate my actions with the investors, but within the company, I've great freedom up to a certain point.*

Despite the obligation to coordinate major actions, managerial discretion was in general untouched by the private equity company, as investors did not want to provoke managers' resigning over their intervention.[749] Freedom of decision by management increased in parallel to the reduction of former family owners' influence. Despite considerable family influence before the buy-out,[750] only two managers explicitly said that freedom from family influence was a motivation for them.[751] A possible explanation for this limited consent might have been that managers did not feel their freedom to be restricted in the family business as they were used to the pre buy-out level of discretion. An alternative explanation might have been that managers still felt loyal to the family managers and family owners they worked with and did not want to comment on this issue.

Commitment to the company was the second most frequent motivation named by managers to participate in the buy-out. All six managers that stressed this motivation worked in their respective companies for a considerable time period between 4 to 17 years – two of the managers had never worked for another company before.[752] Over these years, managers had established an emotional bond to the company they worked for, comparable to the emotional bond between family owner and company. In result, they felt like stewards of the respective company exhibiting lower self-interest and pursuit of joint goals, thus displaying features of a stewardship-relation towards the company.[753] Managers argued that they were rooted in their company, had a very high identification with it, and wanted to build the company's

[749] Cf. subsection 5.3.1.

[750] Cf. subsection 3.2.3.

[751] B and F.

[752] B, D, F, G, H, and M; 40% of 15 respondents.

[753] This underlines the argument in subsection 5.1.1 that internal, non-family managers were likely to behave like stewards.

future.[754] Others emphasized their relation to employees and felt socially responsible for the workforce.[755] The manager of M concluded his case:

> *I joined the company when it had about € 10 million in sales. A certain relation has grown as I took part in the following development. And the reason why I said I support the buy-out – [...] I was interested in the continuation of the company. That was exactly the same [goal] as [the former family owner].*

Four managers mentioned that compensation was a motive to carry out the buy-out.[756] Three of these managers joined the company at the buy-out (E, I) or briefly beforehand (K).[757] The number of managers motivated by the compensation scheme was surprisingly low, given private equity companies increased total compensation considerably. Possibly, some managers did not want to comment on the motivation through compensation, as they thought this motive might leave a bad aftertaste.[758]

The motive to follow the owner's decision was only brought up by three managers but is of particular interest.[759] These managers did not initiate the buy-out, but they wanted to remain on the management board post buy-out and therefore participated in the buy-out. Two of these managers had worked in the company for a long time before the buy-out.[760] The investment manager backing A stated:

> *The management didn't have any motive at all to do the buy-out. In this case, the management wasn't the driving force. The family owner wanted to sell and he wanted to sell to a financial investor. And a financial investor only acquires, if the management is in.*

---

[754] B, G, H, and M.

[755] D and F.

[756] E, I, H, and K; 27% of 15 respondents. Details on the different components of compensation are presented later on in this subsection.

[757] The fourth manager (H) owned his own consultancy with several employees before the buy-out. When he joined the company, he negotiated an agreement with the former family manager on a stake in the company. Despite his considerable tenure of seven years in the company, he might not have given up this profit-minded attitude – or was the only one to speak it out.

[758] This effect is referred to as a social-desirability-bias, which is a common problem of interviewing (cf. Schnell/Hill/Esser (2005), p. 355 et seq.).

[759] A, B, and Q; 20% of 15 respondents.

[760] (A, B). For a critical remark of the investment manager backing B about the company's managers, see his quotation later in this subsection.

Two managers did the buy-out as they were discontented with the former job. One manager working in another family business was not promoted to senior management as this position was reserved to family members (O). The other manager led a corporation whose long pursued strategy was eventually prohibited by anti-trust laws (E).[761]

Private equity companies also changed the **compensation scheme** to motivate management. Changes occurred with respect to the variable share of salary, total salary and equity participation.

The variable share of manager's salaries was increased in four companies and accounted for 50% of total salary in most cases.[762] In family businesses, variable salary components were also widely spread but accounted for a lower percentage of 30-40% of total salary. In three companies, the variable share of total salary was not changed, as this share was already very high pre buy-out.[763] The performance indicator, which variable payments were linked to, changed from mostly gross earnings (EBT) pre buy-out to EBITDA post buy-out.[764] Some managers had a set of different indicators, which variable payment was based on, as the manager of E explained:

> *60% of the bonus depends on achieving EBITDA targets, 10% on working capital targets, 10% on sales targets and 20% on qualitative targets.*

Through the buy-out, goal achievement became more transparent for managers. In B, cash forecast and management accounting were improved to the extent that managers knew about goal achievement during the fiscal year and were able to estimate their bonus. Objective communication and determination of goal achievement was a positive change for management, as some family owners were rather subjective with regard to the computation of bonus payments.

Total salary increased in six companies in consequence of the buy-out, in part due to the increase of the variable share of salary (i.e. the fixed salary has remained

---

761 The manager of E further stated that enthusiasm for the company was another motive for the buy-out. He emphasized outstanding company characteristics like market position, company development or product portfolio.

762 B, D, F, and K; 57% of 7 respondents.

763 A, G, and M; 43% of 7 respondents.

764 Cf. subsection 6.3.3 for a discussion of the change in performance indicators.

constant), in part due to an increase in the base payment.[765] The increase could at most double managers' pre buy-out salary; however, increases also had to be seen in the context of changes in functions and responsibilities. Only the salary of the manager in M remained constant, which the investment manager described as being already decent before the buy-out. Some interviewees added that alike salary increases were unlikely in family businesses, as family owners did not know the market price of qualified managers. The manager of A provided another reason:

> *Financial investors are rather willing to pay management more than a family owner. Family owners will always say: I could do this on my own. [...] They don't see managers as entrepreneurs, because family owners will always stay the entrepreneurs, and only entrepreneurs are to be paid like entrepreneurs. Private equity companies remunerate in a different way.*

While no non-family manager reported an equity stake in the family business, ten managers held an equity stake post buy-out.[766] Most of them held stakes between 5% and 20%. Higher equity stakes were reported by the manager of H, who turned pre buy-out sweet equity into a stake of 25%, and the manager of L, who held 40%. While most interviewees were enthusiastic about future capital gains from their participations, some appeared less positive. These managers said they liked the idea of equity participation but would carry out their duty also without it (I); others felt compelled to purchase equity to remain on the management board (N, Q). The investment manager backing B had to convince the management to purchase equity:

> *We didn't have typical buy-out managers there. [.. The incumbent managers] liked the idea of becoming senior managers and having a greater field of responsibility, in the sense of an employee. But in the sense of an owner-manager, we had to talk them into buying a stake. [...] This was something completely different from managers that are eager to become owner-managers, who we see in other cases. [The idea of becoming owner-managers] was far off for the incumbent managers.*

---

765 A, B, D, F, H, and Q; 86% of 7 respondents.

766 B, C, D, E, F, H, K, L, N, and Q; 83% of 12 respondents. In P, an interim management was leading the company; interim managers were unlikely to be granted equity stakes, given their involvement in the company was only of temporary nature.

In two companies, managers did not hold a stake at the time interviews were conducted.[767] In M, management participation was envisaged but postponed after a major acquisition to prevent dilution of managers' stakes [768], and in J, the manager did not want to acquire an equity stake.

With regard to the **control group**, motivation of managers of the family businesses sold to holding companies was already discussed in subsection 4.2.1.2 and is not included in the motivation pattern discussed in this subsection. With regard to their compensation, holding companies employed the same instruments of motivation like private equity companies. In R, the family manager's variable share accounted for 50% of his total salary and the family held an equity stake of 30%. In S, the family manager received bonus payments upon achievement of certain objectives, as he had to sell all his equity stake for tax reasons.

In the companies funded by semi-public investment companies, all three managers did the buy-out to become entrepreneurs.[769] As these managers were majority owners, they stipulated their compensation independently.

This subsection's **key findings** with regard to motivation can be subsumed as follows: While making money was infrequently indicated as motivation for the buy-out, the most frequent motive was becoming an entrepreneur and thus increasing freedom of decision. The related motive of freedom from family influence was rarely mentioned by interviewed managers, potentially because they were still loyal to the family or because they were used to the low degree of managerial discretion before the buy-out.[770] A particular motive emerged from interviews with managers who had been

---

767 17% of 12 respondents.

768 Equity grants were sometimes postponed until the private equity company had confidence in the management team, possibly half a year after the buy-out. This was a protection against granting shares to managers that had to be replaced after the buy-out.

769 While the manager of V was with his company more than a year before the buy-out, managers of T and U joined the company at the buy-out.

770 The finding, that freedom from family influence was not a major motive for managers, contradicted the opposite expectation derived from the considerable family influence on the management before the buy-out, as described in subsection 5.3.1. The finding that making money was not a key motivator also surprised, given private equity companies increased total compensation considerably after the buy-out. Although both findings lent themselves to

with the bought-out company for a comparably long time before the buy-out: These managers felt an emotional bond to and responsibility for the company.

Proposition 5A: *Commitment to the company was a motivation to do the buy-out for managers, who were with the company for a long period (i.e. at least four years) before the buy-out.*

With regard to the compensation scheme of managers, this subsection has shown that private equity companies used the standard means of compensation in portfolio companies. In family businesses, total compensation levels were in general lower and no equity participation was granted. All family businesses used variable payments, but determination of bonuses was not always comprehensible to managers and in part seemed subjective. Private equity companies changed the performance indicator the variable component of salary was based on and made the bonus payment more transparent for managers.

Proposition 5B: *Compared to the pre buy-out state, management is more incentivized post buy-out through equity participation, increases in total compensation, higher variable shares of compensation and greater transparency in performance determination.*

5.3.6. Decision making process of management

This subsection discusses the changes in the decision making process of management. After a comparison of decision making pre buy-out and post buy-out, resulting changes will be exemplified by analyzing management's approach towards evaluation of business relations and management's cost awareness after the buy-out.

Before the buy-out, family managers were prone to leading the company based on their gut feeling; this pattern of decision making was underlined by interview partners of nine companies that were managed by family manager until or before the buy-out.[771] While decisions were taken very fast, this approach had the shortcoming that decisions were not based on comprehensive analyses and were not linked to

propositions, these were not developed as these findings were likely to be distorted by the self-reporting bias of interviewed managers.

[771] A, B, F, I, J, L, P, R, and T; 60% of 15 respondents.

corporate planning or strategy. Gut feeling was based on the broad experience family managers had gathered during their tenure and could be a substitute for potentially missing plans or poor management accounting.[772] But even if the family business had a thorough planning and a sound management accounting, the family manager was accountable to nobody but himself, as the family manager of R explained:

> *You know, which direction to take, but you don't have substantiated the decision with figures. But, do you want to do it for yourself, if you're alone? To put the figures on the desk and say each quarter: Yippee, I'm so good!*

Family managers also lacked a sparring partner in the business, who could give a second opinion on critical decisions, as they either managed the company alone or did not regard non-family managers as peers. Instead, family managers based their opinions on talks to relatives and other people they had confidence in, though these possibly were far away from the company.[773]

If the company was not managed by a family manager pre buy-out, other problems could arise. The family owner possibly still influenced management's decisions, but his influence could be volatile and possibly influenced by other family members. The manager of A said that this influence might lead non-family managers to take decisions that they did not consider right. But management could not do much more than showing the disadvantages of these decisions and trying to persuade the family owner.[774]

After the buy-out, managers held a minority stake in the company, which restricted managerial discretion.[775] So, managers were accountable to the new majority owners, the private equity company. Investors expected management to grow the company according to the projections in the business plan, in order to maximize company value at exit.[776] Management was more oriented towards financial figures representing value generation and liquidity, and had to base management decisions

---

[772] Cf. subsection 6.3.1 for planning and subsection 6.3.2 for management accounting.

[773] L and T; 13% of 15 respondents.

[774] Cf. subsection 5.3.1 for owner's influence on management.

[775] Before the buy-out, family managers or family owners with a kinship relation to management mostly held the majority in the company.

[776] Cf. subsection 6.3.1.

rationally on these figures. Thus, management by gut feeling was replaced by management by figures through the buy-out.[777] Eight managers reported that the influence of figures has increased through the buy-out.[778] The manager of C said:

If a private equity company owns a company, [the business] is much more driven by figures. Decisions are taken based on facts and figures and not on emotions or gut feeling.

This rational, non-emotional decision making based on figures made management decisions more comprehensible for owners, banks and members of the supervisory board; this increase in comprehensiblity seemed to be the main driver behind changes in decision making (see Figure 38). The private equity company was interested in monitoring company development and expected notification when intervention was needed. Banks needed information to monitor covenants stipulated in the loan contracts.[779] As a breach of these covenants endangered financing of the company, management had to take these restrictions into account in all its decisions. The supervisory board monitored and advised management, as described in subsection 5.3.3. The supervisory board's questioning of proposed decisions forced management to prepare their decision papers thoroughly, as the manager of L explained:

You have to report every month and you should think all propositions through. You have to present reasonable, sound concepts. And you should not bring anything unfinished to the meeting.

The improvements in strategy, planning and management accounting post buy-out provided a framework for management decisions and thus enabled the changes

---

777 Other changes in decision making that occurred in individual cases were that management is more open towards external advice from consultants and that junior managers can challenge decisions by the management, which is rather difficult if senior managers are family members.

778 B, C, D, E, F, I, J, and P; 73% of 11 companies. In contrast, the managers of A, G, and M (27% of 11 companies) said that the influence of numbers on decision making has not increased. In A and M, management controlling was already well established pre buy-out and managers used it intensively. The manager of G (where the buy-out took place shortly before the interview) expected that the importance of figures would increase.

779 Cf. subsection 7.3.2. Covenants serve as "a contract that restricts managers' ability to use value reducing methods to generate cash or take other actions that reduce debtholder value." (Baker/Wruck (1989), p. 169).

described above (see Figure 38).[780] Especially availability of data from management accounting provided management with tools to make plans, set targets and control achievement of objectives. The manager of D stated:

Improvements in management accounting have prepared the ground to take fast and possibly better operational decisions.

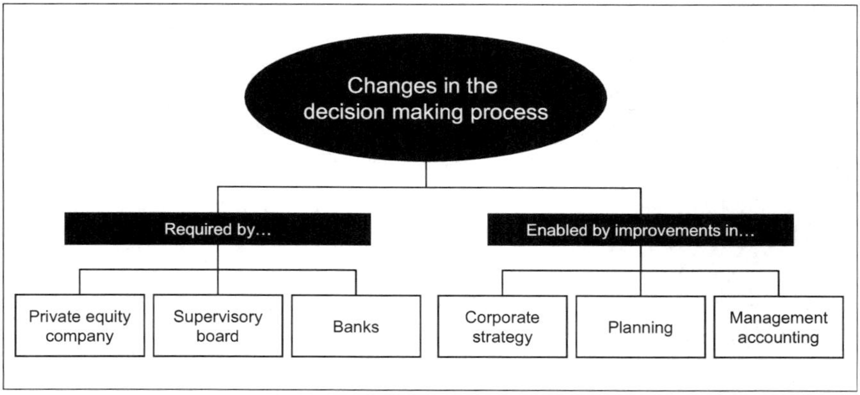

Figure 38: Drivers and enablers of changes in the decision making process

Source: Author's illustration

In the **control group**, the family businesses sold to holding companies provided a diverse picture with regard to changes in the decision making process. In R, the influence of financial figures on management decisions did not change, presumably, because management accounting was not changed and the supervisory board dissolved. In S, decisions were based to a lower degree on gut feeling after the sale, as the family manager had to discuss and justify decisions with the investment manager. Whether a change in decision making occurred, seemed to depend on involvement of the holding company and state of the subsidiary before the sale.

[780] Cf. subsection 5.3.2 for strategy, subsection 6.3.1 for planning and subsection 6.3.2 for management accounting.

In companies backed by semi-public investment companies, decision making was based on figures after the buy-out. This change in decision making style was not due to pressure from investment companies, which was generally low. Instead, managers seemed to have introduced this style of decision making independently. Focus on figures could be explained by managers being a different generation than former family managers, by managers' knowledge on modern tools of managerial control, or by their lack of experience to base gut feeling on.

Consequences of the changes in the decision making process are exemplified by the evaluation of business relations and cost awareness in the following. After the buy-out, management could **evaluate business relations** and either continue relations, renegotiate contracts or end relations. Ten companies reported they renegotiated business relations to increase profitability.[781] Revaluations were enabled by the improved or newly installed management accounting and demanded by private equity companies to increase profitability. Post buy-out management negotiated harder for better conditions and formalized business relationships through setting up contracts that did not exist or were rather relational contracts before the buy-out. This striving for increases in profitability put an end to discounts for friends of the family (J, U) and local sourcing, thus forgoing potential cost savings by sourcing internationally (I, K, P). The manager of K said:

> *Until the family owner resigned, we had the strategic restriction that all consumer products had to be produced in Germany. Since the buy-out, we have turned this paradigm upside down. Today, we source these products from China at a much lower price.*

Three companies did not follow this practice of revaluating business relations for profitability.[782] These companies were either depending on a strong supplier or headed by non-family managers pre buy-out.

---

[781] D, G, I, J, K, O, P, R, U, and V; 77% of 13 respondents. With the exception of G, all these companies were exclusively owned by the family before the buy-out.

[782] A, L, and M; 23% of 13 respondents.

In the context of changes in the decisions making process, interview partners were also asked whether they introduced **measures to cut costs** after the buy-out. In eight companies, cost cutting measures were introduced after the buy-out.[783] In most cases, potential to cut costs had already been identified by management pre buy-out, but family owners refused such steps for focusing less on profits or feeling indebted to employees. Cost cuts were mainly initiated by management and only in one case, the private equity company specifically demanded these cuts. Measures to cut costs included operational improvements in logistics and sourcing, increased cost consciousness throughout the company or optimization of product range.

In contrast, no cost cutting measures were reported in seven companies.[784] In these cases, costs were already low before the buy-out or managers objected cost cuts. For instance, the manager of F objected the private equity company's suggestion to reduce costs by cutting the Christmas bonus. Although private equity companies asked for measures to reduce costs, they mainly focused on growth in these companies.

Measures of cost reduction affected employees directly only in a few companies. While nine companies reported that headcount did not decrease following the buy-out,[785] employees were laid off in four companies.[786] Layoffs to increase profitability (B and E) were relatively low. In contrast, layoffs in the turnaround companies P and Q were considerably higher with about one third in case of P.

In **conclusion**, this subsection has shown that the decision making process of managers changed significantly in consequence of the buy-out. Before the buy-out, gut feeling, particular family objectives and emotions influenced decisions of the management. Gut feeling was based on the comprehensive experience long-serving managers had gathered. Family owners or managers held a stake in their company and were thus free to pursue their preferred goals, which were different from merely profit oriented companies. After the buy-out, separation of ownership and management increased the need for strong corporate governance and improved transparency.

---

783 B, E, H, I, J, K, L, and P; 53% of 15 respondents. With the exception of T, all these companies were exclusively owned by the family pre buy-out.

784 A, C, D, F, G, M, and O; 47% of 15 respondents.

785 A, D, F, G, H, J, K, M, and O; 69% of 13 respondents.

786 B, E, P, and Q; 31% of 13 respondents. All these companies were exclusively owned by the family before the buy-out.

Corporate governance and transparency requirements forced managers to take rationale decisions that were comprehensible for owners, banks and members of the supervisory board. But managers also recognized the advantages of figures to steer the company. These considerations lead to the following proposition:

Proposition 6: *Managers in portfolio companies focus on rational, comprehensible decisions based on figures to steer the company and thus put an end to management by gut feeling, emotions and particular family objectives.*

5.4 Summary of chapter

This chapter discussed changes in several aspects of corporate governance that were induced by buy-outs in former family businesses.

The first aspect of corporate governance examined is owner influence on management decisions. In most family businesses, family owners interfered with strategic and operational decisions of non-family management. After the buy-out, private equity companies influenced strategic decisions but no operational decisions. Management appreciated strategic influence due to investment managers' experience. Owner influence on strategic decisions changed from family owners' patronizing style to investors' interaction based style. Operational influence was precluded by law and by investment managers' objective not to be involved in day-to-day business.

Owners' influence on corporate strategy resulted in a severe change in strategies the sample companies pursued after the buy-out, especially in the fields of acquisitions, internationalization, and increasing profitability. Before the buy-out, family owners were hesitant towards these strategies, due to risk aversion, lack of competence, and lower priority assigned to growth. After the buy-out, owners' goals changed and portfolio companies were thus pressured by private equity companies to grow through acquisitions and internationalize. Investors provided the support for both strategies, which former family owners were unable to provide. Both strategies restored growth potential, as portfolio companies' strong position in the home market hampered organic growth therein. Private equity companies also emphasized increases in profitability, though rarely demanding sale of unused assets or divisions, possibly because operations were already very lean before the buy-out. While acquisitions are a strategy which investors also apply in other types of buy-outs, the focus on internationalization and renouncement of operational improvements distinguish buy-outs in family businesses.

Supervision by and support from the supervisory board changed significantly along with changes in board composition. Not every family business had a supervisory board. In case a family business had a board, it was composed of confidants of the family owners, namely auditors, lawyers, bankers, and acquaintances, who often lacked entrepreneurial thinking and relevant expertise. In consequence, boards members could only provide very limited support to managers. Moreover, board members did not carry out their supervisory function effectively due to insufficient qualification or dependency, or because supervision was unwanted by family owners and managers. After the buy-out, private equity companies appointed new supervisory boards or replaced virtually all board members. New boards were composed of investment managers, who represented the investor, experienced managers, who contributed their expertise, and less frequently members of the formerly owning family. The purpose of family members on the board was not to contribute expertise, but rather to represent their equity stake and allow a bond to the company, possibly to facilitate sale negotiations and emotional separation. The new composition enabled supervisory boards to efficiently supervise and support management through challenging decisions, making propositions and providing business contacts. Board meetings were more open, more structured and thus professionalized.

Management composition was changed substantially through the buy-out. Some of the changes in management were triggered by family owners to groom the company for sale; however, investors made further changes to the remaining teams. Especially CFOs were replaced and their positions upgraded, to reflect the increased importance of financing, and strengthen the interface to investors and banks. Intensity of changes hinted at differences in the recruiting criteria between family owners and private equity companies. Family owners seemed to tolerate weaknesses in managers' skills as they still controlled the company directly through management participation or indirectly through the supervisory board or ownership. Private equity companies looked for managers with a strong profile, high level of qualification, and experience to implement the envisaged strategy. Consequently, many pre buy-out managers did not meet the expectations of private equity companies and were replaced, though this brought about several disadvantages like loss of knowledge or loss of employees' confidence. Family members mostly left deliberately after the sale of the company or were replaced after cooperation failed. Given their experience and resort to external advice private equity companies had an advantage in composing an adequate management team. Private equity companies mostly preferred external over internal candidates to appoint managers, because of the weakness of the second management tier in family businesses. Instead, they capitalized on their broad network to identify and hire external candidates.

Six different motivations for managers to do the buy-out emerged from the interviews: Becoming an entrepreneur, commitment to the company, making money, following owners' decision, discontent with former job, and enthusiasm for the company. The increase in managerial discretion was the most frequent motive for the buy-out. Surprisingly, freedom from family influence was reported seldom as motivation, possibly because non-family managers were still loyal to the family or because they were used to the pre buy-out situation. Commitment to the company was motivation especially for long-serving managers, who thus revealed their self-image as stewards of the company. Some managers seemed to be driven into the buy-out involuntarily, as family owners decided to sell the company. Surprisingly, financial rewards were seldom mentioned as motivation for the buy-out, despite significant improvements in the compensation scheme. Total and variable payments were increased and were made more transparent to managers. Portfolio companies typically wanted managers to buy equity in the company, which was an opportunity family owners virtually never offered non-family managers. Despite being financially very attractive, some managers regarded equity participations less positively because of the inherent risk.

The buy-out also affected the process of decision making. In family businesses, some family managers were reported to base their decisions on intuition and talks to relatives. Gut feeling based on intuition and the considerable experience of family managers might have been the best decision base in the light of family businesses' poor management accounting and strategic planning. After the buy-out, management took non-emotional, rational, and comprehensible decisions based on figures. This decision style was enabled by improved instruments of managerial control and required by private equity companies, bank covenants, and supervisory board's monitoring. Changes in the decision making process lead to revaluation of business relations post buy-out, putting an end to personal preferences of family owners and aiming at increasing profits. Changes in decision making also lead to cutting operational cost, yet rarely implying layoffs.

The discussion of these aspects of corporate governance has shown in detail how buy-outs put an end to the frequent unity of ownership and management in the hands of the family, thus creating space in which to install a veritable corporate governance system. Owners do no more interfere with managements' day to day decisions, but actively monitor management through the supervisory board and stipulate the long-term development of the company through goals and strategy. The supervisory board is professionalized and strengthened to effectively monitor management. Management is significantly changed and professionalized through replacements, as shown in all sample companies.

These changes in corporate governance of former family businesses entail fading and finally vanishing of many of the peculiarities of family businesses: Owners' influence on operational decisions, reluctance to internationalize or grow through acquisitions, renouncement or installation of a weak supervisory board, no delegation of control, appointment of managers who carry out owners' decisions, and intuitive decision making. Discontinuation of these peculiarities of family businesses prepares the ground for professionalizing companies in many different ways. With the discontinuation of non-economic goals pursued by families, an economization of companies takes place[787], i.e. all activities are directed towards increasing a company's value and thus the value of private equity companies' investments.

The separation of ownership and control also puts an end to the stewardship environment in family businesses. While the end of this unity enables private equity companies to appoint more professional managers, ease close supervision and cease paternalism, it turns the portfolio companies into an agency environment. To avoid the costs of agency relationships, investors take the necessary precautions by installing a strong and capable supervisory board, introducing a compensation system to prevent divergence of managers' interests, and demand a more transparent decision making process. Despite these measures, some agency conflicts are nevertheless likely to occur. Existence of agency conflicts is a disadvantage inherent in the organization of portfolio companies compared to family businesses, and thus makes one of the key drivers of value generation of buy-outs in corporations ineffective. In consequence,

[787] Economization refers to the process of aligning a company with basic economic principles. This implies putting an end to non-economic paradigms, which might have guided family businesses before the buy-out. Thus, economization does not refer to cost reductions or rationalizations.

private equity companies must compensate this unavailable value generation through value creation by professionalizing the company. This chapter has shown that changes in all aspects of corporate governance, which were examined, aim at professionalizing the portfolio company compared to the former family business.

6 Changes in instruments of managerial control

This chapter inquires into changes in the instruments of managerial control after buy-outs in family businesses. Similar to chapter 1, this chapter starts with contrasting the instruments and the background of their implementation in section 6.1. Section 6.2 derives expectations about likely changes from the former section, and section 6.3 presents the changes observed in sample companies. Section 6.4 provides a summary of the chapter. The instruments of managerial control under analysis are: planning, management accounting, and performance measurement (see Figure 39).[788]

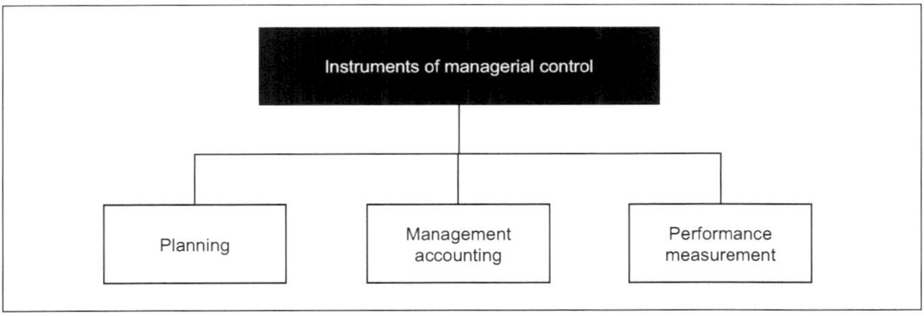

Figure 39: Analyzed instruments of managerial control

Source: Author's illustration

[788] The planning process deals with the conception of plans for a company's future activities (cf. Weber/Schäffer (2008), p. 5). Management accounting is the management function which is responsible for creating reports to inform the management on company activities and coordinating these activities (cf. Weber/Schäffer (2008), pp. 1, 24). Performance measurement refers to the choice of indicators to measure management performance and the monitoring of management performance.

The theoretical discussion of instruments of managerial control in family businesses also draws on literature that investigates into relevant issues in Mittelstand companies, as literature in the field of instruments of managerial control in German family businesses is rather limited. Literature on Mittelstand companies allows for analogical inferences for two reasons: First, the majority of Mittelstand companies are family businesses (estimations range from 83.5% to 95.1%; cf. Wolter/Hauser (2001), p. 71; Kay et al. (2003), p. 49; Kayser/Wallau (2003), p. 57 according to Hauser/Wolter (2007), p. 22). Second, most studies unintentionally refer to family businesses despite their different labeling (e.g., 81% of sample companies are family businesses in the study of Ossadnik/Barklage/van Lengerich (2004); 64% in the study of Günther/Gonschorek (2006); 59% in the study of Schachner/Speckbacher/Wentges (2006)).

6.1 Theoretical comparison of family businesses and portfolio companies

6.1.1. Instruments of managerial control in family businesses

Scholars have provided several **explanations for the less intensive usage of instruments of managerial control**, which are also termed control instruments in the following. First, goals of family owners and family managers differ from those of owners and managers of non-family businesses as family owners and managers draw benefits from achievements of non-financial and financial goals.[789] Given relevance of non-financial goals, the relative importance of financial goals is lower in family businesses than in non-family businesses.[790] In consequence, instruments of managerial control, which aim at increasing organizational efficiency and thus profit, might be less important to family owners and managers.[791]

Second, family owners and managers tend to base decisions rather on experience and intuition than on figures.[792] Thus, the need for control instruments is not only reduced, but these instruments might be seen as a straightjacket for their decisions.[793] The typically strong involvement of family owners and managers in the company's operations further reduces the need of tools to measure and control company performance.[794] Based on considerations in the early years of the family business, family managers regard control instruments superfluous and forgo implementation of these instruments, though the company has grown to a size where more information to control and support decisions might be appropriate.[795]

---

[789] Cf. subsection 4.2.2.2; Schachner/Speckbacher/Wentges (2006), pp. 592, 600; Dunn (1995), pp. 21 et seq.; Andersson/Carlsen/Getz (2002), pp. 100 et seq.; LeCornu et al. (1996), pp. 9-11; Günther/Gonschorek (2006), p. 7; Hirigoyen (1982), p. 590.

[790] Cf. subsection 5.2.5. This is backed by surveys showing that family businesses expect a lower return on equity than non-family businesses (cf. Feldbauer-Durstmüller/Wimmer (2008), p. 41; Schachner/Speckbacher/Wentges (2006), pp. 599 et seq.). However, return expectations in family businesses increases with company size (Schachner/Speckbacher/Wentges (2006), p. 599).

[791] Cf. Weber/Schäffer (2008), p. 19.

[792] Cf. subsection 5.3.6; Filbeck/Lee (2000), p. 204; Schein (1983), p. 26. See footnote 660 for further literature on this issue.

[793] Cf. Ward (1988), p. 114; Forst (1992), p. 37.

[794] Cf. subsection 5.3.1; Speckbacher/Schachner (2004), pp. 424-428; Schachner/Speckbacher/Wentges (2006), p. 607; Mintzberg/Waters (1982), pp. 495 et seq.; Habig/Berninghaus (2003), p. 34.

[795] Cf. subsection 5.2.6; Schröder (1998), p. 288; Daily/Dollinger (1992), p. 124; Charan/Hofer/Mahon (1980), p. 6.

Third, due to their parsimony and the limited benefit they attach to the results of control instruments, family owners and managers might be reluctant to dedicate human resources, significant initial investments, and continuous costs to instruments of managerial control.[796] Disinclination towards dedicating human resources to these tasks might be strengthened by the fact that especially smaller family businesses would hardly be able to utilize these resources to capacity.[797]

Fourth, preparation of data within the instruments of managerial control is time-consuming and might therefore be expected to be delegated by management.[798] However, family owners and managers might object this solution for two reasons: Information would empower the responsible employee, who would be well informed about processes, target values and current values.[799] This would mark the end of tacit knowledge of family owners and managers, which is often described as a competitive advantage of family businesses and serves as an instrument to assure family owners' and managers' power.[800]

Fifth, given rather weak or nonexistent supervisory boards in family businesses and reservation to share information with banks, provision of information to these stakeholders does not increase urgency to install and continuously improve instruments of managerial control.[801] In a survey, only 23% of family businesses provided data from management accounting to banks and only 15% to supervisory boards.[802]

---

796 Cf. Carney (2005), p. 254; Daily/Dollinger (1992), p. 124.

797 Cf. Kosmider (1994), p. 83; Friedl (2003), p. 73. This argument is partly offset by an empirical study showing that employees executing control instruments frequently carry out other tasks not related to instruments of managerial control, mostly accounting (cf. Ossadnik/Barklage/van Lengerich (2004), p. 628; Günther/Gonschorek (2006), p. 11; Horvath (2000), p. 27; Hahn (1994), p. 145).

798 Cf. Hennerkes (1998), p. 80.

799 Cf. Maser (1998), pp. 14 et seq.; Ward (1988), p. 113; Kosmider (1994), p. 83.

800 Cf. Sirmon/Hitt (2003), p. 342; Cabrera-Suarez/De Saa-Perez/Garcia-Almeida (2001), p. 44.

801 Cf. subsections 5.1.1 and 5.3.3 for details on supervisory boards in family businesses and subsection 7.3.2 for reporting of family businesses to banks. FORST underlines that provision of information to non-family investors is neither an argument for introducing or strengthening instruments of managerial control, given family businesses refuse cooperation with these investors (cf. Forst (1992), p. 37).

802 Cf. Feldbauer-Durstmüller/Wimmer (2008), p. 45.

Sixth, instruments of managerial control provide information that can be used to monitor management, e.g. by comparing projected to realized developments. While monitoring is necessary in an agency setting, it is not necessary for stewardship-oriented managers or might even be detrimental to their intrinsic motivation, as monitoring might be taken as sign of owners' distrust.[803] In case of an agency setting between family managers and family owners, who are not involved in the daily business of the company, instruments of managerial control could lower information asymmetries and thus discretion of family managers.[804] Therefore, family managers as well as stewardship-oriented non-family managers have an incentive for not introducing or improving instruments of managerial control.

Besides these arguments suggesting restricted usage, the literature also provides **arguments favoring the usage of instruments of managerial control**. Family businesses with an equally mixed board[805] or exclusive non-family management might exhibit a more intensive usage of instruments of managerial control.[806] On the one hand, non-family managers might demand introduction of these instruments, as they might be used to work with them in their former companies.[807] On the other hand, family owners and managers might use these instruments to monitor non-family managers and ensure that the latter act in the family's best interest.[808] Support for this argument is provided by empirical studies, which have shown that family businesses with non-family managers use instruments of managerial control more intensively.[809]

Banks might ask for implementing certain instruments of managerial control and for getting data from these instruments to determine creditworthiness.[810] These

803 Cf. Davis/Schoorman/Donaldson (1997b), pp. 38-40; Uhlaner/Flören/Geerlings (2007), p. 276.

804 Cf. Horvath (2000), p. 32.

805 Cf. subsection 5.1.1.

806 Cf. Schachner/Speckbacher/Wentges (2006), p. 606; Flacke (2006), p. 248.

807 Cf. Schein (1983), p. 26; Ward (1988), p. 115; Daily/Dollinger (1992), p. 124.

808 Cf. subsection 5.1.1; Feldbauer-Durstmüller/Haas (2008), p. 111; Daily/Dollinger (1992), p. 124.

809 Cf. Filbeck/Lee (2000), p. 210; Kosmider (1994), pp. 156 et seq.

810 Cf. Flacke (2006), pp. 248, 256. For instance, failure to provide a business plan could entail denial of a loan, as lenders might regard this failure as an indicator for unprofessionalism or as lenders are unable to evaluate the business (cf. Coleman/Carsky (1999), p. 82).

demands are in line with the bank regulation Basel II, which requires banks to gather more data on debtors.[811]

The larger and the older family businesses are, the more intensive is their use of instruments of managerial control.[812] Larger companies are more complex, thus necessitating more control instruments, and can more easily afford the costly implementation of these instruments.[813] Ownership of older family businesses might be split among a greater number of family members that are also more distant to the company, who might demand information provided by these control instruments.[814]

Despite these arguments favoring usage of control instruments, the literature suggests in general that instruments of managerial control are used to a lower degree in family businesses compared to non-family businesses. Most empirical studies support this hypothesis.[815] Figure 40 summarizes the theoretical reasons for and against intensive usage of control instruments in family businesses.

---

811 Cf. Flacke (2006), p. 292. Basel II is an accord by the Basel Committee on Banking Supervision, which recommends banks to underlay bank loans with equity depending on the debtor's creditworthiness. Banks require company data to determine the creditworthiness of a company (cf. Kabuth (2004), p. 3)

812 Cf. Filbeck/Lee (2000), pp. 206, 210; Ossadnik/Barklage/van Lengerich (2004), pp. 624 et seq., 627; Schachner/Speckbacher/Wentges (2006), pp. 605 et seq.; Hoque/James (2000), pp. 3, 9.

813 In general, smaller companies have fewer occasions to employ certain tools of management accounting, like investment calculations, make-or-buy analyses, or project management (cf. Ossadnik/Barklage/van Lengerich (2004), p. 628).

814 Cf. Uhlaner/Wright/Huse (2007), p. 233.

815 Cf. Ossadnik/Barklage/van Lengerich (2004), p. 627; Filbeck/Lee (2000), p. 213; Westhead (1997), p. 145. Only FELDBAUER-DURSTMÜLLER/WIMMER do not support the hypothesis (cf. Feldbauer-Durstmüller/Wimmer (2008), p. 44-46).

But even if instruments of managerial control are implemented in a family business, the importance management attaches to this function is crucial for the maximum contribution of control instruments; given the arguments discussed in the beginning of this chapter, not all managers in family businesses seem committed to these instruments (cf. Schröder (1998), p. 331).

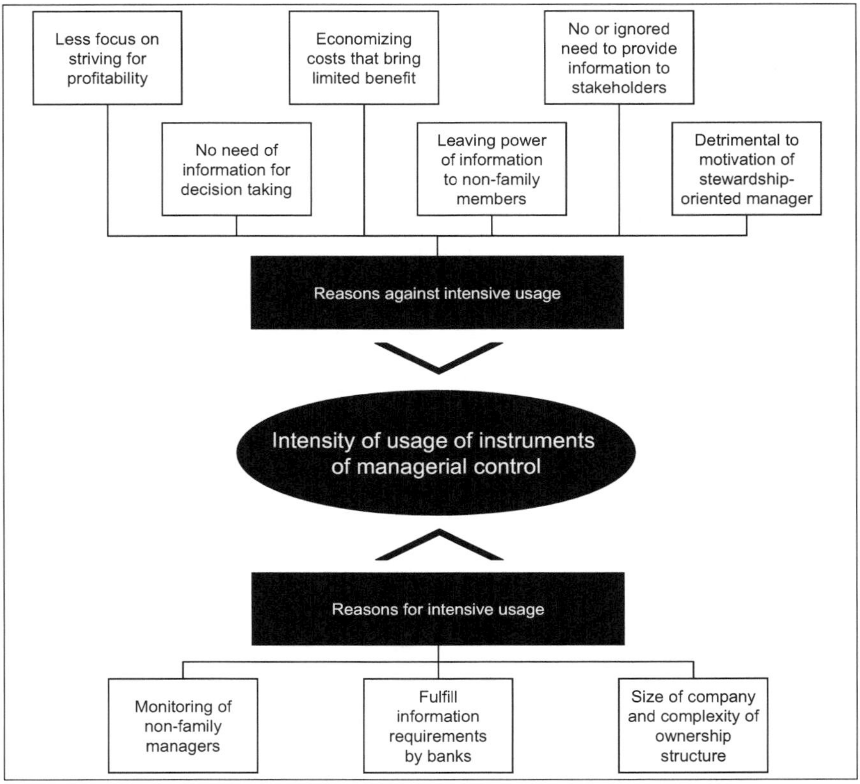

Figure 40: Reasons influencing usage of control instruments in family businesses
Source: Author's illustration

After this discussion of the theoretical background, empirical data on individual control instruments in family businesses will be presented. Starting with the first instrument of managerial control, Table 27 provides an overview of **empirical studies on the usage of planning tools in family businesses.**[816] The studies presented agree

[816] The three samples differ with regard to the size of companies included. The survey on top of the list examines the largest companies and studies below smaller ones. GÜNTHER/GONSCHOREK focused on larger companies with sales between € 20m and € 1,000m; 23% of companies are larger than € 100m (Günther/Gonschorek (2006), p. 5). OSSADNIK/BARKLAGE/VAN LENGERICH included companies with sales between € 0.1m and € 920m; 7% of companies are larger than €

on the fact that the majority of family businesses use planning tools.[817] As pointed out above, company size seems to be a major driver of usage of planning tools. This is reflected by the intensity of usage of the tools liquidity planning, financial planning and business plan, which is highest in the study by GÜNTHER/GONSCHOREK focusing on larger companies.[818] However, findings are inconsistent with regard to some aspects: In the sample of GÜNTHER/GONSCHOREK, virtually all companies employed projections of financial statements and had a business plan, whereas in the other two studies only half or even less sample companies employed these tools.

Author, year	Sample composition	Planning tools
Günther/ Gonschorek (2006)	307 German family (64%) and non-family (36%) businesses; average frequency of usage of selected tools	97% Projected profit and loss statement, balance sheet 90% Business plan 87% Liquidity planning 59% Financial plan
Ossadnik/ Barklage/ van Lengerich (2003)	169 German family (81%) and non-family (19%) businesses; average frequency of usage of selected tools (1 = permanent usage; 5 = never used)	1.9 Liquidity planning 2.6 Financial plan 2.8 Business plan 2.9 Projected profit and loss statement, balance sheet
Feldbauer-Durstmüller/ Wimmer (2008)	236 Austrian family businesses; average frequency of usage of selected tools	88% Sales planning 67% Liquidity planning 60% Projected profit and loss statement 48% Projected balance sheet

Table 27: Surveys on the usage of planning tools in family businesses

Source: Günther/Gonschorek (2006), p. 12; Ossadnik/Barklage/van Lengerich (2003), p. 61; Feldbauer-Durstmüller/Wimmer (2008), p. 46

125m (Ossadnik/Barklage/van Lengerich (2003), p. 52). FELDBAUER-DURSTMÜLLER/WIMMER do not provide minimum or maximum sales of the family businesses included; 23% of companies are larger than € 50m (the largest sales category given) and 29% smaller than € 10m (Feldbauer-Durstmüller/Wimmer (2008), pp. 24 et seq.). Divergences of the results (which are discussed below) seem too significant to be entirely attributable to the non-overlapping of size categories in these studies.

817 Only 4% of family businesses do not engage in a planning process (cf. Feldbauer-Durstmüller/Wimmer (2008), pp. 45 et seq.). The authors find that planning in family businesses is more intensive than in non-family businesses, especially with regard to sales forecasts and liquidity planning. This contrasts findings of several other authors (see footnote 815). The authors provide two explanations for this intensive usage of planning: First, family businesses might be more prudent as capital stems from family fortune. Second, these companies must have a closer look at their budgets given debt financing to bridge liquidity shortages is less available.

818 A survey among Swiss family businesses has found that 24% do not have a business plan (cf. PriceWaterhouseCoopers (2008b), p. 4). This percentage is about the average of the studies of GÜNTHER/GONSCHOREK and OSSADNIK/BARKLAGE/VAN LENGERICH.

With regard to the second control instrument discussed, results of surveys on the **usage of tools of management accounting** are shown in Table 28.[819] These studies show that tools of management accounting are used less intensively than planning tools. Especially strategic and complex tools like balanced scorecards are infrequently used. Besides these insights, Table 28 does not show consistent patterns: While GÜNTHER/GONSCHOREK find that family businesses intensively use a broad range of tools of management accounting, results from OSSADNIK/BARKLAGE/VAN LENGERICH do not support this inference. It is especially remarkable that cost accounting, investment calculations and benchmarking seem to be used less intensive in the study of the latter authors compared to the study of FELDBAUER-DURSTMÜLLER/WIMMER, though these authors focus on smaller companies than the former.[820] Despite these inconsistent results on the usage of management accounting tools, a longitudinal analysis of Austrian family businesses has shown that management accounting has been professionalized over the last years.[821]

[819] For remarks on sample differences with regard to the size of companies included, see footnote 816.

[820] Besides the aforementioned studies, FORST has examined the state of management accounting before buy-outs in family businesses; he has found that family businesses do not employ any tools of management accounting besides those, which are obligatory by law (cf. Forst (1992), p. 37). However, this finding has to be seen in the light of the time past since FORST conducted his study.

[821] A comparison of three surveys shows that the percentage of family businesses forgoing management accounting has decreased from 30% in 1994, over 19% in 2004 to 14% in 2007 (cf. Niedermayr (1994), p. 219; Wimmer (2004), p. 207; Feldbauer-Durstmüller/Wimmer (2008), p. 43). Percentages are not perfectly comparable, as they are not based on a constant panel, but suffice to derive a trend.

FELDBAUER-DURSTMÜLLER/WIMMER find that there is no significant difference between family businesses and non-family businesses in the usage of management accounting (cf. Feldbauer-Durstmüller/Wimmer (2008), p. 43).

Author, year	Sample composition	Tools of management accounting
Günther/ Gonschorek (2006)	307 German family (64%) and non-family (36%) businesses; average frequency of usage of selected tools	92% Cost accounting 88% Product cost calculation 57% Investment calculations 16% Balanced scorecard
Ossadnik/ Barklage/ van Lengerich (2003)	169 German family (81%) and non-family (19%) businesses; average frequency of usage of selected tools (1 = permanent usage; 5 = never used)	2.4 Cost accounting 3.2 Product cost calculation 4.0 Investment calculations 4.1 Benchmarking 4.8 Customer benefit analysis 5.0 Balanced scorecard
Feldbauer-Durstmüller/ Wimmer (2008)	236 Austrian family businesses; average frequency of usage of selected tools	78% Investment calculations 61% Cost accounting 54% Benchmarking 30% Customer benefit analysis 14% Balanced scorecard

Table 28: Surveys on the usage of tools of management accounting in family businesses

Source: Günther/Gonschorek (2006), p. 12; Ossadnik/Barklage/van Lengerich (2003), p. 61; Feldbauer-Durstmüller/Wimmer (2008), pp. 44, 46[822]

Unavailability of more detailed data on the three studies discussed above hinder deeper analyses, which might yield more detailed and more consistent insights than the comparison of average values. In their study on usage of tools of planning and management accounting in family businesses, SIEMES/SEGBERS pursue an interesting approach.[823] They analyze their data using a cluster analysis, which yields three different groups: One group exhibiting high intensity in planning and management accounting; a second group with intensive planning but less intensive management accounting; and a third group with a low intensity in planning and management accounting.[824] Non-existence of a cluster populated by companies with intensive management accounting and relatively weak planning suggests that planning appears to be more important for family businesses.[825] FLACKE also employs a cluster analysis

---

822 For a less detailed study by practitioners, cf. PriceWaterhouseCoopers (2005), p. 19; PriceWaterhouseCoopers (2006), p. 37.

823 Cf. Siemes/Segbers (2005), pp. 312-315.

824 Companies in the first cluster are significantly larger in terms of sales than in the other two clusters. Unfortunately, SIEMES/SEGBERS do not consider characteristics of family businesses (e.g. ownership structure, mixed management, existence of supervisory board), which might possibly account for differences between clusters.

825 This argument is somewhat offset by the fact that the difference in average usage between the clusters is higher for the tools of planning than for those of management accounting. This means

in his study on the state of management accounting in Mittelstand enterprises; he identifies three clusters, which differ with respect to their state of professionalism significantly.[826] In essence, the cluster analysis might be a first indication that the intensity of planning and management accounting in family businesses is very heterogeneous;[827] this heterogeneity would reduce the explanatory power of a mere look at mean values, as done in most previous studies.

Empirical evidence on performance measurement as the third control instrument is very limited for family businesses. Given the lower importance attached to financial goals in family businesses, scarcity of research might reflect the neglect by practitioners. Family managers hardly engage in performance monitoring and thus use of indicators, given there is frequently no independent external shareholder or supervisory board member to monitor them or to provide feedback.[828] The importance of monitoring is further reduced by the overriding importance of family concerns and non-economic goals, not reflected in performance indicators.[829] As delegation of control to non-family managers calls for monitoring, intensive performance measurement should be expected in family businesses led by non-family managers; however, there seems to be hardly research on performance indicators and monitoring used for this purpose.[830] Empirical studies have shown that family businesses using performance indicators focus on net earnings, earning before taxes (EBT) or earnings

---

that the difference between companies with a weak and a strong planning is relatively greater than the difference between the companies with a weak and strong management accounting. This contrasts the argument that planning is more important than management accounting for family businesses.

826 Cf. Flacke (2006), pp. 252 et seq. Company size (in terms of total assets), non-family managers, young managers, and cooperation with banks seem to foster a professional management accounting (cf. Flacke (2006), p. 256).

827 GÜNTHER/GONSCHOREK find that value-oriented tools of management accounting are more often used by larger companies (cf. Günther/Gonschorek (2006), p. 12). This might be taken as indicator that a cluster analysis would have yielded more detailed results in their study as well.

828 Cf. Poza/Alfred/Maheshwari (1997), p. 149.

829 Cf. Ward (1988), p. 105.

830 This scarcity of research is true for most issues relating to non-family managers in family businesses. CHUA/CHRISMAN/SHARMA note that given the importance attached to the relationship between family business and non-family managers, "it is surprising that there have been so few studies on the topic in the literature." (Chua/Chrisman/Sharma (2003), p. 96; cf. Carrasco-Hernandez/Sánchez-Marín (2007), p. 218).

before interest and taxes (EBIT).[831] WARD argues that these indicators best reflect the amount of money available to the family and the business for further investments.[832] Targets are mostly linked to these performance indicators and stipulated on an annual basis.[833] A survey on the expected return on capital in the USA has found that 55% of family owners did not have a target rate of return on their capital invested in the company; another 27% had a rough target rate, but had not stipulated a definite number.[834]

6.1.2. Instruments of managerial control in portfolio companies

In portfolio companies, **instruments of managerial control play a vital role for four reasons**. First, management needs control instruments to prepare planning for upcoming years to base the business plan on.[835] The business plan is pivotal for managers' success to convince a private equity company to invest and to win a bank to contribute debt to the deal.[836] After the buy-out took place, instruments of managerial control stipulate goals, which managers are supposed to achieve, to develop the company according to the business plan, and provide an outline for company development until the exit.[837]

Second, managers also need data from instruments of managerial control to base their rationale decisions on; this increase in importance of control instruments results from the change in the decision making process putting an end to intuitive decisions as observed before the buy-out.[838] The instruments of managerial control are

---

831 Cf. Ward (1988), p. 113; Günther/Gonschorek (2006), p. 13; European Private Equity & Venture Capital Association (2005), p. 20.

832 Cf. Ward (1988), p. 113.

833 Cf. Günther/Gonschorek (2006), p. 15.

834 Cf. Upton/Petty (2000), p. 34.

835 Cf. Sharp (2003), p. 37; Wright/Coyne (1985), pp. 26-28.

836 Cf. Becker (2000), pp. 62, 106; Sharp (2003), pp. 35 et seq.; Sander (2006), p. 203; Wright/Robbie (1996), p. 160. Instruments of managerial control are a requirement of private equity companies and poor state of implementation might lead to investment denial (cf. Mitchell/Reid/Terry (1995), p. 190).

837 Cf. 5.3.5; Becker (2000), p. 90; Bruining/Bonnet/Wright (2004), p. 160; Houlden (1990), pp. 73 et seq. Information requirements of private equity companies are adapted to the performance of the portfolio companies. They typically increase in case of under-performance and decrease in case of over-achievement or at a later stage of the holding period (cf. Mitchell/Reid/Terry (1995), p. 191).

838 Cf. subsection 5.3.6; Jones (1992), p. 162.

employed by managers to monitor their own performance in terms of goal achievements.[839] If members of the management team were replaced through the buy-out, new managers are likely to demand and implement instruments of managerial control, because they are used to work with these instruments.[840] But also pre buy-out managers who remained on the management board, might put greater emphasis on control instruments, given they do not want to risk their own money invested in the company.[841]

Third, separation of ownership and control as discussed in subsection 5.1.2 creates an agency setting. Therefore, investment managers and members of the supervisory board need data from the instruments of managerial control to monitor managers.[842] Results from control instruments permit investment managers and board members to assess company development, reconfigure goals and compensation, and thus incentivize managers.[843] Moreover, board members need data from these instruments as background knowledge of the company to support and advise management best.[844]

Fourth, banks also require intensive usage of control instruments. Banks need the data generated by these instruments during buy-out negotiations and post buy-out: During negotiations, data on company development as envisaged in the business plan is needed to determine debt capacity and, thus, post buy-out capital structure of the portfolio company.[845] Post buy-out, data from control instruments is used to monitor

---

839 Cf. Bruining/Bonnet/Wright (2004), p. 160.

840 Cf. subsection 6.1.1.

841 Cf. Jones (1992), p. 166. After the buy-out, non-family managers of portfolio companies have enhanced freedom to adjust control instruments and the power to effect these adjustments (cf. Jones (1992), p. 152).

842 Cf. sources in footnote 576; Sharp (2003), pp. 98 et seq.; Sander (2006), p. 170; Meier (2006), p. 21. JONES rejects this reason (cf. Jones (1992), p. 163).

843 Cf. Bruining/Bonnet/Wright (2004), p. 166; Robbie/Wright (1996), pp. 53 et seq.; Reid (1996), pp. 242 et seq.; Mitchell/Reid/Terry (1995), p. 194; Reid (1996), p. 243. Monitoring of managers has been discussed in the context of venture capital investments in portfolio companies, which are mostly fast-growing start-ups by Mitchell/Reid/Terry (1997), p. 59.

844 Cf. Achleitner et al. (2004), p. 34; Bruining/Bonnet/Wright (2004), p. 166; Anders (1992), p. 84.

845 Cf. Thompson/Wright (1995), p. 693; Huydts (1992), p. 148; Becker (2000), p. 36; Robbie/Wright (1996), p. 50.

whether the company fulfills at all times loan covenants and thus whether debt service might be endangered.[846]

The only **counterargument against intensive usage** of control instruments is the increased costs the instruments entail. Therefore, this discussion suggests that control instruments are intensively used in portfolio companies.[847] The existing, very limited research on instruments of managerial control backs this inference.[848]

After this general discussion of influences on instruments of managerial control in portfolio companies, a closer look will be given on the individual instruments, though this more detailed analysis is complicated by the scarcity of research on these instruments.[849] Most research in this field focuses on spin-off buy-outs and shows that after the buy-out, instruments of managerial control are better adapted to the portfolio companies' organizational context, as companies are freed from conformity constraints by their former holding company.[850] HOWORTH/WESTHEAD/WRIGHT and ACHLEITNER/SCHRAML/TAPPEINER find first evidence on professionalization of instruments of managerial control following buy-outs in former family businesses.[851] Without providing precise details, a survey in Switzerland has shown that 38% of Swiss family businesses improve their control instruments in anticipation of the sale, as discussed in subsection 4.2.1.3.[852] Despite focusing on spin-off buy-outs, JONES conducted the

---

846 Cf. subsection 7.1.2; Huydts (1992), p. 176; Citron/Robbie/Wright (1997), p. 284. Like private equity companies, banks intensify their monitoring if company performance falls short of projections (cf. Angwin/Contardo (1999), p. 501).

847 In a study among UK private equity companies, only 2 out of 20 respondents indicated that costs of control instruments were considered as a critical factor when deciding how to change instruments (cf. Mitchell/Reid/Terry (1995), p. 192).

848 Cf. Jones (1992), p. 166.

849 Research on buy-outs seems to focus on issues related to corporate governance or financing instead.

850 Cf. Jones (1992), p. 166; Bruining/Bonnet/Wright (2004), p. 170; Geidner (2009), p. 280. Relevance of the study by BRUINING/BONNET/WRIGHT for this subsection is limited due to the focus on changes in control instruments related to strategy. Changes in control instruments in the study by JONES depend on the specific state of these instruments in the former corporation before the buy-out and are thus not perfectly transferable to buy-outs in family businesses.

851 Cf. Howorth/Wright/Westhead (2007), pp. 13, 22 et seq.; Achleitner/Schraml/Tappeiner (2008), p. 70 (the latter study examines minority stakes of private equity companies in family businesses). Both studies do not provide concrete details on professionlization.

852 Cf. PriceWaterhouseCoopers (2005), p. 19.

most detailed study on changes in instruments of management control after buy-outs.[853] As this study allows for analogical inferences about effects of buy-outs in family businesses, study results are presented in the following in detail.

Table 29 shows the **usage of selected planning tools** after the buy-out. In general, the importance of planning tools increases or remains unchanged; only a few companies reported planning tools were abandoned or lost importance.[854] These findings have to be seen in the context that examined portfolio companies were former corporate divisions, which presumably used planning tools more intensively than family businesses. Private equity companies did not stipulate usage of certain tools or details of their implementation; but investors expected that plans were updated at least on an annual basis.[855] HOWORTH/WESTHEAD/WRIGHT find that especially successful buy-outs in family businesses put an emphasis on strategic planning and specific goal setting.[856]

	Usage of planning tools		
Tool	Tool introduced or retained with increased importance	Tool retained at unchanged importance	Tool abandoned or retained with lower importance
Long-term planning	46%	27%	27%
Short-term planning	67%	27%	6%
Capital expenditures	35%	59%	6%
Fixed period budgets	18%	82%	0%
Revised forecasts	44%	56%	0%

Table 29: Usage of planning tools after spin-off buy-outs

Source: Modifiedly taken from Jones, C. S. (1992), p. 168 (n=17)[857]

[853] Cf. Jones (1992). Results are based on interviews with senior managers in 17 portfolio companies.

[854] In contrast to this general trend, 27% of companies discontinued long term planning completely after the buy-out. JONES explains the relatively high percentage of companies abandoning or lowering the importance of long term planning with the fact that in some companies, pre buy-out long term plans were based on poor planning processes, and results were mostly created to fulfill holding companies' demands (cf. Jones (1992), p. 157).

[855] Cf. Jones (1992), p. 156.

[856] Cf. Howorth/Wright/Westhead (2007), p. 23. The authors do not compare these findings to the pre buy-out state.

[857] Selected tools. Data is based on interviews with 17 buy-outs in divisions of UK corporations (cf. Jones (1992), pp. 154 et seq.).

Changes in management accounting are similar to those in planning (see Table 30): Most companies retain their tools or attach greater importance to them.[858] Increases in importance or new introductions aimed at improving performance of portfolio companies.[859] Again, results stem from spin-off buy-outs in corporate divisions, which are likely to exhibit a more intensive usage of management accounting pre buy-out than family businesses and might thus understate potential changes after buy-outs. Private equity companies do not seem to impose certain tools on the company, but to develop and improve usage of tools together with managers through the supervisory board.[860] After the buy-out, results have to be reported more frequently and within a strict time limit.[861]

	Usage of tools of management accounting		
Tool	Tool introduced or retained with increased importance	Tool retained at unchanged importance	Tool abandoned or retained with lower importance
Cost accounting	31%	63%	6%
Product contributions	29%	59%	12%
Variance analyses	41%	59%	0%
Cash flow reports	43%	43%	14%

Table 30: Usage of tools of management accounting after spin-off buy-outs

Source: Modifiedly taken from Jones, C. S. (1992), p. 168 (n=17)[862]

[858] MITCHELL/REID/TERRY confirm that private equity companies demand a more detailed form of accounts than typical shareholders (cf. Mitchell/Reid/Terry (1995), p. 191).

[859] Cf. Jones (1992), p. 158. JONES uses this argument also for the planning tools newly introduced or appreciated.

[860] Cf. Bruining/Bonnet/Wright (2004), pp. 165-167, 171; Jones (1992), p. 155. In contrast, MITCHELL/REID/TERRY argue that over a third of private equity companies have fixed requirements for information provision (cf. Mitchell/Reid/Terry (1995), p. 191). This low share of investors with pre-defined information requirements is surprising, given private equity companies' reporting to fund investors might favor a higher degree of standardization. Possibly, investors have stipulated basic information requirements every portfolio company has to fulfill; information requirements beyond these might be more tailored to the specific portfolio company.

[861] Cf. Bruining/Bonnet/Wright (2004), p. 166; Mitchell/Reid/Terry (1995), p. 191.

[862] Cf. footnote 857.

With regard to changes in **performance measurement**, private equity companies are expected to focus on earnings before interest, taxes, depreciation and amortization (EBITDA) or cash flows as most important performance indicator. These indicators reflect liquidity in the company, which is needed to service debt and pay interest, both resulting from the significant leverage following the buy-out.[863] A survey by the EUROPEAN PRIVATE EQUITY AND VENTURE CAPITAL ASSOCIATION has supported this expectation with first empirical evidence. The study has shown that after buy-outs in family businesses, performance indicators become more important for management and that the most important performance indicator changes from net earnings to cash flow through buy-outs in family businesses (see Table 31).

	Importance	
Performance indicator	Pre buy-out	Post buy-out
Cash flow	4.19	4.72
Net earnings	4.38	4.64
Long-term profitability	4.14	4.48
Sales growth	4.17	4.32

Table 31: Change in importance of performance indicators in buy-outs

Source: European Private Equity & Venture Capital Association (2005), p. 20[864]
Selected average values on Likert scale (5= very important; 1 = very unimportant)

Importance of both indicators can be derived from the increased reporting frequency demanded by investors: BRUINING/BONNET/WRIGHT found reporting on a monthly basis, JONES reporting on a daily basis.[865] The business plan underlying the buy-out specifies target values of the indicators, which management is expected to achieve.

[863] Cf. Becker (2000), p. 90; Sander (2006), p. 166; Ballwieser/Schmid (1990b), p. 359.

[864] n=111 (cash flow and long-term profitability); n=112 (net earnings); n=109 (sales growth).

[865] Cf. Bruining/Bonnet/Wright (2004), p. 167; Jones (1992), pp. 157 et seq., 163. MITCHELL/REID/TERRY also reported outstanding importance of cash flows for private equity companies without providing a reporting interval (cf. Mitchell/Reid/Terry (1995), p. 190).

6.2 Expected changes based on the literature

6.2.1. Planning

The general discussion about the importance of instruments of managerial control in family businesses and portfolio companies suggests that the importance of all control instruments will increase through the buy-out; hence, the importance of planning can also be expected to increase.[866] Studies on planning in family businesses showed a rather frequent usage, which surprises, given the theoretical considerations on lower importance attached to this instrument by family owners and managers. However, diverging results could be explained by the cluster analysis presented in subsection 6.1.1, namely that family businesses are not perfectly homogeneous with regard to the intensity of usage of planning tools. Instead there seem to be several groups whose usage of planning tools ranges from very professional and intensive to rather rudimentary. After the buy-out, general importance of planning increases given information requirements by the investor, the professionalized supervisory board, and the heavily lending banks. Besides, managers' demand for planning is very high in order to derive decisions and outline company development. Given this internal desire by management and external pressure by stakeholders to develop the planning process, even family businesses with relatively strong planning tools are likely to further improve this control instrument to account for the increased risk and financial constraints of the buy-out.[867] Planning as antecedent of monitoring might be more problematic for stewardship-oriented managers in family businesses than for agency-oriented managers in portfolio companies, as the comparison of planned and realized company performance (i.e. monitoring) might crowd out motivation of stewardship-oriented managers. In consequence of all these considerations, planning is expected to become professionalized, more intensive and based on a broader set of planning tools

---

866 Comparability of the surveys on usage of selected instruments of managerial control in family businesses and portfolio companies is limited for three reasons: First, the study of JONES on control instruments in portfolio companies uses UK data, whereas the other studies refer to Germany or German-speaking Europe. Second, JONES' study is rather old as it dates from 1992; meanwhile usage of control instruments is likely to have changed. Third, JONES' results are based on buy-outs in corporate divisions, which differ from buy-outs in family businesses most prominently with regard to state of professionalism and organizational size.

867 Cf. Jones (1992), p. 158.

through the buy-out;[868] however, the degree of this change depends on the state of the planning process pre buy-out and might thus range from a minor revision to a new conception starting from scratch. Empirical evidence on this expected change was provided by JONES, who has shown that importance of planning tools increases or remains unchanged – abandonment is infrequent.[869]

6.2.2. Management accounting

The discussion of management accounting in family businesses and portfolio companies suggests changes similar to those in planning. Despite the expected low importance of management accounting in family businesses, these companies show a somewhat frequent usage of tools of management accounting though intensity of usage is lower than for planning tools. Similar to the usage of planning tools, usage of tools of management accounting is not homogeneous in all family businesses. The greater importance family businesses assign to planning compared to management accounting suggests that the share of family businesses with poor management accounting systems is even higher than the share of companies with poor planning. After the buy-out, portfolio companies in general make intensive usage of tools of management accounting. As in the case of planning, there are two addressees for data from management accounting: On the one hand, management needs information on the business and its environment to base its decisions on, especially with regard to the high risk of the buy-out and the newly introduced non-emotional, fact-based decision making.[870] On the other hand, investment managers and members of supervisory boards need this information to monitor and support management. Therefore, data is supposed to be timely available and to be reliable.[871] Post buy-out managers, who are aware of acting in an agency setting, accept this monitoring, whereas before the buy-out, stewardship-oriented managers might be frustrated by the monitoring function of

---

868 This formulation of an expected change is not intended to be a pre-state of a proposition (cf. footnote 598).

869 Cf. subsection 6.1.2 for results of the study by JONES and footnote 850 for a critical remark on the transferability of JONES' results.

870 Cf. Jones (1992), p. 153; subsection 5.3.6.

871 Cf. subsection 5.3.6; Sander (2006), p. 172. Private equity companies demand frequent reporting of data particularly to quickly detect deteriorating situations in portfolio companies (cf. Mitchell/Reid/Terry (1995), p. 195).

management accounting. To groom the company for the exit, management accounting is expanded from cost accounting and calculation of financial indicators to comprise strategic tools allowing identification of market trends and comparison to competitors.[872] So, management accounting is expected to become more important and more professionialized through the buy-out. With regard to empirical evidence on this expected change, the study of JONES underlines this inference, as most companies newly introduced or retained tools of management accounting after the buy-out, whereas only very few abandoned them.[873] HOWORTH/WESTHEAD/WRIGHT and FORST find similar evidence in buy-outs in former family businesses, without substantiating it with precise details or statistics.[874] Management accounting is professionalized before the buy-out by 38% of Swiss family owners, to increase transparency of the company and facilitate the sale process.[875]

Changes in management accounting help managers to achieve their goals. This increases the buy-out's likelihood of success and increases managers' compensation. Therefore, managers' attitude towards the changes in management accounting is likely to be positive. This positive attitude might be negatively affected by managers' dislike of closer monitoring, which is enabled by an improved management accounting. However, this dislike is expected to be limited, as most post buy-out managers are external managers, who are used to this practice from their former employers.[876] Thus, managers are expected to appreciate the changes in management accounting after the buy-out.

---

872 Cf. PriceWaterhouseCoopers (2005), p. 19; Howorth/Wright/Westhead (2007), p. 14.

873 Cf. subsection 6.1.2 for results of the study by JONES and footnote 850 for a critical remark on the transferability of JONES' results. JONES' finding that existing tools of management accounting are rather improved than new ones introduced related to buy-outs in divisions of corporations; given limited usage of certain tools in some family businesses, these companies are rather expected to introduce new tools after the buy-out (cf. Jones (1992), p. 161).

874 Cf. Howorth/Wright/Westhead (2007), pp. 13 et seq.; Forst (1992), p. 39. FORST found that in 70% of buy-outs in former family businesses, significant changes in management accounting take place.

875 Cf. PriceWaterhouseCoopers (2005), p. 19.

876 Cf. subsection 5.3.4.

6.2.3. Performance measurement

Based on the comparison of family businesses and portfolio companies, significant changes can also be expected in the last instrument of managerial control discussed: performance measurement. Family businesses do not attach greatest importance to performance indicators. This might be explainable by the relatively lower importance of company performance and the moderate state of other control instruments, which limits interest in and measurability of performance. If family businesses employ performance indicators, they focus on net earnings, EBT and EBIT.[877] After the buy-out, performance indicators become one of the most important tools for management and owners, to guarantee the company's ability to service debt and monitor company development. Therefore, performance indicators closely related to liquidity like EBITDA or cash flow are predominant post buy-out. So, performance indicators are expected to be introduced or altered by the buy-out to reflect EBITDA or cash flow. A case study of a German buy-out in a family business has shown that earnings and sales as performance indicators used by the family owners have been substituted by performance indicators relating to cash flow and working capital.[878]

In line with introducing or altering performance indicators, performance monitoring might change. Given the absence or low importance of performance indicators in family businesses, monitoring is either not possible or of minor importance. After the buy-out, private equity companies closely monitor targets for management. These targets are derived from the business plan, on which the financial structure was based and which therefore has to be fulfilled. In consequence, formulation of targets and monitoring are expected to be introduced or intensified.

[877] Usage of cash flow as performance indicator seems to depend on company size: A study among rather smaller German family businesses has found that about 58% of managers are provided with updated information on cash flows (cf. PriceWaterhouseCoopers (2006), p. 37). In contrast, a survey among larger family businesses has shown that cash flow is the fourth most frequently used performance indicator employed by 73% of family businesses (cf. Günther/Gonschorek (2006), p. 13).

[878] Cf. F.A.Z. Institut (2005), p. 34.

6.3 Observed changes based on empirical evidence

6.3.1. Planning

This subsection sheds light on changes in planning which are induced by a buy-out. After a description of planning in family businesses, changes in the planning process are highlighted and implementation of these changes will be discussed.

With regard to the quality of their planning **before the buy-out**, three different types of family businesses emerged from the interviews.[879] The first group consists of five companies that had an advanced planning process in place prior to the buy-out.[880] Their well structured planning comprised projections several years into the future and a detailed plan for the next year. In two companies, the thorough state of planning resulted from preparations of the company for sale, as discussed in subsection 4.2.1.3.[881] Two managers reported that they planned very conservatively in order to avoid missing their own goals.[882] The manager of C said that conservative projections and permanent fulfillment of these were the main reasons for the good relation with banks.

The second group of family businesses had an intermediate planning with some weaknesses. Plans in the 11 companies of this group were less detailed, less up-to-date and less reliable.[883] Three managers said their companies only had detailed figures for the next year, but no long-term oriented plans.[884] Other shortcomings were that planning ended three months after the beginning of the year to plan (D) or that plans

---

879 Categorization was based on individual interviewees' statements and assessments and did not involve stringent, objective criteria, which had to be fulfilled by a company to qualify for a certain category.

880 A, B, C, M, and R; 25% of 20 respondents.

881 B and C.

882 C and R.

883 D, E, F, G, H, I, K, L, P, S, and V; 55% of 20 respondents.

884 P, S, and V.

were not strictly binding (H).[885] In I, top-down planning[886] was not coordinated with employees who had to achieve the goals according to the manager:

> *[Before the buy-out], relevant employees weren't included in the planning process. Headquarters planned for all subsidies worldwide. Then, a manager in China realized with great surprise, what he was supposed to deliver. Funny enough, that usually worked out. However, this might be due to the low growth projection of 2-3% that was quite achievable.*

The four family businesses in the third group were characterized by poor planning – these companies did not plan before the buy-out.[887] In U, no plans existed and in consequence no measures or strategic steps to achieve any targets could be taken. Two companies lacked a business plan with a clear description of business purpose, product range, market and strategy.[888]

In summary, the majority of companies[889] showed weaknesses in their planning before the buy-out. As derived from the literature, quality of planning seemed to be correlated to company size: The larger the company, the more professional the planning process. Family owners and family managers did not attach great importance to detailed plans about the company's future. They might have put more emphasis on their gut feeling and business understanding instead of projected figures. This would be in line with Proposition 6.[890] The manager of H supported this assertion:

> *Now, there is someone who puts emphasis on planning. The former family manager didn't care.*

---

885 In some cases, this rudimentary state was only achieved in consequence of pressure from the banks (E), or plans were particularly made for the due diligence process (G, K, and L).

886 Top-down planning means that planning takes place at the top level of the company and subordinated departments have to adhere to specifications of superior organizational units in their planning. In contrast, bottom-up planning means that planning takes place at the lowest level of the company and plans are aggregated in superior organizational units (cf. Wöhe/Döring (2008), p. 88; Lück (2004), pp. 104 et seq.).

887 J, O, T, and U; 20% of 20 respondents.

888 O and V.

889 75% of 20 respondents.

890 Cf. subsection 5.3.6.

After the buy-out, planning changed significantly in 12 companies.[891] Changes occurred in one or several of the following seven ways (see Figure 41): First, plans were conceived in greater detail. In E, plans were made for every business entity, product line, and international subsidiary. Second, plans did not only consist of budgets, but also included key performance indicators, cash planning, personnel planning, investment planning, and indicators on earnings as well as on other financial parameters. Third, the time horizon of planning was increased to three or five years. This was equal to the period of planning, advanced family businesses had before the buy-out. Fourth, planning became more standardized and better structured to deliver more reliable and aggregated data, reduce lead time, and ensure clear results.[892] Fifth, planning was performed bottom-up.[893] Employees who were responsible for achieving a certain plan had a say about their plans. Accordingly, the manager of F stated:

> *We have a bottom-up planning according to different criteria including sound cash planning and planning of the balance sheet. This is a proper planning process that we have set up in the meantime [after the buy-out].*

Sixth, in case a business plan had not existed in a family business, post buy-out the plan was conceived and coordinated with the private equity company and finally documented in written form. After the buy-out, this business plan was the binding road map for management and stipulated company development and assumptions thereof. Seventh, the planning process was accelerated and adjusted to fulfill reporting requirements of private equity companies. While this acceleration of planning was rather limited in companies with a thorough process before the buy-out, this acceleration was significant in other companies: The sound planning process in B was advanced by nine weeks. In contrast, planning in D was finished nine months earlier in the fiscal year than it had been in the family business.

---

891 D, E, F, G, H, I, J, K, N, O, P, and Q; 71% of 17 respondents.

892 An example for these changes is the professionalization of sales planning in company J. Before the buy-out, the sales department gave a first estimation of units sold at the end of the former season. About four months before the beginning of the new season, these numbers were specified more precisely and used to plan the production process. After the buy-out, sales planning had become a continuous process: An online-based monitoring system showed for each sales representative, how many units customers had ordered and which customers the employee contacted next.

893 See footnote 886.

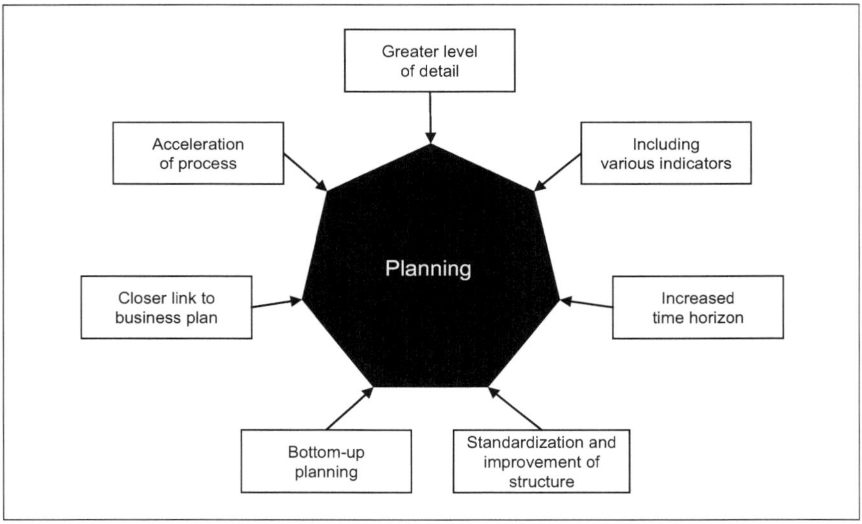

Figure 41: Changes in planning

Source: Author's illustration

In consequence of these changes, the importance of the planning process, of resulting plans and of the business plan increased significantly. After the buy-out, plans had been a crucial instrument for managers to steer the company and for the investor, the supervisory board and the banks to monitor company development. The manager of H said:

> *Before, we simply extrapolated the prior year. If we planned to grow by 15% and actually grew by 10%, we patted ourselves on the back. [...] Now, if we plan to grow by 12% and realize 9%, we have to justify where the deviation has come from. Plans are more binding.*

If the planning process was already changed before the buy-out to prepare the company for sale, these modifications seemed rarely sufficient. In most of these cases, planning was improved further after the buy-out, as the manager of E explained:

> *I think, after the acquisition of the private equity company, [the portfolio company] has further changed in a significant way. [...] If I should evaluate [planning over time] on a 100% scale: I think planning was at 20% before the*

buy-out, increased to 40-50% through the bank's influence [before the buy-out] and is now at 80-90%.

In five companies, planning was hardly changed after the buy-out.[894] In four of the five companies, non-family managers were already responsible for the respective company before the buy-out. In L, the new manager appreciated the former family manager's planning despite initial criticism of lack of a long-term planning. The manager of C stated that the investment manager criticized the management for their conservative planning. In consequence, planning became more ambitious; but changes remained limited as the manager objected more ambitious changes given he had to achieve the planned targets.

A comparison of the occurrence of changes in planning with the pre buy-out level of professionalism shows that changes in companies with sound planning pre buy-out reported virtually no changes, whereas planning was changed significantly in all other companies (see Table 32).

	Pre buy-out level of professionalism		
Occurence of changes through the buy-out	Advanced	Intermediate	Poor
No changes	A, B, C, M, R*	L	
Changes		D, E, F, G, H, I, K, P, S*, V*	J, O, T*, U*

Table 32: Correlation between changes in planning and pre buy-out professionalism

Source: Interview data (n=20)
* Company of the control group

With regard to the **implementation of the described changes**, the planning process and the resulting plans were mainly changed by the management team. After the buy-out, some managers finally had the discretion to implement the planning they considered necessary. The manager of H said that he always wanted a thorough planning, but the family manager did not attach importance to it. Especially if a new CFO or head of the department in charge of planning was hired, this person brought

894 A, B, C, L, and M; 29% of 17 respondents.

his experience and professional requirements with regard to risk management and cash planning into the revision of planning.[895]

Besides management's influence on the changes in planning, investment managers were also involved in these changes by articulating information requirements of the private equity company and stipulating these in contracts so that the management was obliged to comply. These stipulations also included information requirements of banks. Managers did not regard these requirements as restrictions of their managerial freedom as the stipulations were mostly in line with the improvements in planning managers envisaged. The pre and post buy-out family manager of G was fond of the planning that had improved significantly after the buy-out. Access to this know-how was one of the reasons why he had decided to do the owner buy-out.[896]

With regard to the **control group**, the two family businesses sold to holding companies reported rather different developments with regard to their planning process. In R, which had a sophisticated planning process before the sale, the process was not changed. The holding company had suggested to all subsidiaries a three year forecast, while R already had a five year forecast in place. In S, which had a decent planning process before the sale, planning was carried out in greater detail, was more frequently adjusted during the fiscal year, and reached further into the future.

Companies backed by semi-public investment companies were rather small so that their planning was very limited or non existent before the buy-out. In these companies, new managers conceived the planning process from scratch to satisfy personal information requirements and those of investors. Given the size of these companies, the process was somewhat restricted and focused on sales projections, cash planning, and three year forecasts. The backing semi-public investment companies received a short version of corporate plans.[897]

---

[895] Cf. subsection 5.3.4 for changes in the management and subsection 5.3.6 for the increased importance of numbers for management.

[896] Room for improvement of the planning process was often detected during the due diligence process. External consultants supported the changes by tailoring the process to the company's needs and providing help with the implementation.

[897] The investment manager backing T said that the investment company was not interested in greater detail as they would not be able to assess the additional data, given the great number of portfolio companies an investment manager monitors (see footnote 672).

To sum up, this subsection has shown changes in planning after the buy-out. Before the buy-out, family businesses attached a rather low importance to planning. In consequence, the process had diverse weaknesses in most companies. After the buy-out, planning was significantly modified and professionalized. Changes were reported in every sample company, but varied considerably depending on the level of professionalism in pre buy-out planning. In particular, new management promoted professionalization of planning recognizing its importance for steering the company. Private equity companies and other external stakeholders demanded a sound planning process to monitor company development. These considerations lead to the following propositions:

Proposition 7A:	*Through the buy-out, planning is professionalized: Planning is carried out in greater detail, reaches further into the future and includes cash planning.*
Proposition 7B:	*After the buy-out, the importance of planning is higher compared to its importance in the pre buy-out company.*

The importance management assigned to planning provides support for proposition 6.

6.3.2. Management accounting

This subsection compares the state of management accounting pre buy-out to the state post buy-out in the sample companies. Reasons for observed changes, their implementation and management's evaluation of changes will be discussed.

Before the buy-out, three different states of management accounting could be identified (see Table 33): advanced, intermediate, and poor.[898] In four companies, a system of management accounting was in place that can be described as advanced.[899] Managers of these companies appreciated management accounting as important help to steer their companies. Possible explanations for the sound state of management accounting are that the company was prepared for sale or that non-family managers

[898] Categorization was based on individual interviewees' statements and assessments, and was thus not based on stringent, objective criteria (cf. footnote 879).

[899] A, H, M, and R; 25% of 16 respondents. A, M, and R also had a sound planning process (see footnote 880).

had learned about the advantages in companies, they worked with before joining the family business. Company M had to fulfill the increased requirements of transparency, after it became a corporation years before the buy-out. External consultants revised the management accounting system and implemented for instance a balanced scorecard, which was further enhanced internally.

In eight companies, management accounting seemed to be intermediate according to interviewees' descriptions.[900] In these companies, management accounting was simplistic and thus hardly had significant explanatory power. In C, earnings statement and profit contribution were not available on a product or customer base. In I, the basic concept of cash flow was unknown, as the manager explained:

> *Cash flow was completely unknown – no one knew what it was. Cash flow was the balance of the bank account. They looked at this balance and in case it was alright, the cash flow was also alright.*

Reports of management accounting were less standardized and less frequent, thus lowering transparency. In two companies, only very basic data was generated on a monthly base.[901] Unreliable results from management accounting as in C made it difficult for management to recognize unprofitable business areas and to determine which measures to take in order to counteract business problems.[902]

In four companies, management accounting can be described as poor.[903] The investment manager backing S stated that most management accounting systems in smaller companies were extremely weak and unreliable. These systems mostly consisted of some spreadsheet tables that were not integrated – company V exactly fitted that description. In U, no figures were computed besides sales and the balance sheet, and in T, management accounting merely consisted of a system to record work time.

---

900 B, C, G, I, J, K, P, and S; 50% of 16 respondents.

901 I and P. The very basic data included orders, sales, major cost accounts and income statements.

902 The manager of K exemplified the limited explanatory power of management accounting before the buy-out. He said that in a cost calculation, 80% of costs were transfer prices from different departments in the company. The manager felt results from management accounting were unsatisfactory. In consequence, he based many decisions on his gut feeling.

903 O, T, U, and V; 25% of 16 respondents. Most of these four companies were relatively small with sales of less than € 20m, so that they possibly could not afford dedicating personnel to management accounting. O, T, and U also exhibited a very poor planning process (see footnote 887).

Pre buy-out level of professionalism		
Advanced	Intermediate	Poor
A, H, M, R	B, C, G, I, J, K, P, S	O, T, U, V

Table 33: Pre buy-out level of professionalism in management accounting
Source: Interview data (n=16)

This moderate professionalism of management accounting might result from the decision making process discussed in subsection 5.3.6: Pre buy-out managers mostly based decisions rather on gut feeling and experience than on figures, so that results from management accounting played a negligible role. The manager of J provided support for this presumption by saying that data from management accounting was not used given the company had always been profitable; management accounting only existed to satisfy bank requirements. The investment manager backing B provided another evidence for this presumption:

The family manager recognized by personal investigation and business understanding whether a process was okay or not. He didn't manage by figures. Instead, he went to the container with scrap metal and had a look whether the parts therein were raw metal or almost finished products that were recognized as defective after completion.

Besides this main explanation, interviewees put forward most of the theoretical arguments presented in subsection 6.1.1 that suggest low importance and a poor state of management accounting. First, technology focus and low orientation towards commercialization reduced the necessity of management accounting to improve organizational efficiency. The investment manager backing I said:

There are companies that are mainly technology-driven and that are managed this way. In these cases, we must address [management accounting].

Second, some family owners or managers were too parsimonious to dedicate employees and money to management accounting, which they deemed a non-productive activity. Third, as information is power, family owners or managers might not want anyone in their family business to have access to the analyses management accounting created. Fourth, there might have been no need for data from management accounting as families frequently owned and managed the company or were very familiar with the business. This argument underlines the stewardship setting before the buy-out.

After the buy-out, management accounting changed in all sample companies independent of the pre buy-out status. When comparing the different management accounting systems, a fairly homogeneous standard emerges. In general, post buy-out management accounting provided figures in greater detail and faster compared to the pre buy-out state. No interviewee mentioned a change in data reliability – but presumably reliable data was a precondition of private equity companies that was not worth to be mentioned.

The differences between the pre buy-out and post buy-out state of management accounting led to significant changes in 14 companies.[904] Only in three companies, limited changes occurred; these three companies belonged to the group of companies that already had a good management accounting before the buy-out.[905] In these companies, the underlying system did not change; only the reporting output was adapted to investors' needs (A and M) or management accounting was extended to generate certain financial indicators (H).

After the changes through the buy-out, management accounting comprised several tools: Earnings and different levels of profit contribution could be broken down by product, customer segment, legal entity and individual customer. A detailed cost accounting enabled monitoring of cost centers and profit centers. Current liquidity, cash flow and cash forecasts were provided. For projects, pre-calculation and post-calculation were prepared. Key performance indicators showed operational performance. Variance analyses comparing planned and realized figures were computed. All data was available on different levels of consolidation, what required standardization of figures in all subsidiaries. In turnaround companies, the state of restructuring measures was tracked. Through all these measures, transparency increased significantly. The manager of I said accordingly:

---

[904] B, C, D, E, F, G, I, J, K, L, N, O, P, and Q; 82% of 17 respondents.

[905] A, H, and M; 18% of 17 respondents.

Management accounting has improved significantly. [...] Now, we have indicators on productivity, cash, and earnings, variance analyses, forecasts – basically, we have everything.

Besides the breadth of analysis, also timeliness of data from management accounting changed after the buy-out. As explained above, in several companies only limited data was available during the fiscal year pre buy-out. After the buy-out, many financial figures – including the most important ones – had to be available on a monthly basis.[906] In some companies, key indicators were even updated on a daily basis.

Interview partners named four **addressees that required the changes** in management accounting (see Figure 42); some of these were briefly discussed before.[907] First, managers needed data from management accounting in order to monitor internal processes, to control whether company development was in line with the business plan, and to take the right measures to achieve certain goals.[908] Thus, new and old managers required and appreciated improvements in management accounting, as the investment manager backing B noticed:

The top management consists of persons that would never run a company without such a system of management accounting. We have an incredibly experienced CFO, who would never work in a company that has a management accounting worse than the current one. [...] And I think that especially the two [pre buy-out] managers have simply learned how useful this instrument is.

Moreover, company development called for improvements in management accounting. After the buy-out, companies were more oriented towards growth through acquisitions and internationalization.[909] In consequence, complexity of companies increased and

906 According to the investment manager backing K, demand for monthly availability of data applied to earnings statements, balance sheet, cash flow and basic variance analyses. However, requirements were likely to differ between various private equity companies.

907 Cf. subsection 6.1.1.

908 Management especially needed a sound management accounting to achieve the strategic goal of improving profitability (cf. subsection 5.3.2).

909 Cf. subsection 5.3.2.

rendered an improved management accounting indispensable. The anticipation of dynamic future growth further strengthened this requirement.

Second, private equity companies demanded changes to enable monitoring of the portfolio company. Thus, investors monitored whether the company was on track according to the business plan. While a family owner or manager knew the company inside out through his close interference, the newly owning investor and its investment managers needed information to complement their limited company know-how and to base decisions on.[910] Data from management accounting was also needed for the private equity company's reporting to its fund-investors and as a basis for company valuation at the exit. For these purposes, private equity companies demanded timely reporting, which put management and employees in charge of management accounting under pressure as the manager of K stated:

> *With regard to monthly reporting, you have to fulfill the requirements and you have to fulfill them promptly. If you don't do that, you have an investment manager on your back requiring the figures. So, there is a certain time pressure. No one cared about [timeliness] in the past.*

Third, supervisory board members depended on reliable and detailed data from management accounting. The company was obliged to report results from management accounting to the supervisory board, so that board members were able to recognize critical developments early, initiate adequate measures, and thus support management.

Fourth, reporting to banks required sound management accounting, so that banks were able to control compliance with covenants and supervise company development. Given the company's financial structure after the buy-out, banks were a very important stakeholder and supervised compliance with loan covenants.[911] Private equity companies incorporated the reporting requirements of banks into their own information requirements.

---

[910] E.g. if certain actions require owners' approval.

[911] Cf. subsection 7.1.1 for the capital structure and subsection 7.3.2 for reporting to banks.

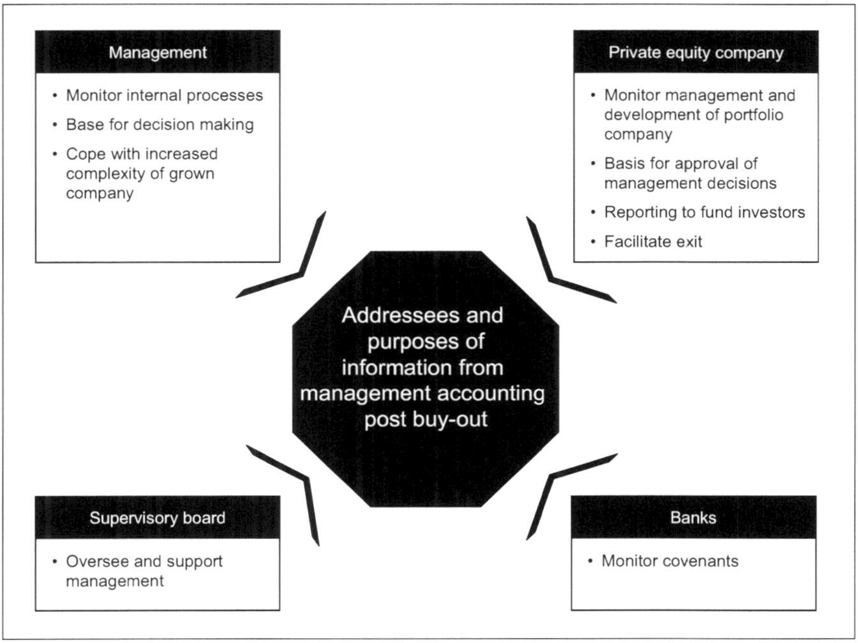

Figure 42: Addressees and purposes of information from management accounting post buy-out

Source: Author's illustration

Implementation of the new system of management accounting can be considered as a joined product of the four parties mentioned before: The private equity company and the banks defined reporting requirements.[912] Managers – and in particular a new CFO – took these basic requirements, combined them with own ideas and their knowledge of the company and the market, and conceived a draft of the new management accounting. Members of the supervisory board provided their opinion on the draft and possibly external consultants contributed their special knowledge.

---

912 However, investors did not stipulate details of the new system of management accounting.

The changes in management accounting comprehended organizational changes. In light of the greater number of tasks and the increase in importance, headcount dedicated to management accounting was increased.[913] The manager of E said:

We invest more money into management accounting – private equity companies are the guys, who create most jobs for management accountants.

Pre buy-out employees either adapted to the new tasks or were dismissed. New and more complex processes often required installation of a new IT system for management accounting. Additional staff and investments into IT entailed higher costs of management accounting post buy-out.

As changes in management accounting were very profound, implementation required some time. For instance, organizational, personnel and procedural changes took two years until completion in company D.[914] Therefore, private equity companies pressured portfolio companies to implement financial indicators first, as they allowed investors to monitor management and recognize potential problems in the company at an early stage.

Managers' evaluations of the changes in management accounting were mostly positive. Of the 15 managers that reported major changes in management accounting, 10 appreciated these modifications.[915] These managers mainly emphasized improved transparency and better support for decision making as results from these changes. The manager of C said:

Management is based on drastically improved figures we have at hand on a monthly basis. [...] Now, we have a management information system that differs considerably from the one we had [before the buy-out] with regard to the quality and scope of information.

---

913 Cf. subsection 5.3.4 for appointment of a new CFO or head of management accounting.

914 Transformation of management accounting can be delayed by other important business activities like integration of an acquired company or search for a new CFO.

915 B, C, D, E, G, H, I, K, O, and P; 67% of 15 respondents.

When asked for evaluating the changes in management accounting, five managers raised criticism.[916] These managers disapproved the considerable time and effort management had to invest into implementation. They feared an excess of data produced by management accounting that would not be used. Costs of implementation for new employees, new IT and consultants were also disapproved. The manager of A rephrased his disapproval:

> *We tried to say: Let's stop here. [...] There are other figures that mean the same. [...] Otherwise, we have to hire two additional employees, who only do [management accounting] and who aren't productive at the end of the day.*

This criticism presumably stemmed from different perceptions what figures management accounting should create. However, disapproval of the requirements demanded by private equity companies was not shared by all interviewees. The manager of D explained that it took him some time to fully appreciate the new data from management accounting after initial skepticism:

> *With every improved figure we realized that we could use better analyses for us. We came to understand, that we primarily generate the figures for us – i.e. the company and the management – and secondarily as reporting instrument.*

Interviewed managers stated that the enormous change in management accounting would have been very unlikely, if the company was still a family business. Family owners and managers mostly attached lower importance to management accounting and lacked the know-how to implement changes.[917] The manager of H expressed that he would have loved to have the post buy-out management accounting already in the family business, but he was not allowed to implement it. The manager of G approved the pressure to implement modifications, as before the buy-out, improvements were always forgone giving priority to more urgent projects.

With regard to the **control group**, management accounting in family businesses sold to holding companies was less affected by the sale. Company R had an advanced management accounting in place that already exceeded requirements of the holding

[916] A, I, G, H, and N; 33% of 15 respondents.

[917] Underpinning his experience, the investment manager backing B said that improving management accounting was a commodity service that every private equity company would implement.

company before the sale. The holding company backing S pursued a different approach, which the family manager appreciated: Portfolio companies sent predefined internal data to the holding company, which processed this data and returned a complete analysis covering the most important figures to the subsidiary.

In the companies backed by semi-public investment companies, changes in management accounting were immense. Given the absence of a well-organized management accounting, this system was introduced from scratch after the buy-out.[918] But unlike private equity companies, investment companies only stipulated some reporting requirements in the participation agreement and left all other modifications of management accounting entirely to managers. Managers stated that these changes were very positive for the company development.

In conclusion, this subsection has shown that buy-outs profoundly changed management accounting in portfolio companies. Before the buy-out, most family owners and managers neglected management accounting so that its state can be characterized as moderate on average. After the buy-out, management accounting was modified in every sample company. Management accounting was assigned a greater importance, personnel dedicated to it increased, processes were professionalized, and results were expected in greater quality. These considerations lead to the following proposition:

Proposition 8A: *Through the buy-out, management accounting is professionalized: Figures are expected to be in greater detail, more up-to-date and more reliable.*

In contrast to pre buy-out neglect, management accounting was of considerable importance post buy-out to several parties: Private equity companies needed the results for monitoring and reporting to its fund investors. Banks supervised adherence to their covenants. Supervisory boards required the results to oversee and support management. Besides these external parties, management also depended on the figures of management accounting to base its decisions on and make them more comprehensible to the external parties mentioned before.

---

918 All three companies belonged to the group of family businesses with poor management accounting before the buy-out (see footnote 903).

Proposition 8B: *The importance of management accounting post buy-out is higher compared to its importance pre buy-out.*

Proposition 8C: *Management appreciates the results of management accounting despite increased costs and time-consuming implementation.*

The importance management assigned to data from management accounting provides support for proposition 6. Changes in management accounting seem similar to changes in planning, as suggested by the similarity between propositions 7A and 8A as well as 7B and 8B.

6.3.3. Performance measurement

This subsection discusses the change in performance indicators used to measure achievement of targets in portfolio companies.

In five companies, performance indicators and thus objectives were not used **prior to the buy-out**.[919] Two managers said that family managers simply used statements of the bank to steer their company.[920] The post buy-out manager of V was astonished about the company's success pre buy-out, though no performance indicator and no targets had been stipulated.

There might have been four possible explanations for this lack of performance measurement: First, there might be no business plan to derive target values of the indicator from.[921] Second, the management accounting system was insufficient to provide timely data about the indicator.[922] Third, in case the manager was a family manager, he might not have wanted targets to restrict his discretion. Fourth, a family manager might not have seen the necessity to stipulate targets for himself and thus did not need a clear performance indicator, as the investment manager backing S said:

> *Typically, the family manager hasn't stipulated objectives for himself. This is an instrument that is frequently newly introduced [after the buy-out]. [The*

---

[919] G, J, O, T, and V; 42% of 11 respondents.

[920] G and O.

[921] O and V.

[922] Companies O, T, and V belonged to the group of family businesses that had virtually no management accounting in place before the buy-out and companies G and J had a rather moderate management accounting (cf. subsection 6.3.2).

family manager] has put all his effort into the company, while stipulating the objectives as he thought best.

In contrast, seven family businesses used performance indicators to determine management's achievements. While six of these companies either focused on EBT,[923] B was the only company to focus on sales growth. In two companies, earnings were combined with another performance indicator: In M, management was also assessed in terms of EBITDA and in I, in terms of sales growth.

Despite the use of performance indicators and targets, family owners and managers did not seem to attach great importance to these indicators. In some companies, this might have been due to the rudimentary state of planning, which hampered derivation of targets.[924] In company K, targets were merely presented to the banks despite virtually no significance for the company. In F, there was no continuous monitoring of the performance indicator but real performance was reported once a year; if targets were missed this was accepted without any consequences. Underlining this indifference towards achievements of specific objectives, the manager of I reported that the family manager was only interested in positive earnings and company growth – the precise figures of profitability or sales growth were of lower interest.

After the buy-out, the predominant performance indicator was EBITDA and similar indicators monitoring cash flow. All managers reported to focus on these indicators.[925] The manager of H said:

Now, we're by far more cash flow-oriented. This is more oriented towards performance indicators, but this isn't annoying. I have to say, we missed that a bit before [the buy-out]. Cash flow was a performance indicator actually no one was interested in.

In five companies, sales growth was also reported as important performance indicator, but it was always subordinated to EBITDA in importance.[926] Other performance indicators of lower importance were indicators on productivity, sales in certain

923 A, F, I, K, M, and P; 58% of 11 respondents.

924 Cf. subsection 6.3.2.

925 Due to limited time of the interviewee, this question was not asked to the manager of P in the interview.

926 B, C, E, I, and M; 31% of 16 respondents.

geographical regions, individual targets for certain managers or the reduction of debt. Instead of being subordinated, indicators on operational performance were of equal importance than EBITDA in portfolio companies in turnaround situations, thus, reflecting the need to restructure operations in these companies.[927] Most objectives, especially those linked to EBITDA and sales growth, were derived from the business plan and from strategic discussions between private equity company and management.[928]

In two companies, the main performance indicators used did not change significantly after the buy-out, since EBITDA was already used as performance indicators before the buy-out (M) or because the manager, who joined the company pre buy-out, introduced objectives linked to performance indicators upon his appointment (C).

The importance of sales growth and the outstanding importance of EBITDA are not surprising. As proxy for the company's ability to generate liquidity, EBITDA was the key performance indicator that ensured the company's ability to service and redeem debt. Besides the private equity company, this was also in the interest of the banks which provided debt to finance the buy-out. Banks stipulated covenants in their loan contracts that forced management to achieve certain EBITDA values.[929] EBITDA and sales growth are the main drivers of company valuation and were thus of paramount interest for the private equity company. While EBITDA directly increases the company value based on the typically used comparable company method of valuation[930], sales growth can be seen as indicator for future EBITDA growth. The manager of K said:

---

927 Cf. subsection 5.3.2 on owners' influence on strategy.

928 Management's evaluation of how demanding the objectives were varied. Three managers stated that the targets were very demanding with expected EBITDA and sales growth being double-digit percentages. Pressure to achieve these goals was described as intense and estimated to be higher than in companies not owned by a private equity company. Despite this intense pressure, the manager of E perceived these objectives as fair given the performance-oriented compensation, he described as extremely attractive. In contrast, the manager of H said that the objectives he agreed on with the private equity company were not more ambitious than the targets he would have set himself anyways. These differences might be explainable by different levels of managers' eagerness, by different management objectives pre buy-out, or by different types of private equity companies backing the respective companies.

929 Cf. subsection 7.3.2.

930 The comparable company method of valuation is a valuation technique, which computes the company value by multiplying a performance indicator (e.g. EBITDA) with valuation multiples of comparable companies (cf. Thommen/Achleitner (2006), p. 653).

We had to present a five-year plan with sales and earnings [...] and especially with EBITDA projections. [...] Based on these assumptions the transaction price was paid. For the private equity company and the financing banks [...], this is the bible.

With regard to the **control group**, in the two family businesses sold to holding companies performance indicators did hardly change. Company R already had a well established set of targets prior to the sale with EBIT as performance indicator and the holding company merely stipulated target ranges. These targets were equal for all portfolio companies, so that R overachieved them. In S, the holding company accepted the objectives proposed by the family manager, namely earnings, sales growth and cash flow.[931] With regard to the time horizon of ownership, the family manager of R noted a change through the sale:

The tenor [of the holding company] is more short-term oriented than I thought. [The holding company] is quoted on the stock market and therefore has to disclose results. [...] One could say that they are mostly interested in short-term oriented performance indicators, while I am more interested in the ones with a long-term orientation.

The companies backed by a semi-public investment company also adopted EBITDA as main performance indicator after the buy-out. These changes seemed to be driven by the investment company to ensure portfolio companies' ability to service and redeem mezzanine capital. However, neither investment companies nor managers set clear target values, as the manager of U stated:[932]

We care for decent margins but whether we earn 1% more or less with a certain product, we don't care.

---

[931] These performance indicators were a mixture of the typical objectives family businesses had before the buy-out (earnings and sales growth) and portfolio companies had after the buy-out (cash flow).

[932] This freedom from targets for managers might be explainable by two facts: On the one hand, investment companies either held no equity stake or only a minority stake, so that managers as majority owners had a strong word in the discussion about objectives for the company. On the other hand, investment companies were arguably less interested in company development and increases in company value. Investment companies held mostly silent partnerships and not equity, and were thus not entitled to participate in value increases. Given this lower importance of increases in company value, investment companies are less incentivized to set and monitor targets.

This subsection has shown that prior to the buy-out, family businesses either do not use a performance indicator or focus on earnings. But even in the latter case, some interview partners cast doubt on the real importance of targets linked to this indicator. After the buy-out, performance was measured in all companies through EBITDA and clear targets were derived from the business plan. The differences in the performance indicator used could be explainable by the main interest the respective owner had in the company: Family owners were interested in earning their living with the family business and therefore focused on an indicator close to the net amount of money they received from the company. Private equity companies were interested in a high exit value and focused on EBITDA as the base of typical valuation models. Moreover, EBITDA indicated a portfolio company's ability to service and repay debt and thus, whether the company was in danger of becoming insolvent. These considerations suggest the following propositions:[933]

Proposition 9A: *Private equity companies introduce EBITDA as key performance indicator.*

Proposition 9B: *Post buy-out, objectives of the management will be clearly stipulated by private equity companies.*

6.4 Summary of chapter

This chapter has analyzed changes in three instruments of managerial control after buy-outs in former family businesses.

The first instrument of managerial control analyzed in this chapter was planning. Before the buy-out, the state of planning differed significantly between the sample companies. Three groups emerged from the analysis with one group exhibiting sound planning, a second group made up of most sample companies showing rather simple planning, and a third group having poor planning. Size seemed a main determinant of the level of professionalism before the buy-out. After the buy-out, the planning process changed in all companies: Post buy-out planning became more detailed, more timely, more standardized, and was linked closer to the business plan.

[933] Due to the frequent changes in performance indicators, no proposition could be derived on the tightening of targets stipulated by private equity companies compared to targets demanded by family owners.

Resulting plans were composed bottom-up, included more indicators, and reached further into the future. Depending on the state of professionalism before the buy-out, these changes corresponded to minor revisions or new conceptions. Planning processes which were changed pre buy-out to prepare the company for sale were mostly improved further. Planning became more important for managers to take decisions and for investors, supervisory board members and banks to monitor the company.

The second control instrument under examination was management accounting. Similar to the state of planning in family businesses, no homogeneous state of management accounting emerged before the buy-out: The state of management accounting ranged from highly professional to lacking most basic tools. On average, professionalism of management accounting was rather moderate. This was the consequence of low importance attached to management accounting in family businesses as data was not needed for decision making and various other reasons. After the buy-out, management accounting changed in almost all companies significantly: Resulting figures were more detailed, more up-to-date and more reliable using a broader set of tools of management accounting. Importance of management accounting increased as management needed data for decision making, the company became more complex given its growth, and members of the supervisory board needed figures to oversee and support management. Further, banks and private equity companies needed results from management accounting to monitor company development. Implementation of the new system of management accounting entailed significant costs for staff and IT. Nevertheless, most managers appreciated the figures or even demanded them for their work; only a few managers criticized information requirements as exaggerated.

The third instrument of managerial control analyzed was performance measurement. With regard to this control instrument, family businesses can be split into two groups: The first group of family businesses did not employ performance indicators and targets at all. The second group of family businesses mostly focused on earnings (either net earnings or EBT) as performance indicator, but managers cast doubt on the importance and immutability of the targets linked to it. After the buy-out, EBITDA was established as the main performance indicator in all portfolio companies, in some companies combined with sales growth. EBITDA provides an overview of portfolio companies' ability to service and redeem debt stemming from the buy-out transaction.[934] Moreover, EBITDA in combination with sales growth are the basis for company valuation at exit.

The analysis of changes in these three instruments of managerial control has shown that after the buy-out, usage of all instruments was intensive and took place on a homogenous, professional level. Installation of this professional level meant different degrees of change for companies, depending on the respective state of the control instruments before the buy-out.

Intensification of control instruments formalizes and enhances the instruments to support management decisions. These improvements seem necessary given the lower experience of post buy-out managers (compared to former family managers), the heavy burden of debt resulting from the buy-out and the easier transferability of formalized instruments to other managers in case of replacements.

These changes enable intensified control of management by owners, supervisory board members and banks and thus are a consequence of the separation of ownership and control. The tightness of the post buy-out control also underlines the company's transformation from a stewardship setting to an agency setting. While in the former, close control might be detrimental to managers' motivation and performance, control post buy-out is needed to reduce agency conflicts.

The changes in control instruments are also in line with two developments discussed earlier: On the one hand, companies are professionalized not only to improve monitoring and ensure debt service and redemption, but also to support company development and thus increase company value. On the other hand, planning, management accounting and performance monitoring increase the companies' ability to grow and generate profits. Therefore, these changes show the growing importance of economic goals and the decline of importance of non-economic goals – an economization of the company takes place.

[934] Cf. subsection 7.1.1 for the financing structure of portfolio companies after the buy-out.

7 Changes in financial practices

This chapter examines changes in financial practices after buy-outs in family businesses. In line with the chapters 5 and 6, the chapter starts with a comparison of financial practices in family businesses and portfolio companies in section 7.1, proceeds with derivation of expected changes in section 7.2 and continues with description and analysis of empirically observed changes in section 7.3. Section 7.4 summarizes the chapter. Analysis of financial practices focuses on the following three aspects: financing, reporting to banks, and investment activity (see Figure 43).

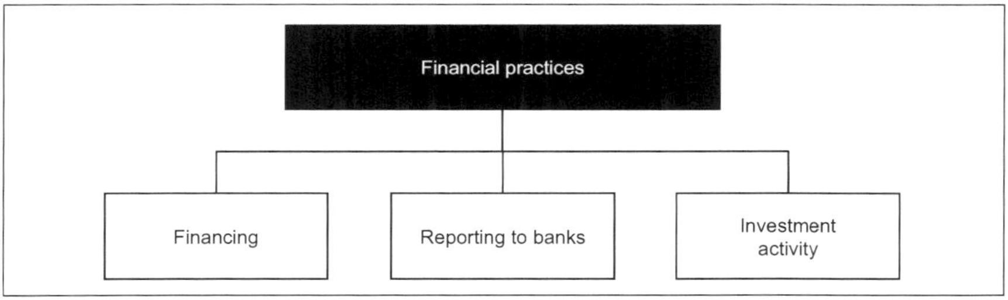

Figure 43: Analyzed aspects of financial practices

Source: Author's illustration

7.1 Theoretical comparison of family businesses and portfolio companies

7.1.1. Financial practices in family businesses

Financing in family businesses are characterized by two particular features: On the one hand, conserving and defending the **family's ownership of the company** is an outstanding goal for family owners.[935] This goal aims at preserving income for the current generation and estate of future family generations.[936] German family businesses are to a large extent exclusively owned by the family: According to KLEIN,

[935] Cf. Tagiuri/Davis (1992), p. 52; Achleitner/Klöckner (2006), pp. 10 et seq.; Achleitner/Schraml/Klöckner (2008), p. 18; Mishra/McConaughy (1999), p. 60; Sirmon/Hitt (2003), p. 343; McConaughy/Phillips (1999), p. 130; Jaskiewicz (2006), p. 94; Pernsteiner (2008), pp. 63 et seq.

[936] Cf. Denison/Lief/Ward (2004), p. 63.

84% of family businesses are entirely owned by the family.[937] In consequence, the vast majority of family businesses does not have access to the public market for equity.[938]

On the other hand, **family owners are** more **risk averse** than owners of public companies. The main explanation for risk aversion is the lack of diversification in the financial portfolio of family owners, as a major share of the family estate is tied up in the family business.[939] Risk aversion can also be explained by the family's human capital bound in the family business. The company might provide employment to family members, and prestige to the whole family – especially to the family manager – for the entrepreneurial daringness to start and run a business.[940] Potential loss of family estate, employment and prestige is exacerbated by the fact that these assets are not only lost for the current generation, but also for future generations.[941] Empirical studies have confirmed risk aversion of family owners.[942] In consequence, these are less inclined to pursue risky innovations and grow the company.

These two particular features drive the financial goals of family businesses (see Figure 44).[943] Longevity of the family business is reflected in the goals of "flexibility / liquidity" and "reliability / long-term orientation", which ensure solvency of the family business and sustainable availability of capital. The preservation of ownership exclusively in the hands of the family is mirrored by the goals "preventing influence of non-family investors/lenders" and "independence". These two goals categorically obstruct any equity provision by non-family investors.[944]

---

937 Cf. Klein (2004), p. 108.

938 Cf. Coleman/Carsky (1999), p. 74; Sirmon/Hitt (2003), p. 343. Especially larger family businesses might have the possibility to access the public capital market, but renounce to use this source of capital.

939 Cf. Ang (1991) according to Coleman/Carsky (1999), p. 74; Dreux (1990), p. 230.

940 Cf. Mishra/McConaughy (1999), pp. 53 et seq.

941 Cf. Mishra/McConaughy (1999), p. 54.

942 Cf. Lyagoubi (2006), p. 549; Donckels/Fröhlich (1991), p. 159.

943 For similar studies on financial goals of family businesses, see Redlefsen/Eiben (2006), p. 5; Tagiuri/Davis (1992), pp. 46-48; Hirigoyen (1982), p. 593; Günther/Gonschorek (2006), p. 7.

944 Cf. Poutziouris (2001), p. 282; Natermann/Schönecker (2001), p. 411. FORST suggests that besides the family owners' refusal of external investors, the latter would not invest their money into family businesses due to the lack of transparency with regard to business planning and accounting (cf. Forst (1992) pp. 53-55).

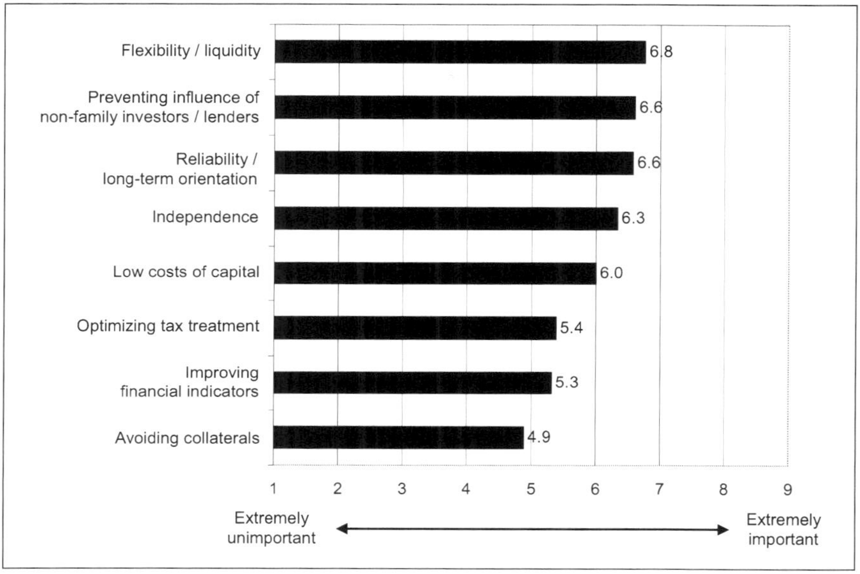

Figure 44: Importance of financial goals for family businesses

Source: Achleitner/Schraml/Klöckner (2008), p. 19 (n=237)

The goal "preventing influence of non-family investors / lenders" shown above deserves a second look: This goal does not only include investors who provide equity capital, but also embraces lenders who provide debt capital to the family business. Provision of debt from non-family investors would make family managers accountable to these parties – an obligation family managers want to avoid in general.[945] Several studies provide support for this **debt aversion** by showing that family businesses aim at avoiding debt and display a lower debt level than non-family businesses.[946] Despite this debt aversion, family owners still prefer debt over equity, as borrowing does not

---

945 Cf. Lyagoubi (2006), p. 549; Sharma (2004), p. 21; Westhead/Cowling (1996), p. 19.

946 Cf. López-Gracia/Sánchez-Andújar (2007), p. 276; Lyagoubi (2006), pp. 546-548; Zellweger (2006), p. 49; Craig/Moores (2005), p. 113; F.A.Z. Institut et al. (2004), p. 9; Astrachan et al. (2003), p. 8; Mishra/McConaughy (1999), pp. 59 et seq.; Gallo/Vilaseca (1996), p. 3; Albach/Freund (1989), p. 175. In contrast, COLEMAN/CARSKY do not find a significant difference in leverage between family businesses and non-family businesses (cf. Coleman/Carsky (1999), p. 78).

affect ownership and control of the company.[947] Debt aversion seems to decrease with company size; owners of small family businesses seem to attach greater importance to keeping non-family investors out of the company, while owners of larger family business stronger emphasize company growth (which necessitates capital).[948]

MISHRA/MCCONAUGHY attribute this debt aversion to family owner's fear of losing control.[949] The increased risk aversion among family businesses described above equals a virtual premium on costs of debt. The virtually increased costs of debt cause family businesses to borrow less.[950] While recent studies confirm the aversion against debt, these studies point out that family businesses have the advantage of reduced agency costs versus public companies and should therefore obtain resources easier at lower capital costs.[951] Costs of debt are further lowered by the accord of goals between family owners and lenders with regard to the long-term orientation and risk aversion.[952]

The general striving of family businesses to avoid equity or debt from non-family members might be the attempt to preserve the stewardship-setting in the family businesses. Striving for common family goals aligns interests of family members as owners and managers;[953] this stewardship-setting eliminates agency conflicts. Injection of capital from non-family members implies that non-family owners or creditors might pursue different goals than family members; pursuit of different goals might give rise to agency conflicts. Fearing agency conflicts, non-family owners might demand accountability from family members and might thus turn the company into an agency-setting.

---

947 Cf. Berger/Udell (1998), p. 48.

948 Cf. Romano/Tanewski/Smyrnios (2001), p. 303.

949 Cf. Mishra/McConaughy (1999), p. 60.

950 Cf. Mishra/McConaughy (1999), p. 54. In contrast, ELLUL AT AL. find that conflicts within the group of family owners adversely affect credit costs, if family owners do not provide a high degree of creditors' protection (cf. Ellul/Guntay/Lel (2007), pp. 27, 38).

951 Cf. López-Gracia/Sánchez-Andújar (2007), p. 281; Anderson/Mansi/Reeb (2003), p. 283; Poza/Hanlon/Kishida (2004), p. 115. In contrast, BOPAIAH finds that being a family business facilitates availability of debt, but does not affect credit conditions (cf. Bopaiah (1998), pp. 83 et seq.).

952 Cf. Sharma (2004), p. 21; Anderson/Mansi/Reeb (2003), p. 283; Bopaiah (1998), p. 84.

953 Cf. subsection 2.1.1.

A particular feature of debt provision in Germany is the close relationship between a company and one or two banks, which are called housebanks.[954] The companies' relations to their housebanks are characterized by long-term orientation, high level of trust between banks and companies, and the banks' major share in the provision of total debt to the respective companies.[955] Housebanks ensure the provision of liquidity to companies in slightly adverse business situation. In return, housebanks are presumably compensated by a prerogative offer of profitable services to the company. However, these relations are not exclusive as ACHLEITNER/SCHRAML/ KLÖCKNER have shown that 88.4% of German family businesses cooperate with more than one bank.[956]

As family owners' refuse to leave equity shares to non-family members and have an aversion against debt, internal financing remains the preferred capital source. Internal financing through accruing profits saves taxes compared to distributing profits; given optimizing taxes is an important goal in family businesses as shown in Figure 44, this is another motivation for internal financing.[957] ROMANO/TANEWSKI/ SMYRNIOS present empirical data supporting the order of preference: internal financing, then debt, and then equity. This is perfectly in line with **Pecking Order Theory**, which is thus well suited to describe the financing behavior of family businesses.[958]

Pecking Order Theory is also backed by a survey of ACHLEITNER/SCHRAML/ KLÖCKNER on German family businesses (see Figure 45).[959] The study shows that retained earnings representing internal financing is the dominant financial instrument. Debt from banks and shareholder's is frequently used, though less common than retained earnings, with preference for short-term credits over long-term loans.[960]

---

[954] Cf. Segbers (2006), p. 2. 69% of housebanks are mid-sized local banks, i.e. cooperative bank or savings bank ("Sparkasse") (cf. Schmidt (2001), pp. 45 et seq.).

[955] Cf. Elsas/Krahnen (1998), pp. 1284-1286, 1313; von Tippelskirch (2000), p. 113.

[956] Cf. Achleitner/Schraml/Klöckner (2008), p. 31.

[957] Cf. Corbetta (1995), p. 263.

[958] Cf. Romano/Tanewski/Smyrnios (2001), p. 303. Applicability of Pecking Order Theory is confirmed by Poutziouris (2001), p. 288. Pecking Order Theory suggests that companies prefer internal finance over external finance and debt over equity (cf. Myers (1984), p. 581).

[959] Empirical results are in line with Redlefsen/Eiben (2006), pp. 6-8; F.A.Z. Institut et al. (2004), pp. 9-16.

[960] Cf. Poutziouris (2001), p. 283.

Usage of equity depends on the investor: Equity from family members seems acceptable and is regularly used, though less often than debt. Equity from non-family members, be it private equity companies or the public market for capital seem to be out of question and are very rarely used.

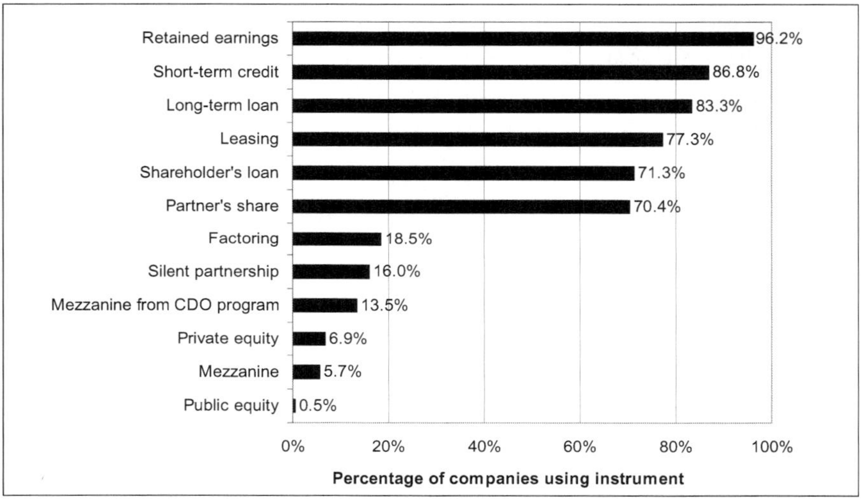

Figure 45: Usage of financial instruments by family businesses

Source: Achleitner/Schraml/Klöckner (2008), p. 28 (n=237)[961]

ACHLEITNER/SCHRAML/ KLÖCKNER also shed light on the usage of **innovative financial instruments**. Family businesses seem to dislike these instruments. Factoring, standardized mezzanine through a CDO program[962] and general mezzanine are used by less than 20% of family businesses. Private equity participation is also very unpopular with family businesses, which is not surprising from Pecking Order

961 These results are in line with Redlefsen/Eiben (2006), p. 7.

962 A collateralized debt obligation (CDO) "is an asset-backed security whose underlying collateral is typically a portfolio of bonds or bank loans" (Duffie/Gârleanu (2001), p. 41). Mezzanine from CDO program means provision of mezzanine capital in a program refinanced using a CDO structure (cf. Achleitner (2006), pp. 310-313). For a more detailed explanation of this financial instrument, see Schmidtbleicher (2006).

Theory as described above.[963] The general disinclination towards innovative financial instruments could be explained by the fact that plain debt is available at lower costs than most innovative financial instruments due to the comparatively high equity ratios of family businesses.[964] Another explanation might be that many family managers and owners seem to lack a comprehensive overview and understanding of the increasingly complex offer of financial instruments.[965] This is underlined by financial intermediaries' criticism of financial skills in family businesses.[966]

By and large, family businesses exhibit **high equity ratios** compared to non-family businesses according to several studies.[967] The survey of ACHLEITNER/SCHRAML/KLÖCKNER confirms a high equity ratio for German family businesses with an average equity ratio of 44.7%.[968] This is well above the ratio projected from aggregated data of financial statements of all German companies, which estimates the average equity ratio of German companies for 2006 at 25.2%.[969]

A particular character trait of some family businesses seems to be the attempt to avoid usage of debt capital completely (see Table 34). The resulting high equity ratios are suboptimal from an economic point of view, as increased leverage would decrease the tax burden of the company and increase the return on capital invested by the family. LEYHERR points out that high equity ratios might also be an indicator for unprofessional financial management.[970]

---

963 Leasing is not considered as innovative financial instrument given its rather long history (cf. Marek (2001), pp. 5-13).

964 Cf. F.A.Z. Institut et al. (2004), p. 9.

965 Cf. Redlefsen/Knöll (2005), p. 3.

966 Cf. Coleman/Carsky (1999), p. 82.

967 Cf. López-Gracia/Sánchez-Andújar (2007), p. 276; Gallo/Tàpies/Cappuyns (2004), p. 310; Poutziouris (2001), p. 285; Agrawal/Nagarajan (1990), p. 1329; for further references, see footnote 946. ZELLWEGER tested the equity ratio of Swiss family businesses for a correlation to the SFI but did not find a significant correlation (cf. Zellweger (2006), p. 50).

968 Cf. Achleitner/Schraml/Klöckner (2008), p. 28. The study of Redlefsen/Eiben (2006) found the average equity ratio of German family businesses to amount to 36.3% (cf. Redlefsen/Eiben (2006), p. 3).

969 Cf. Deutsche Bundesbank (2007), pp. 44-46. The estimated value refers to the average of all German companies regardless of company size, which somewhat reduces comparability with the figure provided above, as the study of Achleitner/Schraml/Klöckner (2008) includes companies with sales between € 1m and € 7,000m (cf. Achleitner/Schraml/Klöckner (2008), p. 13).

970 Cf. Leyherr (2000), p. 96.

Author, year	Sample composition	Equity ratio ≥ 50%	Equity ratio ≥ 70%
Achleitner/Schraml/Klöckner (2008)	237 German family businesses	35.1%	19.7%
Pernsteiner (2008)	189 Austrian family businesses	19.1%	n/a
Redlefsen/Eiben (2006)	297 German family businesses	26.4 %	9.8%
Leyherr (2000)	122 Austrian family businesses	29.8%	n/a

Table 34: Overview of surveys on equity ratios of family businesses

Source: Achleitner/Schraml/Klöckner (2008), p. 26; Pernsteiner (2008), pp. 62 et seq.; Redlefsen/Eiben (2006), p. 3; Leyherr (2000), pp. 95 et seq.

Three reasons could explain the high equity ratios among family businesses: First, a comparatively high equity ratio is the result of family owners' debt aversion and inclination towards retained earnings. Second, this difference is in line with risk aversion of family owners, as debt obliges the borrower to service debt and failure to fulfill this obligation in difficult times might endanger companies' existence and independence. Third, family owners might decide to retain equity in the company for future investments of considerable size, as equity injection from non-family investors is not an option and equity injection from family members might be restricted in volume.

Financial interactions between family and family business are rather limited. The possibility for the family business to raise money from its owners is restricted by the family's estate, which is in most cases already largely invested in the company. Despite this limitation, financial backing from the family is a frequently used instrument.[971] Withdrawal of capital from the family business is always an option for family owners. While tax implications reduce the attraction of withdrawing capital for private consumption, private incidents like divorce, retirement, or estate planning might require family owners to take money out of the business.[972] As these incidents are rather rare, capital withdrawals can be assumed to be limited. Family businesses have a lower

[971] Cf. Coleman/Carsky (1999), p. 79; Achleitner/Schraml/Klöckner (2008), p. 28; Haynes et al. (1999), p. 237; Natermann/Schönecker (2001), pp. 410 et seq.

[972] Cf. Ward (1988), p. 107; Sorenson (2000), p. 140.

pay-out ratio than non-family businesses, which leaves retaining profits as a major financial instrument as presented above.[973] This also explains the considerable equity ratio of family businesses and underlines the financial health of these companies.

7.1.2. Financial practices of portfolio companies

As explained in subsection 2.1.2, the acquisition of a portfolio company through a private equity company in a buy-out is typically financed with a significant share of debt, which is also referred to as acquisition loan and the resulting financial structure is termed **acquisition financing**.[974] In buy-outs, debt is predominantly secured by cash flows of portfolio companies, not by their assets or shareholders' guarantees.[975]

---

973 Cf. Gallo/Tàpies/Cappuyns (2004), p. 311; F.A.Z. Institut et al. (2004), p. 9; Poutziouris (2001), p. 288; Hirigoyen (1982), p. 593. In a survey among German family businesses, only 5% of respondents indicated they pay out all profits, while 22% accrued all profits in the company (cf. PriceWaterhouseCoopers (2006), p. 20). The low pay-out ratio of family businesses can be possibly explained by other forms of compensation instead of dividends, like free use of corporate goods, attribution of improper costs to the firm (e.g. for personal household staff), or salaries for family members above their market value (cf. Corbetta (1995), p. 263). HAYNES ET AL. found that family businesses with sole proprietors are more likely to exhibit resource flows from the family to the business, while businesses that are incorporated and thus presumably more mature are more likely to exhibit resource flows from business to family (cf. Haynes et al. (1999), pp. 225, 237).

974 Cf. Diem (2005), p. 1; Kühn (2006), pp. 65 et seq. The total volume of financing in buy-outs includes the acquisition price, the transaction fees, and the provision of working capital and capital for investments. For studies on the increase of leverage after buy-outs in public companies, see Kaplan (1989a), p. 223; Marais/Schipper/Smith (1989), p. 156.

Financing of the acquisition is organized as follows: First, a financial vehicle, called the NewCo, is founded to acquire the family business. The NewCo is endowed with equity predominantly by the private equity company and with debt by banks. Redemption and interest payments are generated by the portfolio company and all risks relating to the transaction are pooled in the NewCo. Liability of the NewCo is mostly limited through its incorporation as corporation or exclusion of liability through the legal form of a GmbH & Co. KG (cf. Weitnauer (2003b), pp.170-181; Diem (2001), pp. 3 et seq.; Achleitner (2002), p. 201).

975 Cf. Kühn (2006), p. 220; Kessel (1995), p. 88; Diem (2001), p. 4; Achleitner (2002), p. 201; Kitzmann (2005), p. 31. This financing structure is also called cash flow-based lending. Besides cash flow-based lending, KITZMANN discusses that there are also two other forms of buy-out deals: First, in asset based deals, assets of the company are used as collaterals. Second, in asset sales deals, the acquisition price is largely financed by selling assets not necessary for company operations (cf. Kitzmann (2005), p. 29). Applicability of asset-sale deals for buy-outs in family businesses may be doubted, given family owners' parsimony leads to less diversified companies with fewer unutilized assets (cf. Chrisman/Chua/Steier (2005), p. 240; Carney (2005), pp. 254-257).

Debt capacity of the portfolio company is limited by the company's future cash flows projected in the business plan, as the company must be able to service debt at all times. The business plan also stipulates a repayment schedule management of the portfolio company must adhere to.[976]

The acquisition loan is provided in a multitude of forms with different maturities, collateralization, subordination and other characteristics. Essentially, debt can be differentiated into two broad categories: Mezzanine capital[977] and senior loans. Mezzanine capital is subordinated to senior loans with regard to access to collaterals and debt service. This increased risk of mezzanine is compensated by a higher interest rate or an option to buy equity of the company (so called equity kicker).[978]

The remainder between the acquisition price and total debt must be financed by equity. Given the considerable leverage, equity investments in portfolio companies bear a high risk. The risk is further increased by limited fungibility of shares in portfolio companies, as 95% of family businesses are not publicly traded.[979] Table 35 presents an overview of surveys on the capital structure of German portfolio companies at the buy-out.

---

976 Cf. Thompson/Wright (1995), p. 693; Huydts (1992), p. 148. Debt capacity is also influenced by attractiveness of the industry, speed of redemption, company size and the relation between private equity company and lender (cf. Becker (2000), p. 36; Robbie/Wright (1996), p. 50).

977 Different forms of mezzanine capital include: subordinated debt, vendor loan, silent partnerships, profit participating certificates (granting right to participate in profits and liquidation dividends, but not to vote or share in capital ("partiarisches Darlehen" or "Genussschein") (cf. Jakoby (2000), pp. 264 et seq.; Ballwieser/Schmid (1990a), p. 304).

978 Cf. Hug/Ernst (2003), pp. 444 et seq.; Beitmann (2003), pp. 106 et seq.; Weitnauer (2003a), pp. 66-68; Diem (2001), pp. 22 et seq.; Jakoby (2000), pp. 262-269; Huydts (1992), pp. 148 et seq., 153-158; Arbeitskreis Finanzierung der Schmalenbach-Gesellschaft - Deutsche Gesellschaft für Betriebswirtschaft e.V. (1990), pp. 841 et seq. Senior debt mostly amounts to four or five times the cash flow. Mezzanine capital can be added so that total debt does not exceed six or seven times the cash flow. These multiples vary depending on stability of cash flows, market, products and further characteristics (cf. Diem (2001), p. 23).

If equity, mezzanine capital and senior loan do not suffice to finance the acquisition price, junk bonds might be emitted to close the financing gap (cf. Achleitner (2002), p. 202; Kessel (1995), pp. 90 et seq.).

979 Cf. Klein (2004), p. 114; Kühn (2006), pp. 93-95; Jakoby (2000), p. 257.

Author, year	Sample composition	Capital structure		
		Equity	Mezzanine capital	Senior loans
Kühn (2006)	94 Institutional buy-outs in European family and non-family businesses	36%	11%	53%
Jakoby (2000)	62 Buy-outs in German family and non-family businesses	36.3%	n/a	n/a
Vest (1995)	16 Buy-outs in German non-family businesses	20.3%	20.3%	59.4%
Gräper (1993)	36 Buy-outs in German family and non-family businesses	30.2%	13.0%	56.8%
Forst (1992)	24 Buy-outs in German family businesses	20.7%	n/a	n/a

Table 35: Survey results on the capital structure of portfolio companies at the buy-out

Source: Kühn (2006), pp. 165 et seq.; Jakoby (2000), p. 262; Vest (1995), p. 245; Gräper (1993), p. 110; Forst (1992), p. 25[980]

Figure 46 draws a comparison between buy-outs in family businesses and all types of buy-outs with regard to the development of equity ratios. The figure shows that equity ratios in buy-outs in family businesses are continuously higher than ratios in all buy-outs except for 2007. The figure further exhibits that the average equity ratio in buy-outs varies over time in line with cyclical trends.

[980] JAKOBY does not provide an average percentage for mezzanine capital, as mezzanine was only used in 14 companies of his sample group; he asserts that this low usage of mezzanine capital might be linked to the fact that only 40% of the buy-outs in his sample were backed by a private equity company (cf. Jakoby (2000), pp. 266 et seq.). The equity ratio in the study of GRÄPER might be overstated as he included nine buy-outs, where the management team provided 100% of equity; these companies are presumably small given the restriction by the managers' personal funds (cf. Gräper (1993), pp. 110-112).

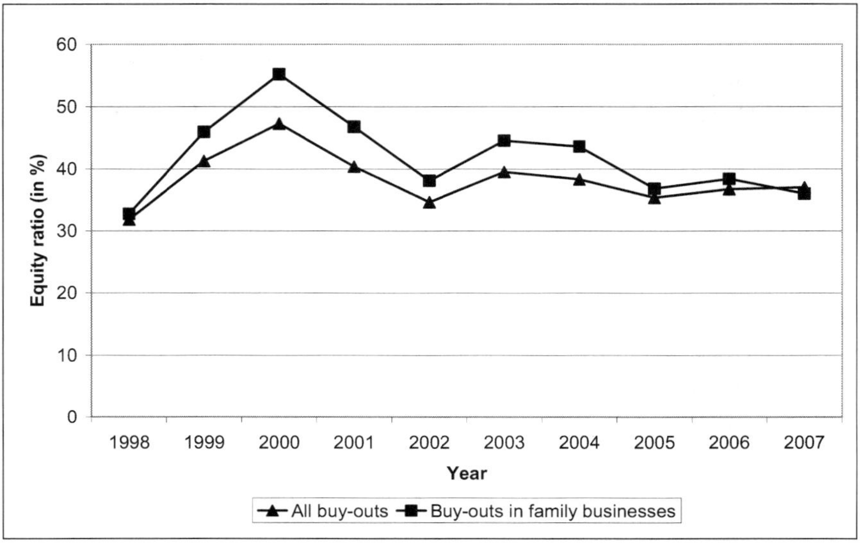

Figure 46: Comparison of equity ratios of buy-outs in family businesses with all buy-out averages

Source: Klöckner (2008), p. 24 (n=12,600 (all buy-outs); n=3,900 (buy-outs in family businesses))

The considerable **leverage in buy-outs has** five main **advantages**: First, the leverage increases the return on capital invested for the private equity company by lowering the amount of capital needed and reducing tax payments.[981] Second, concrete stipulation of the repayment schedule bonds management to deliver on the business

[981] Cf. Hug/Ernst (2003), p. 443; Brealey/Myers/Allen (2006), pp. 469-476; Modigliani/Miller (1963), p. 442; Fox/Marcus (1992), pp. 71 et seq.; Newbould/Chatfield/Anderson (1992), p. 56; Kaplan (1989b), p. 630; Thompson/Wright/Robbie (1992), p. 66; Amihud (2002), p. 22. Cf. Diem (2001), pp. 5 et seq.

Another explanation of the high leverage is that in the past, many buy-outs were done with the purpose to divide the company after the acquisition, as sale of the company in independent parts promised a higher value than the acquisition price (private equity companies pursuing this strategy were termed corporate raiders). In this case, a very high leverage is tolerable as the capital structure is not intended to last for a long time (cf. Achleitner (2002), p. 200). However, this approach seems more appropriate for buy-outs in undervalued corporations than for buy-outs in family businesses, given the latter's growth opportunities and limited scope for divestments.

plan.[982] Third, leverage enables a private equity company to make competitive bids despite the lack of strategic premia a strategic buyer could offer.[983] Fourth, this reduction in the total amount of equity involved in the buy-out increases the maximum number of shares in the company managers can afford given the restriction of their personal funds.[984]

The fifth advantage of high leverage will be discussed in greater detail as it is subject of an intense theoretical discussion relating to the Free Cash Flow Hypothesis. "Free cash flow is cash flow in excess of that required to fund all projects that have a positive net present value."[985] The hypothesis states that managers tend to invest free cash flow in projects with a negative net present value to increase their power, prestige, and compensation.[986] Debt service, which is evoked by the typically high level of debt in buy-outs, withdraws capital from managerial discretion. Thus, the hypothesis closes, buy-outs ensure more efficient utilization of capital.[987] However, empirical studies on the applicability of the hypothesis have yielded inconclusive results.[988]

---

[982] Cf. Thompson/Wright (1995), p. 693; Cotter/Peck (2001), p. 102; Seth/Easterwood (1993), p. 252. Obligation to deliver on the business plan implies a reduction in agency costs, i.e. losses in wealth incurred by owners and lenders. These losses stem from the separation of capital provision and management (cf. Jensen/Meckling (1976), p. 308).

[983] Cf. Achleitner (2002), p. 201.

[984] Cf. Jakoby (2000), p. 259.

[985] Jensen (1986), p. 323. The net present value (NPV) is the result of discounting all cash flows of a cash flow stream at the relevant cost of capital and subtracting the investment costs; projects with a positive NPV create value for the company, while projects with a negative NPV do not cover capital costs and are thus disadvantageous (cf. Copeland/Weston/Shastri (2005), p. 27).

[986] Cf. Jensen (1986), p. 323; Murphy (1985), pp. 32, 34.

[987] Cf. Jensen (1986), pp. 323 et seq.; Fox/Marcus (1992), pp. 67 et seq., While the explanation provided above explains how debt improves efficiency of investments, it does not relate this efficiency to gains for shareholders. Shareholders would prefer companies with free cash flows to pay it out to them instead of investing it into projects with a negative net present value. Debt does not only induce managers to make investments into projects with a positive net present value, it can also be used to buy back shares and thereby pay out current cash to shareholders (Jensen (1986), pp. 323 et seq.).

[988] The following studies confirm the Free Cash Flow Hypothesis: Green (1992), p. 531; Opler/Titman (1993), p. 1996; Lehn/Poulsen (1989), p. 783. In contrast, the following studies do not support the hypothesis: Kosedag/Lane (2002), p. 269; Kieschnick (1998), pp. 187, 199; Kieschnick (1989), p. 57. All these studies were performed using data on buy-outs in public companies.

The main disadvantages of high leverage are twofold: On the one hand, the company incurs significant expenses for interest and redemption, which withdraw cash from the company. On the other hand, high leverage increases the likelihood of financial distress, if performance falls short of projections due to unfavorable market conditions and the company has difficulties to service debt.[989] Different empirical studies have confirmed that higher leverage is associated with higher probability of failure.[990]

To finance the acquisition, **capital can be raised from four** different **parties** (see Figure 47). The equity participation of management fulfills two reasons: On the one hand, equity participation turns an employed manager into a veritable entrepreneur. On the other hand, equity participation incentivizes managers to put their full effort into the company as their personal investment could promise a very high return or could be lost in case the company files for bankruptcy.[991]

Former family owners might also contribute to financing the buy-out – this is another peculiarity of buy-outs in family businesses. Family owners can provide equity or mezzanine (through vendor loans). There are two reasons for family owners' financial commitment after the buy-out: Either family owners want to safeguard some influence on the company post buy-out – what would be in line with the strategy of fading, minor influence – or family owners and private equity companies could not agree on a company value and chose vendors' loans or equity stakes to overcome differences in valuation.[992]

---

989 Cf. Diem (2001), p. 6. This risk of financial distress is contrasted with the advantages of leverage in the so called trade-off theory (cf. Kühn (2006), pp. 72-77; Brealey/Myers/Allen (2006), p. 477). KÜHN has found that trade-off theory predicts the financial structure of buy-outs well (cf. Kühn (2006), p. 220).

990 Cf. Wright et al. (1996), p. 67; Kaplan/Stein (1993), pp. 325, 349 et seq., 355 et seq.; Bruner/Eades (1992), p. 47.

991 Cf. subsection 5.3.5; Jakoby (2000), p. 272; Cotter/Peck (2001), p. 102; Jensen (1986), pp. 325 et seq.

992 Cf. subsection 4.1.2.5 and 4.2.2.5 (for strategies of emotional separation of the family from the company); Jakoby (2000), pp. 281 et seq. JAKOBY provides as further possible explanations that the former family owners wanted either to secure feasibility of the buy-out or sell gradually for tax reasons. While the first argument only seems to make sense in small buy-outs potentially without participation of a private equity company, the latter argument was objected by the family manager of S, who wanted to keep a stake in the company but had to sell the company completely for tax reasons.

Private equity companies contribute mezzanine, rarely debt and typically the lion's share of equity from the funds they manage.[993] The equity stake of private equity companies entitles investors to a claim on a share of the sale price at exit.[994] Private equity companies might withdraw capital from a portfolio company; this withdrawal is called a recapitalization and refers to a special dividend of the portfolio company to owners financed through borrowing new debt.[995] Different authors point out that private equity companies have established a reputation among banks given they are repeated players on the market for debt. This reputation facilitates access to debt and allows investors to borrow at more favorable conditions.[996]

Loans to acquire a company are not provided by a single bank, given the considerable risk of buy-outs. Instead, one or a small group of banks (termed underwriters or lead arrangers) assure provision of debt and gather other banks interested to form a bank pool and syndicate the loan to pool members.[997] In addition, lead arrangers can pass loans on to insurances, hedge funds or other investors through securitization to reduce risk on their own books.[998]

---

993 Cf. Baur (2003), p. 77; Thompson/Wright (1995), p. 692; Jensen (1986), p. 326. Private equity companies syndicate buy-outs to reduce risk, increase deal flow and improve value adding activites. (cf. Manigart et al. (2006), pp. 147 et seq. For an overview on motives for syndication, see Nathusius (2005), pp. 75-113).

994 Cf. Kessel (1995), pp. 93 et seq.

995 Cf. Gaughan (1999), pp. 217 et seq.

996 Cf. Baur (2003), p. 79; Cotter/Peck (2001), p. 103; DeAngelo/DeAngelo (1987), p. 43; DeAngelo/DeAngelo/Rice (1984), p. 373. However, LUIPPOLD reported an increase in costs of debt following a buy-out, as mentioned above (cf. Luippold (1991), pp. 312, 327).

997 Cf. Diem (2001), p. 7.

998 Cf. Financial Services Authority (2006), pp. 38-43. Through this passing on, banks reduce their credit risk exposure to 19.4% of total initial exposure within 120 days after the buy-out. Securitization refers to "the transformation of (relatively) illiquid financial claims [here: the loan] held by financial intermediaries into (more) tradable ones. Physically, the process involves pooling and repackaging loans into other transformed assets (asset backed securities), thus making them marketable." (Chandy/Sriram (1990), p. 86).

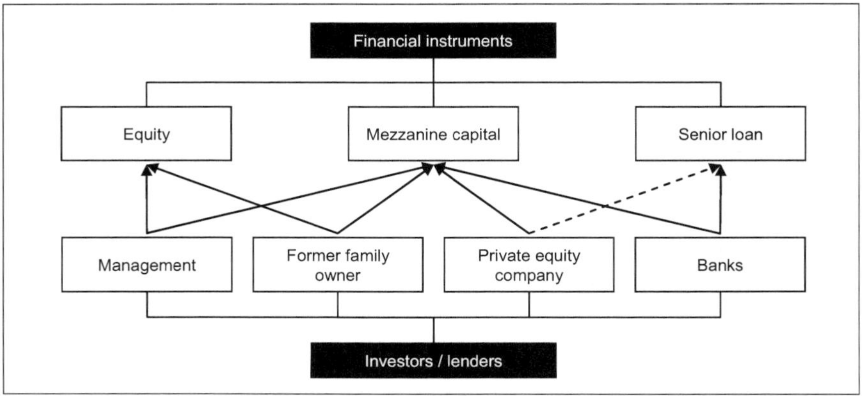

Figure 47: Financial instruments and their investors/lenders

Source: Modifiedly taken from Jakoby (2000), p. 272
The dashed line is a less typical capital provision

Given the considerable, inherent risk in buy-outs, banks have certain requirements potential portfolio companies have to fulfill to qualify for acquisition financing. These requirements are mostly in line with the characteristics, private equity companies look for in a portfolio company: financial strength, attractive product-market combination, experienced management, and hidden reserves.[999] However, a major difference in requirements between private equity companies and banks is that while the former focus on potential for value generation in portfolio companies, the latter focus on sustainability of the cash flow even under adverse market conditions.[1000]

Over the life of the debt agreement, banks continuously monitor portfolio companies using **covenants**.[1001] Two groups of covenants can be distinguished: Accounting-based covenants and non-accounting-based covenants. The first group of covenants provides an overview over the company's financial performance and, thus, enables monitoring of the company's ability to pay interest and redeem loans. Accounting based covenants are financial indicators, which are based on the business

---

999 Cf. subsections 4.1.2.1 and 4.2.2.1; Hug/Ernst (2003), pp. 442 et seq.; Baur (2003), p. 70.

1000 Cf. Diem (2001), pp. 18 et seq.

1001 Cf. Hug/Ernst (2003), p. 446; Jakoby (2000), p. 263; Huydts (1992), pp. 170 et seq.; Baker/Wruck (1989), pp. 169 et seq. For a definition of the term covenant, see footnote 779.

plan and define target ranges management must adhere to. Exemplary covenants are leverage ratio, debt cover ratio, interest cover ratio, and capital expenditures.[1002] The second group consisting of the non-accounting-based covenants relates to information requirements and restrictions of management behavior. Exemplary covenants are availability of audited accounts and management accounts within a certain period, or restrictions on additional borrowings or asset disposals.[1003] If covenants are breached, loans might be renegotiated or recalled. However, in two of three cases, negotiations lead to a waiver of the contractually stipulated consequences.[1004]

7.2 Expected changes based on the literature

7.2.1. Financing

The comparison of capital structures in family businesses and portfolio companies suggests a dramatic shift following the buy-out. Family businesses tend to be financed excessively with equity due to family owners' debt aversion and fear to lose control of the family business. In contrast, the high leverage of portfolio companies is a major key for value generation in buy-outs and increases the private equity companies' returns. Therefore the private equity company is likely to turn the capital structure of the portfolio company upside down.[1005] This inference is backed by the study of FORST, who found that the equity ratio of family businesses falls from 31.0% pre buy-out to 20.7% post buy-out.[1006]

Family businesses cover their needs for debt capital mostly through their local housebanks.[1007] Long established relationships create the level of trust family owners

---

[1002] Leverage ratio indicates the ratio of total debt to total equity. Debt cover ratio corresponds to the ratio of redemption payments to cash flow. Interest cover ratio stands for the ratio of interest payments to cash flow (cf. Diem (2001), p. 15; Citron/Robbie/Wright (1997), p. 284; Baker/Wruck (1989), p. 171.).

[1003] Cf. Diem (2001), p. 14.; Citron/Robbie/Wright (1997), pp. 284 et seq.; Kessel (1995), p. 89; Baker/Wruck (1989), p. 171.

[1004] Cf. Citron/Robbie/Wright (1997), p. 293; Kester/Luehrman (1995), p. 127.

[1005] This formulation of an expected change is not intended to be a pre-state of a proposition (cf. footnote 598).

[1006] Cf. Forst (1992), p. 25.

[1007] Cf. F.A.Z. Institut et al. (2004), pp. 10, 15; Schmidt (2001), pp. 45 et seq.

might need to overcome debt aversion and fear to open their books.[1008] Both characteristics support intensive cooperation with a small number of housebanks.[1009] Private equity companies might look for rather different qualities of banks, given the increased demand for know how in acquisition financing and housebanks' potential unwillingness to finance buy-outs due to considerable risk of these transactions. Thus, portfolio companies are expected to break with their long bank relations and switch to new banks.

Given backing of the private equity company, debt can be expected to be provided at greater ease to portfolio companies. This implies that borrowing is likely to be facilitated. Concerning costs of debt, the buy-out might have two effects: On the one hand, reputation of the investor and greater transparency towards banks suggest lower costs of debt. On the other hand, the increase in leverage suggests an increase in costs of debt. LUIPPOLD found evidence that costs of debt in German buy-outs have increased by about 1.5% for collateralized debt and more than 2% for non-collateralized debt compared to the respective costs of debt before the buy-out.[1010]

Many studies have shown that buy-outs trigger operational improvements in portfolio companies through improvements in working capital management or sale of unutilized assets.[1011] KITCHING has shown that portfolio companies halved working capital within two years after the buy-out.[1012] This might be triggered by access to know how on improvements in these operations and increased pressure stemming from high leverage. Although, family businesses are renowned for being parsimoniously managed, private equity companies are likely to improve operational measures even further.[1013]

1008 Cf. Wimmer et al. (2005), pp. 164 et seq.; Natermann/Schönecker (2001), p. 419; Hennerkes (1998), p. 307.

1009 REDLEFSEN/EIBEN have found that German family businesses cooperate with 3.2 banks on average (cf. Redlefsen/Eiben (2006), p. 9). This constriction to a small number of banks implies that family businesses even forgo comparing credit or loan conditions between different banks or addressing other banks for financing acquisitions (cf. F.A.Z. Institut et al. (2004), pp. 14 et seq.).

1010 Cf. Luippold (1991), pp. 312, 327. Jakoby (2000) found in his survey, that in 76% of German buy-outs interest rates are fixed (cf. Jakoby (2000), p. 269).

1011 Cf. Hug/Ernst (2003), p. 443; Smith (1990), pp. 151 et seq.; Malone (1989), p. 358. However, WEIR/LANG do not find support for the hypothesized improvements in working capital management (cf. Weir/Laing (1998), p. 265).

1012 Cf. Kitching (1989), p. 79.

1013 Cf. Carney (2005), p. 254.

Financial backing of a company by its owners seems limited in both cases before and after the buy-out. In general, family owners accrue a major share of profits in the company, but they are hardly able to support the company in case of distress given limited financial resources. Private equity companies would have the financial means to support a portfolio company, but might prefer either to sell off the company or leave it to bankruptcy.[1014] Possible reasons for this lack of support might be that a turnaround would either demand too much attention from investment managers or would take too long given the limited holding period.[1015] Although private equity companies typically realize their investment in the portfolio company at exit, recapitalizations during the holding period are occasionally used to withdraw capital from the portfolio company. So, great changes are not expected with regard to owners' backing of the company.

7.2.2. Reporting to banks

Reporting to banks is already expected from family businesses, if they have taken out loans. However, this reporting obligation contradicts the exemption from external scrutiny typically associated with private ownership and mostly aimed at by family owners.[1016] Therefore, family businesses report only limited information to banks und thus infrequently fulfill all reporting requirements.[1017] Reporting to banks after the buy-out may be expected to be extensive. Given the considerable amount of debt involved in buy-outs, banks require portfolio companies of private equity companies to be very transparent.[1018] This includes generation of regular reports on financial performance and financial covenants as well as timely information of all important business activities.[1019] Given the importance of leverage in the financing structure after the buy-out, profound changes in the reporting to banks may be expected.

In parallel to this expected increase in reporting requirements post buy-out, banks will stipulate tight covenants, which will be strictly monitored in detail. Tight

---

[1014] Cf. Wright et al. (1994), p. 25.

[1015] Cf. Wright et al. (1994), p. 35. Literature on bankruptcy of private equity companies seems quite scarce.

[1016] Cf. Coleman/Carsky (1999), p. 82.

[1017] Cf. Siemes/Segbers (2005), pp. 316 et seq.; Günther/Gonschorek (2006), pp. 8 et seq.

[1018] Cf. Geidner (2009), pp. 192-194.

[1019] Cf. Diem (2001), p. 14.

restrictions of managerial discretion stemming from these covenants can be assumed to be a significant change for non-family managers, who are likely to have no restrictions of their discretion due to financial indicators.

7.2.3. Investment activity

The changes in ownership and in the goals the new owners pursue suggest that considerable changes might occur in the investment activity. Before the buy-out, family businesses might be expected to exhibit an intensive investment activity for two reasons:[1020] First, family businesses have to invest continuously into equipment to achieve their goal of providing excellent products or services to customers.[1021] Second, family businesses can make investments regardless of bank approval, given their healthy equity ratios.[1022] However, some investments might be economically inefficient or ineffective overinvestments due to weaknesses in planning and management accounting.[1023] After the buy-out, the high leverage obliges management to pay interest and redeem debt. Thus, debt service cannibalizes new investments and is likely to cause a decrease in investment activity.[1024]

Taking investment decisions in family businesses is very quick and unbureaucratic given family owners or managers frequently decide alone. Decisions are frequently not based on precise calculations of the respective investment project.[1025] The decision making process is very likely to change profoundly.[1026] Banks and private equity companies stipulate investments in the business plan and want to know about the purpose and the time, when investments pay off. Checks by the supervisory board or banks force managers to consider carefully, which investments to make.

[1020] In contrast, some authors stress family owners' parsimony, which entails neglect of investments (cf. Wimmer et al. (2005), p. 169; Carney (2005), p. 254; Hickey (2005), p. 31; Forst (1992), p. 38).

[1021] Cf. Tagiuri/Davis (1992), p. 46.

[1022] Cf. Mühlebach (2004), p. 87, Carney (2005), p. 259 et seq.

[1023] Cf. Wimmer et al. (2005), p. 169; subsection 5.3.6 for decision making and subsections 6.3.1 and 6.3.2 for weaknesses in planning and management accounting pre buy-out.

[1024] Cf. Jakoby (2000), p. 311; Kester/Luehrman (1995), p. 120; Wright et al. (1991), pp. 109-111.

[1025] Cf. Wimmer et al. (2005), p. 168.

[1026] Cf. Forst (1992), p. 40.

In parallel with investment activity, purposes of investments might change. Family businesses have patient capital, which describes capital that is invested for long periods without thread of being withdrawn.[1027] Thus, family businesses do not refrain from investments that have a long lead time until they pay off.[1028] Empirical studies have shown that family businesses outspend non-family businesses in investments into research and development, or property, plant and equipment.[1029] After the buy-out, especially long-term investments into research and development (R&D) or entries into new markets might suffer under the heavy burden debt service puts on the company; as diligent buyers would critically point to severe neglect in these areas (e.g. an empty R&D portfolio), investments into R&D and new markets are not forgone entirely, but can be expected to decrease given their long pay-off period.[1030] So, purposes of investments might change through the buy-out: Investments into maintenance and new equipment are expected to remain on their high pre buy-out level due to their short pay-off period. Investments into research and development are expected to decline, given their long pay-off period.

7.3 Observed changes based on empirical evidence

7.3.1. Financing

This subsection sheds light on the profound changes in financing after a buy-out in a former family business. First, the situation before the buy-out will be described. Then, post buy-out capital structure, relations to banks, provision of debt, operational measures, and financial backing of owners will be discussed. Managers' evaluations of the changes close this subsection.

As discussed before in this chapter, **before the buy-out**, family businesses have a reputation for their disinclination towards the use of debt capital. Despite differences with regard to industry, company size or state of professionalism of financial practices

[1027] Cf. Sirmon/Hitt (2003), p. 343; Bertrand/Schoar (2006), pp. 75 et seq.

[1028] Cf. Hofbauer/Pernsteiner (2008), p. 147; James (1999), p. 52.

[1029] Cf. Miller/Le Breton-Miller (2006), p. 78.

[1030] Cf. Fox/Marcus (1992), pp. 76-78; Houlden (1990), p. 47; Easterwood/Seth/Singer (1989), p. 40; Zahra (1995), p. 242. However, another study on UK buy-outs does not support this finding (cf. Thompson/Wright/Robbie (1992) pp. 65 et seq.).

(as will be shown later), family businesses in the sample backed this cliché: Nine interview partners reported that the former family owners or managers aimed at limiting or even entirely avoiding debt.[1031] Equity ratio in these companies was in general higher than 50%; some companies did not have any bank loan outstanding.[1032] When talking about equity ratio and debt aversion, the family manager of R said his company was healthy and did not need bank loans. Non-family managers had to follow the debt aversion of family owners and stated that absolute independence from banks was a major objective (manager of M) or that avoidance of any bank loan was the highest principle (manager of U).

Besides different attitudes towards debt, family businesses can be clustered into three groups according to the state of professionalism of their financial practices: advanced, intermediate and poor financial practices (see Table 36).[1033] Five companies exhibited an advanced level of professionalism in their financial practices.[1034] These companies cooperated with several banks and had good credit conditions. They disposed of decent credit lines that did not restrict their operational business. Professionalism in their financial practices was underlined by the use of sophisticated or rather innovative financial instruments such as mezzanine capital, interest rate hedging and leasing.

The second group comprising seven companies had financial practices that can be described as intermediate.[1035] Most of these companies cooperated with one or two banks and did not use innovative financial instruments or techniques. In most of these companies, family owners and management did not attach great importance to financing. Interview partners reported that the capital structure, bank loans from

---

[1031] A, G, H, I, K, M, O, R, and U; 43% of 21 respondents. The only observable characteristic these companies had in common was that most of them were rather mid-sized companies with sales between € 20m – 100m.

[1032] Interview partners were reserved with regard to revealing precise equity ratios before the buy-out. Only three interview partners stated the exact values, so that no overview of the values is provided.

[1033] Categorization was based on individual interviewees' statements and assessments, and was thus not based on stringent, objective criteria (cf. footnote 879).

[1034] A, G, L, M, and R; 24% of 21 respondents. Four of the five companies in this group aimed at avoiding debt as explained in the paragraph above. This can be seen as indicator that the phenomenon of disinclination and distrust towards debt and banks was not restricted to companies with poor financial practices.

[1035] B, D, H, K, O, S, and U; 33% of 21 respondents.

different banks, development of interest rates and other key financial determinants were insufficiently considered.[1036] The manager of O expressed this attitude:

If you have a family business with fair financial resources, financing isn't important for you.

The last group, which consisted of nine companies, exhibited poor financial practices.[1037] This group comprises companies that either had experienced restrictions in their business activities before the buy-out; or financial problems were one of the reasons why the company was sold. In companies P and Q financial distress triggered the buy-out. Exemplary financial weaknesses of companies in this group were lack of a simplistic working capital management (I), insufficient credit line combined with the need to renegotiate every bank loan (J), or financial restrictions deterring the company from carrying out certain projects (T).

Pre buy-out level of professionalism		
Advanced	Intermediate	Poor
A, G, L, M, R	B, D, H, K, O, S, U	C, E, F, I, J, N, P, Q, T

Table 36: Pre buy-out level of professionalism in financial practices

Source: Interview data (n=21)

On average, the level of professionalism in financial practices can be described as moderate before the buyout.[1038] This view was shared by most investment managers. The investment manager backing S said:

In most family businesses, there are obvious shortcomings in financing. They went to a mid-sized local bank for the provision of capital at conditions, which are far from being attractive.

[1036] The family manager of company B had a poor relation to his bank, as he was upset by a past incident: An upswing in working capital combined with an earnings crisis in a subsidiary entailed a financial crisis for the whole company and banks were not willing to support the company despite its long track record of success in business.

[1037] C, E, F, I, J, N, P, Q, and T; 43% of 21 respondents.

[1038] 76% of family businesses exhibited weaknesses in their financial practices.

Another weakness of family businesses was the financial backing of their owners. Family owners' ability to provide further capital to the family business in case the company needed additional funding was rather limited, given most of family fortune was already bound in the company.

Through the buy-out, the capital structure of the companies changed fundamentally from low to high leverage and from asset-based to cash flow-based borrowing. The structuring of this acquisition financing was almost exclusively conceived and determined by private equity companies and banks. Management had almost no direct influence on capital structure after the buy-out.[1039]

As shown in subsection 3.2.4, family owners held equity stakes in ten companies after the buy-out; this equity participation was either a way to overcome valuation differences in negotiations or it was a consequence of former family owners' wish to retain a minor influence on the company post buy-out.[1040] Post buy-out equity stakes of vendors seem very untypical in other types of buy-outs like spin-off buy-outs or going privates, and might thus be a characteristic feature of buy-outs in family businesses.

Directly after the buy-out, equity ratio was on average about 30%, with the highest value being 60% and the lowest value being 6%.[1041] For most companies, the

[1039] In the interviews, management directly influenced the financial structure to a certain degree in only two cases: When looking for a private equity company to do the secondary buy-out in this company, the two managers in F selected the investor with the lowest leverage. As bids of several private equity companies for this secondary buy-out were within the price range the first investor expected, the two managers selected the private equity company which convinced them most and proposed the lowest leverage. They communicated this as maximum leverage they would accept to the remaining potential buyers and these withdrew their offers.

The managers of L had the choice between mezzanine capital and a bank loan to complete the financing of the acquisition of the company. The two managers forwent the private equity company's offer of mezzanine capital and took out a cheaper loan from a bank. Two years after the buy-out, the company incurred losses and had difficulties to service debt. With hindsight, the manager would have taken the mezzanine capital to reduce risk.

Besides these exceptions of direct influence, management could influence capital structure indirectly through its influence on the business plan, as the business plan was the central determinant of the capital structure post buy-out.

[1040] A, C, E, F, G, H, M, N, O, and Q; 59% of 17 respondents. Cf. subsection 4.2.2.3 for the sale process and subsection 4.2.2.5 for the family's separation from its business.

[1041] Similar to disclosure of the equity ratio pre buy-out, interview partners were reserved with regard to revealing the equity ratio after the buy-out. Only two interview partners stated the exact values;

high levels of leverage, which are typical for buy-outs, marked a turnaround in their financing strategy. In H, the family manager had pursued the goal to become independent of banks over several years; when he had finally achieved this goal, the buy-out took place. Before the buy-out, the highly leveraged capital structure typical for buy-outs could not be realized by companies, as the investment manager backing I stated:

> *This form of financing wouldn't have been possible for a company owned by a family. These syndicated loans are tailored to financial investors and are based on the trust in a financial investor to develop a company according to the business plan.*

Management had to comply with the covenants, which were stipulated at the buy-out based on the business plan. Deviations from the plan endangered the whole financial structure.[1042] Given this inflexibility of the financial structure, financial planning had to allow for working capital, credit line, and other financial parameters that were flexible after the buy-out. In most cases, interview partners assessed these allowances as sufficient. However, the manager of N reported that allowances in his case were insufficient. Management learned from these restrictions and conceived the business plan for the secondary buy-out with a higher degree of generosity. Another deviation from the business plan was reported by the investment manager backing B: His private equity company created separate scenarios in the business plan particularly for the banks. The company would be able to achieve these conservative bank scenarios even in the most adverse business environment.

The post buy-out financial structure also included mezzanine instruments. This was a novelty for many companies that sometimes also had disinclinations against innovative financial instruments.

---

data for four other sample companies could be retrieved from the CMBOR database. Given this restricted availability of data, no overview of the values could be provided.

The average equity ratio of 30% provided above includes the highest value of 60% for company E according to the CMBOR database. This value could be considered as an outlier given the typical levels of leverage in buy-out transactions. Removing the high value yielded an average equity ratio of 24%.

[1042] Cf. subsection 7.3.2 for manager's evaluation of covenants.

Reorganization of the financing structure affected the **company's relations to banks**. Before the buy-out, most sample companies cooperated with more than two banks. Post buy-out, one or two banks become the lead arranger of the acquisition loan and syndicated this loan further to other banks. This concentration on a smaller number of banks accelerated the decision processes, which the banks were involved in, as the investment manager backing K stated:

> *We reorganize the financial structure of the company and refinance the acquisition loan through the lead arranger. We always do this to ensure actionability. If you think of insolvency: Banks always cause problems. Members of a bank pool rarely reach an agreement. It's not a rare case that the smallest bank causes the biggest problems. This is something we don't like. So, we take a lead arranger who acts as the leader of the bank pool. And if there are problems, we talk to that leader. And if we have a good relation, we solve the problem by talking to this bank only, instead of talking to ten banks individually.*

When choosing a bank as lead arranger for the acquisition loan, investment managers could choose between a new bank and the pre buy-out housebank of the company. If the pre buy-out bank was a local branch of a large national or international bank, the local branch was familiar with the bought-out company's development in the past and could provide a valuable internal reference for the department specialized in acquisition financing. But if the pre buy-out bank was a mid-sized local bank[1043], it might not have access to the specialized know-how to provide an acquisition loan or might not want to become the lead arranger given the considerable risk of the transaction.

In three companies, pre buy-out banks became lead arrangers of the acquisition loan.[1044] In seven companies, the lead arranger was a bank the company did not work with before the buy-out.[1045] Cooperation with new banks was appreciated by two managers for professionalism of the new banks (I) and for its reputational effect, if

[1043] Cf. footnote 954.

[1044] A, F, and L; 30% of 10 respondents.

[1045] C, D, E, G, I, J, and M; 70% of 10 respondents.

banks were international and well-known (E).[1046] Many pre buy-out banks that did not become lead arrangers joined the syndication pool. In two cases, management asked for this inclusion in the syndication pool, given the long established business relation or a special competence of the bank.[1047]

Acquisition financing affected the **provision of debt capital** with regard to credit costs and availability of debt. In most companies, costs of debt decreased after the buy-out. In the case of company K, the interest rate for the credit line decreased by about 2.5%. This might appear surprising at first sight, as leverage had increased in many companies and thus absolute interest payments increased as well. However, there are three factors that might explain the decrease in cost of debt (see Figure 48): First, backing of the private equity company increased the trustworthiness of the company given the track record of financial investors and personal contacts of investment managers. The investment manager backing company M said:

> *It is very interesting to see that conditions depend on who negotiates with the banks: if management negotiates on its own or if they use our backing. [In the latter case] typically, conditions are significantly more favorable.*

Second, if the CFO was replaced, the company would be represented more professionally in credit negotiations.[1048] Third, planning, management accounting and reporting to banks were improved so that companies became more transparent to banks.[1049] Only companies that had a high degree of professionalism in their financial practices before the buy-out did not report a change in debt conditions, like company A.

[1046] The manager of J added that it was quite understandable that the pre buy-out bank did not send the most professional bankers to the company, as J had a very low level of debt before the buy-out.

[1047] J and M.

[1048] Cf. subsection 5.3.4.

[1049] Cf. subsection 6.3.1 for changes in the planning process, subsection 6.3.2 for management accounting and subsection 7.3.2 for reporting to banks.

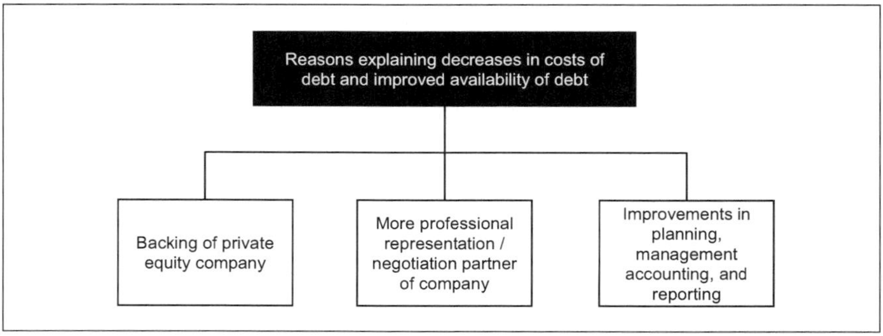

Figure 48: Reasons for decreases in costs of debt and improved availability of debt

Source: Author's illustration

Availability of debt differed with regard to the amount needed: The credit line was extended, which put an end to pre buy-out credit line restrictions. Loans that exceeded credit lines were more difficult to get. This greater ease of receiving debt might be explainable by the same factors that enabled lower interest rates as discussed above. For turnaround company Q, backing of the private equity company increased the company's reputation with banks, and thus restored availability of debt and reduced credit costs.

If capital needs exceeded the credit line and were not designated in the acquisition loan, availability of debt became difficult. The manager of H said that capital needs, which were not included in the planning, were at least as difficult to realize as before the buy-out. In F, loans for new investments were taken out easily before the buy-out, so that restrictions of the acquisition financing were disapproved by the manager. In exceptional cases, the acquisition loan could be adapted to provide the additional funding, if capital was needed for a new investment that was proven to be profitable. Company B was refinanced six months after the buy-out to be able to finance an acquisition. The manager of N had more negative experiences as growth of his company was slowed down by difficulties to borrow from banks.[1050]

[1050] Despite his negative attitude, the manager of N also told that backing of the financial investor helped company N to finance the purchase of a patent that was crucial for further company

Besides the change to acquisition financing, sample companies reported the launch of **operational measures to improve their financial practices**: reducing working capital, leasing and introducing further company-specific improvements. In company I the term working capital was practically unknown before the buy-out. Upon his appointment, the manager of I claimed to reduce working capital by € 5 million – one year later, working capital had decreased by € 9 million. In retrospect, the manager learned that employees laughed at him at first for the initial claim. But also in two companies, in which working capital was permanently monitored and kept to a low level pre buy-out, improvements were achieved.[1051]

After the buy-out, leasing was used more often and at better conditions compared to before the buy-out. Company M, which invested heavily into its pool of machines, used an even mix of debt and leasing to finance the considerable investments pre buy-out. After the buy-out, the company almost exclusively used leasing.

Three more company-specific improvements of financial practices emerged from the interviews: First, hedging instruments were introduced where applicable.[1052] Second, backing of a private equity company and increased internal know-how through appointing a new CFO helped companies in the rating process.[1053] Third, some financial services were brought back into the company: J stopped the cash-in of letters of credit at the bank and processed them in house, saving considerable bank fees.

Private equity companies gave impulses for most of these improvements based on their financial know-how and experience. The investment manager backing M said:

---

development. As a family business, the company would not have been able to take out a loan for this purchase. Cf. footnote 1070 for a more detailed description of the case.

[1051] B and L.

[1052] Hedging instruments are precautionary measures that protect the company from adverse effects of changes in interest rates or foreign exchange rates on earnings (cf. Brealey/Myers/Allen (2006), pp. 727-733).

[1053] Reports how the buy-out affected the company's rating diverged: Company J received a better rating, B kept its very good, pre buy-out rating and M was downgraded. I was rated by a rating agency during the time of the buy-out transformation, when the NewCo was already founded and had borrowed debt capital to finance the transaction. At that time, the company including its assets had not been merged into the NewCo. In consequence, the NewCo was about to receive a bad rating though there were no changes in the original company. After the rating agency was informed that a buy-out had taken place, the bad rating was withdrawn.

I think we know the specific benchmarks for these companies. I would say that every company has room for improvement when it is sold to a private equity company for the first time.

With regard to **financial backing of the private equity company** after the buy-out, statements of managers and investment managers diverged significantly. Investment managers argued that the private equity company was a better owner for the company as the investor did not withdraw liquidity from the company for personal reasons unlike family owners. This behavior of family owners before the buy-out was confirmed by only one manager (H). But also private equity companies wanted to withdraw equity from the company through a recapitalization like in C. The manager reported that he had fierce discussions with the investor; eventually, the private equity company refrained from its intention.

Opinions between managers and investors diverged on the question whether a private equity company would provide support if a portfolio company was in financial distress. The investment manager of A said that provision of capital depended on the company's situation: In certain situations, the investor would back the company; but if the situation was hopeless, the investor would withdraw from the investment. Managers were rather critical about the possibility of financial support. The manager of H said that he himself would not inject fresh capital, so why should the private equity company. The manager of L argued:

If performance is bad and the business plan is missed by far, [...] the financial investor won't inject money. The investor doesn't consider this support his duty. I know of an entrepreneur who needed the financial investor to bail him out – he went bankrupt. I don't believe that financial investors inject additional capital.

Another issue of owner's backing was the question whether the private equity company would provide further capital for investments. In general, portfolio companies were expected to use internal financing or debt capital to finance investments or acquisitions. If capital needs exceeded these sources – which was mostly the case in acquisitions – the private equity company might negotiate a new acquisition loan and might provide further equity if needed, given profitability of the investment purpose. If more capital was needed for a certain investment, financial power of a private equity company might be of help: An investor is able to provide large amounts of capital or could theoretically even underwrite an acquisition alone. Thus, even if banks were unwilling to provide sufficient debt capital, an investment could be completed. The manager of N made rather different experiences when he asked the backing investor for additional capital to finance a profitable investment:

> *[The investment manager] said the company had already received the capital designated for our company – he couldn't provide more. All the capital was invested and the fund had been closed and there was nothing left.*

Managers' evaluations of the changes in financing were mixed (see Table 37). While six managers (42%) said that the changes had strengthened competitiveness of the company, four (29%) said the company was weakened. Another four managers (29%) were undecided which means that they recognized the advantages as well as the disadvantages of the changes. In general, managers appreciated the professionalism of financial practices, the improvement of relations to banks, and the support by the private equity company post buy-out. Managers disapproved the high leverage. An analysis of the answers yielded that managers of smaller companies tended to think their company was weakened. The stronger family influence was on the management pre buy-out, the more managers regarded the changes as strengthening. Obviously, managers of companies that were sold for their financial problems indicated the company was strengthened.

Effect of the changes in financing on the company's competitiveness		
Strengthened	Undecided	Weakened
C, E, H, I, J, P	B, F, L, N	D, K, M, O

Table 37: Evaluation of the changes in financing

Source: Interview data (n=14)

With regard to the **control group**, financing also changed in the family businesses taken over by holding companies: But buyers did not use acquisition financing and both sample companies had no debt after the acquisition. In case of R, the investment was leveraged on the level of the holding company to capitalize on the holding company's more favorable debt conditions and higher level of financial professionalism. Similarly, company S did not have significant debt outstanding after the transaction. However, S was an exception with regard to this capital structure. Typically, subsidiaries of the holding company of S were considerably leveraged, as the holding company of S wanted subsidiaries to have an equity ratio of 30%. In general, debt conditions of the subsidiaries improved due to solution of the succession problem, reputation of the backing holding company, and support in financial planning by the investor.[1054] Investment managers expected their portfolio companies to autonomously finance their growth, but were also willing to back companies directly. As holding companies did not realize capital gains, they demanded subsidiaries to pay out a major share of their profits.[1055]

The capital structure of companies backed by semi-public investment companies consisted of equity from the new owner, mezzanine capital of the semi-public investment company and bank loans. In V, the semi-public investment company also injected equity into the new company. So, acquisition financing was used in no transaction of this group. In T and U, solution of the succession problem and backing of the investment company also led to better conditions of debt capital.[1056] In contrast, the manager of V reported higher credit costs due to the lower equity ratio. Besides capital, investment companies also provided financial advice to the new managers. Portfolio companies reported operational improvements in their financial practices like use of working capital management and leasing.

To sum up, this subsection has examined changes in financing after buy-outs. Pre buy-out, family businesses showed a rather limited level of professionalism with regard to financial practices. Many family owners exhibited the debt aversion

[1054] The investment manager backing S said that the help to negotiate with banks and to optimize financing was the main support his holding company provided. Investment managers joined management in negotiations with banks. Due to his experience from similar negotiations, the investment manager had a clear idea of how the capital structure should look like and what were good credit conditions. The investment manager concluded that financing was an area of the company, in which there could be a lot to gain.

[1055] The investor backing S demanded from its portfolio companies to distribute 70% of profits. The portfolio companies could choose to retain earnings above this hurdle rate, but would have to pay interest that was higher than typical bank interest rates on these retained earnings.

[1056] The investment manager backing T added that typically, buy-out managers in deals with semi-public investment companies had to provide considerable private guarantees to receive bank loans.

suggested in the literature and did not attach great importance to financing. The buy-out changed this financial structure. Transactions were structured like typical buy-outs, thus erasing all peculiarities of the former family business: leverage increased significantly and a broader set of financial instruments including mezzanine capital was used. Management had to adhere to a strict payment schedule to service and redeem the acquisition loan, which restricted managerial discretion. However, frequent equity participation of former family owners after the buy-out differed from typical post buy-out capital structures.

Proposition 10A: *Greater importance is attached to financing post buy-out compared to its importance pre buy-out.*

Proposition 10B: *Frequently, former family owners retain an equity stake in the company post buy-out.*

Post buy-out, debt provision was concentrated on one or two banks, which served as lead arrangers that syndicated the loan to a pool of banks. Only in onw of three cases, lead arrangers were pre buy-out banks of the company. After the buy-out, companies paid lower interest rates on debt. Availability of additional debt depended on the amount needed and the financing purpose, but became more difficult.

Proposition 10C: *Private equity companies aim at cooperating with banks experienced in acquisition financing and might therefore induce portfolio companies to switch banks.*

Proposition 10D: *Backing by the private equity company, increased transparency, and improved proficiency in financing reduce credit costs.*

Financing practices were professionalized by reductions of working capital, use of mezzanine capital and leasing, and further company-specific improvements. Managers expressed doubts about the financial backing of private equity companies to finance further growth or support a company in financial distress. Managers' evaluations of all these changes were mixed. Managers appreciated professionalization through support of the private equity company, but disapproved the considerable leverage.

Proposition 10E: *Through the buy-out, financial practices are professionalized: Mezzanine capital, working capital management, leasing and other financial practices are used.*

7.3.2. Reporting to banks

The changes in financing are reflected in the companies' reporting to banks. This subsection compares reporting before the buy-out to reporting after the buy-out and includes findings on the covenants.

Before the buy-out, reporting by most family businesses was restricted to limited financial data including simplified overviews of sales and costs, and preliminary computations of earnings ("Betriebswirtschaftliche Auswertung", (BWA)). Some interviewees indicated they also provided earnings statements or balance sheets to their banks. Variance analyses were hardly included in these reports, possibly due to the lack of updated figures during the fiscal year that could be compared to annual budgets and plans.

Reporting information was provided in different intervals but usually less frequently than on a monthly basis.[1057] Standard intervals were quarterly or biannually with a more detailed overview provided once a year in some companies. An example of very limited reporting is company O, which merely reported a balance sheet once a year. This low level of transparency towards the banks might be explainable by family businesses' debt aversion, distrust towards banks, and rather limited use of debt as discussed in the previous subsection. Distrust and disinclination led so far that some sample companies rejected certain reporting requirements to prevent bank influence like company G. Company J also did not adhere to all reporting requirements but had to bear the consequence of lower credit lines, as the manager recalled:

> *Banks didn't receive reporting at all or not in the required form. The balance sheet was sent to the banks once a year, but not on a monthly or quarterly basis. And as these were mid-sized local banks, bankers took balances and mutual trust into account – but in consequence, the credit line was rather limited. I think the credit line was about a third of what it was after the buy-out.*

[1057] The only exception was company A, which reported an earnings statement to its bank every month.

An example of superficial compliance to bank requirements was the implementation of management accounting in J, as described in subsection 6.3.2. Although a person dedicated to management accounting was hired, his reports were not used internally. In contrast to this closeness towards banks, two companies also reported deliberately in a shorter interval than required by their banks (M, S).

After the buy-out, reporting to banks was more frequent, more timely and more detailed. The standard reporting interval after the buy-out was one month. Timeliness of reporting was increased significantly. The manager of I said that reports were sent to the bank ten days after the end of the reporting period compared to a lead time of six weeks pre buy-out. Content of reporting became rather standardized post buy-out. Reporting packages included monthly updates on earnings statements, balance sheets, performance indicators, covenants and a verbal description of the company's situation by management. However, reporting content was not strictly dictated by banks; the manager of H agreed with the banks on a level of detail which diverged from the initial requirements the banks had, but which was suitable for the company. Reported data was available on a consolidated basis, what was a novelty for most companies.

Increased transparency was a precondition to borrow from banks. Changes in reporting mirror increased importance of banks, typical rises in leverage, and discontinuation of aversion and distrust towards debt and banks by former family owners and family managers. To comply with these increased reporting requirements of banks, companies had to professionalize departments and processes of financing, planning and management accounting, as the manager of K stated:

> *Given the [pre buy-out] structures and people, we would have failed to comply with the increased requirements for financing and accounting [data] especially requested by the banks. We would have been able to fulfill these requirements in no way.*[1058]

[1058] The manager of L added that increased reporting requirements were partly due to the more general changes in bank practices as a consequence of Basel II (for a description of Basel II, see Albrecht/Maurer (2005), p. 852).

Thus, a competent and experienced CFO was crucial to adapt the internal processes according to banks' requirements and represent the company towards the banks.[1059]

In the two turnaround companies, reporting only changed to a minor degree, as these companies already had comprehensive reporting requirements before the buy-out, given the companies' situations. Reporting content in these two companies was extended to provide information on the status of restructuring measures. However, in Q, the general level of detail of reporting was reduced post buy-out, since the company was no longer in the workout department of banks.[1060]

As explained earlier in this chapter, **important elements of reporting to banks were covenants**, which indicated the company's ability to service debt. Interviewed managers had a rather negative attitude towards covenants as they restricted investment activity and managerial discretion. The manager of D stated:

> *You always have to meet these covenants. If you do not adhere to covenants, this might endanger the financial structure of the company. This danger puts pressure on all decisions we take.*

If the company kept the covenants or even exceeded the underlying plans, relations with banks were described as fairly good. But a breach of covenants put major stress on the relation between management and banks. Company N missed some covenants for a month, as a major customer delayed a market launch and thus payments for the new product. The manager of N told:

> *All hell broke loose. Immediately, a meeting of the bank pool took place. The lead arranger made us look like fools. He articulated utter incomprehension for missing such an important figure. He imposed a fine on us and announced that financing would be recalled if we missed the covenant once more.*[1061]

[1059] The importance, which the position of the CFO gained through adaptation of processes and representation towards the banks, was a major explanation for the changes of the CFO in many portfolio companies, as the pre buy-out CFO might not have had the profile required for this position (cf. section 5.3.4).

[1060] The workout department supervises companies, which have violated the terms of the debt agreement, but entered a negotiated (workout) agreement with the bank outside the bankruptcy process (cf. Gaughan (1999), p. 449; Brealey/Myers/Allen (2006), p. 925).

[1061] This statement has to be seen in the context, that company N missed covenants for the first time and this was the only time it happened. The following month, all covenants were kept.

With regard to the **control group**, reporting changed in a different way in the family businesses sold to holding companies, given both companies were not using debt after the buy-out.[1062] The manager of S provided less information in less frequent intervals after the sale. A short version of the balance sheet and the earnings statement was sent to banks biannually, instead of quarterly like before the sale. The manager of R could not provide any information on this issue as the company used debt neither before nor after the acquisition through the holding company.

Reporting became more frequent and more detailed in the companies backed by semi-public investment companies. The financing investment companies received BWAs every month; other banks received their reports either on a monthly (U) or a quarterly basis (V). The manager of T reported that relations to banks had improved significantly given his open and pro-active communication style.

In conclusion, this subsection has analyzed the changes in reporting to banks after the buy-out. Reporting pre buy-out was rather infrequent and limited with regard to its content. These limitations reflected distrust of family owners and family managers towards banks. After the buy-out, reporting was more frequent, more timely and more detailed. This in turn mirrored the elementary importance of debt capital for private equity companies. Managers disapproved covenants as they restricted managerial discretion. These considerations lead to the following proposition:

Proposition 11: *After the buy-out, transparency for banks is increased significantly through more frequent, more timely, and more detailed reporting.*

The improvements in reporting provide support for proposition 10A.

7.3.3. Investment activity

In this subsection, effects of the buy-out on investment activity in the portfolio company will be discussed. After a look at investment activity in family businesses, the analysis will focus on the relation between investment activity and business plan, the process of taking investment decisions and the purpose of investments.

[1062] Cf. subsection 7.3.1.

Interviewed managers reported that investment activity **before the buy-out** had not followed a clearly stipulated long-term investment plan. Either investments were not planned at all or family managers used their discretion to deviate from plans. In three companies neither a budget for investments existed nor did managers calculate an investment plan to analyze payback time of the investment pre buy-out.[1063] The manager of K reported a very arbitrary decision making process for investments: To acquire machines worth several € 100,000 responsible managers sat together with the family owner in the evening and tried to convince him in a conversation to do the investment. No objective decision criteria were used in these cases.

This unplanned investment activity led to three characteristics of investments in family businesses: First, investments were not always efficient, i.e. directed to increasing profits most. The manager of A reported that the former family manager invested money into increasing sales without knowing whether these investments would pay off. The manager explained this behavior by the fact that the former family manager earned more than he and his family needed. Instead of increasing family income even further, this family manager preferred to develop the company. While this approach to investments did not maximize profits in the short-term, it might increase long-term profits of the company and was thus in line with the investment behavior of family businesses described in subsection 7.2.3. Investment projects, which were funded by the family, but did not pay off until after the sale of the former family business, constituted a windfall profit for private equity companies in three cases.[1064]

The second characteristic followed from insufficient planning and ignoring impact on profits: With family businesses' focus on organic growth, these companies tended to overinvest, i.e. investing too heavily given the target market or economic considerations.[1065] In K, machines were bought on suspicion, without analysis of

[1063] E, J, and U.

[1064] A, K, and O.

[1065] Overinvestment did not seem to occur in small family businesses according to the investment manager backing S. Many small companies needed investments into their obsolete infrastructure (like IT or Enterprise Resource Planning (ERP)) after the buy-out. This statement was underlined by companies S, T, and U, as will be discussed later in this subsection.

The contradiction between overinvesting and parsimony, both being characteristics of family businesses, is not explained in literature up to now. Based on the sample companies, a possible reconciliation might be the following: Overinvestment refers to investments targeted at improving the product of the family business. In consequence, products frequently exceed market demand. In contrast, parsimony refers to investments not directly related to the product, like perquisites for

market potential. In B, which was a very technology-oriented company, machines were replaced because a new technology was on the market, though the new technology was not necessarily needed and machines in place had not been written off completely.[1066]

Third, investment decisions were not taken because of business reasons but to minimize taxes or to build capital reserves, as the investment manager backing K explained:

Most companies that we see are overinvested. [Investments] focus on profit minimization to lower taxes. Real estate is considered as pension for the family owners' retirement. Thus, [many former family owners] invested heavily into property. And they always wanted to have the newest production facilities.

After the buy-out, investment activity changed significantly with regard to the purpose of investments and the process of decision making (see Figure 49). Post buy-out, the business plan contained allowances for investments and mostly directed investments to pre-stipulated measures. Thus, the business plan provided a road map, which investments would be done in the years following the transaction. In the business plan, management outlined future purposes of investments. Through its acquisition of the company at the buy-out, the private equity company committed itself to fund these investments. The manager of C said:

In the strategic paper we conceived before the buy-out, all these investments were included as part of our global growth strategy.

In contrast to predictions by the buy-out literature, interviewees did not report a decline but an increase in investments. Seven companies reported an increase in total investments.[1067] Most of these increases were significantly: Company B reported the

employees or investments into property. In their striving for improving the quality of their products, family managers overinvest into projects seemingly affecting products and are reluctant to invest into projects without a direct impact on the product (parsimony)

[1066] The manager of B defended the investment activity of the company before the buy-out, thus objecting overinvestments: He stated that the company used calculations based on the return on investment (RoI) before the buy-out to determine profitability.

[1067] B, C, E, F, M, P, and Q; 64% of 11 respondents.

highest investments in the year following the buy-out. F built two new production plants to the previously existing three plants. Investments in M increased by about 25%. Investment activity also increased in the two turnaround companies after restructuring; in these companies, investments were badly needed as capital expenditures were delayed or forgone before the buy-out. Four companies reported that the sum of total investments had remained approximately the same through the buy-out.[1068] No interviewee reported that overall investment activity decreased through the buy-out. However, the manager of F noted that investment activity was cut back after some time with regard to the exit on the horizon.

There were three possible reasons for this increase in investment activity: First, the general strategy of fostering company growth after the buy-out necessitated investments into the company.[1069] Second, pre buy-out, family owners might have lacked financial means and access to capital to make these investments. Third, private equity companies supported investments to groom the company for the exit, as a diligent buyer would recognize forgone investments and deduct these from company value.

Private equity companies' assessment of investment opportunities seemed to depend strongly on the time the investment paid off: Investments that paid off within the remaining holding period were supported while equally profitable projects that paid off after the intended exit were mostly forgone. Two managers reported major difficulties to get approval for profitable investments that were not anticipated in the business plan.[1070] The argument that private equity companies only approved investments that paid off during the remaining holding period might be a possible explanation why investment activity was reported to increase shortly after the buy-out but seemed to decrease the more, the closer the exit came.

[1068] H, I, L, and O; 36% of 11 respondents.

[1069] Cf. subsection 5.3.2.

[1070] F and N. Despite major difficulties to receive approval for unanticipated investments, the manager of N told that the private equity company helped him to make a strategically important investment. Company N had identified a technology in a non-related market that could revolutionize N's products. After securing the rights of sale, the licensor went bankrupt. To prevent the technology from falling into a competitor's hands, N wanted to buy the patent. Although this investment was not designated in the business plan, the private equity company backed N in buying the patent.

The buy-out changed **the way how investment decisions were taken**. Investment budgets were derived from the business plan and defined a framework for investments in the company. For investments exceeding a certain value, a written investment proposal was composed that showed initial investment, annual return and break-even of the investment project.[1071] While the manager of H said that these calculations were essential to bring about approval post buy-out, the manager of K said that computations like these were not needed and not considered important before the buy-out.

Investment proposals were scrutinized by the supervisory board or the private equity company directly. Private equity companies judged all investments on their capacity to increase company profits and thus the company's sale price at exit. This contrasts to family owners, who also made investments not directed to increase profit.

In general, managers appreciated the possibility to discuss investment opportunities with members of the supervisory board and investment managers. Managers agreed that the way investment decisions were taken lead to more efficient investments and a less capital-intensive management style after the buy-out.[1072] The manager of E stated:

> *With a private equity company [as owner], you have to present an investment proposal, though this is less typical for Mittelstand companies. This is quite usual, but [the family manager] didn't do it. [...] Investments are more controlled, more specific, and more conscious.*

However, investments had to be planned with greater diligence to be approved by the supervisory board or the private equity company. Scrutiny of this process made investments more laborious and made some managers of H less aggressive and more hesitant with regard to investment proposals.

[1071] Investments below this threshold can be approved by management alone.

[1072] D, K, and L.

Purposes of investments could be distinguished into four groups according to interviewees: acquisitions, internationalization, organic growth[1073] and maintenance. First, investments into acquisitions increased significantly in three companies.[1074] The most prominent example is company B, which was in negotiations of its third acquisition after the buy-out.

Second, investments were directed towards other countries to gain market access or foster growth. Company C pursued internationalization by acquiring a company in North America, entering the South American market and establishing a plant in Eastern Europe.

Third, investment activity with regard to organic growth was evaluated more ambivalent by managers: On the one hand, investments into organic growth in H remained unchanged; N purchased a patent that was of strategic importance for the company;[1075] and I increased the investments into research and development as antecedents of organic growth, after years of neglect before the buy-out.[1076] On the other hand, two managers reported that investments into products or processes were reduced and redirected into acquisitions and internationalization.[1077] However, redirection of investments in company B might be due to overinvestments into products and processes before the buy-out.

Fourth, investments into maintenance depended on urgency. If investments were overdue, they were made: Company M invested into its overaged pool of machines and Q built a new plant and invested into IT. In case investments were not behind schedule, private equity companies were less interested in investing into fixed assets, and, hence, increased scrutiny of investments into equipment.

The increase of investments into acquisitions and internationalization was in line with the changes in corporate strategy after the buy-out as discussed in subsection 5.3.2. Increases in acquisition activity were expected, as family businesses forwent op-

---

[1073] For disambiguation of the strategies of internationalization and organic growth in this context, see footnote 601.

[1074] B, C, and M.

[1075] Cf. footnote 1070.

[1076] Investments in R&D were neglected after the death of the former family manager as management and family owners did not take crucial decisions, according to the manager of I (cf. subsection 4.2.1.1).

[1077] B and C.

portunities before the buy-out and private equity companies could provide valuable support in pursuing a buy-and-build strategy. Investments in organic growth and maintenance remained constant or decreased slightly. This was in line with expectations, as the former investments had a payback period beyond the holding period and the latter investments were not appropriate to grow the company. The increase in investments into internationalization was surprising, given these investments might be expected to have a rather long leadtime until they pay off; their increase could be explained by increasing the strategic value of the company or even making the company more attractive for potential buyers.[1078]

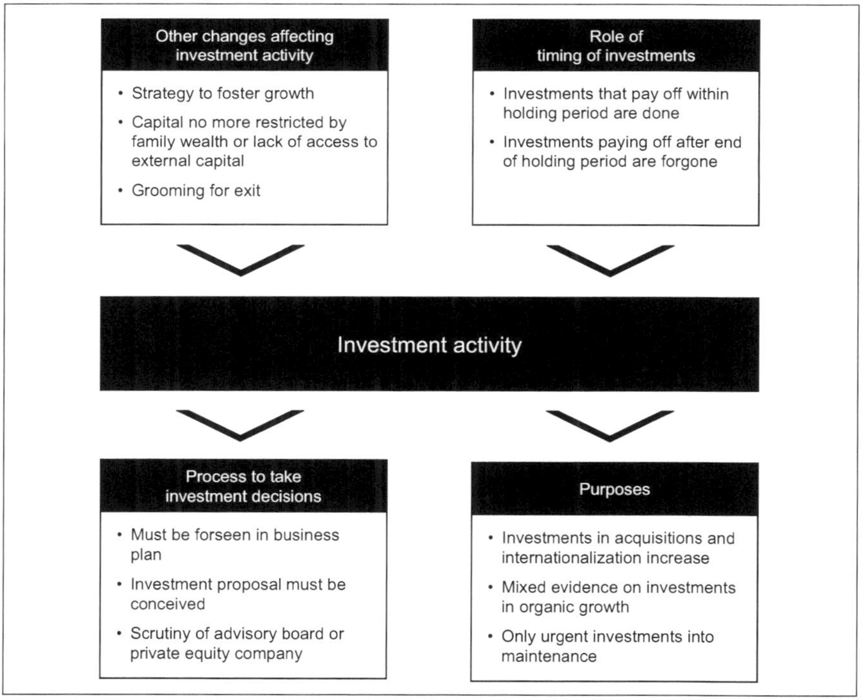

Figure 49: Antecedents and consequences of changes in investment activity

Source: Author's illustration

[1078] Cf. subsection 5.3.2.

With regard to the **control group**, investment activity in the former family businesses, which were acquired by holding companies, was positively affected by the buy-out. Company R was about to make a considerable investment relative to company size in North America. While this investment purpose was in line with that of private equity companies, holding companies also encouraged their subsidiaries to invest into maintenance and keep their pool of machines up to date. This support for maintenance investment might be explainable by the long holding period these investors envisaged. Investment activity was closely coordinated with the holding company and fostered by investor's backing. Restrictions of investments based on the business plan were not mentioned.

Investment activity in companies backed by semi-public investment companies increased as well. In these companies, investments focused besides specialized machines mostly on company infrastructure like IT; infrastructure seemed to be obsolete or inadequate in all three companies before the buy-out. Company T also attempted to acquire a competitor post buy-out, but the deal failed. Investment decisions in these companies were based on investment proposals. As investment companies were not major shareholders in these companies, they did not influence purpose or scope of investments.

To sum up, this subsection has analyzed changes in the investment activity after a buy-out. Before the buy-out, investment activity was not based on a detailed, long-term planning of the company and no objective process to take investment decisions was reported. Post buy-out, investments were stipulated in the business plan underlying the buy-out. Investment activity increased in most companies or remained constant in some – no decrease was reported. Investment decisions were based on investment proposals and approval of the supervisory board or the private equity company. Investments were mainly made in line with corporate strategy, thus focusing on acquisitions and internationalization. These considerations lead to the following propositions:

Proposition 12A:	*After the buy-out, investment decisions are more professional – including pre-definition in the business plan, profitability analyses, and scrutiny of different parties.*
Proposition 12B:	*Total investment activity tends to increase after the buy-out.*
Proposition 12C:	*Post buy-out, investment activity is more in line with corporate strategy and thus oriented towards acquisitions and internationalization.*

7.4 Summary of chapter

This chapter shed light on changes in financing, reporting and investing induced by a buy-out in former family businesses.

With regard to financing of the companies examined, family businesses behave as predicted by the literature: Many companies avoided debt, which was questionable from an economic point of view but driven by the fear to lose control of the company. Further, many family businesses (though not the same that exhibited debt aversion) showed weaknesses in their financial practices. After the buy-out, private equity companies used their whole toolset of financial engineering: they increased leverage considerably, employed innovative financial instruments and improved financial practices in portfolio companies. Especially implementation of cash-flow based acquisition financing marked a turning point for portfolio companies, which entailed closer cooperation with experienced banks that frequently differed from pre buy-out banks. Costs of debt decreased, but availability of debt was aggravated besides provisions in the business plan. Financial relationships of portfolio companies to private equity companies were less intensive than those with family owners before the buy-out: This meant on a positive side that investors only rarely withdrew capital from portfolio companies; but this looser relationship also implied that private equity companies were less likely to rescue a portfolio company from financial distress. A peculiarity of buy-outs in family businesses seemed that former family owners frequently retained an equity stake in the company after the sale.

Reporting of portfolio companies to banks also differed significantly from reporting of family businesses. The latter frequently did not completely fulfill reporting requirements by banks. Given the importance of bank loans within the capital structure of portfolio companies, it was not surprising that companies had to change their reporting behavior fundamentally. They professionalized reporting by providing reports more often, more timely and in greater detail. The strict covenants banks stipulated in loan agreements constricted managerial discretion to managers' regret.

Investment activity in family businesses was also changed profoundly by the buy-out. The mostly unplanned and in part arbitrary investment activity in family businesses was characterized by economically inefficient investments, ineffective overinvestments or investments triggered by goals like tax minimization or estate planning of the family owner. After the buy-out, investment activity remained unchanged or increased, which marked a surprising difference from the expected decrease in investments derived from the literature. This investment strategy was pursued to implement the growth strategy defined by owners, to groom the company for the exit, and to seize investment opportunities forgone under family ownership due to capital restrictions. However, investments were only done if they paid off during the remaining holding period of the private equity company. This entailed significant investments shortly after the buy-out and a fading investment activity as the company approached the exit. The process to take investment decisions was professionalized by provision in the business plan, conception of investment proposals, and scrutiny by the supervisory board or the private equity company. Lastly, purposes of investments changed as capital was directed towards acquisitions and internationalization. Investments into maintenance seemed to decline if they were not urgent and evidence on investments into organic growth was mixed.

This chapter has shown that the capital structure and reporting behavior to banks changed as predicted in the literature. The predicted decrease in investments was not confirmed by interview partners. These results underline that buy-outs in family businesses deserve a separate analysis and that findings from other types of buy-outs cannot be generally applied. The changes in capital structure, financial practices and reporting to banks are consequences of the increased leverage. The outstanding importance of financial engineering as a lever of value generation is thus stressed. With regard to investment activity, buy-outs in family businesses seem special. Investments in acquisitions and internationalization seemed more promising than repaying debt, possibly because some of these opportunities were neglected by former family owners.

This chapter has also shown the economization of portfolio companies. Family ownership before the buy-out has given family businesses some particular characteristics that in part even contradict economic thinking: Aversion to debt, forgoing of investment opportunities to remain independent from external investors, and ignorance of reporting requirements by banks cannot be explained economically – but rather by the peculiarity of family owners. Post buy-out, private equity companies merely focus on economic results of every action in the portfolio company – thus there is no room for peculiarities of family businesses any more. This whole process can be described as the economization of the former family business.

8 Conclusion, implications and outlook

The eighth chapter closes this thesis. Section 8.1 summarizes the most important findings and draws a conclusion from those findings. Section 8.2 derives implications for researchers and practitioners and section 8.3 provides a final outlook.

8.1 Conclusion

The omnipresence of family businesses in Germany and around the globe, the succession problem as the Achilles' heel of these distinctive companies, and the buy-out as an increasingly frequent solution to this problem have motivated this thesis. Despite the economic and social importance of buy-outs in family businesses, there is a research gap with regard to the consequences of this solution to the succession problem. This leads to the research question underlying this thesis: **How do buy-outs in family businesses change corporate governance, instruments of managerial control, and financial practices?**

The thesis draws on the literature from the fields of family businesses and buy-outs as well as on the contrast between stewardship theory (as a theoretical explanation of pre buy-out family businesses) and agency theory (for post buy-out portfolio companies). To build theory with regard to the research question, the thesis pursues an **exploratory research approach**. As an empirical base, interviews with 17 managers of portfolio companies and 7 investment managers backing these companies are complemented by 8 interviews with managers and investment managers of former family businesses sold through transactions other than buy-outs. **Qualitative content analysis** was applied to these interviews to extract the evidence. For this analysis, the three dimensions of the research question were broken down into their most important aspects. These dimensions and aspects provide the framework of analysis that guides the derivation of propositions from the evidence. In the following, the propositions on the three dimensions, namely corporate governance, instruments of managerial control, and financial practices, are presented.

Within the first dimension of **corporate governance**, six aspects are analyzed, and the results are depicted below.[1079] As a general trend, private equity companies institutionalize and strengthen corporate governance to mitigate agency conflicts arising from the buy-out. In particular, investors change the composition, incentivization and decision making of management.

First, an examination of owner influence on management decisions shows that private equity companies differ from family owners as they hardly influence operational decisions of the management. In contrast, the influence on strategic decisions is similar to that of family owners, though the former's influence is more interaction-oriented, while the latter stipulate specific details of the strategy.

Second, private equity companies use their influence on the corporate strategy of portfolio companies to increase the latter's profitability and to foster growth through acquisitions and internationalization. The publicly debated lay-offs or closures of plants are typically only reported by portfolio companies in turnaround situations.

Third, investors' influence is largely channeled through investment managers or experienced outside managers on the supervisory board. These newly appointed board members tighten supervision of and provide more valuable support to the management, thus professionalizing the supervisory board. Family members remain on the board, rather, to represent their equity stake or to maintain a relationship with the company; family members' experience does not seem to be the reason for their appointment.

Fourth, not only does supervision and support of managers change, but also composition of the management team. Due to retirement, insufficient management skills, or failed cooperation, only every fourth manager remains in his position after the buy-out. Although some managers are replaced before the buy-out to prepare the company for the buy-out, this seems insufficient to private equity companies, which replace some or all of the remaining managers after the buy-out. Their broad network and the discontinuation of family influence endow investors with an advantage in recruiting over family businesses. Lack of capable internal managers and ease of access to external human resources explain why three of four newly appointed managers post buy-out come from another company. In particular, CFOs are replaced

[1079] See Table A-1 in Appendix A for an extensive overview.

by more competent managers, and their positions are upgraded, reflecting the importance of communication to banks and investors.

Fifth, managers are mainly motivated to participate in the buy-out by the opportunity to be an entrepreneur or by personal commitment to the company, frequently evoked by long affiliation with the company. Another, although less important, motivation is compensation, which is made more attractive through increases in variable and total compensation, equity shares, and greater transparency in performance determination.

Sixth, replacements in the management team and tighter supervision professionalize managers' decision making processes: Instead of decisions being based on gut feelings, emotions and particular family objectives, post buy-out decisions are rational, substantiated with figures and understandable for investors, banks and board members

The second dimension covered in this thesis is **instruments of managerial control**, which consist of three aspects: planning, management accounting and performance measurement.[1080] Changes in these aspects increase transparency of the portfolio company. Thus, changes are the basis for the managers' rational decision making processes based on figures and they enable tighter supervision by investors and supervisory boards.

First, as an important indicator of future company development, the planning process is given greater importance and professionalized through the buy-out. Plans are conceived in greater detail, reach further into the future and contain liquidity projections. The intensity of these changes depends on the professionalism of pre buy-out planning.

Second, to supervise internal processes, management accounting is professionalized in a way similar to planning: Data from post buy-out management accounting are more up-to-date, more reliable and available in greater detail. The changes in management accounting increase the importance of this control instrument and are appreciated by managers.

[1080] See Table A-2 in Appendix A for an extensive overview.

Third, besides planned company development and efficiency of processes, investors monitor the performance of managers more closely. Private equity companies stipulate clear targets and switch the key performance indicator from earnings to EBITDA to ensure solvency and track development of the company value.

Financial practices is the third dimension analyzed and consists of three aspects: financing, reporting to banks, and investing.[1081] The changes in corporate governance and instruments of managerial control enable the highly leveraged capital structure typical for buy-outs. This goes along with professionalization of financing and investing and closer relationships to banks.

First, financing is given greater importance to and executed more professionally: Mezzanine capital, working capital management, and leasing are introduced. Some portfolio companies switch to banks experienced in buy-outs, which provide acquisition financing. Investors' backing and increased transparency reduce relative credit costs. Despite the sale of their family business and all of the associated changes, family owners frequently retain an equity stake after the buy-out.

Second, transparency for banks is improved through more frequent, more timely and more detailed reporting.

Third, investment activity increases and is carried out more professionally. Investment decisions are pre-defined in the business plan, are based on profitability analyses, and are scrutinized by the board or investors. In line with corporate strategy, investments focus on acquisitions and internationalization.

After this summary of the findings, conclusions are drawn with regard to the drivers of the observed changes and the major effects of buy-outs in family businesses. The analysis of the observed changes suggests that general and specific **drivers of change** can be distinguished. Arguably, there are two most prominent general drivers of changes after buy-outs: First, private equity companies give support to and articulate expectations of portfolio companies. Investors support portfolio companies with their know-how and resources and expect management to foster growth, increase profitability and prepare the company for the exit. Second, the financial structure of buy-outs characterized by high leverage affects the financial practices and

[1081] See Table A-2 in Appendix A for an extensive overview.

transparency of portfolio companies. Besides these general drivers, there are two drivers specific to buy-outs in family businesses. First, discontinuation of the family influence puts an end to the pursuit of non-economic family goals. Second, the transition from a stewardship setting to an agency setting calls for the introduction of measures to mitigate newly arising agency conflicts.

These drivers result in **three major effects** on bought-out family businesses: professionalization, economization[1082], and prevention of agency conflicts (see Figure 50). Virtually all changes identified in this thesis can be attributed to one or several of these effects.[1083]

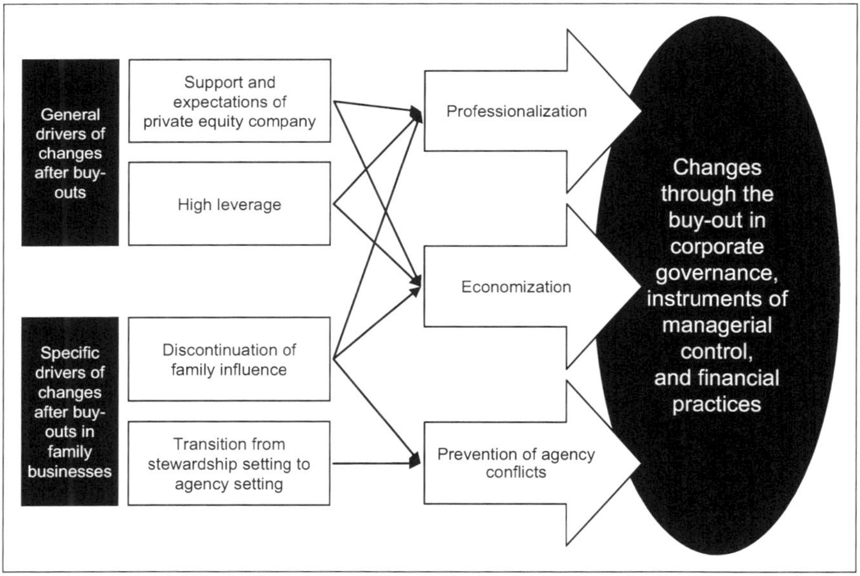

Figure 50: Major effects of buy-outs in family businesses and their drivers

Source: Author's illustration

[1082] Economization here refers to the process of aligning a company with basic economic principles. Thus, economization does not refer to cost reductions or rationalizations (see footnote 787).

[1083] See Table A-1 and Table A-2 in Appendix A for the attribution of changes to the major effects.

Professionalization improves the organizational processes and the institutions of corporate governance, so that these are more appropriate to developing the company according to the private equity company's vision. Professionalization is a consequence of private equity companies' support and expectations and of the financial structure, which is sponsored by banks demanding professionalism before investing. Striving for professionalism ensues from the discontinuation of family influence, which can potentially hinder this development pre buy-out. Professionalization affects most aspects of the changes discussed in this thesis.

Economization refers to the discontinuation of pursuit of non-economic family goals; post buy-out management focuses on economic goals like growth, profitability and increasing company value. Economization results from the expectations of the private equity company with regard to the aforementioned economic goals. Stronger focus on these goals also ensues from the highly leveraged financial structure post buy-out and the discontinuation of family influence, which can hinder economization before the buy-out. Economization affects corporate strategy, management compensation, investment activity, instruments of managerial control, and financial practices. While professionalization improves the quality of organizational processes, economization alters the aims of these processes.

Prevention of agency conflicts includes monitoring of management's actions, incentivization of managers, and direct control of management through replacement of managers. The buy-out dissolves the unity of ownership and management in the hands of the family; post buy-out separation of ownership and management gives rise to agency conflicts. Thus, this transition from a stewardship-setting to an agency-setting calls for prevention of agency conflicts. This is an important difference from buy-outs in non-family businesses, where buy-outs usually reduce agency conflicts by tightening corporate governance. The prevention of agency conflicts affects supervisory boards, compensation, all instruments of managerial control and reporting to banks.

With regard to **value creation**, combination of these three major effects marks another considerable difference between buy-outs in family businesses and in non-family businesses. As stated above, investors' rigid corporate governance of portfolio companies reduces agency conflicts in former public companies; reduction of agency costs is a major lever of value generation in these buy-outs. In contrast, buy-outs in family businesses break up the predominating unity of ownership and control in the hands of the family; this creates agency conflicts not existing before the buy-out and obviously does not create value for investors.

Value creation in buy-outs is achieved by the professionalization and the economization of family businesses. These two effects compensate for the losses from additional agency costs and create excess value for private equity companies. Thus, professionalization and economization render buy-outs in family businesses profitable and therefore attractive for private equity companies.

8.2 Implications

8.2.1. Implications for researchers

This thesis makes a variety of contributions to the fields of family business research and buy-out research.

Implications for research on family businesses are threefold. First, the thesis found that **professionalization** post buy-out is a main lever of value creation for private equity companies. Analyses of the pre buy-out state of planning, management accounting, and financing has shown that levels of professionalism varied significantly. Despite emerging research interest among scholars on professionalization in family businesses,[1084] drivers of professionalization that might explain the observed variations are far from clear. Moreover, it is not clear why family businesses do not use the same or similar methods that private equity companies employ to professionalize portfolio companies.

Second, while family business research is aware of the need for further research on professionalization, researchers seem to be unaware of the second major effect identified in this thesis: **economization**. While the disadvantageous peculiarities of family businesses and their effects on company growth, profitability or other goals are discussed in the literature,[1085] efforts of family businesses to overcome these adverse effects are neglected. Motivation to more strongly emphasize economic goals over

---

1084 Cf. Achleitner/Schraml/Klöckner (2008); Songini (2006); Chittoor/Das (2007).

1085 Cf. Habbershon/Williams (1999); Vinton (1998); Harvey/Evans (1994); Dreux (1990); Dyer (1989); Schein (1983); Bertrand/Schoar (2006); Habbershon/Williams (1999); Arregle/Durand/Very (2004).

non-economic goals might be triggered by family members' desire for increased dividends or by generational transition in ownership or management.

Third, this thesis finds strong support for the application of **stewardship theory** to explain cooperative mechanisms in family businesses. This support might encourage scholars to elaborate this theory and intensify its application. With regard to the longevity of stewardship theory, results of this thesis find that following the buy-out, stewardship-minded behavior is replaced by agency-minded behavior. This contrasts with the findings of HOWORTH/WRIGHT/WESTHEAD and calls for explanation of the different results.[1086]

The thesis also raises three implications for research on buy-outs. First, the discussion of the changes has shown that **buy-outs in family businesses deserve a separate analysis** from other types of buy-outs. The distinctiveness of family businesses entails a specific approach by private equity companies to account for these peculiarities. While researchers studying family businesses might regard buy-outs in family businesses as being out of their realm, research on buy-outs has focused on other types of buy-outs, which were more prominent in the past.

Second, identification and empirical support of **professionalization and economization** as major effects of buy-outs broaden the existing understanding of the levers of **value generation in buy-outs**; current frameworks are based on spin-off buy-outs and going-private buy-outs, and they overlook effects specific to buy-outs in family businesses.[1087] Identification of these two effects also contributes to the discussion on the entrepreneurial character of buy-outs; while buy-out research has from early on focused on efficiency gains, recent research results indicate that this is only half of the story. In particular, authors such as WRIGHT and BRUINING emphasize that bought-out companies are more entrepreneurial than they were before the buy-out. Evidence on professionalization and economization underline this entrepreneurial impetus after the buy-out.[1088]

[1086] Cf. Howorth/Wright/Westhead (2007).

[1087] Cf. Kaserer et al. (2007), pp. 94-99, 190; Berg/Gottschalg (2005), pp. 11-13.

[1088] Cf. Wright et al. (2000), p. 592; Bruining/Bonnet/Wright (2004), p. 171 et seq.; Bruining/Verwaal (2005), pp. 22 et seq.; Zahra (1995), p. 241; Robbie/Wright (1995), pp. 528 et seq.

Third, the thesis casts **doubts on the predominant typology of buy-outs** according to the type of buyer besides the private equity company.[1089] Typically, the differentiation between management buy-outs and management buy-ins is used to assess whether management is able to reduce information asymmetries before the buy-out, or whether management has thorough know-how of the company and can start company transformation the first day after the buy-out. This differentiation seems inappropriate for buy-outs in family businesses, as many changes in the management team occurred either before the buy-out to prepare the company for the sale or soon after the buy-out to professionalize management.

Results of this thesis also **call for further research**. The propositions derived await empirical validation, which could be achieved in a large scale survey. As many details of the changes could not be analyzed in depth, propositions leave room for specification and determination of interdependencies or antecedents. To better explain some results, the evidence could also be interpreted using agency theory combined with altruism instead of stewardship theory. Results of this thesis could also be compared to family businesses sold through an IPO or to strategic investors, who either maintained companies as independent entities or integrated them into a larger corporation. A longitudinal study could deepen the understanding about timing, magnitude, and causes for changes. To conclude, variation of the research approach seems promising to gain further insights into the changes after buy-outs in family businesses.

8.2.2. Implications for practitioners

The results presented in this thesis have a multitude of implications for family owners, private equity companies investing in family businesses and managers interested in buy-outs in family businesses.

The discussion of the buy-out background has shown that there are still family owners and family managers, who are either **unaware or ignoring the urgency of the succession problem**. This attitude lowers the sale price of the family business and might eventually endanger its existence. Therefore, family owners and family

[1089] Cf. Wright et al. (2001), p. 241 et seq.

managers are advised to critically ask themselves when to hand over the company and whether a relative is motivated and qualified to take over.

If the company is to be sold, **preparations for the sale** should be made to improve salability of the company, accelerate the sale process and increase the sale price. Preparatory measures include increasing profitability, conceiving or revising the business plan, increasing transparency of the company through improvements in the instruments of managerial control, and preparing the management team. Consultants specialized in company sales and professional processes like auctions help to achieve a fair sale price.

Private equity companies compete with other potential buyers for family businesses. While the identification of potential target companies seems uncritical, approach and negotiations are adversely affected by the bad reputation of private equity. Current reservations of investors, prejudices stemming from ignorance, and negative media coverage shed a gloomy light on private equity companies. To appreciate buy-outs as an accepted and attractive sale alternative among the general public and family owners in particular, **private equity companies should improve their public relations** through increased transparency and better cooperation with the media.

In sale negotiations, private equity companies should **pay due respect to vendors' interests**. Family owners are not exclusively interested in the highest sale price. Therefore, sale negotiations should also emcompass talks on concessions like lay-offs, relocations, and continuation of company expansion. As most buy-outs in family businesses are growth stories, concessions could be considered and might motivate family owners to agree to lower sale prices (as already done by holding companies). Although investment managers are aware of soft factors like trust and respectfulness, interviewees suggested that these are still not addressed adequately.

With regard to the **role of the family post buy-out**, two strategies can be distinguished: First, family members can make a clear cut and discontinue all involvement in the company. Second, family owners can retain a fading minor influence in the company. While the first strategy might be hard to handle emotionally, the second strategy is prone to conflicts with the private equity company and post buy-out managers. Family managers remaining in their position post buy-out have to comply with expectations of the new owners concerning management style, decision making approach and general management skills. Nevertheless, cooperation seems problematic as witnessed by failure in two of three sample companies. To prevent such conflicts, private equity companies, fellow managers and potential post buy-out family managers should discuss openly and in detail their expectations, and investors should assess family managers diligently.

As described above, value generation of buy-outs in family businesses depends on professionalization and economization. To maximize return on their investments, private equity companies are advised to **focus investment activity on** companies that promise the greatest **potential for professionalization and economization**. The stronger the impact of both effects, the higher might be the return from the buy-out.

Family businesses could also achieve **professionalization and economization** of the company **without the buy-out**. Given the importance assigned to non-economic goals or particular family interests, the two effects might not be in the interest of all family owners. However, family owners striving to increase the value and profitability of their family business could independently initiate the same or similar changes that private equity companies employ. Consultants, experienced members of the supervisory board, or external non-family managers could contribute professional knowledge to the company. The motivation and impact of non-family managers could be increased by empowerment, more attractive compensation schemes, and potentially equity participation. Non-family managers seemed to be aware of many possibilities for improvement before the buy-out, but they needed the buy-out to receive the permission to implement them. Data which improved the decision making process resulted from the changes in the instruments of managerial control. All these changes could help to overcome the idleness or obsolescence of family managers approaching retirement, and to restore the growth dynamics of the company. The feasibility of professionalization and economization without buy-outs is exemplified by the companies of the control group.

Lastly, interview partners have frequently complained about the **lack of background information on buy-outs in family businesses**. This thesis, along with other publications quoted herein, is intended to close this gap.

8.3 Outlook

At the beginning of this thesis, a recent surge in the number and volume of buy-outs in German family businesses was noted. Despite this considerable increase, the German market is presumably not exhausting its full potential yet but will continue to grow for two reasons: On the supply side of private equity, more investors and more capital may be attracted to the comparably young and underdeveloped German buy-out market. On the demand side, myriads of German family businesses are aging and a significant share may be expected to face the succession problem, which might be solved through a buy-out. With a greater number of buy-outs taking place and improved transparency of the private equity industry, the notoriety of failed examples and prejudices will be overcome and buy-outs may represent an accepted and appealing solution to the succession problem.

A more mature market in the future implies more variety and more competition. Private equity companies will have to refine their interactions with family owners to attract deals and to succeed in this market. Moreover, private equity companies will have to develop specific methods of value creation for family businesses to deliver adequate returns to their fund investors despite the fierce competition. Hence, the question of how buy-outs change former family businesses is expected to become increasingly relevant and important for future family owners, investment managers, managers of portfolio companies, and the general public.

Given the increasing relevance and importance of the topic, this thesis provides the first insights on changes after buy-outs in family businesses. The evidence analyzed, the propositions derived, and the underlying main effects identified give an initial, unprecedented overview of the antecedents, reasons, and consequences of changes after buy-outs in family businesses. This groundwork and the intriguing character of the research object will hopefully attract and inspire more research on buy-outs in family businesses.

Appendix

A: Overview of propositions

Dimension	Aspect	Number	Proposition	Effects of buy-outs: Professionalization	Economization	Prevention of agency conflicts
Corporate governance	Owner influence on management decisions	1A	Private equity companies' influence on strategic decisions is as intensive as the influence of former family owners.			
		1B	Private equity companies influence strategic decisions through an interaction-oriented approach, whereas family owners stipulate a concrete strategy.			
		1C	Private equity companies do not exert influence on operational decisions.	X		
	Owner influence on corporate strategy	2A	Private equity companies urge their portfolio companies to grow through acquisitions and/or internationalization and/or increase profitability.		X	
		2B	Apart from portfolio companies in turnaround situations, private equity companies hardly demand operational improvements following buy-outs.			
	Supervision and support from the supervisory board	3A	Private equity companies professionalize the supervisory board by appointing experienced and intervening members to the board.	X		X
		3B	Post buy-out supervisory boards tighten supervision and stronger support management compared to pre buy-out supervisory boards.	X		X
		3C	Family members remain on supervisory boards post buy-out to represent their equity stake and keep in touch with the company rather than to contribute their experience.			
	Composition of the management team	4A	Private equity companies have requirements for managers of portfolio companies that differ from requirements demanded by family owners.	X	X	X
		4B	Pre buy-out managers seldom fulfill the requirements expected by private equity companies and are therefore replaced.	X		X
		4C	In particular, CFOs are replaced by more competent managers and their position is upgraded.	X		X
		4D	Most family managers leave deliberately due to incapacity to carry out the strategy agreed on, or after a conflict with the private equity company about different management styles.	X		X
		4E	Private equity companies have an advantage over family businesses in composing a management team suitable for implementing needed changes.	X		
		4F	Private equity companies prefer appointing external managers over promoting internal junior managers to the management.	X		X
		4G	Family owners appoint non-family managers before the sale to ensure continuity and thus increase salability of the company.			
		4H	Private equity companies continue to change the management in most companies in which management was already changed before the buy-out.	X		X
	Motivation and compensation of management	5A	Commitment to the company was a motivation to do the buy-out for managers, who were with the company for a long period (i.e. at least four years) before the buy-out.			
		5B	Compared to the pre buy-out state, management is more incentivized post buy-out through equity participation, increases in total compensation, higher variable shares of compensation and greater transparency in performance determination.	X	X	X
	Decision making process of management	6	Managers in portfolio companies focus on rational, comprehensible decisions based on figures to steer the company and thus put an end to management by gut feeling, emotions and particular family objectives.	X	X	X

Table A-1: Overview of propositions (1/2)

Source: Author's illustration

Not all propositions could be attributed to one or several effects of buy-outs.

Dimension	Aspect	Number	Proposition	Effects of buy-outs		
				Professionalization	Economiza-tion	Prevention of agency conflicts
Instruments of managerial control	Planning	7A	Through the buy-out, planning is professionalized: Planning is carried out in greater detail, reaches further into the future and includes cash planning.	X	X	X
		7B	After the buy-out, the importance of planning is higher compared to its importance in the pre buy-out company.			X
	Management accounting	8A	Through the buy-out, management accounting is professionalized: Figures are expected to be in greater detail, more up-to-date and more reliable.	X	X	X
		8B	The importance of management accounting post buy-out is higher compared to its importance pre buy-out.			X
		8C	Management appreciates the results of management accounting despite increased costs and time-consuming implementation.			
	Performance measurement	9A	Private equity companies introduce EBITDA as key performance indicator.		X	X
		9B	Post buy-out, objectives of the management will be clearly stipulated by private equity companies.	X	X	X
Financial practices	Financing	10A	Greater importance is attached to financing post buy-out compared to its importance pre buy-out.	X	X	
		10B	Frequently, former family owners retain an equity stake in the company post buy-out.			
		10C	Private equity companies aim at cooperating with banks experienced in acquisition financing and might therefore induce portfolio companies to switch banks.	X		
		10D	Backing by the private equity company, increased transparency, and improved proficiency in financing reduce credit costs.	X	X	
		10E	Through the buy-out, financial practices are professionalized: Mezzanine capital, working capital management, leasing and other financial practices are used.	X	X	
	Reporting to banks	11	After the buy-out, transparency for banks is increased significantly through more frequent, more timely, and more detailed reporting.			X
	Investing	12A	After the buy-out, investment decisions are more professional – including pre-definition in the business plan, profitability analyses, and scrutiny by different parties.	X	X	
		12B	Total investment activity tends to increase after the buy-out.		X	
		12C	Post buy-out, investment activity is more in line with corporate strategy and thus oriented towards acquisitions and internationalization.		X	

Table A-2: Overview of propositions (2/2)

Source: Author's illustration

Not all propositions could be attributed to one or several effects of buy-outs.

B: Cover letter

TECHNISCHE
UNIVERSITÄT
MÜNCHEN

Center for Entrepreneurial
and Financial Studies

Arcisstr. 21
80333 München

Telefon: 089-289-25192
Telefax: 0721-151-412990
oliver.kloeckner@cefs.de
www.cefs.de

Mit freundlicher Unterstützung durch:

Bundesministerium
für Wirtschaft
und Technologie

Bayerisches Staatsministerium für
Wirtschaft, Infrastruktur, Verkehr und Technologie

Center for Entrepreneurial and Financial Studies (CEFS)
TU München · Arcisstr. 21 · 80333 München

Bitte um ein persönliches Interview

München, 11.09.2008

Sehr geehrter XXX,

bitte erlauben Sie, dass wir uns mit einer großen Bitte an Sie wenden, die für unsere Forschungsarbeit von großer Bedeutung ist. Im Rahmen eines Forschungs- und Dissertationsprojektes beschäftigen wir uns mit Buyouts in Familienunternehmen. Der Fokus liegt hierbei auf den Auswirkungen des Buyouts auf das Unternehmen in den Bereichen Corporate Governance, Management, Finanzierung und Controlling.

Sie haben in der XXX sicherlich erlebt, dass mit dem Buyout und in der nachfolgenden Zeit wesentliche Veränderungen im Unternehmen stattgefunden haben. In einem persönlichen Interview würden wir Sie gerne zu diesen Veränderungen in der XXX seit dem Buyout befragen. Wir wissen, dass Ihre Zeit knapp ist, allerdings sind wir überzeugt, dass gerade die Perspektive des Unternehmers dringend notwendig ist, um ein realistisches Bild der Veränderungen wiederzugeben. Wir würden uns daher freuen, wenn wir Sie – oder, sofern dies nicht möglich ist, alternativ einen Ihrer Mitarbeiter – in einem persönlichen Gespräch zu Ihren Buyout-Erfahrungen befragen könnten.

Das Interview nimmt maximal eine Stunde in Anspruch und kann auf Ihren Wunsch entweder telefonisch oder bei Ihnen vor Ort stattfinden. Der Termin wäre für Sie frei wählbar im Zeitraum bis Mitte August dieses Jahres. Selbstverständlich werden Ihre Antworten anonym behandelt. Die Ergebnisse der Gespräche fließen zugleich in die Dissertation von Herrn Klöckner ein. Bei Interesse erhalten Sie gerne nach der Veröffentlichung ein Exemplar. Wir hoffen, durch diese Forschungsarbeit auf dem Gebiet erste, wertvolle Erkenntnisse gewinnen zu können, welche einen Buyout als attraktive Lösungsmöglichkeit für Nachfolgeprobleme in Familienunternehmen aufzeigen.

Im Anhang finden Sie ein Formular für Ihre Antwort. Wir würden uns sehr freuen, wenn wir zur Unterstützung des Forschungsvorhabens und der Dissertation von Herrn Klöckner auf Sie zählen könnten!

Mit besten Grüßen

Prof. Dr. Dr. Ann-Kristin Achleitner Oliver Klöckner

Wissenschaftliche Direktoren: Univ.-Prof. Dr. Dr. Ann-Kristin Achleitner, KfW-Stiftungslehrstuhl für Entrepreneurial Finance; Univ.-Prof. Dr. Christoph Kaserer, Lehrstuhl für BWL / Finanzmanagement und Kapitalmärkte

C: Interview guide

Interviewleitfaden

im Rahmen des Forschungsprojekts „Buyouts in Familienunternehmen"

Einleitungsfragen

Transaktion

1. Könnten Sie den Ablauf des Buyouts kurz darstellen?
2. Was war der Grund für den Verkauf durch die Familie?

Einfluss der Familie vor dem Buyout

3. Wie sah die Eigentümerstruktur vor dem Buyout aus?
4. Wie war die Geschäftsführung besetzt?
5. Wir setzte sich der Aufsichtsrat / Beirat zusammen?

Corporate Governance

Einfluss der Eigentümer

6. Was denken Sie, wie hat sich durch den Buyout der Einfluss der Eigentümer auf strategische und operative Entscheidungen des Managements geändert?
   6.1 Hat sich in Folge des Buyouts der Einfluss der Eigentümer (dh. der Private-Equity-Gesellschaft im Vergleich zu den vorherigen Familieneigentümern) auf operative Entscheidungen im Tagesgeschäft verstärkt, vermindert oder ist dieser unverändert geblieben?
   6.2 Hat sich in Folge des Buyouts der Einfluss der Eigentümer auf strategische Entscheidungen verstärkt, vermindert oder ist dieser unverändert geblieben?
7. Hält die Eigentümerfamilie noch Anteile an dem Unternehmen?
   Wie bewerten Sie deren Einfluss?
8. Haben die neuen Eigentümer dem Unternehmen eine neue Strategie vorgegeben?

Zielvereinbarung und -überprüfung

9. Wie hat sich die Zielvereinbarung durch den Buyout geändert?
   9.1 Gab es Zielvereinbarungen vor dem Buyout?
   Werden Zielvereinbarungen seit dem Buyout verwendet?
   Wurden bereits bestehende Renditeziele nach dem Buyout angehoben?

9.2 Wird das Management durch die Eigentümer anhand des Erreichens finanzieller Ziele gemessen (durch Kennzahlen wie Cash Flow, Return on Equity oder andere Finanzkennzahlen)?
Wird das Management an der Erreichung strategischer Ziele gemessen (Marktanteil, Eintritt in neue Marktsegmente, Internationalisierung)? Hat sich in Folge des Buyouts die Gewichtung zwischen finanziellen und strategischen Zielen geändert?

Aufsichtsgremium

10. Wie hat sich der Buyout auf den Aufsichtsrat / Beirat ausgewirkt?
    10.1 Gab es personelle Veränderungen im Aufsichtsrat/Beirat?
    10.2 Haben Sie das Gefühl, dass der Aufsichtsrat in seiner Zusammensetzung nach dem Buyout das Unternehmen aktiver unterstützt?
    10.3 Hinterfragt der Aufsichtsrat die Entscheidungen des Managements stärker seit dem Buyout?

Teilfazit

11. Gab es weitere entscheidende Veränderungen im Bereich der Corporate Governance?
12. Würden Sie sagen, dass das Unternehmen in der Dimension Corporate Governance durch den Buyout gestärkt oder geschwächt wurde oder unverändert geblieben ist?

Management

13. Welche personellen Veränderungen fanden in der Geschäftsführung nach dem Buyout statt?

Entscheidungsprozess

14. Wie hat sich der Buyout auf den Prozess der Entscheidungsfindung im Management ausgewirkt?
    14.1 Würden Sie sagen, dass seit dem Buyout Daten aus dem Controlling und der Marktforschung einen größeren Einfluss auf die Entscheidungen des Managements haben?
    14.2 Hat sich der Grad der Formalisierung, im Hinblick auf den Entscheidungsprozess des Managements, erhöht?
    14.3 Fanden unmittelbar nach dem Buyout Kostensenkungsmaßnahmen statt, deren Möglichkeiten das vorherige Management zwar erkannt hatte, die es jedoch nicht umgesetzt hat?

Investitionstätigkeit

15. Wie hat sich nach Ihrer Einschätzung die Investitionstätigkeit des Unternehmens durch den Buyout verändert?
    15.1 Wurden seit dem Buyout Investitionen in größerem Umfang getätigt? Hätte es darüber hinaus betriebswirtschaftlich sinnvolle Möglichkeiten für solche Investitionen gegeben? Wurden diese aufgrund des Buyouts zurückgestellt?

Beziehung zu Kunden und Zulieferern

16. Wie wurde der Eigentümerwechsel der Öffentlichkeit und den Stakeholdern gegenüber kommuniziert?
17. Wie schätzen Sie hat sich der Buyout auf die Beziehung des Unternehmens zu Kunden und Zulieferern ausgewirkt?
    17.1 Hat in der Folge des Buyouts die Kundenfluktuation zugenommen? Sind Stammkunden gewechselt?
    17.2 Wurden Geschäftsbeziehungen zu Kunden und Zulieferern nach dem Buyout auf Profitabilität hin überprüft? Hat dies zu Neuverhandlungen oder zur Beendigung von Geschäftsbeziehungen geführt?
    17.3 Haben sich Kunden oder Zulieferer darüber negativ geäußert, dass sie nicht mehr mit einem Familienmitglied sprechen können?

Beziehung zu Arbeitnehmern

18. Wie schätzen Sie hat sich die Beziehung des Unternehmens zu den Arbeitnehmern in Folge des Buyouts verändert?
    18.1 Hat sich im Generellen die Bezahlung der Mitarbeiter geändert? Hat sich die Arbeitsatmosphäre im Unternehmen verändert? Gab es unter den Mitarbeitern Vorbehalte gegenüber der Private-Equity-Gesellschaft als neue Eigentümerin?
    18.2 Gab es deutlichen Arbeitsplatzabbau? Warum wurde dieser nicht im Familienunternehmen durchgeführt?

Motivation des Managements

19. Welches waren die zentralen Beweggründe, den Buyout durchzuführen? Wie hat sich der Buyout auf die Entlohnung des Managements ausgewirkt?
    19.1 Ist der variable Anteil des Gehalts angestiegen?
    19.2 Wenn die Ziele erreicht werden, ist die Entlohnung nun attraktiver als vor dem Buyout?

Teilfazit

20. Würden Sie sagen, dass das Unternehmen in der Dimension Management durch den Buyout gestärkt oder geschwächt wurde oder unverändert geblieben ist?

Finanzierung

Ausgestaltung der Unternehmensfinanzierung

21. Würden Sie sagen, dass seit dem Buyout die Finanzierung des Unternehmens professioneller betrieben wird?
    - 21.1 Wird seit dem Buyout ein breiteres Spektrum an Finanzierungsinstrumenten genutzt?
    - 21.2 Gab es Veränderungen bei den Geschäftspartnern (Banken, Rating-Agenturen, Corporate Finance Beratungen) im Bereich der Unternehmensfinanzierung?
      Ist diese Veränderung auf eine Professionalisierung der Unternehmensfinanzierung zurückzuführen oder auf die Buyout-Transaktion?
    - 21.3 Wie hat sich die Beteiligung der Private Equity Gesellschaft auf die Verfügbarkeit von Fremdkapital ausgewirkt?
      War es möglich die Finanzierungskosten von Fremdkapital zu verringern?

CFO

22. Gibt es einen neuen CFO im Unternehmen?
    Würden Sie sagen, dass der neue CFO über mehr relevante Erfahrung oder mehr Wissen in den Bereichen Finanzierung, Controlling und Rechnungswesen verfügt?
    - 22.1 Gab es Veränderungen in der Arbeit und der Stellung des CFOs? Wurde die Bedeutung des CFOs aufgewertet?

Finanzkommunikation

23. Hat sich das Reporting gegenüber den Banken nach Ihrer Einschätzung verändert?

Teilfazit

24. Gab es weitere entscheidende Veränderungen in der Dimension Finanzierung?
25. Würden Sie sagen, dass das Unternehmen in der Dimension Finanzierung durch den Buyout gestärkt oder geschwächt wurde oder unverändert geblieben ist?

Controlling

Planungsprozess

26. Wie hat sich der Buyout auf den Planungsprozess ausgewirkt?
    - 26.1 Gab es einen regelmäßigen Planungsprozess (Business Plan, Budgets, Planungsgrößen für Cashflow, GuV, Bilanz) vor dem Buyout?
      In welcher Weise hat sich der Planungsprozess durch den Buyout verändert?

Veränderung des Controllingsystems

27. Ist aufgrund des Buyouts das Controllingsystem verändert worden?
    - 27.1 Wurde das Controllingsystem im Zuge des Buyouts überprüft und verändert?
      Sind infolge dessen die Kosten für das Controlling angestiegen?
    - 27.2 Wurde die Erhebung zusätzlicher Kennzahlen von der Private Equity Gesellschaft oder den Banken verlangt?
      Welche sind dies?
    - 27.3 Schätzen Sie, dass das Management mithilfe des veränderten Controllings das Unternehmen nun besser lenken kann?

Schlüsselgröße der Unternehmenssteuerung

28. Gab es eine oder mehrere Schlüsselgrößen, nach der das Unternehmen vor dem Buyout gesteuert wurde?
    Hat sich die Bedeutung dieser Schlüsselgröße(n) nach dem Buyout verändert?
29. Was ist die Schlüsselgröße zur Steuerung des Unternehmens nach dem Buyout? (EBITDA, Umsatzwachstum, working capital)

Teilfazit

30. Gab es weitere entscheidende Veränderungen in der Dimension Controlling?
31. Würden Sie sagen, dass das Unternehmen in der Dimension Controlling durch den Buyout gestärkt oder geschwächt wurde oder unverändert geblieben ist?

Fazit

32. Was würden Sie als die markantesten Einflüsse der Private-Equity-Gesellschaft auf Ihr Unternehmen bezeichnen – im Positiven wie im Negativen?
    - 32.1 Was waren die entscheidendsten Maßnahmen, die die Wettbewerbsfähigkeit des Unternehmen verbessert haben?
    - 32.2 Und was waren Maßnahmen, die sich eher ungünstig auf das Unternehmen ausgewirkt haben?

33. Welche Maßnahmen infolge des Buyouts würden Sie heute anders angehen? Auf welche würden Sie gänzlich verzichten?

34. Wie haben sich seit dem Buyout Umsatz, EBIT und Mitarbeiterzahl entwickelt?

Vielen Dank für das Gespräch

List of References

Achleitner, A.-K. (2002): Handbuch Investment Banking, Ed. 3, Gabler, Wiesbaden.

Achleitner, A.-K. (2005): Vom Guten der Heuschrecken-Debatte, in: Die Betriebswirtschaft, 65 (4), pp. 327-329.

Achleitner, A.-K. (2006): Die Bedeutung organisierter Kapitalmärkte für das mittelständische Unternehmen, in: Biner, A. / Brockhaus, M. / Kirchschläger, A. / Stämpfli, R. / Tanner, R. (Ed.): International Public Affairs: Im Spannungsfeld von Freiheit und Verantwortung – Festschrift zum 60. Geburtstag von Herrn Prof. Dr. h.c. Wolfgang Schürer, Stämpfli, Bern, pp. 305-321.

Achleitner, A.-K. / Achleitner, P. (2000): Die Finanzierung von Familienunternehmen durch Beteiligungsgesellschaften, in: Jeschke, D. / Kirchdörfer, R. / Lorz, R. (Ed.): Planung, Finanzierung und Kontrolle im Familienunternehmen, C.H. Beck, München, pp. 127-148.

Achleitner, A.-K. / Bassen, A. / Jais, S.D. / Nietzer, P. (2004): Controlling von Buyout-Transaktionen durch Private-Equity-Gesellschaften, in: Die Zeitschrift für Controlling & Management (Sonderheft 1), pp. 32-45.

Achleitner, A.-K. / Braun, R. / Bender, M. / Geidner, A. (2008a): Community Development Venture Capital - Concept and Status Quo in Germany, in: International Journal of Entrepreneurship and Innovation Management - Special Issue on: The Role of Public Venture Capital Financing Towards Creating New Entrepreneurial Businesses and Innovations (forthcoming).

Achleitner, A.-K. / Ehrhart, N. / Zimmermann, V. (2006): Beteiligungsfinanzierung nach der Marktkonsolidierung, KfW Bankengruppe, Frankfurt a.M.

Achleitner, A.-K. / Fingerle, C.H. (2003): Unternehmenswertsteigerung durch Management Buyout, in: TUM EF Working Paper Series.

Achleitner, A.-K. / Fingerle, C.H. (2004): Finanzierungssituation des deutschen Mittelstands, in: Achleitner, A.-K. / von Einem, C. / von Schröder, B. (Ed.): Private Debt - alternative Finanzierung für den Mittelstand, Schäffer-Poeschel, Stuttgart, pp. 5-40.

Achleitner, A.-K. / Heister, P. / Stahl, E. (2007): Social Entrepreneurship - Ein Überblick, in: Achleitner, A.-K. / Pöllath, R. / Stahl, E. (Ed.): Finanzierung von Sozialunternehmen, Schäffer-Poeschel, Stuttgart, pp. 3-25.

Achleitner, A.-K. / Herman, K. / Nathusius, E. / Lerner, J. (2008b): European private equity cases: introduction, in: World Economic Forum (Ed.): Globalization of alternative investments - The global economic impact of private equity report 2008, World Economic Forum, Geneva, pp. 87-89.

Achleitner, A.-K. / Herman, K. / Nathusius, E. / Lerner, J. (2008c): Messer Griesheim, in: World Economic Forum (Ed.): Globalization of alternative investments - The global economic impact of private equity report 2008, World Economic Forum, Geneva, pp. 91-102.

Achleitner, A.-K. / Herman, K. / Nathusius, E. / Lerner, J. (2008d): New Look, in: World Economic Forum (Ed.): Globalization of alternative investments - The global economic impact of private equity report 2008, World Economic Forum, Geneva, pp. 103-114.

Achleitner, A.-K. / Klöckner, O. (2005): Employment contribution of Private Equity and Venture Capital in Europe, European Venture Capital & Private Equity Association, Zaventem.

Achleitner, A.-K. / Klöckner, O. (2006): Finanzierung von Familienunternehmen: Wunderwaffe oder Achillesferse, in: Mach, A.E. (Ed.): Familienunternehmen im Zeichen des Wandels, Alphazirkel, Munich, pp. 7-18.

Achleitner, A.-K. / Poech, A. (2004): Familienunternehmen und Private Equity: Die psychologischen Bruchstellen, Apax Partners Beteiligungsberatung, Munich.

Achleitner, A.-K. / Schraml, S.C. / Klöckner, O. (2008): Wie professionell ist die Unternehmensfinanzierung tatsächlich?, Center for Entrepreneurial and Financial Studies, Alphazirkel, Droege & Comp., Munich.

Achleitner, A.-K. / Schraml, S.C. / Tappeiner, F. (2008): Private Equity in Familienunternehmen - Erfahrungen mit Minderheitsbeteiligungen, Books on Demand, Norderstedt.

Agrawal, A. / Nagarajan, N.J. (1990): Corporate Capital Structure, Agency Costs, and Ownership Control: The Case of All-Equity Firms, in: Journal of Finance, 45 (4), pp. 1325-1331.

Albach, H. / Freund, W. (1989): Generationswechsel und Unternehmenskontinuität, Bertelsmann Stiftung, Gütersloh.

Albanese, R. / Dacin, M.T. / Harris, I.C. (1997): Agents as Stewards, in: Academy of Management Review, 22 (3), pp. 609-611.

Albrecht, P. / Maurer, R. (2005): Investment- und Risikomanagement, Ed. 2, Schäffer-Poeschel, Stuttgart.

Allen, M.P. / Panian, S.K. (1982): Power, Performance and Succession in the Large Corporation, in: Administrative Science Quarterly, 27 (4), pp. 538-547.

Amihud, Y. (2002): Leveraged Management Buyouts and Shareholders' Wealth, in: Amihud, Y. (Ed.): Leveraged Management Buyouts, Beard Books, Washington D.C., pp.

Anders, G. (1992): The "Barbarians" in the Boardroom, in: Harvard Business Review, 70 (4), pp. 79-87.

Anderson, R.C. / Mansi, S.A. / Reeb, D.M. (2003): Founding family ownership and the agency cost of debt, in: Journal of Financial Economics, 68, pp. 263-285.

Anderson, R.C. / Reeb, D.M. (2003): Founding-Family Ownership and Firm Performance: Evidence from the S&P 500, in: Journal of Finance, 58 (3), pp. 1301-1328.

Andersson, T. / Carlsen, J. / Getz, D. (2002): Family Business Goals in the Tourism and Hospitality Sector: Case Studies and Cross-Case Analysis from Australia, Canada, and Sweden, in: Family Business Review, 15 (2), pp. 89-106.

Ang, J.S. (1991): Small business uniqueness and the theory of financial management, in: Journal of Small Business Finance, 1 (1), pp. 1-13.

Ang, J.S. / Cole, R.A. / Lin, J.W. (2000): Agency Costs and Ownership Structure, in: Journal of Finance, 55 (1), pp. 81-106.

Angwin, D. / Contardo, I. (1999): Unleashing Cerberus: Don't Let Your MBOs Turn on Themselves, in: Long Range Planning, 32 (5), pp. 494-504.

Angwin, D. / Stern, P. / Bradley, S. (2004): Agent or Steward: The Target CEO in a Hostile Takeover - Can a Condemned Agent be Redeemed?, in: Long Range Planning, 37 (3), pp. 239-257.

Arbeitskreis Finanzierung der Schmalenbach-Gesellschaft - Deutsche Gesellschaft für Betriebswirtschaft e.V. (1990): Analyse der für die Entwicklung eines Buy-out-Marktes notwendigen Bedingungen in der Bundesrepublik Deutschland unter besonderer

Berücksichtigung von MBOs, in: Zeitschrift für betriebswirtschaftliche Forschung, 42 (10), pp. 830-850.

Arnet, P. / Hartmann, H. (2004): Nachfolgeregelung bei Familienunternehmen - Verkauf als Option, in: Der Schweizer Treuhänder, 10, pp. 833-840.

Arregle, J.-L. / Durand, R. / Very, P. (2004): Origines du capital social et avantages concurrentiels des firmes familiales, in: M@n@gement, 7 (1), pp. 13-36.

Arrow, K.J. (1999): Foreword, in: Carroll, G. / Teece, D. (Ed.): Firms, Markets and Hierarchies, Oxford University Press, New York, NY, pp. vii–viii.

Arthurs, J.D. / Busenitz, L.W. (2003): The Boundaries and Limitations of Agency Theory and Stewardship Theory in the Venture Capitalist/Entrepreneur Relationship, in: Entrepreneurship Theory & Practice, 28 (2), pp. 145-162.

Arzac, E.R. (2004): Valuation for Merger, Buyouts, and Restructuring, John Wiley & Sons, New York, NY.

Asquith, P. / Wizman, T.A. (1990): Event risk, covenants, and bondholder returns in leveraged buyouts, in: Journal of Financial Economics, 27, pp. 195-213.

Astrachan, J.H. (2003): The emergence of a field. Commentary on the special issue of Journal of Business Venturing - The evolving family/entrepreneurship relationship, in: Journal of Business Venturing, 18 (5), pp. 567-572.

Astrachan, J.H. / Allen, E. / Spinelli, S. / Wittmeyer, C. / Glucksman, S. (2003): American Family Business Survey 2002, The George and Robin Raymond Family Business Institute, Alfred, NY.

Astrachan, J.H. / Jaskiewicz, P. (2008): Emotional Returns and Emotional Costs in Privately Held Family Businesses: Advancing Traditional Business Valuation, in: Family Business Review, 21 (2), pp. 139-149.

Astrachan, J.H. / Klein, S.B. / Smyrnios, K.X. (2002): The F-PEC Scale of Family Influence: A Proposal for Solving the Family Business Definition Problem, in: Family Business Review, 15 (1), pp. 45-58.

Astrachan, J.H. / Kolenko, T.A. (1994): A Neglected Factor Explaining Family Business Success: Human Resource Practices, in: Family Business Review, 7 (3), pp. 251-262.

Astrachan, J.H. / Shanker, M.C. (2006): Family business' contribution to the US economy: a closer look, in: Poutziouris, P.Z. / Smyrnios, K. / Klein, S.B. (Ed.): Handbook of Research on Family Business, Edward Elgar, Cheltenham, pp.

Atteslander, P. (2003): Methoder der empirischen Sozialforschung, Ed. 10, Walter de Gruyter, Berlin.

Bächle, C.M. / Hager, P. (1999): Anreizstrukturen für das Management im Rahmen von Buy-Outs, in: M&A-Review (9), pp. 380-384.

Baker, G.P. / Wruck, K.H. (1989): Organizational changes and value creation in leveraged buyouts : The case of the O.M. Scott & Sons Company, in: Journal of Financial Economics, 25 (2), pp. 163-190.

Ball, R. / Watts, R. (1979): Some Additional Evidence on Survival Biases, in: Journal of Finance, 34 (1), pp. 197-206.

Ballwieser, W. / Schmid, H. (1990a): Charakteristika und Problembereiche von Management Buy-Outs (I), in: Das Wirtschaftsstudium (5), pp. 299-305.

Ballwieser, W. / Schmid, H. (1990b): Charakteristika und Problembereiche von Management Buy-Outs (II), in: Das Wirtschaftsstudium (6), pp. 358-364.

Barney, J.B. (1990): The Debate between Traditional Management Theory and Organizational Economics: Substantive Differences or Intergroup Conflict?, in: Academy of Management Review, 15 (3), pp. 382-393.

Barney, J.B. / Ouchi, W.G. (1986): Agency Theory: How Market Forces Affect the Management of a Firm, in: Barney, J.B. / Ouchi, W.G. (Ed.): Organizational Economics, Jossey-Bass, San Francisco, CA, pp. 205-213.

Baron, R.A. / Markman, G.D. (2000): Beyond social capital: How social skills can enhance entrepreneurs' success, in: Academy of Management Executive, 14 (1), pp. 106-116.

Basu, A.K. / Lal, R. / Srinivasan, V. / Staelin, R. (1985): Salesforce Compensation Plans: An Agency Theoretic Perspective, in: Marketing Science, 4 (4), pp. 267-291.

Baur, W. (2003): Finanzierung von unternehmergesteuerten Buy-Outs, in: Weitnauer, W. (Ed.): Management Buy-Out - Handbuch für Recht und Praxis, C.H. Beck, Munich, pp. 68-100.

Becker, F.G. (2007): Fremdmanagement in Familienunternehmen: Annäherung an eine vielschichtige Thematik, in: Letmathe, P. / Eigler, J. / Welter, F. / Kathan, D. / Heupel, T. (Ed.): Management kleiner und mittlerer Unternehmen, Deutscher Universitäts-Verlag, Wiesbaden, pp. 205-224.

Becker, G.S. (1981): A Treatise on the Family, Harvard University Press, Cambridge.

Becker, R. (2000): Buy-outs in Deutschland: Handbuch für Manager, Consultants und Investoren, Deutscher Wirtschaftsdienst, Köln.

Becker, R. (2001): Praktische Vorgehensweise des Managements in einem Buy-out, in: Achleitner, A.-K. / Thoma, G.F. (Ed.): Handbuch Corporate Finance, Ed. 2, Deutscher Wirtschaftsdienst, Cologne, chapter 6.4.2.

Beehr, T.A. / Drexler, J.A. / Faulkner, S. (1997): Working in small family businesses: empirical comparisons to non-family businesses, in: Journal of Organizational Behavior, 18 (3), pp. 297-312.

Beitmann, B. (2003): Finanzierung von Institutionellen Buy-Outs, in: Weitnauer, W. (Ed.): Management Buy-Out - Handbuch für Recht und Praxis, C.H. Beck, Munich, pp. 101-118.

Berelson, B. (1954): Content Analysis, in: Lindzey, G. (Ed.): Handbook of Social Psychology, Addison-Wesley, Cambridge, pp. 488-522.

Berg, A. / Gottschalg, O.F. (2005): Understanding Value Generation in Buyouts, in: Journal of Restructuring Finance, 2 (1), pp. 9-37.

Berger, A.N. / Udell, G.F. (1998): The economics of small business Finance: The roles of private equity and debt markets in the financial growth cycle, in: Journal of Banking & Finance, 22, pp. 613-673.

Berle, A.A. / Means, G.C. (1932): The Modern Corporation and Private Property, Macmillan, New York, NY.

Bertrand, M. / Schoar, A. (2006): The Role of Family in Family Firms, in: Journal of Economic Perspectives, 20 (2), pp. 73-96.

Bettis, R.A. / Donaldson, L. (1990): Market Discipline and the Discipline of Management, in: Academy of Management Review, 15 (3), pp. 367-368.

Bhattacharya, U. / Ravikumar, B. (2004): From Cronies to Professionals: The Evolution of Family Firms, in: Klein, E. (Ed.): Capital Formation, Governance and Banking, Nova Science, Hauppauge, NY, pp. 23-38.

Birley, S. (2001): Owner-manager attitudes to family and business issues: A 16 country study, in: Entrepreneurship Theory & Practice, 26 (2), pp. 63-76.

Birley, S. / Ng, D. / Godfrey, A. (1999): The Family and the Business, in: Long Range Planning, 32 (6), pp. 598-608.

Block, J.H. / Thams, A. (2008): Long-Term Orientation in Family Firms: A Bayesian Analysis of R&D Spending, SSRN.

Blumentritt, T.P. / Keyt, A.D. / Astrachan, J.H. (2007): Creating an Environment for Successful Nonfamily CEOs: An Exploratory Study of Good Principals, in: Family Business Review, 20 (4), pp. 321-335.

Bopaiah, C. (1998): Availability of Credit to Family Businesses, in: Small Business Economics, 11 (1), pp. 75-86.

Bousek, H. / Ehringer, G. / Fischer, M. / Hackl, E. / Jandl, H. / Maurer, M. / Mittendorfer, R. / Untergrabner, G. (2003): Management Buy-Out und Management Buy-In - Ein Leitfaden für Eigentümer und Manager, Investkredit Bank, Vienna, pp.

Brealey, R.A. / Myers, S.C. / Allen, F. (2006): Principles of corporate finance, McGraw-Hill, New York.

Brockhaus, R.H. (2004): Family Business Succession: Suggestions for Future Research, in: Family Business Review, 17 (2), pp. 165-177.

Bruining, H. / Bonnet, M. / Wright, M. (2004): Management control systems and strategy change in buyouts, in: Management Accounting Research, 15 (2), pp. 155-177.

Bruining, H. / Verwaal, E. (2005): Successful Management Buyouts: Are They Really More Entrepreneurial? , ERIM Report Series Reference No. ERS-2005-076-STR, Erasmus University Rotterdam, 11/2005.

Bruner, R.F. / Eades, K.M. (1992): The crash of the Revco leveraged buyout: The hypothesis of inadequate capital in: Journal of the Financial Management Association, 21 (1), pp. 35-49.

Brunninge, O. / Nordqvist, M. / Wiklund, J. (2007): Corporate Governance and Strategic Change in SMEs: The Effects of Ownership, Board Composition and Top Management Teams, in: Small Business Economics, 29 (3), pp. 295-308.

Bruton, G.D. / Keels, J.K. / Scifres, E.L. (2002): Corporate restructuring and performance: An agency perspective on the complete buyout cycle, in: Journal of Business Research, 55 (9), pp. 709-724.

Bryman, A. (2004): Social research methods, Ed. 2, Oxford University Press, New York, NY.

Bull, I. (1989): Financial performance of leveraged buyouts: An empirical analysis, in: Journal of Business Venturing, 4 (4), pp. 263-279.

Bundesministerium der Finanzen (2003): Einkommensteuerliche Behandlung von Venture Capital und Private Equity Fonds; Abgrenzung der privaten Vermögensverwaltung vom Gewerbebetrieb, BMF-Schreiben IV A 6 - S 2240 - 153/03, Bundesfinanzministerium, 12/2003.

Burger-Calderon, M. / Näther, C. (2001): Buy-outs als Finanzierungsinstrument für eigentümergeführte Unternehmen, in: Achleitner, A.-K. / Thoma, G.F. (Ed.): Handbuch Corporate Finance, Ed. 2, Deutscher Wirtschaftsdienst, Cologne, chapter 6.4.5.

BVK (2008): BVK Statistik - Das Jahr 2007 in Zahlen, Bundesverband Deutscher Kapitalbeteiligungsgesellschaften, 02/2008.

Cabrera-Suarez, K. / De Saa-Perez, P. / Garcia-Almeida, D. (2001): The Succession Process from a Resource- and knowledge-based View of the Family Firm, in: Family Business Review, 14 (1), pp. 37-47.

Caers, R. / Dubois, C. / Jegers, M. / Gieter, S.D. / Schepers, C. / Pepermans, R. (2006): Principal-Agent Relationships on the Stewardship-Agency Axis, in: Nonprofit Management, 17 (1), pp. 25-47.

Cappuyns, K. (2006): Internationalization of family businesses through strategic alliances: an exploratory study, in: Poutziouris, P.Z. / Smyrnios, K.X. / Klein, S.B. (Ed.): Handbook of Research on Family Business, Edward Elgar, Cheltenham, pp. 445-459.

Carney, M. (2005): Corporate Governance and Competitive Advantage in Family-Controlled Firms, in: Entrepreneurship Theory & Practice, 29 (3), pp. 249-265.

Carney, M. / Gedajlovic, E. (2002): The Coupling of Ownership and Control and the Allocation of Financial Resources: Evidence from Hong Kong, in: Journal of Management Studies, 39 (1), pp. 123-146.

Carrasco-Hernandez, A. / Sánchez-Marín, G. (2007): The Determinants of Employee Compensation in Family Firms: Empirical Evidence, in: Family Business Review, 20 (3), pp. 215-228.

Chandy, P.R. / Sriram, R. (1990): Securitization in the Market Place, in: American Business Review, 8 (2), pp. 86.

Charan, R. / Hofer, C.W. / Mahon, J.F. (1980): From Entrepreneurial to Professional Management: A Set of Guidelines, in: Journal of Small Business Management, 18 (1), pp. 1-10.

Chittoor, R. / Das, R. (2007): Professionalization of Management and Succession Performance - A Vital Linkage in: Family Business Review, 20 (1), pp. 65-79.

Chrisman, J.J. / Chua, J.H. / Kellermanns, F.W. / Chang, E.P.C. (2007): Are family managers agents or stewards? An exploratory study in privately held family firms, in: Journal of Business Research, 60 (10), pp. 1030-1038.

Chrisman, J.J. / Chua, J.H. / Kellermanns, F.W. / Matherne, I.I.I. / Curtis, F. / Debicki, B.J. (2008): Management Journals as Venues for Publication of Family Business Research, in: Entrepreneurship Theory & Practice, 32 (5), pp. 927-934.

Chrisman, J.J. / Chua, J.H. / Litz, R.A. (2004): Comparing the Agency Costs of Family and Non-Family Firms: Conceptual Issues and Exploratory Evidence, in: Entrepreneurship Theory & Practice, 28 (4), pp. 335-354.

Chrisman, J.J. / Chua, J.H. / Sharma, P. (1996): A Review and Annotated Bibiliography of Family Business Studies, Kluwer Academic, Norwell.

Chrisman, J.J. / Chua, J.H. / Sharma, P. (1998): Important Attributes of Successors in Family Businesses: An Exploratory Study, in: Family Business Review, 10 (3), pp. 19-34.

Chrisman, J.J. / Chua, J.H. / Sharma, P. (2003): Current Trends and Future Directions in Family Business Management Studies: Toward a Theory of the Family Firm, Coleman White Paper Series, 01/2003.

Chrisman, J.J. / Chua, J.H. / Sharma, P. (2005): Trends and Directions in the Development of a Strategic Management Theory of the Family Firm, in: Entrepreneurship Theory & Practice, 29 (5), pp. 555-575.

Chrisman, J.J. / Chua, J.H. / Steier, L.P. (2005): Sources and Consequences of Distinctive Familiness: An Introduction, in: Entrepreneurship Theory & Practice, 29 (3), pp. 237-247.

Chrisman, J.J. / Chua, J.H. / Steier, L.P. (2007): Agency Issues in the Management Buy-Out and Buy-in Alternatives of Family Firms, Paper for the 5th conference on: Theories of the family enterprise, Mississippi State University.

Chua, J.H. / Chrisman, J.J. / Sharma, P. (2003): Succession and Nonsuccession. Concerns of Family Firms and Agency Relationship with Nonfamily Managers, in: Family Business Review, 16 (2), pp. 89-107.

Citron, D. / Robbie, K. / Wright, M. (1997): Loan Covenants and Relationship Banking in MBOs, in: Accounting & Business Research, 27 (4), pp. 277-294.

Coleman, S. / Carsky, M. (1999): Sources of Capital for Small Family-Owned Businesses: Evidence from the National Survey of Small Business Finances, in: Family Business Review, 12 (1), pp. 73-85.

Copeland, T.E. / Weston, J.F. / Shastri, K. (2005): Financial Theory and Corporate Policy, Ed. 4, Pearson Addison Wesley, Boston.

Corbetta, G. (1995): Patterns of Development of Family Businesses in Italy, in: Family Business Review, 8 (4), pp. 255-265.

Corbetta, G. / Salvato, C. (2004a): Self-Serving or Self-Actualizing? Models of Man and Agency Costs in Different Types of Family Firms: A Commentary on "Comparing the Agency Costs of Family and Non-family Firms: Conceptual Issues and Exploratory Evidence", in: Entrepreneurship Theory & Practice, 28 (4), pp. 355-362.

Corbetta, G. / Salvato, C.A. (2004b): The Board of Directors in Family Firms: A Contingency Perspective, in: Family Business Review, 17 (2), pp. 119-134.

Cornelli, F. / Karakas, Ö. (2008): Private equity and corporate governance: do LBOs have more effective boards?, in: World Economic Forum (Ed.): Globalization of alternative investments - The global economic impact of private equity report 2008, World Economic Forum, Geneva, pp. 65-84.

Cotter, J.F. / Peck, S.W. (2001): The structure of debt and active equity investors: The case of the buyout specialist, in: Journal of Financial Economics, 59, pp. 101-147.

Craig, J. / Moores, K. (2005): Balanced Scorecards to Drive the Strategic Planning of Family Firms, in: Family Business Review, 18 (2), pp. 105-122.

Daily, C.M. / Dollinger, M.J. (1992): An Empirical Examination of Ownership Structure in Family and Professionally Managed Firms, in: Family Business Review, 5 (2), pp. 117-136.

Davis, J.H. / Schoorman, F.D. / Donaldson, L. (1997a): Reply: The Distinctiveness of Agency Theory and Stewardship Theory, in: Academy of Management Review, 22 (3), pp. 611-613.

Davis, J.H. / Schoorman, F.D. / Donaldson, L. (1997b): Toward a stewardship theory of management, in: Academy of Management Review, 22 (1), pp. 20-47.

Dean, S.M. (1992): Characteristics of African American Family-Owned Businesses in Los Angeles, in: Family Business Review, 5 (4), pp. 373-395.

DeAngelo, H. / DeAngelo, L. (1985): Managerial ownership of voting rights : A study of public corporations with dual classes of common stock, in: Journal of Financial Economics, 14 (1), pp. 33-69.

DeAngelo, H. / DeAngelo, L. (1987): Management Buyouts of Publicly Traded Corporations, in: Financial Analysts Journal, 43 (3), pp. 38-49.

DeAngelo, H. / DeAngelo, L. / Rice, E.M. (1984): Going Private: Minority Freezeouts and Stockholder Wealth, in: Journal of Law and Economics, 27 (2), pp. 367-401.

Dees, G.J. (2001): The Meaning of "Social Entrepreneurship", Duke University's Fuqua School of Business, 05/2001.

Demski, J.S. / Feltham, G.A. (1978): Economic Incentives in Budgetary Control Systems, in: Accounting Review, 53 (2), pp. 336-359.

Denis, D.J. (1994): Organizational form and the consequences of highly leveraged transactions - Kroger's recapitalization and Safeway's LBO, in: Journal of Financial Economics, 36, pp. 193-224.

Denison, D. / Lief, C. / Ward, J.L. (2004): Culture in Family-Owned Enterprises: Recognizing and Leveraging Unique Strengths, in: Family Business Review, 17 (1), pp. 61-70.

Deutsche Bundesbank (2007): Ertragslage und Finanzierungsverhältnisse deutscher Unternehmen im Jahr 2006, http://www.bundesbank.de/download/volkswirtschaft/monatsberichte/2007/200712mb_bbk.pdf [Access: 20.10.2008].

Diem, A. (2001): Finanzierung von Leveraged Buy-outs, in: Achleitner, A.-K. / Thoma, G.F. (Ed.): Handbuch Corporate Finance, Ed. 2, Deutscher Wirtschaftsdienst, Cologne, chapter 6.4.4.

Diem, A. (2005): Akquisitionsfinanzierungen - Kredit für Unternehmenskäufe, C.H. Beck, Munich.

Donaldson, L. (1990a): The Ethereal Hand: Organizational Economics and Management Theory, in: Academy of Management Review, 15 (3), pp. 369-381.

Donaldson, L. (1990b): A Rational Basis for Criticisms of Organizational Economics: A Reply to Barney, in: Academy of Management Review, 15 (3), pp. 394-401.

Donaldson, L. / Davis, J.H. (1991): Stewardship Theory or Agency Theory: CEO Governance and Shareholder Returns, in: Australian Journal of Management, 16 (1), pp. 49-64.

Donckels, R. / Fröhlich, E. (1991): Are Family Businesses Really Different? European Experiences from STRATOS, in: Family Business Review, 4 (2), pp. 149-160.

Donckels, R. / Lambrecht, J. (1999): The Re-emergence of Family-Based Enterprises in East Central Europe: What Can Be Learned from Family Business Research in the Western World?, in: Family Business Review, 12 (2), pp. 155-164.

Donnelley, R.G. (1964): The Family Business, in: Harvard Business Review, 42 (4), pp. 93-105.

Dreux, D.R. (1990): Financing Family Business: Alternatives to Selling Out or Going Public, in: Family Business Review, 3 (3), pp. 225-243.

Duffie, D. / Gârleanu, N. (2001): Risk and Valuation of Collateralised Debt Obligations, in: Financial Analysts Journal, 57 (1), pp. 41-59.

Dumas, C. (1992): Integrating the Daughter into Family Business Management, in: Entrepreneurship Theory & Practice, 16 (4), pp. 41-55.

Dunemann, M. / Barrett, R. (2004): Family Business and Succession Planning, Family and Small Business Research Unit Working Paper, Monash University.

Dunn, B. (1995): Success Themes in Scottish Family Enterprises: Philosophies and Practices Through the Generations, in: Family Business Review, 8 (1), pp. 17-28.

Dyer, W.G. (1989): Integrating Professional Management into a Family Owned Business, in: Family Business Review, 2 (3), pp. 221-235.

Easterby-Smith, M. / Thorpe, R. / Lowe, A. (2002): Management Research, Ed. 2, Sage, London.

Easterwood, J.C. / Seth, A. / Singer, R.F. (1989): The Impact of LBOs on Strategic Direction, in: California Management Review, 32 (1), pp. 30-43.

Eaton, C. / Yuan, L. / Wu, Z. (2002): Reciprocal altruism and the theory of the family firm, Paper presented at the Second Annual Conference on Theories of the Family Enterprise: Search for a Paradigm, Wharton School of Business, Philadelphia, 12/2002.

Eddleston, K.A. / Kellermanns, F.W. (2007): Destructive and productive family relationships: A stewardship theory perspective, in: Journal of Business Venturing, 22 (4), pp. 545-565.

Eisenhardt, K.M. (1989): Agency Theory: An Assessment and Review, in: Academy of Management Review, 14 (1), pp. 57-74.

Ellul, A. / Guntay, L. / Lel, U. (2007): External Governance and Debt Agency Costs of Family Firms, FRB International Finance Discussion Paper No. 908, Federal Reserve Bank, 11/2007.

Elsas, R. / Krahnen, J.P. (1998): Is relationship lending special? Evidence from credit-file data in Germany, in: Journal of Banking & Finance, 22 (10/11), pp. 1283-1316.

Ensley, M.D. / Pearson, A.W. (2005): An Exploratory Comparison of the Behavioral Dynamics of Top Management Teams in Family and Nonfamily New Ventures: Cohesion, Conflict, Potency, and Consensus, in: Entrepreneurship Theory & Practice, 29 (3), pp. 267-284.

European Commission (2003): Commission Recommendation of 6 May 2003 concerning the definition of micro, small and medium-sized enterprises, in: Official Journal of the European Union, 46 (L 124), pp. 36-41.

European Private Equity & Venture Capital Association (2005): Private Equity and Generational Change - The Contribution of Private Equity to the Succession of Family Businesses in Europe, European Private Equity & Venture Capital Association, Zaventem.

F.A.Z. Institut (2002): MBO als Nachfolgelösung, Boschen Offsetdruck, Frankfurt a.M.

F.A.Z. Institut (2005): Interne und externe Nachfolgelösungen im Mittelstand, Boschen Offsetdruck, Frankfurt a.M.

F.A.Z. Institut / APAX Partners / KPMG / WestLB Equity Investments (2004): Unabhängig erfolgreich - Wachstums- und Finanzierungsstrategien von großen Familienunternehmen, Boschen Offsetdruck, Frankfurt a.M.

Fama, E. / Jensen, M.C. (1983): Separation of ownership and control, in: Journal of Law and Economics, 26, pp. 301-325.

Fama, E.F. (1980): Agency Problems and the Theory of the Firm, in: Journal of Political Economy, 88 (2), pp. 288-307.

Family Business Center / Ernst & Young (2005): Finanzielles Risiko- und Investitionsverhalten von Familienunternehmen.

Feldbauer-Durstmüller, B. / Haas, T. (2008): Controlling-Konzeption für kleine und mittlere Familienunternehmen, in: Feldbauer-Durstmüller, B. / Pernsteiner, H. / Rohatschek, R. / Tumpel, M. (Ed.): Familienunternehmen - Controlling, Finanzmanagement, Unternehmensrechung und Wirtschaftsprüfung, Steuern, Linde, Vienna, pp. 107-136.

Feldbauer-Durstmüller, B. / Wimmer, B. (2008): Familienunternehmen und Controlling - Ergebnisse der emprischen Studie, in: Feldbauer-Durstmüller, B. / Pernsteiner, H. / Rohatschek, R. / Tumpel, M. (Ed.): Familienunternehmen - Controlling, Finanzmanagement, Unternehmensrechung und Wirtschaftsprüfung, Steuern, Linde, Vienna, pp. 31-52.

Fenn, G.W. / Liang, N. / Prowse, S. (2005): The Economics of the Private Equity Market, Staff Studies, No.168, Board of Governors of the Federal Reserve System, 12/1995.

Fernández, Z. / Nieto, M.J. (2005): Internationalization Strategy of Small and Medium-Sized Family Businesses: Some Influential Factors, in: Family Business Review, 18 (1), pp. 77-89.

Fiegener, M.K. (2005): Determinants of Board Participation in the Strategic Decisions of Small Corporations, in: Entrepreneurship Theory & Practice, 29 (5), pp. 627-650.

Filatotchev, I. / Wright, M. (2005): The corporate governance life cycle, in: Filatotchev, I. / Wright, M. (Ed.): The Life Cycle of Corporate Governance, Edward Elgar, Cheltenham, pp. 1-19.

Filbeck, G. / Lee, S. (2000): Financial Management Techniques in Family Businesses, in: Family Business Review, 13 (3), pp. 201-216.

Financial Services Authority (2006): Private equity: A discussion of risk and regulatory engagement, Discussion Paper 06/6, Financial Services Authority, 11/2006.

Fischhoff, B. / Bar-Hillel, M. (1984): Focusing techniques: A shortcut to improving probability judgments?, in: Organizational Behavior and Human Performance, 34 (2), pp. 175-194.

Flacke, K. (2006): Controlling in mittelständischen Unternehmen - Ausgestaltung, Einflussfaktoren der Instrumentennutzung und Einfluss auf die Bankenkommunikation, Doctoral thesis at the Westfälische Wilhelms-Universität Münster, Münster.

Fleischhauer, Hoyer & Partner (2006): Coming of age - the European buyout mid-market, Fleischhauer, Hoyer & Partner Private Equity Consultants, Munich.

Flören, R.H. (2002): Crown Princes in the Clay, Van Gorcum, Assen.

Forst, M. (1992): Management Buy-out und Buy-in als Form der Übernahme mittelständischer Unternehmen, Schäffer-Poeschel, Stuttgart.

Fox, I. / Marcus, A. (1992): The Causes and Consequences of Leveraged Management Buyouts, in: Academy of Management Review, 17 (1), pp. 62-85.

Fox, M.A. / Hamilton, R.T. (1994): Ownership and diversification: Agency theory or stewardship theory, in: Journal of Management Studies, 31 (1), pp. 69-81.

Frankfurter Allgemeine Zeitung (2005): Der Fall Grohe liefert Zündstoff, 27.05.2005.

Freund, W. (2004): Unternehmensnachfolgen in Deutschland, in: Institut für Mittelstandsforschung (Ed.): Jahrbuch zur Mittelstandsforschung 1/2004, Deutscher Universitäts-Verlag, Wiesbaden, pp. 57-88.

Friedl, B. (2003): Controlling, Lucius & Lucius, Stuttgart.

Gallo, M.A. / Sveen, J. (1991): Internationalizing the Family Business: Facilitating and Restraining Factors, in: Family Business Review, 4 (2), pp. 181-190.

Gallo, M.A. / Tàpies, J. / Cappuyns, K. (2004): Comparison of Family and Nonfamily Business: Financial Logic and Personal Preferences, in: Family Business Review, 17 (4), pp. 303-318.

Gallo, M.A. / Vilaseca, A. (1996): Finance in Family Business, in: Family Business Review, 9 (4), pp. 387-401.

Gaughan, P.A. (1999): Mergers, Acquisitions, and Corporate Restructurings, John Wiley & Sons, New York, NY.

Geidner, A. (2009): Der Wandel der Unternehmensführung in Buyouts - Eine Führungssystem-orientierte Sicht von Private-Equity-finanzierten Desinvestitionen von Konzerneinheiten, Gabler (forthcoming), Wiesbaden.

Goffee, R. / Scase, R. (1985): Proprietorial control in family firms: some functions of "quasi-organic" management systems, in: Journal of Management Studies, 22 (1), pp. 53-68.

Gomez-Mejia, L.R. / Larraza-Kintana, M. / Makri, M. (2003): The determinants of executive compensation in family-controlled public corporations, in: Academy of Management Journal, 46 (2), pp. 226-237.

Gomez-Mejia, L.R. / Nuñez-Nickel, M. / Gutierrez, I. (2001): The role of family ties in agency contracts, in: Academy of Management Journal, 44 (1), pp. 81-95.

Gompers, P. / Lerner, J. (2001): The Venture Capital Revolution, in: Journal of Economic Perspectives, 15 (2), pp. 145-168.

Gossens, L. / Manigart, S. / Meuleman, M. (2007): The Change in Ownership After a Buy-out: Impact on Performance, Vlerick Leuven Gent Working Paper Series 2007/26, Vlerick Leuven Gent Management School, 01/2007.

Gräper, M. (1993): Management Buy-Out - Eine empirische Analyse zur deutschen Entwicklung bis 1990, Vauk, Kiel.

Green, S. (1992): The Impact of Ownership and Capital Structure on Managerial Motivation and Strategy in Management Buy-Outs: A cultural Analysis, in: Journal of Management Studies, 29 (4), pp. 513-535.

Greenwood, R. (2003): Commentary on: "Toward a theory of agency and altruism in family firms", in: Journal of Business Venturing, 18 (4), pp. 491-494.

Gubitta, P. / Gianecchini, M. (2002): Governance and Flexibility in Family-Owned SMEs, in: Family Business Review, 15 (4), pp. 277-297.

Gudmundson, D. / Hartman, E.A. / Tower, C.B. (1999): Strategic Orientation: Differences between Family and Nonfamily Firms, in: Family Business Review, 12 (1), pp. 27-39.

Gummesson, E. (2006): Qualitative research in management: addressing complexity, context and persona, in: Management Decision, 44 (2), pp. 167-179.

Günther, T. / Gonschorek, T. (2006): Wert(e)orientierte Unternehmensführung im Mittelstand - Erste Ergebnisse einer empirischen Untersuchung, Dresdner Beiträge zur Betriebswirtschaftslehre, Nr. 114/2006, Universität Dresden, 01/2006.

Habbershon, T.G. / Astrachan, J.H. (1997): Research Note - Perceptions Are Reality: How Family Meetings Lead to Collective Action, in: Family Business Review, 10 (1), pp. 37-52.

Habbershon, T.G. / Williams, M.L. (1999): A Resource-Based Framework for Assessing the Strategic Advantages of Family Firms, in: Family Business Review, 12 (1), pp. 1-22.

Habbershon, T.G. / Williams, M.L. / MacMillan, I.C. (2003): A Unified Systems Theory of Family Firm Performance, in: Journal of Business Venturing, 18 (4), pp. 451-465.

Habig, H. / Berninghaus, J. (2003): Die Nachfolge im Familienunternehmen ganzheitlich regeln, Ed. 2, Springer, Berlin.

Hahn, D. (1994): Controlling in mittelständischen Familienunternehmungen, in: Hinterhuber, H.H. / Rechenauer, O. / Stumpf, M. (Ed.): Die mittelständische Familienunternehmung, Peter Lang - Europäischer Verlag der Wissenschaften, Frankfurt a.M., pp. 125-153.

Hall, A. / Nordqvist, M. (2008): Professional Management in Family Businesses: Toward an Extended Understanding, in: Family Business Review, 21 (1), pp. 51-69.

Handler, W.C. (1989): Methodological Issues and Considerations in Studying Family Businesses, in: Family Business Review, 2 (3), pp. 257-276.

Handler, W.C. (1994): Succession in Family Business: A Review of the Research, in: Family Business Review, 7 (2), pp. 133-157.

Harris, D. / Martinez, J.I. / Ward, J.L. (1994): Is Strategy Different for the Family-Owned Business?, in: Family Business Review, 7 (2), pp. 159-174.

Harvey, M. / Evans, R.E. (1994): Family Business and Multiple Levels of Conflict, in: Family Business Review, 7 (4), pp. 331-348.

Haubrock, A. (2005): Wie gestalte ich den Ausstieg und den Einstieg?, in: Nagl, A. (Ed.): Wie regele ich meine Nachfolge? Leitfaden für Familienunternehmen, Wiesbaden, pp. 55-84.

Institut für Mittelstandsforschung (2007): Die volkswirtschaftliche Bedeutung der Familienunternehmen, Bonn.

Haynes, G.W. / Walker, R. / Rowe, B.R. / Hong, G.-S. (1999): The Intermingling of Business and Family Finances in Family-Owned Businesses, in: Family Business Review, 12 (3), pp. 225-239.

Heck, R.K. / Trent, E.S. (1999): The Prevalence of Family Business from a Household Sample, in: Family Business Review, 12 (3), pp. 209-219.

Heel, J. / Kehoe, C. (2005): Why some private equity firms do better than others, in: The McKinsey Quarterly, 1/2005, pp. 24-26.

Hennerkes, B.-H. (1998): Familienunternehmen sichern und optimieren, Campus, Frankfurt a.M.

Hennerkes, B.-H. / Pleister, C. (1999): Erfolgsfaktor Nachfolgeregelung, in: Hennerkes, B.-H. / Pleister, C. (Ed.): Erfolgsmodell Mittelstand, Gabler, Wiesbaden, pp. 273-276.

Herzberg, F. / Mausner, B. / Snyderman, B.B. (1959): The Motivation to Work, John Wiley & Sons, New York, NY.

Hickey, J. (2005): Family business buyouts, in: European Venture Capital & Private Equity Journal, July/August 2005, pp. 30-31.

Hill, M. (2003): Buyout-Finanzierungen - Struktur und wesentliche Elemente eines Buyout, in: Wolf, B. / Ditt, T. / Hill, M. (Ed.): Strukturierte Finanzierungen: Projektfinanzierung, Buy-out-Finanzierung, Asset-backed-Strukturen, Schäffer-Poeschel, Stuttgart, pp. 125-167.

Hinterhuber, H.H. / Minrath, R. (1994): Der Beirat einer mittelständischen Familienunternehmung, in: Hinterhuber, H.H. / Rechenauer, O. / Stumpf, M. (Ed.): Die mittelständische Familienunternehmung, Peter Lang - Europäischer Verlag der Wissenschaften, Frankfurt a.M., pp. 71-99.

Hirigoyen, G. (1982): Le comportement financier des moyennes entreprises industrielles familiales, in: Banque, 417, pp. 588-593.

Hirsch, P.M. / Friedman, R. / Koza, M.P. (1990): Collaboration or Paradigm Shift?: Caveat Emptor and the Risk of Romance with Economic Models for Strategy and Policy Research, in: Organization Science, 1 (1), pp. 87-97.

Hite, G.L. / Vetsuypens, M.R. (1989): Management Buyouts of Divisions and Shareholder Wealth, in: Journal of Finance, 44 (4), pp. 953-970.

Hofbauer, E. / Pernsteiner, H. (2008): Bewertungsfragen von nicht börsennotierten Familienunternehmen, in: Feldbauer-Durstmüller, B. / Pernsteiner, H. / Rohatschek, R. / Tumpel, M. (Ed.): Familienunternehmen - Controlling, Finanzmanagement, Unternehmensrechung und Wirtschaftsprüfung, Steuern, Linde, Vienna, pp. 139-166.

Holland, P.G. / Boulton, W.R. (1984): Balancing the "Family" and the "Business" in Family Business, in: Management Horizons, 27 (2), pp. 16-21.

Hollander, B.S. / Elman, N.S. (1988): Family-Owned Businesses: An Emerging Field of Inquiry, in: Family Business Review, 1 (2), pp. 145-164.

Holliday, A. (2007): Doing and Writing Qualitative Research, Ed. 2, Sage, London.

Hoque, Z. / James, W. (2000): Linking Balanced Scorecard Measures to Size and Market Factors: Impact on Organizational Performance, in: Journal of Management Accounting Research, 12, pp. 1-17.

Horvath, P. (2000): Der Consigliere – Der Controller im Familienunternehmen, in: Jeschke, D. / Kirchdörfer, R. / Lorz, R. (Ed.): Planung, Finanzierung und Kontrolle im Familienunternehmen, C.H. Beck, Munich, pp. 23-34.

Houlden, B. (1990): Buy-outs and Beyond - Motivations, Strategies and Ownership Changes, in: Long Range Planning, 23 (4), pp. 73-77.

Howorth, C. / Westhead, P. / Wright, M. (2004): Buyouts, information asymmetry and the family management dyad, in: Journal of Business Venturing, 19 (4), pp. 509-534.

Howorth, C. / Wright, M. / Westhead, P. (2007): Professionalization, stewardship and performance: A longitudinal case study analysis of family firm succession by management buyout, Lancaster University Management School, 01/2007.

Hug, J. / Ernst, D. (2003): Finanzierungsmodelle von Leveraged Buy-outs, in: M&A-Review (10), pp. 441-446.

Hutchinson, P. (1999): Small enterprise: finance, ownership and control, in: International Journal of Management Reviews, 1 (3), pp. 343-365.

Huydts, H.J. (1992): Management Buyout als strategische Option zur Regelung der Nachfolge in mittelgroßen Familenunternehmen - Erfolgsfaktor und Gestaltungsvarianten, Brönners Druckerei, Frankfurt a.M.

IMAP M&A Consultants (2008): Studie 2008 - Nachfolge im Mittelstand, IMAP M&A Consultants, Mannheim, 07/2008.

Isenberg, D.J. (1986): Thinking and Managing: A Verbal Protocol Analysis of Managerial Problem Solving, in: Academy of Management Journal, 29 (4), pp. 775-788.

Handelsblatt (2008a): Kunert stellt US-Beratung Alix bloß, 05.09.2008.

Handelsblatt (2008b): Märklin legt sich mit Beratern an, 14.08.2008.

Jackson-Cookland, C. / Crowe, A. / Pratt, M. (1998): Management Buy-Outs, in: Bank of England - Financial Stability Review, 38 (4), pp. 57-64.

Jakoby, S. (2000): Erfolgsfaktoren von Management Buyouts in Deutschland, Josef Eul, Lohmar.

James, H.S. (1999): Owners as Manager, Extended Horizons and the Family Firm, in: International Journal of the Economics of Business, 6 (1), pp. 41-55.

Jaskiewicz, P. (2006): Performance-Studie börsennotierter Familienunternehmen in Deutschland, Frankreich und Spanien, Josef Eul, Lohmar.

Jensen, M.C. (1983): Organization Theory and Methodology, in: Accounting Review, 58 (2), pp. 319-338.

Jensen, M.C. (1986): Agency Costs of Free Cash Flow, Corporate Finance, and Takeovers, in: American Economic Review, 76 (2), pp. 323-329.

Jensen, M.C. (1989a): Active Investors, LBOS, and the Privatization of Bankruptcy, in: Journal of Applied Corporate Finance, 2 (1), pp. 35-44.

Jensen, M.C. (1989b): Eclipse of the Public Corporation, in: Harvard Business Review, 67 (61-74), pp. 61-74.

Jensen, M.C. / Meckling, W.H. (1976): Theory of the firm: Managerial Behavior, Agency Costs and Ownership Structure, in: Journal of Financial Economics, 3 (4), pp. 305-360.

Johannisson, B. / Huse, M. (2000): Recruiting outside board members in the small family business: an ideological challenge, in: Entrepreneurship & Regional Development, 12 (4), pp. 353-378.

Johnson, J.L. / Daily, C.M. / Ellstrand, A.E. (1996): Boards of Directors: A Review and Research Agenda, in: Journal of Management, 22 (3), pp. 409-438.

Jones, C.S. (1992): The Attitudes of Owner-Managers towards Accounting Control Systems following Management Buyout, in: Accounting, Organizations and Society, 17 (2), pp. 151-168.

Jones, T.M. (1995): Instrumental stakeholder theory: A synthesis of ethics and economics, in: Academy of Management Review, 20 (2), pp. 404-437.

Joskow, P.L. (2004): Introduction to New Institutional Economics: A Report Card, in: Brousseau, E. / Glachang, J.-M. (Ed.): New Institutional Economics - A Guidebook, Cambridge University Press, Cambridge, pp. 1-20.

Jost, P.-J. (2001): Die Prinzipal-Agenten-Theorie im Unternehmenskontext, in: Jost, P.-J. (Ed.): Die Prinzipal-Agenten-Theorie in der Betriebswirtschaft, Schäffer-Poeschel, Stuttgart, pp. 11-43.

Kabuth, A. (2004): Impulse zur Ratingberatung durch Basel II, in: Achleitner, A.-K. / Everling, O. (Ed.): Handbuch Rating Praxis, Gabler, Wiebaden, pp. 3-14.

Kaplan, S.N. (1989a): The effects of management buyouts on operating performance and value, in: Journal of Financial Economics, 24 (2), pp. 217-254.

Kaplan, S.N. (1989b): Management Buyouts: Evidence on Taxes as a Source of Value, in: Journal of Finance, 44 (3), pp. 611-632.

Kaplan, S.N. / Stein, J.C. (1993): The Evolution of Buyout Pricing and Financial Structure in the 1980s, in: The Quarterly Journal of Economics, 108 (2), pp. 313-357.

Kaserer, C. / Achleitner, A.-K. / von Einem, C. / Schiereck, D. (2007): Private Equity in Deutschland - Rahmenbedingungen, ökonomische Bedeutung und Handlungsempfehlungen, Books on Demand, Norderstedt.

Kaufman, A. / Englander, E.J. (1993): Kohlberg Kravis Roberts & Co. and the restructuring of American capitalism, in: Business History Review, 67 (1), pp. 52-97.

Kay, R. / Günterberg, B. / Holz, M. / Wolter, H.-J. (2003): Unternehmerinnen in Deutschland, Bundesministerium für Wirtschaft und Arbeit, Berlin.

Kayser, G. / Wallau, F. (2003): Der industrielle Mittelstand - ein Erfolgsmodell, Bundesverband der deutschen Industrie, Berlin.

Kayser, G. / Wallau, F. / Adenäuer, C. (2006): BDI-Mittelstandspanel - Ergebnisse der Online Mittelstandsbefragung, Institut für Mittelstandsforschung, Bonn.

Kellersmann, D. / Winkeljohann, N. (2007): Die Bedeutung von Corporate Governance für den Mittelstand/Familienunternehmen, in: Finanzbetrieb (7-8), pp. 406-412.

Kessel, A. (1995): Der Leveraged Buyout in den USA und der Bundesrepublik Deutschland: Eine Agency-theoretische Betrachtungsweise, Europäischer Verlag der Wissenschaften, Frankfurt a.M.

Kester, W.C. / Luehrman, T.A. (1995): Rehabilitating the Leveraged Buyout, in: Harvard Business Review, 73 (3), pp. 119-130.

Kieschnick, R.L. (1989): Management Buyouts of Public Corporations: An Analysis of Prior Characteristics, in: Amihud, Y. (Ed.): Leveraged Management Buyouts, Beard Books, Washington D.C., pp. 35-67.

Kieschnick, R.L. (1998): Free Cash Flow and Stockholder Gains in Going Private Transactions Revisited, in: Journal of Business Finance & Accounting, 15 (1/2), pp. 187-202.

Kitching, J. (1989): Early returns on LBOs, in: Harvard Business Review, 67 (6), pp. 74-81.

Kitzmann, J. (2005): Private Equity in Deutschland, Deutscher Universitäts-Verlag, Wiesbaden.

Klein, S.B. (2000): Family Businesses in Germany: Significance and Structure, in: Family Business Review, 13 (3), pp. 157-181.

Klein, S.B. (2004): Familienunternehmen - Theoretische und empirische Grundlagen, Ed. 2, Gabler, Wiesbaden.

Klein, S.B. / Astrachan, J.H. / Smyrnios, K.X. (2005): The F-PEC Scale of Family Influence: Construction, Validation, and Further Implication for Theory, in: Entrepreneurship Theory & Practice, 29 (3), pp. 321-339.

Klein, S.B. / Bell, F.-A. (2007): Non-family executives in family businesses - a literature review, in: Electronic Journal of Family Business Studies, 1 (1), pp. 19-37.

Klöckner, O. (2008): Buy-outs/ins in Family Firms – A Statistical Overview, in: Wright, M. / Scholes, L. / Ball, R. / Howorth, C. / Klöckner, O. /Westhead, P. / Burrows, A. (Ed.): Private Equity in Family Firms – A report on private equity investments in family firms across Europe, CMBOR, Nottingham, pp. 12-34.

Klughardt, B. (1994): Psychologie der Nachfolgeplanung im Familienunternehmen - theoretische und praktische Aspekte, in: Hinterhuber, H.H. / Rechenauer, O. / Stumpf, M. (Ed.): Die mittelständische Familienunternehmung, Peter Lang - Europäischer Verlag der Wissenschaften, Frankfurt a.M., pp. 101-124.

Koeberle-Schmid, A. / Nützel, O. (2005): Family Business Governance: Herausforderungen und Mechanismen, INTES Zentrum für Familienunternehmen, Vallendar.

Kohlberg Kravis Roberts (1989): Leveraged buy-outs, in: Journal of Applied Corporate Finance, 2 (1), pp. 67-70.

Kosedag, A. / Lane, W.R. (2002): Is it Free Cash Flow, Tax Savings, or Neither? An Empirical Confirmation of Two Leading Going-private Explanations: The Case of ReLBOs, in: Journal of Business Finance & Accounting, 29 (1/2), pp. 257-271.

Kosmider, A. (1994): Controlling im Mittelstand: Eine Untersuchung der Gestaltung und Anwendung des Controllings in mittelständischen Industrieunternehmen, Ed. 2, Schäffer-Poeschel, Stuttgart.

Kosnik, R.D. (1987): Greenmail: A study of board performance in corporate governance, in: Administrative Science Quarterly, 32 (2), pp. 163-185.

KPMG (2004): Echte Alternative - Management Buy-out mit Private Equity, in: Edit Value, Sommer 2004, pp. 20-22.

Kramer, J. (1990): Die Welle wird überschwappen, in: Continental Bank (Ed.): Management Buy-Out, Knapp, Frankfurt a.M., pp. 9-19.

Kramer, J.W. (2006): Die Rolle der mittelständischen Unternehmensnachfolge im bankinternen Rating - Bedeutung der "geregelten Nachfolge", in: Achleitner, A.-K. / Everling, O. / Klemm, S. (Ed.): Nachfolgerating, Gabler, Wiesbaden, pp. 125-141.

Kropp, M. (1992): Management-Buyouts und die Theorie der Unternehmung, Gabler, Wiesbaden.

Kühn, C. (2006): Capital Structure Decisions in Institutional Buyouts, Deutscher Universitäts-Verlag, Wiesbaden.

Lamnek, S. (2005): Qualitative Sozialforschung, Ed. 4, Beltz PVU, Weinheim.

Lansberg, I.S. / Astrachan, J.H. (1994): Influence of Family Relationships on Succession Planning and Training: The Importance of Mediating Factors, in: Family Business Review, 7 (1), pp. 39-59.

Lansberg, I.S. / Perrow, E.L. / Rogolsky, S. (1988): Family Business as an Emerging Field, in: Family Business Review, 1 (1), pp. 1-8.

Le Breton-Miller, I. / Miller, D. / Steier, L.P. (2004): Toward an Integrative Model of Effective FOB Succession, in: Entrepreneurship Theory & Practice, 28 (4), pp. 305-328.

LeCornu, M.R. / McMahon, R.G. / Forsaith, D.M. / Stanger, A.M. (1996): The Small Enterprise Financial Objective Function, in: Journal of Small Business Management, 34 (3), pp. 1-14.

Lee, C.I. / Rosenstein, S. / Rangan, N. / Davidson, W.N. (1992): Board Composition and Shareholder Wealth: The Case of Management Buyouts, in: Financial Management, 21 (1), pp. 59-72.

Lee, P.M. / O'Neill, H.M. (2003): Ownership Structures and R&D Investments of U.S. and Japanese Firms: Agency and Stewardship Perspectives., in: Academy of Management Journal, 46 (2), pp. 212-225.

Lee, S.K. / Tan, F. (2001): Growth of Chinese Family Enterprises in Singapore, in: Family Business Review, 14 (1), pp. 49-74.

Lehmann-Tolkmitt, A. (2008): Die wichtigsten Regeln für den Beirat im Familienunternehmen, in: May, P. (Ed.): Das INTES-Handbuch Familienunternehmen, INTES - Akademie für Familienunternehmen, Bonn, pp. 352-361.

Lehn, K. / Poulsen, A. (1989): Free Cash Flow and Stockholder Gains in Going Private Transactions, in: Journal of Finance, 44 (3), pp. 771-787.

Lerner, J. (1994): The Syndication of Venture Capital Investments, in: Journal of the Financial Management Association, 23 (3), pp. 16-27.

Levinthal, D. (1988): A survey of agency models of organiations, in: Journal of Economic Behavior and Organization, 9 (2), pp. 153-185.

Leyherr, M. (2000): Die Situation von Familienunternehmen in Österreich unter besonderer Berücksichtigung der Finanzierung und Unternehmensnachfolge, Universität Stuttgart, Stuttgart.

Lichtenberg, F.R. / Siegel, D. (1990): The effects of leveraged buyouts on productivity and related aspects of firm behavior, in: Journal of Financial Economics, 27 (1), pp. 165-194.

Liebeskind, J. / Wiersema, M. / Hansen, G. (1992): LBOs, Corporate Restructuring, and the Incentive-Intensity Hypothesis, in: Financial Management, 21 (1), pp. 73-88.

Lin, T.H. / Smith, R.L. (1998): Insider reputation and selling decisions: the unwinding of venture capital investments during equity IPOs, in: Journal of Corporate Finance, 4 (3), pp. 241-263.

Littunen, H. / Hyrsky, K. (2000): The Early Entrepreneurial Stage in Finnish Family and Nonfamily Firms, in: Family Business Review, 13 (1), pp. 41-54.

Litz, R.A. (1995): The Family Business: Toward Definitional Clarity, in: Family Business Review, 8 (2), pp. 71-81.

Loos, N. (2006): Value Creation in Leveraged Buyouts - Analysis of Factors Driving Private Equity Investment Performance, Deutscher Universitäts-Verlag, Wiesbaden.

Lopes, C. (2003): Bewertung und Preisfindung, in: Weitnauer, W. (Ed.): Management Buy-Out - Handbuch für Recht und Praxis, C.H. Beck, Munich, pp. 41-64.

López-Gracia, J. / Sánchez-Andújar, S. (2007): Financial Structure of the Family Business: Evidence From a Group of Small Spanish Firms, in: Family Business Review, 20 (4), pp. 269-287.

Lossen, U. (2007): Portfolio Strategies of Private Equity Firms - Theory and Evidence, Deutscher Universitäts-Verlag, Wiesbaden.

Lück, W. (2004): Lexikon der Betriebswirtschaftslehre, Ed. 6, Oldenbourg, Munich.

Lueger, M. (2000): Grundlagen qualitativer Forschung, WUV-Universitätsverlag, Vienna.

Luippold, T.L. (1991): Management Buy-Outs - Evaluation ihrer Einsatzmöglichkeiten in Deutschland, Haupt, Bern.

Lütjen, G. (1992): Statt einer Einführung: ein konzeptioneller Ansatz, in: Lütjen, G. (Ed.): Management Buy-out: Firmenübernahme durch Management und Belegschaft, Frankfurter Allgemeine Zeitung, Frankfurt a.M., pp. 5-12.

Lyagoubi, M. (2006): Family firms and financial behavior: how family shareholder preferences influence firms' financing, in: Poutziouris, P.Z. / Smyrnios, K.X. / Klein, S.B. (Ed.): Handbook of Research on Family Business, Edward Elgar, Cheltenham, pp. 537-551.

Lyman, A.R. (1991): Customer Service: Does Family Ownership Make a Difference?, in: Family Business Review, 4 (3), pp. 303-324.

Madslien, J. (2005): Reshaping Germany's companies, http://news.bbc.co.uk/2/hi/business/4238438.stm [Access: 20.10.2008].

Malone, S.C. (1989): Characteristics of smaller company leveraged buyouts, in: Journal of Business Venturing, 4 (5), pp. 349-359.

Manigart, S. / Lockett, A. / Meuleman, M. / Wright, M. / Landström, H. / Bruining, H. / Desbrières, P. / Hommel, U. (2006): Venture Capitalists' Decision to Syndicate, in: Entrepreneurship Theory & Practice, 39 (2), pp. 131-153.

Marais, L. / Schipper, K. / Smith, A. (1989): Wealth effects of going private for senior securities, in: Journal of Financial Economics, 23 (1), pp. 155-191.

Marek, M. (2001): Geschichte des Leasing - Abriss einer beeindruckenden Entwicklung, University Paderborn working paper series, University Paderborn, 10/2001.

Maser, S. (1998): Controlling in mittelständischen Unternehmen, Expert-Verlag, Renningen-Malmsheim.

Matthews, R.C. (1986): The Economics of Institutions and the Sources Of Economic Growth, in: Economic Journal, 96 (384), pp. 903-918.

May, P. (2001): Der Beirat im Familienunternehmen-Wie gut kann er werden? Wie kann er gut werden?, in: Hennerkes, B.-H. / Kirchdörfer, R. (Ed.): Unternehmenshandbuch Familiengesellschaften. Sicherung von Unternehmen, Vermögen und Familie, Ed. 2, Heymanns, Köln, pp. 359-374.

May, P. / Redlefsen, M. / Knappe, C. (2005): Fremdmanager in Familienunternehmen, in: May, P. / Rieder, G. (Ed.): Familienunternehmen heute - Jahrbuch 2006, INTES - Akademie für Familienunternehmen, Bonn, pp. 99-108.

Mayring, P. (2003): Qualitative Inhaltsanalyse - Grundlagen und Techniken, Ed. 8, Beltz Verlag, Weinheim.

Mazzola, P. / Marchisio, G. (2002): The Role of Going Public in Family Businesses' Long-Lasting Growth: A Study of Italian IPOs, in: Family Business Review, 15 (2), pp. 133-148.

Mazzola, P. / Marchisio, G. / Astrachan, J.H. (2008): Strategic Planning in Family Business: A Powerful Developmental Tool for the Next Generation, in: Family Business Review, 21 (3), pp. 239-258.

McClelland, D. (1961): The Achieving Society, Van Nostrand, Princeton.

McConaughy, D.L. (2000): Family CEOs vs. Nonfamily CEOs in the Family-Controlled Firm: An Examination of the Level and Sensitivity of Pay to Performance, in: Family Business Review, 13 (2), pp. 121-131.

McConaughy, D.L. / Phillips, G.M. (1999): Founders versus Descendants: The Profitability, Efficiency, Growth Characteristics and Financing in Large, Public, Founding-Family-Controlled Firms, in: Family Business Review, 12 (2), pp. 123–131.

McConaughy, D.L. / Walker, M.C. / Henderson, G.V. / Mishra, C.S. (1998): Founding Family Controlled Firms: Efficiency and Value, in: Review of Financial Economics, 7 (1), pp. 1-19.

McGoldrick, M. (1992): Ethnicity and the Family Life Cycle, in: Family Business Review, 5 (4), pp. 437-459.

McGregor, D. (1960): The Human Side of Enterprise, McGraw-Hill, Boston.

Meier, D. (2006): Post-Investment Value Addition to Buyouts, Deutscher Universitäts-Verlag, Wiesbaden.

Menendez-Requejo, S. (2006): Ownership structure and firm performance: evidence from Spanish family firms, in: Poutziouris, P.Z. / Smyrnios, K.X. / Klein, S.B. (Ed.): Handbook of Research on Family Business, Edward Elgar, Cheltenham, pp. 575-592.

Mertens, R. (2004): Effiziente Gestaltung der familienexternen Unternehmernachfolge - Fremdmanagement, Stiftung, MBO/MBI, Verlag Dr. Kovac, Hamburg.

Milgrom, P. / Roberts, J. (1992): Economics, organization and management, Prentice-Hall International, Englewood Cliffs.

Miller, D. / Le Breton-Miller, I. (2006): Family Governance and Firm Performance: Agency, Stewardship, and Capabilities, in: Family Business Review, 19 (1), pp. 73-87.

Mintzberg, H. / Waters, J.A. (1982): Tracking Strategy in an Entrepreneurial Firm, in: Academy of Management Journal, 25 (3), pp. 465-499.

Mishra, C.S. / McConaughy, D.L. (1999): Founding Family Control and Capital Structure: The Risk of Loss of Control and the Aversion to Debt, in: Entrepreneurship Theory & Practice, 23 (4), pp. 53-64.

Mitchell, F. / Reid, G.C. / Terry, N.G. (1995): Post Investment Demand for Accounting Information by Venture Capitalists, in: Accounting & Business Research, 25 (99), pp. 186-196.

Mitchell, F. / Reid, G.C. / Terry, N.G. (1997): Venture Capital Supply and Accounting Information System Development, in: Entrepreneurship Theory & Practice, 21, pp. 45-62.

Mitnick, B.M. (1992): The Theory of Agency and Organizational Analysis, in: Bowie, N.E. / Freeman, R.E. (Ed.): Ethics and Agency Theory, An Introduction, Oxford University Press, New York, pp. 75-96.

Modigliani, F. / Miller, M.H. (1963): Corporate Income Taxes and the Cost of Capital: A Correction, in: American Economic Review, 53 (3), pp. 433-444.

Moldenhauer, B. (2007): Insider Ownership, Shareholder Structures and Corporate Governance, Verlag Wissenschaft & Praxis, Sternenfels.

Mühlebach, C. (2004): Familyness als Wettbewerbsvorteil. Ein integrierter Strategieansatz für Familienunternehmen, Haupt, Bern.

Müller, K. (2008): Investing in Private Equity Partnerships: The Role of Monitoring and Reporting, Gabler, Wiesbaden.

Murphy, K.J. (1985): Corporate performance and managerial remuneration : An empirical analysis, in: Journal of Accounting and Economics, 7 (1-3), pp. 11-42.

Mustakallio, M. / Autio, E. / Zahra, S.A. (2002): Relational and Contractual Governance in Family Firms: Effects on Strategic Decision Making, in: Family Business Review, 15 (3), pp. 205-222.

Muth, M.M. / Donaldson, L. (1998): Stewardship Theory and Board Structure: a contingency approach, in: Corporate Governance: An International Review, 6 (1), pp. 5-28.

Myers, S.C. (1984): The Capital Structure Puzzle, in: Journal of Finance, 39 (3), pp. 575-592.

Nagl, A. (2005): Was ist, wenn ich aufhöre?, in: Nagl, A. (Ed.): Wie regele ich meine Nachfolge? Leitfaden für Familienunternehmen, Wiesbaden, pp. 13-34.

Nahapiet, J. / Ghoshal, S. (1998): Social Capital, Intellectual Capital, and the Organizational Advantage, in: Academy of Management Review, 23 (2), pp. 242-266.

Natermann, E. / Schönecker, L. (2001): Die Finanzierung des Familienunternehmens, in: Hennerkes, B.-H. / Kirchdörfer, R. (Ed.): Unternehmenshandbuch Familiengesellschaften: Sicherung von Unternehmen, Vermögen und Familie, Ed. 2, Heymanns, Köln, pp. 407-424.

Nathusius, E. (2005): Syndizierte Venture-Capital-Finanzierung, Verlag Wissenschaft & Praxis, Sternenfels.

Newbould, G.D. / Chatfield, R.E. / Anderson, R.F. (1992): Leveraged buyouts and tax incentives, in: Journal of the Financial Management Association, 21 (1), pp. 50-57.

Niedermayr, R. (1994): Entwicklungsstand des Controlling: Systeme, Kontext und Effizienz, Deutscher Universitäts-Verlag, Wiesbaden.

North, D.C. (1992): Institutions and Economic Theory, in: American Economist, 36 (1), pp. 3-7.

North, D.C. (1993): The new institutional economics and development, Working paper, Washington University, St. Louis, 01/1993.

Oberpracht, D. / Engelstädter, R. (2006): Management-Beteiligungen: Gestaltung im Rahmen von LBO-Transaktionen, in: M&A-Review (2), pp. 71-74.

Opler, T. / Titman, S. (1993): The Determinants of Leveraged Buyout Activity: Free Cash Flow vs. Financial Distress Costs, in: Journal of Finance, 48 (5), pp. 1985-1999.

Ossadnik, W. / Barklage, D. / van Lengerich, E. (2003): Controlling mittelständischer Unternehmen in der Region Osnabrück-Emsland: Empirische Bestandsaufnahme, Evaluierung und Handlungsempfehlungen, Institut für Mittelstandsfragen, Osnabrück.

Ossadnik, W. / Barklage, D. / van Lengerich, E. (2004): Controlling im Mittelstand - Ergebnisse einer empirischen Untersuchung, in: Controlling, 11/2004, pp. 621-629.

Pernsteiner, H. (2008): Familienunternehmen und Finanzmanagement, in: Feldbauer-Durstmüller, B. / Pernsteiner, H. / Rohatschek, R. / Tumpel, M. (Ed.): Familienunternehmen - Controlling, Finanzmanagement, Unternehmensrechung und Wirtschaftsprüfung, Steuern, Linde, Vienna, pp. 53-80.

Perrigo, A.E. (1975): Delegation and succession in the small firms, in: Personnel Management, May 1975, pp. 35-37.

Perrow, C. (1986): Complex Organizations - A Critical Essay, Ed. 3, McGraw-Hill, New York, NY.

Phan, P.H. / Hill, C.W. (1995): Organizational Restructuring and Economic Performance in Leveraged Buyouts: An Ex Post Study, in: Academy of Management Journal, 38 (3), pp. 704-739.

Picot, A. / Dietl, H. / Franck, E. (2005): Organisation - Eine ökonomische Perspektive, Schäffer-Poeschel, Stuttgart.

Pieper, T.M. / Klein, S.B. / Jaskiewicz, P. (2008): The impact of organizational culture on corporate governance – An agency and stewardship theoretical analysis of the relevance of a board of directors in family influenced businesses, in: Journal of Small Business Management, 46 (3), pp. 372-394.

Poech, A. / Achleitner, A.-K. / Burger-Calderon, M. (2005): Private Equity in Familienunternehmen: Eine empirische Untersuchung zu psychologischen Aspekten der Transaktionsentscheidung, in: Finanzbetrieb, 5/2005, pp. 289-295.

Ponemon, L.A. / Gabhart, D.R.L. (1990): Auditor independence judgments: A cognitive-developmental model and experimental evidence, in: Contemporary Accounting Research, 7 (1), pp. 227-251.

Poutziouris, P.Z. (2001): The Views of Family Companies on Venture Capital: Empirical Evidence from the UK Small to Medium-Size Enterprising Economy, in: Family Business Review, 14 (3), pp. 277-291.

Poutziouris, P.Z. / Smyrnios, K.X. / Klein, S.B. (2006): Introduction: the business of researching family enterprises, in: Poutziouris, P.Z. / Smyrnios, K.X. / Klein, S.B. (Ed.): Handbook of Research on Family Business, Edward Elgar, Cheltenham, pp. 1-10.

Poza, E.J. / Alfred, T. / Maheshwari, A. (1997): Stakeholder Perceptions of Culture and Management Practices in Family and Family Firms - A Preliminary Report, in: Family Business Review, 10 (2), pp. 135-156.

Poza, E.J. / Hanlon, S. / Kishida, R. (2004): Does the Family Business Interaction Factor Represent a Resource or a Cost?, in: Family Business Review, 17 (2), pp. 99-118.

Preston, L.E. (1998): Agents, Stewards, and Stakeholders, in: Academy of Management Review, 23 (1), p. 9.

PriceWaterhouseCoopers (2005): Nachfolger gesucht! - Empirische Erkenntnisse und Handlungsempfehlungen für die Schweiz, PriceWaterhouseCoopers, Zurich.

PriceWaterhouseCoopers (2006): Familienunternehmen Deutschland 2006, PriceWaterhouseCoopers, Frankfurt am Main.

PriceWaterhouseCoopers (2008a): Familienunternehmen 2008, PriceWaterhouseCoopers, Frankfurt a.M.

PriceWaterhouseCoopers (2008b): Was bewegt schweizerische Familienunternehmen?, PriceWaterhouseCoopers, Zurich.

Pütter, T. (2001): Grundlagen des Management-Buy-Outs, in: Achleitner, A.-K. / Thoma, G.F. (Ed.): Handbuch Corporate Finance, Ed. 2, Deutscher Wirtschaftsdienst, Cologne, chapter 6.4.1.

Ram, M. / Holliday, R. (1993): Relative Merits: Family Culture and Kinship in Small Firms, in: Sociology, 27 (4), pp. 629-648.

Redlefsen, M. (2004): Der Ausstieg von Gesellschaftern aus großen Familienunternehmen, Deutscher Universitäts-Verlag, Wiesbaden.

Redlefsen, M. / Eiben, J. (2006): Finanzierung von Familienunternehmen, http://www.whu.edu/cms/fileadmin/redaktion/Z-Intes/Finanzierung_von_Familienunternehmen.pdf [Access: 20.10.2008].

Redlefsen, M. / Knöll, A. (2005): Finanzierung von Familienunternehmen, in: INTES Unternehmer Newsletter, October 2005, pp. 1-6.

Reid, G.C. (1996): Fast growing small entrepreneurial firms and their venture capital backers: An applied principal-agent analysis, in: Small Business Economics, 8 (3), pp. 235-248.

Robbie, K. / Wright, M. (1995): Managerial and Ownership Succession and Corporate Restructuring: The Case of Management Buy-Ins, in: Journal of Management Studies, 32 (4), pp. 527-549.

Robbie, K. / Wright, M. (1996): Management Buy-ins - Entrepreneurship, Active Investors and Corporate Restructuring, Manchester University Press, Manchester.

Robbie, K. / Wright, M. / Thompson, S. (1992): Management Buy-ins in the UK, in: Omega, 20 (4), pp. 445-456.

Roberts, J. / McNulty, T. / Stiles, P. (2005): Beyond Agency Conceptions of the Work of the Non-Executive Director: Creating Accountability in the Boardroom, in: British Journal of Management, 16 (Supplement 1), pp. 5-26.

Romano, C.A. / Tanewski, G.A. / Smyrnios, K.X. (2001): Capital structure decision making: A model for family business, in: Journal of Business Venturing, 16 (3), pp. 285-310.

Rue, L.W. / Ibrahim, N.A. (1996): The Status of Planning in Smaller Family-Owned Business, in: Family Business Review, 9 (1), pp. 29-43.

Sahlman, W.A. (1990): The structure and governance of venture-capital organizations, in: Journal of Financial Economics, 27, pp. 473-521.

Sander, J.G. (2006): Gestaltungsfaktoren von Management Buyouts aus der Perspektive von Finanzinvestoren, Tectum, Marburg.

Schachner, M. / Speckbacher, G. / Wentges, P. (2006): Steuerung mittelständischer Unternehmen: Größeneffekte und Einfluss der Eigentums- und Führungsstruktur, in: Zeitschrift für Betriebswirtschaft, 76 (6), pp. 589-614.

Schefczyk, M. (2000): Erfolgsstrategien deutscher Venture Capital-Gesellschaften, Ed. 2, Schäffer-Poeschel, Stuttgart.

Schein, E.H. (1983): The Role of the Founder in Creating Organizational Culture., in: Organizational Dynamics, 12 (1), pp. 13-28.

Schmidt, T. (2001): Die neue Rolle des Firmenkundenbetreuers im mittelständischen Firmenkundengeschäft, Shaker, Aachen.

Schmidtbleicher, R. (2006): Mittelbarer Kapitalmarktzugang für KMU durch Genussrechtepooling, Arbeitspapiere Nr. 128 // Institut für Bankrecht, Johann Wolfgang Goethe-Universität, 03/2006.

Schnell, R. / Hill, P.B. / Esser, E. (2005): Methoden der empirischen Sozialforschung, Ed. 7, Oldenbourg, Munich.

Scholes, L.M. / Westhead, P. / Burrows, A. (2008): Family firm succession: the management buy-out and buy-in routes, in: Journal of Small Business and Enterprise Development, 15 (1), pp. 8-30.

Scholes, L.M. / Wright, M. / Westhead, P. / Burrows, A. / Bruining, H. (2005): Ownership, Governance, Objectives and the Family Firm Succession Process: Evidence from Management Buy-outs, CMBOR working document, Nottingham University, 09/2005.

Scholes, L.M. / Wright, M. / Westhead, P. / Burrows, A. / Bruining, H. (2007): Information Sharing, Price Negotiation and Management Buy-outs of Private Family-owned Firms, in: Small Business Economics, 29 (3), pp. 329-349.

Schröder, E.F. (1998): Controlling-Unternehmenssteuerung im Familienunternehmen, in: Hennerkes, B.-H. / Kirchdörfer, R. (Ed.): Unternehmenshandbuch Familiengesellschaften: Sicherung von Unternehmen, Vermögen und Familie, Ed. 2, Heymanns, Köln, pp. 286-331.

Schröer, S. / Kayser, G. (2006): Beratungsbedarf und Beratungspraxis bei Unternehmensnachfolgen, in: Institut für Mittelstandsforschung Bonn (Ed.): Jahrbuch zur Mittelstandsforschung 1/2006, Institut für Mittelstandsforschung, Bonn, pp. 1-44.

Schulze, W.S. / Lubatkin, M.H. / Dino, R.N. (2002): Altruism, Agency, and the Competitiveness of Family Firms, in: Managerial and Decision Economics, 23 (4-5), pp. 247-259.

Schulze, W.S. / Lubatkin, M.H. / Dino, R.N. (2003a): Exploring the agency consequences of ownership dispersion among the directors of private family firms, in: Academy of Management Journal, 46 (2), pp. 179-194.

Schulze, W.S. / Lubatkin, M.H. / Dino, R.N. (2003b): Toward a theory of agency and altruism in family firms, in: Journal of Business Venturing, 18 (4), pp. 473-490.

Schulze, W.S. / Lubatkin, M.H. / Dino, R.N. / Buchholtz, A.K. (2001): Agency Relationships in Family Firms: Theory and Evidence, in: Organization Science, 12 (2), pp. 99-116.

Schwartz, M.A. / Barnes, L.B. (1991): Outside Boards and Family Businesses: Another Look, in: Family Business Review, 4 (3), pp. 269-285.

Schwenkedel, S. (1991): Management Buyout : ein neues Geschäftsfeld für Banken, Gabler, Wiesbaden.

Segbers, K. (2006): Die Geschäftsbeziehung zwischen mittelständischen Unternehmen und ihrer Hausbank, Peter Lang - Europäischer Verlag der Wissenschaften, Frankfurt a.M.

Seth, A. / Easterwood, J. (1993): Strategic Redirection in Large Management Buyouts: The Evidence from Post-Buyout Restructuring Activity, in: Strategic Management Journal, 14 (4), pp. 251-273.

Shanker, M.C. / Astrachan, J.H. (1996): Myths and Realities: Family Businesses' Contribution to the US Economy–A Framework for Assessing Family Business Statistics in: Family Business Review, 9 (2), pp. 107-123.

Sharma, P. (2004): An Overview of the Field of Family Business Studies: Current Status and Directions for the Future, in: Family Business Review, 17 (1), pp. 1-36.

Sharma, P. / Chrisman, J.J. / Chua, J.H. (1997): Strategic Management of the Family Business: Past Research and Future Challenges, in: Family Business Review, 10 (1), pp. 1-35.

Sharma, P. / Chrisman, J.J. / Chua, J.H. (2003): Predictors of satisfaction with the succession process in family firms, in: Journal of Business Venturing, 18 (5), pp. 667-687.

Sharma, P. / Manikutty, S. (2005): Strategic Divestments in Family Firms: Role of Family Structure and Community Culture, in: Entrepreneurship Theory & Practice, 29 (3), pp. 293-311.

Sharp, G. (2003): Buyouts: A Guide for the Management Team, Euromoney Books, London.

Shleifer, A. / Vishny, R.W. (1997): A Survey of Corporate Governance, in: Journal of Finance, 52 (2), pp. 737-783.

Siemes, A. / Segbers, K. (2005): Mittelständische Unternehmen und ihr Kommunikationsverhalten gegenüber der Bank, in: Finanzbetrieb, 5/2005, pp. 311-320.

Silva, J. (2006): Venture Capital Investments in Family Businesses: The Investee Perspective, Working paper, School of Business and Economics, University of Jyväskylä, 02/2006.

Simon, H.A. (1993): Altruism and economics, in: American Economic Review, 83 (2), pp. 156-161.

Simpson, R.S. / Wright, M. (1991): UK Management Buy-outs: Debt, equity and Agency Cost Implications, in: Managerial and Decision Economics, 12 (1), pp. 15-26.

Singh, H. (1990): Management Buyouts: Distinguishing characteristics and operating changes prior to public offering, in: Strategic Management Journal, 11 (4), pp. 111-129.

Sirmon, D.G. / Hitt, M.A. (2003): Managing Resources: Linking Unique Resources, Management, and Wealth Creation in Family Firms, in: Entrepreneurship Theory & Practice, 27 (4), pp. 339-358.

Smith, A. (1937): The Wealth of Nations, Modern Library, New York.

Smith, A.J. (1990): Corporate ownership structure and performance - The case of management buyouts, in: Journal of Financial Economics, 27 (1), pp. 143-164.

Smyrnios, K. / Tanewski, G. / Romano, C. (1998): Development of a Measure of the Characteristics of Family Business, in: Family Business Review, 11 (1), pp. 49-60.

Songini, L. (2006): The professionalization of family firms: theory and practice, in: Poutziouris, P.Z. / Smyrnios, K.X. / Klein, S.B. (Ed.): Handbook of Research on Family Business, Edward Elgar, Cheltenham, pp. 269-297.

Sonnenfeld, J.A. / Spence, P.L. (1989): The Parting Patriarch of a Family Firm, in: Family Business Review, 2 (4), pp. 355-375.

Sorenson, R.L. (2000): Planning for Family and Financial Success in Family Businesses, in: Family Business Review, 13 (2), pp. 133-142.

Speckbacher, G. / Schachner, M. (2004): Performance Management in mittelständischen Unternehmen, in: Seicht, G. (Ed.): Jahrbuch für Controlling und Rechnungswesen, LexisNexisORAC, Vienna, pp. 423-438.

Spence, M. / Zeckhauser, R. (1971): Insurance, Information, and Individual Action, in: American Economic Review, 61 (2), pp. 380-387.

Steen, A. / Welch, L.S. (2006): Dancing With Giants: Acquisition and Survival of the Family Firm, in: Family Business Review, 19 (4), pp. 289-300.

Stewart, A. (2003): Help One Another, Use One Another: Toward an Anthropology of Family Business, in: Entrepreneurship Theory & Practice, 27 (4), pp. 383-396.

Strömberg, P. (2008): The new demography of private equity, in: World Economic Forum (Ed.): Globalization of alternative investments - The global economic impact of private equity report 2008, World Economic Forum, Geneva, pp. 3-26.

Stulz, R.M. (1990): Managerial Discretion and Optimal Financing Policies, in: Journal of Financial Economics, 26 (1), pp. 3-27.

Szyperski, N. / Nathusius, K. (1999): Probleme der Unternehmensgründung, Ed. 2, Josef Eul, Lohmar.

Tagiuri, R. / Davis, J.A. (1992): On the Goals of Successful Family Companies, in: Family Business Review, 5 (1), pp. 43-62.

Tagiuri, R. / Davis, J.A. (1996): Bivalent Attributes of the Family Firm, in: Family Business Review, 9 (2), pp. 199-208.

Thommen, J.-P. / Achleitner, A.-K. (2006): Allgemeine Betriebswirtschaftslehre, Ed. 5, Gabler, Wiesbaden.

Thompson, S. / Wright, M. (1989): Bonding, Agency Costs and Management Buyouts, in: Bulletin of Economic Research, 41 (1), pp. 69-75.

Thompson, S. / Wright, M. (1995): Corporate governance: the role of restructuring transactions, in: Economic Journal, 105 (430), pp. 690-703.

Thompson, S. / Wright, M. / Robbie, K. (1992): Buy-outs, Divestment, and Leverage: Restructuring Transactions and Corporate Governance, in: Oxford Review of Economic Policy, 8 (3), pp. 58-69.

Tobler, S. (1998): Financial Engineering: Die Suche nach innovativen MBO-Finanzierungsstrukturen, in: Krebs, A.E. / Studer, T. (Ed.): Management Buyout, Rüegger, Zurich, pp. 39-77.

Tosi, H.L. / Brownlee, A.L. / Silva, P. / Katz, J.P. (2003): An Empirical Exploration of Decision-making Under Agency Controls and Stewardship Structure, in: Journal of Management Studies, 40 (8), pp. 2053-2071.

UBS (2005): Nachfolge im Unternehmen - Eine Herausforderung für Unternehmer, Verwaltungsräte und Familienaktionäre, UBS, Zurich.

Uhlaner, L. / Wright, M. / Huse, M. (2007): Private Firms and Corporate Governance: An Integrated Economic and Management Perspective, in: Small Business Economics, 29 (3), pp. 225-241.

Uhlaner, L.M. / Flören, R.H. / Geerlings, J.R. (2007): Owner Commitment and Relational Governance in the Privately-Held Firm: An Empirical Study, in: Small Business Economics, 29 (3), pp. 275-293.

Upton, N. / Petty, W. (2000): Venture capital investment and US family business, in: Venture Capital, 2 (1), pp. 27-39.

Upton, N. / Teal, E.F. / Felan, J.T. (2001): Strategic and Business Planning Practices of Fast Growth Family Firms, in: Journal of Small Business Management, 39 (1), pp. 60-72.

van Maanen, J. (1983): Qualitative Methodology, Sage, London.

van Slyke, D.M. (2007): Agents or Stewards: Using Theory to Understand the Government-Nonprofit Social Service Contracting Relationship, in: Journal of Public Administration Research and Theory, 17 (2), pp. 157-187.

Vargas Sanchez, A. (2004): Development of Corporate Governance Systems: Agency Theory versus Stewardship Theory in Welsh Agrarian Cooperative Societies, Working Paper, University of Huelva, 05/2004.

Vest, P. (1995): Der Verkauf von Konzernunternehmen durch Management Buy-Out, Deutscher Universitäts-Verlag, Wiesbaden.

Villalonga, B. / Amit, R. (2006): How do family ownership, control and management affect firm value?, in: Journal of Financial Economics, 80 (2), pp. 385-417.

Vinton, K.L. (1998): Nepotism: An Interdisciplinary Model, in: Family Business Review, 11 (4), pp. 297-303.

von Boxberg, F. (1991): Das Management Buyout-Konzept, Verlag Dr. Kovac, Hamburg.

von Tippelskirch, A. (2000): Der langfristige Kredit als tragende Säule der Finanzierung im deutschen Mittelstand, in: Jeschke, D. / Kirchdörfer, R. / Lorz, R. (Ed.): Planung, Finanzierung und Kontrolle im Familienunternehmen, C.H. Beck, Munich, pp. 111-126.

Wagner, E. (2008): Besonderheiten der Kapitalstrukturpolitik von Familienunternehmen, in: Feldbauer-Durstmüller, B. / Pernsteiner, H. / Rohatschek, R. / Tumpel, M. (Ed.): Familienunternehmen - Controlling, Finanzmanagement, Unternehmensrechung und Wirtschaftsprüfung, Steuern, Linde, Vienna, pp. 167-199.

Ward, J.L. (1987): Keeping The Family Business Healthy: How to Plan for Continuing Growth, Profitability and Family Leadership, Jossey-Bass, San Francisco, CA.

Ward, J.L. (1988): The Special Role of Strategic Planning for Family Businesses, in: Family Business Review, 1 (2), pp. 105-117.

Ward, J.L. (1997): Growing the Family Business: Special Challenges and Best Practices, in: Family Business Review, 10 (4), pp. 323-337.

Ward, J.L. / Handy, J.L. (1988): A Survey of Board Practices, in: Family Business Review, 1 (3), pp. 289-308.

Wasserman, N. (2006): Stewards, agents, and the founder discount: executive compensation in new ventures, in: Academy of Management Journal, 49 (5), pp. 960-976.

Webb, I. (1985): Management Buy-out: a guide for prospective entrepreneur, Gower, Aldershot.

Weber, J. / Schäffer, U. (2006): Einführung in das Controlling, Ed. 11, Schäffer-Poeschel, Stuttgart.

Weber, J. / Schäffer, U. (2008): Introduction to Controlling, Schäffer-Poeschel, Stuttgart.

Weir, C. / Laing, D. (1998): Management buy-outs: The impact of ownership changes on performance, in: Journal of Small Business and Enterprise Development, 5 (3), pp. 261-269.

Weitnauer, W. (2003a): Ausgangssituation der Finanzierung eines Buy-Out, in: Weitnauer, W. (Ed.): Management Buy-Out - Handbuch für Recht und Praxis, C.H. Beck, Munich, pp. 65-68.

Weitnauer, W. (2003b): Rechtliche Gestaltung eines Buy-Out, in: Weitnauer, W. (Ed.): Management Buy-Out - Handbuch für Recht und Praxis, C.H. Beck, Munich, pp. 157-210.

Wellendorff, C. (1999): Nachfolgeoptimierung - mehr als nur Paragraphen, in: Hennerkes, B.-H. / Pleister, C. (Ed.): Erfolgsmodell Mittelstand, Gabler, Wiesbaden pp. 277-296.

Welsch, J.H. (1993): The Impact of Family Ownership and Involvement on the Process of Management Succession, in: Family Business Review, 6 (1), pp. 31-54.

Werner, S. / Tosi, H.L. (1995): Other people's money: The effects of ownership on compensation strategy and managerial pay, in: Academy of Management Journal, 38 (6), pp. 1672-1691.

Westhead, P. (1997): Ambitions, external environment and strategic factor differences between family and non-family companies, in: Entrepreneurship & Regional Development, 9 (2), pp. 127-157.

Westhead, P. / Cowling, M. (1996): Management and Ownership Issues in Family and Non-family companies, Working Paper No. 42, Warwick Business School, 08/1996.

Westhead, P. / Cowling, M. (1998): Family Firm Research: The need for a Methodological Rethink, in: Entrepreneurship Theory & Practice, 14 (3), pp. 31-56.

Westhead, P. / Cowling, M. / Storey, D.J. (1997): The management and performance of unquoted family companies in the United Kingdom, Working paper, Centre for Small and Medium Sized Enterprises, Warwick Business School, 01/1997.

Whisler, T.L. (1988): The Role of the Board in the Threshold Firm, in: Family Business Review, 1 (3), pp. 309-321.

White, H.C. (1985): Agency as Control, in: Pratt, J.W. / Zeckhauser, R.J. (Ed.): Principals and Agents: The Structure of Business, Harvard Business School Press, Boston, pp. 187-214.

Willard, G.E. / Krueger, D.A. / Feeser, H.R. (1992): In order to grow, must the founder go, in: Journal of Business Venturing, 7 (3), pp. 181-194.

Williamson, O.E. (2000): The New Institutional Economics: Taking Stock, Looking Ahead, in: Journal of Economic Literature, 38 (3), pp. 595–613.

Wimmer, B. (2004): Unternehmensplanung und -kontrolle: Integrative Konzepte und Stand der Praxis unter besonderer Berücksichtigung von Wertorientierung und informationstechnischer Gestaltungsmöglichkeiten, Doctoral thesis at the Johannes Kepler Universität, Linz.

Wimmer, R. / Domayer, E. / Oswald, M. / Vater, G. (2005): Familienunternehmen - Auslaufmodell oder Erfolgstyp?, Ed. 2, Gabler, Wiesbaden.

Winter, M. / Fitzgerald, M.A. / Heck, R.K.Z. / Haynes, G.W. / Danes, S.M. (1998): Revisiting the Study of Family Businesses: Methodological Challenges, Dilemmas, and Alternative Approaches, in: Family Business Review, 11 (3), pp. 239-252.

Witt, P. (2003): Corporate Governance - Systeme im Wettbewerb, Deutscher Universitäts-Verlag, Wiesbaden.

Wöhe, G. / Döring, U. (2008): Einführung in die Allgemeine Betriebswirtschaftslehre, Ed. 23, Franz Vahlen, Munich.

Wolter, H.-J. / Hauser, H.-E. (2001): Die Bedeutung des Eigentümerunternehmens in Deutschland, in: Institut für Mittelstandsforschung (Ed.): Jahrbuch zur Mittelstandsforschung 1/2001, Deutscher Universitäts-Verlag, Wiesbaden, pp. 27-78.

Wong, B. / McReynolds, B.S. / Wong, W. (1992): Chinese Family Firms in the San Francisco Bay Area, in: Family Business Review, 5 (4), pp. 355-372.

Wortman, M.S. (1994): Theoretical Foundations for Family-Owned Business: A Conceptual and Research-Based Pradigm, in: Family Business Review, 7 (1), pp. 3-27.

Wright, M. / Coyne, J. (1985): Management Buy-Outs, Croom Helm, Dover.

Wright, M. / Hoskisson, R.E. / Busenitz, L.W. (2001): Firm rebirth: Buyouts as facilitators of strategic growth and entrepreneurship, in: Academy of Management Executive, 15 (1), pp. 111-125.

Wright, M. / Hoskisson, R.E. / Busenitz, L.W. / Dial, J. (2000): Entrepreneurial Growth Through Privatization: The Upside of Management Buyouts, in: Academy of Management Review, 25 (3), pp. 591-601.

Wright, M. / Hoskisson, R.E. / Busenitz, L.W. / Dial, J. (2001): Finance and management buyouts: agency versus entrepreneurship perspectives, in: Venture Capital, 3 (3), pp. 239-261.

Wright, M. / Lockett, A. (2003): The Structure and Management of Alliances: Syndication in the Venture Capital Industry, in: Journal of Management Studies, 40 (8), pp. 2073-2102.

Wright, M. / Robbie, K. (1996): Venture Capitalists, Unquoted Equity Investment Appraisal and the Role of Accounting Information, in: Accounting & Business Research, 26 (2), pp. 153-168.

Wright, M. / Robbie, K. / Yves, R. / Thompson, S. / Joachimsson, R. / Bruining, J. / Herst, A. (1993): Harvesting and the Longevity of Management Buy-outs and Buy-ins: A Four-Country Study, in: Entrepreneurship: Theory & Practice, 18 (2), pp. 90-109.

Wright, M. / Thompson, S. / Chiplin, B. / Robbie, K. (1991): Buy-ins and Buy-outs - New Strategies in Corporate Management, Kluwer Law International, London.

Wright, M. / Thompson, S. / Robbie, K. (1992): Venture capital and management-led, leveraged buy-outs: A European perspective, in: Journal of Business Venturing, 7 (1), pp. 47-71.

Wright, M. / Wilson, N. / Robbie, K. / Ennew, C. (1994): Restructuring and Failure in Buy-outs and Buy-ins, in: Business Strategy Review, 5 (2), pp. 21-40.

Wright, M. / Wilson, N. / Robbie, K. / Ennew, C. (1996): An Analysis of Management Buy-Out Failure, in: Managerial and Decision Economics, 17 (1), pp. 57-70.

Wruck, K.H. (1994): Financial policy, internal control, and performance: Sealed Air Corporation's leveraged special dividend, in: Journal of Financial Economics, 36 (2), pp. 157-192.

Yin, R.K. (1994): Case Study Research - Design and Methods, Ed. 2, Sage, Thousand Oaks.

Zahra, S.A. (1995): Corporate entrepreneurship and financial performance: The case of management leveraged buyouts, in: Journal of Business Venturing, 10 (3), pp. 225-247.

Zahra, S.A. (2003): International expansion of U.S. manufacturing family businesses: the effect of ownership and involvement, in: Journal of Business Venturing, 18 (4), pp. 495-512.

Zellweger, T.M. (2006): Risk, Return and Value in the Family Firm, Difo-Druck, Bamberg.

Zellweger, T.M. / Nason, R.S. (2008): A Stakeholder Perspective on Family Firm Performance, in: Family Business Review, 21 (3), pp. 203-216.

Zenz-Spitzweg, S.R. (2001): Strategische Rahmenbedingungen von Unternehmensverkäufen und -käufen, in: Achleitner, A.-K. / Thoma, G.F. (Ed.): Handbuch Corporate Finance, Ed. 2, Deutscher Wirtschaftsdienst, Cologne, chapter 6.1.1.